Narratives of Sorrow
and Dignity

O | R | S

OXFORD RITUAL STUDIES

Series Editors
Ronald Grimes
Ute Hüsken, University of Oslo
Eric Venbrux, Radboud University Nijmegen

THE PROBLEM OF RITUAL EFFICACY
Edited by William S. Sax, Johannes Quack, and Jan Weinhold

PERFORMING THE REFORMATION
Public Ritual in the City of Luther
Barry Stephenson

RITUAL, MEDIA, AND CONFLICT
Edited by Ronald L. Grimes, Ute Hüsken, Udo Simon, and Eric Venbrux

KNOWING BODY, MOVING MIND
Ritualizing and Learning at Two Buddhist Centers
Patricia Q. Campbell

SUBVERSIVE SPIRITUALITIES
How Rituals Enact the World
Frédérique Apffel-Marglin

NEGOTIATING RITES
Edited by Ute Hüsken and Frank Neubert

THE DANCING DEAD
Ritual and Religion among the Kapsiki/Higi of North Cameroon
and Northeastern Nigeria
Walter E.A. van Beek

LOOKING FOR MARY MAGDALENE
Alternative Pilgrimage and Ritual Creativity at Catholic Shrines in France
Anna Fedele

THE DYSFUNCTION OF RITUAL IN EARLY CONFUCIANISM
Michael David Kaulana Ing

A DIFFERENT MEDICINE
Postcolonial Healing in the Native American Church
Joseph D. Calabrese

NARRATIVES OF SORROW AND DIGNITY
Japanese Women, Pregnancy Loss, and Modern Rituals of Grieving
Bardwell L. Smith

Narratives of Sorrow and Dignity

Japanese Women, Pregnancy Loss, and Modern Rituals of Grieving

BARDWELL L. SMITH

OXFORD
UNIVERSITY PRESS

OXFORD
UNIVERSITY PRESS

Oxford University Press is a department of the University of Oxford.
It furthers the University's objective of excellence in research, scholarship,
and education by publishing worldwide.

Oxford   New York

Auckland   Cape Town   Dar es Salaam   Hong Kong   Karachi
Kuala Lumpur   Madrid   Melbourne   Mexico City   Nairobi
New Delhi   Shanghai   Taipei   Toronto

With offices in

Argentina   Austria   Brazil   Chile   Czech Republic   France   Greece
Guatemala   Hungary   Italy   Japan   Poland   Portugal   Singapore
South Korea   Switzerland   Thailand   Turkey   Ukraine   Vietnam

Oxford is a registered trademark of Oxford University Press in
the UK and certain other countries.

Published in the United States of America by
Oxford University Press
198 Madison Avenue, New York, NY 10016

© Oxford University Press 2013

Library of Congress Cataloging–in–Publication
Data Smith, Bardwell L., 1925–
Narratives of sorrow and dignity: Japanese women, pregnancy loss, and modern
rituals of grieving/Bardwell L. Smith. pages cm. —(Oxford ritual studies)
Includes bibliographical references and index. ISBN 978–0–19–994213–8 (alk. paper)—ISBN
978–0–19–994215–2 (pbk. : alk. paper)—ISBN 978–0–19–994214–5 (ebook)
1. Fetal propitiatory rites—Buddhism.   2. Fetal propitiatory rites—Japan.   3. Abortion—
Religious aspects—Buddhism.   4. Buddhist women—Religious life—Japan. I. Title.
BQ5030.F47S65 2013
294.3'4388—dc23
2012042673

1 3 5 7 9 8 6 4 2
Printed in the United States of America
on acid-free paper

To Charlotte
Lifelong companion, friend, and dearly beloved

Contents

Preface

PRIOR TO THE beginning of studying *mizuko kuyō* in 1984, the experience of Japanese women and child loss was still abstract to me. It did not take long, however, to become aware that, to many of these women, whether they had induced abortion or lost a child involuntarily, their experience had for one reason or another been profound. And, with that loss, there was a longing to incorporate that "lost presence" into their life in one form or another.

On the other hand, before studying this movement I had begun to realize how devastating child loss can be and how vital the process of mourning that loss is. Within our own family and among some of our closest friends, that reality was vividly apparent.

- As our older daughter was giving birth to her only child, the surgeon discovered that the umbilical cord was embedded in the uterus and that, to save her life, the uterus had to be removed. And that meant, since the child was stillborn, she could never give birth to a child. The consequence of that loss was life changing.
- At about the same time, the families of two colleagues lost sons, who were in their early adult years, to AIDS. A third faculty family lost a fourth grade son from a head accident on school grounds. A married daughter of close faculty friends went through the experience of multiple miscarriages, each adding to the sorrow of being unable to give birth to a child.
- In addition, a faculty couple's college-age daughter who was receiving a heart transplant after a lifetime of congenital heart disease tragically died on the operating table. As the cardiologist consulting with them before the operation said, "I know what you must be going through... " Immediately after making that comment, he stopped and said, "No, I

could not possibly know what you are going through." At that point, in
their eyes, his humanity showed through. It also says worlds about how
often one is unable to fathom the pain of another.

My introduction to this relatively new Japanese practice of mourning the
loss of a *mizuko* (a child or a fetus) was through a course that Elizabeth
Harrison and I jointly taught for the Associated Kyoto Program at Doshisha
University in spring 1984. The class included thirty American undergrad-
uates who were spending their junior year in Japan continuing Japanese
language study, living with Japanese families for ten months, and taking
courses in the history and culture of Japanese society. The intent of this
course was to involve students in small groups, throughout the semester,
in a field-study approach to a particular temple or shrine or one of the
newer forms of religions in the Kyoto area.

One of these groups focused on a temple of the Pure Land school
(Jōdoshū), known popularly as Mizukokuyō-dera. Its name suggests the
prominence given to memorial services for the spirits of *mizuko*. The head
priest allowed his temple to be one of the fieldwork sites for this course.
During that semester we visited his temple with a small group of students
on at least eight occasions. This included attending memorial services
(*kuyō*), observing other activities of the temple, talking frequently with
the head priest, and meeting informally with a number of women who
came to this temple to attend the services, to talk with the priest and his
wife, and to listen to each other's experiences. By the end of the semester,
Beth Harrison and I decided that this phenomenon was worthy of further
study. Two years later, in 1986, I received a Fulbright research grant, and
we began what turned out to be a twenty-five-year research project.

Assisted further by a three-year National Endowment for the Humanities
(NEH) Collaborative Research Grant (1991–94), we were able to continue
our research in Japan, to have regular discussions with each other, and
to write different chapters of our joint manuscript. As the time spent on
this project went beyond what we had originally anticipated, and because
of the demands of our personal and professional lives, the decision was
made to discontinue our collaboration and to proceed on our own, with
the intention of publishing separate manuscripts.

Throughout this time I have benefited by the depth of Beth's scholarship in the area of Japanese history and religion and for her insight into
the issues that this research explored. I could not have participated in such
a project without her competence as a research scholar, and I am also

indebted to her as colleague and friend. Because this has been a cooperative project from the start, Chapter 1 explains how we planned this research and how we shaped it as "our" approach or "our" study. The remainder of the book represents my own work, though, again, it was influenced by innumerable discussions with her over the years.

It is a pleasant piece of irony that had this project been completed ten or fifteen years ago it would not have profited from the wealth of research in gender studies, rituals of mourning, and comparative work in many fields and especially from Tokugawa studies and their influence on how we look at social and religious history in modern and postmodern Japan. Hopefully, that influence will be obvious in this treatment of Japanese women and pregnancy loss.

This is not just another book about *mizuko kuyō*. It is better viewed as a case study by which to understand how ingredients of the social and cultural environment have shaped this movement and how the shortcomings of that environment in its response to the various forms of pregnancy loss are revealed in the process.

At the heart of this research is the issue of how human beings experience the death of a life that has been and remains precious to them. This applies not just to pregnancy loss or even to child loss, though these are the focus of this story. The issue is clearly universal, though it is always personal and unique. The role of society in helping people to heal from these experiences comes in infinite forms, though the demands upon this role have changed enormously in recent decades. It is through examples of grieving these kinds of losses that one finds narratives not only of deep sorrow but also of remarkable dignity. The significance of what constitutes a *mizuko* is an entrée into a larger world. The very meaning of the term *mizuko* is challenged in the process.

Previous Studies of Mizuko Kuyō *in English* (1981–2012)

The literature on *mizuko kuyō* varies from innumerable newspaper and magazine articles, in Japanese especially, to more serious academic study by a number of Japanese and Western scholars. A 1981 article by Anne Page Brooks was perhaps the first account of this movement in English and was based on field study interviews with a dozen or so Japanese scholars and Buddhist priests. In 1987 the English translation of an important article published originally in Japanese by Hoshino Eiki and Takeda Dōshō appeared in the *Japanese Journal of Religious Studies*. This was followed by articles from a variety of perspectives by Elizabeth Harrison, Bardwell Smith, R. J. Zwi Werblowsky, and Richard Fox Young. Werblowsky's (1991) article is a critique of the medical profession, especially ob-gyns for preferring abortion over contraception, and maintains that Buddhist temples implicitly condone abortion by the very fact of conducting these memorial services. He also highlights the excesses of the movement, particularly the degree to which financial profit has been a conspicuous ingredient of *mizuko kuyō* practice. In contrast, Richard Young sees in the phenomenon of child loss the potential across religious and cultural boundaries for more adequate grief therapy, including among Christians in Japan.

The first lengthy account in English was the 1991 Harvard Honors B.A. thesis of Mark Makoto Tanaka. This study utilizes a variety of Japanese sources as well as extensive interviews with priests and other informants, largely in the Kyoto area in summer 1990. Its approach deals with theoretical issues, the history of abortion and family planning in Japan, and abortion rituals in the context of Japanese religion with a substantial focus on *mizuko kuyō*, concluding with interpretations and criticisms of this practice. Following this, William LaFleur's *Liquid Life: Abortion and Buddhism in Japan* (1992) is an extended reflection on the many ways Japanese Buddhists appear to reconcile the classical Buddhist position on abortion as a form of taking human life not by protests against abortion but by ritualized offerings of regretful sorrow in *mizuko kuyō*. Among his concerns was how the United States might learn from Japanese ways of approaching the issue of abortion in a less volatile fashion. His book has been widely reviewed.

The discussion of Japan's sexual culture in Helen Hardacre's book *Marketing the Menacing Fetus in Japan* (1997) helps to locate the phenomenon of *mizuko kuyō* in contemporary Japanese society, especially in the chapter titled "Abortion in Contemporary Sexual Culture." The book discusses the meaning of *sexual culture* not just on the societal level but also on how diverse negotiations can be between an individual man and an individual woman in the experiences of intercourse, contraception, pregnancy, and abortion in the evolving culture of Japanese society's attitudes toward heterosexual behavior within marriage or outside it. The subtleties involved in these sexual negotiations are inevitably, if not entirely, political in nature. The dominant image she presents is one of "male initiative" in tandem with "female passivity," a mode of relationship that is further compromised by the relative absence of women-borne forms of contraception and by a low level of contraceptive responsibility on the part of most males in Japan. While her depiction of Japan's sexual culture contributes to the discussion of *mizuko kuyō* by situating it prominently within this culture, there are significant examples of women who do not fit the stereotype of the passive Japanese woman but who have sought some ritualized conclusion to an experience society rarely acknowledges as important but that particular women may seek. There are also examples of priests who, while offering *kuyō* for the death of a child or the abortion of a fetus, do not trade upon women's feelings of vulnerability or charge exorbitant fees for services rendered but who acknowledge that this kind of abuse does occur.

The December 1999 issue of the *Journal of the American Academy of Religion* carries a set of four "thematically related papers" on *mizuko kuyō* by Meredith Underwood, Elizabeth Harrison, William LaFleur, and Ronald Green. LaFleur's article is a review essay that challenges various assumptions of the Hardacre book, and the focus of Green's essay is how the debate about *mizuko kuyō* reveals that moral positions are "endemic to cross-cultural study." Underwood's article "Strategies of Survival: Women, Abortion, and Popular Religion in Contemporary Japan" approaches *mizuko kuyō* from the standpoint of cultural studies, seeing women who take part in the practice not as "passive recipients but as active participants in the ongoing struggle over cultural meaning and power." Underwood views the *mizuko* phenomenon and its many rituals as standing at the "intersection of several crossroads: between ancient and modern Japan, between the conflicted gender roles of Japanese men and women, between women's agency and their 'victimization,' between 'authentic' and 'inauthentic' religion." She observes that the principal places where one is apt to find repressive attitudes toward women who have chosen to terminate a pregnancy are the very places that one would associate with "conservative religious and political organizations." By implication, she is saying that such repressive attitudes are not universally found.

Marc Moskowitz's *The Haunting Fetus: Abortion, Sexuality, and the Spirit World in Taiwan* (2001) was the first book-length discussion of abortion and rituals connected with it outside of Japan. While its subject matter deals primarily with Taiwan, it details how this society adopts a variety of Japanese elements yet significantly modifies what comes to be known in Taiwan as "fetus–ghost appeasement." Because Taiwan and Japan are different societies, the differences become more sharply distinct, while the similarities take on greater prominence. In his book *Mourning the Unborn Dead: A Buddhist Ritual Comes to America* (2009) Jeff Wilson provides the first genuinely cross-cultural perspective on *mizuko kuyō* as a ceremony for aborted and miscarried fetuses. Focusing primarily on how this ritual has adapted to various social and religious groups in the United States beginning in the 1970s, he presents extensive evidence of how this ritual in its American forms has been "appropriated by non-Buddhists as well as Buddhist practitioners" to become a major source of healing to large numbers of women in their experiences of child loss and abortion.

Another valuable cross-cultural study of the bonds between the living and the dead in religious traditions is the work by Robert E. Goss and Dennis Klass, *Dead but Not Lost: Grief Narratives in Religious Traditions* (2005). Of the six chapters in their volume, the ones that are especially pertinent here are those that deal with the psychology of Japanese ancestor rituals, the process in which Buddhist grief narratives have become Americanized, and an important analysis of grief and continuing bonds in contemporary culture. Because of this recent study and the one by Jeff Wilson, it became important to include them in this research not just because they deal with pregnancy loss material in Japanese society and culture but also because they extend the discussion of grieving and mourning to include and go beyond child loss. Had this kind of research in grief narratives not expanded as it has in the past couple of decades, this wider coverage would not have been possible.

As a corollary to the loss of a child or a fetus, yet distinctly different, are two works that focus on animals and a variety of objects that have been especially treasured by Japanese men and women in recent decades. In her published doctoral dissertation, *Kuyō in Contemporary Japan: Religious Rites in the Lives of Laypeople* (2000), Angelika Kretschmer provides a historical summary of *kuyō* rites for the deceased in Japan as well as for *mizuko* and a useful discussion of *kuyō*-type rites or ceremonies for animals, plants and objects of various kinds. The most historically rich discussion of rites for animals, especially domestic pets (*petto*), may be found in Barbara Ambros, *Bones of Contention: Animals and Religion in Contemporary Japan* (Honolulu: University of Hawaii Press, 2012). This work has enormous value not only for ritual and comparative studies but also for providing through great detail the changing significance of the human–animal relationship in Japan. In her own words, a central part of her study is expressed in these words: "Because of their liminal and hybrid status between humans and nonhuman animals, pets can serve as a particularly fruitful topic of inquiry in delineating how cultures construct boundaries between the species" (p. 14).

A final work to cite is among a small handful of books that have greatly informed my understanding of the medieval antecedents in Japan of what emerged five decades ago in the form of *mizuko kuyō*. This is not to suggest any causal connection between these antecedents and this modern phenomenon that appeared to have few roots in the past. While the term *antecedent* can be problematic, it is the accomplishment of Hank Glassman's study *The Face of Jizō: Image and Cult in Medieval Japanese Buddhism* (2012) to have explored in detail the cultural, artistic, literary, and ritualistic expressions by which the bodhisattva cult, especially that of Jizō, raises questions about contemporary forms of Japanese religious and cultural history and, in particular, how they differ and how they seem to be more than remnants of the past.

Because my own study has also taken seriously the concept of *muen-botoke* (the unconnected dead), especially as it relates to what is *marginalized* by society and how these influences have shaped attitudes toward women in Japan, I have profited by Glassman's narrative and performance oriented approach, first, to whatever suffering may have been experienced and expressed in medieval Japan through child loss and, second, how this experience was at times opened up, healed, and transformed by means of the Jizō cult. As he writes, it was especially through this cult's "connection to the journey of the soul in the otherworld [that Jizō] became the champion and special protector of those on the margins of personhood itself: women, children, and 'the unconnected dead', or *muen*" (p. 6). While Glassman's study was published after my manuscript had been completed, his careful documentation reveals how in medieval Japanese Buddhism there existed forms of cultural sensitivity to women in their experiences of child loss that were addressed in many forms of protective and healing rituals centuries before *mizuko kuyō*.

Narratives of Sorrow
and Dignity

PART ONE

Approaching the Worlds of Mizuko

I

Mizuko Kuyō

MEMORIAL SERVICES FOR CHILD LOSS IN JAPAN

WHILE WALKING ON a two-week portion of the Shikoku pilgrimage in fall 1996, my wife, Charlotte, and I, along with Eshin and Akiko Nishimura, had an experience that is pertinent to the subject of this book.[1] At Kirihataji (Temple #10), after walking up the long flight of 330 steps, we came to the top where the main temple is located. After chanting the Hannya Shingyō (Heart Sutra) and placing *ofuda* (prayers on inscribed slips of paper) in a large metal container at both the main hall (*hondō*) and the hall honoring Kōbō Daishi (*daishidō*), we met an elderly Japanese couple who had an interesting story to tell. As this was their third or fourth time walking the roughly 1300 km ancient path, they showed us their pilgrim's album (*nōkyōchō*) stamped with the seals from all eighty-eight temples, with calligraphy added by the priest at each temple. We assumed they must be devout Buddhists, but they said this was not the case (Figure 1.1).

The impetus for what had become an important ingredient in their life was the loss of their only offspring, an exceptionally gifted son who had died suddenly in his early forties. They were devastated. Their grief was so profound and extended that a close friend urged them to consider this pilgrimage, for he had heard how the discipline of doing this had enabled another person to deal with a similar loss. This meant little to the couple at the start, but in time they recognized they must somehow deal with their distress if they were to regain any meaning to their life.[2] By the time we met them, the ritual of walking this ancient path had stitched their life together in ways they never could have imagined.

The story goes on, and there are many such stories, but the point is clear. In virtually every life there are experiences of irreplaceable loss. A loss of this magnitude brings forms of grief that seem inconsolable. If one

FIGURE I.I Elderly couple at Temple 10 Kirihataji (Shikoku pilgrimage).

is not to be stuck in grief, there must be a process of healing in which one discovers the "ability to mourn," as Peter Homans called it.³ It is by means of mourning that new life breaks through.

To cite the loss incurred by this elderly couple is not to compare it with other experiences of loss, though it would be akin to the forms of death mentioned in the Preface. The white robe (*oizuru*) worn by pilgrims is a symbol of death; pilgrimage is a means of practicing one's mortality. For this couple, performing the ritual began to heal the pain of losing their son, and, to their surprise, the new form of his presence in their life linked them to a wider world they were just discovering. The irony of deep loss is that, with the miracle of healing, life's finitude becomes more treasured, bringing greater sensitivity to the pain of others.

How does one compare the death of that son to whatever sense of loss felt by a woman alone or by a couple in the throes of early child death, stillbirth, multiple miscarriages, or even induced abortion? One learns to be cautious about comparisons. The common factor is the death of what is part of oneself. Coming to terms with this, in whatever form it occurs, is a path to healing on a larger scale. It is a personalized form of suffering and of freedom from attachment to suffering. This is what *kuyō* is all about.

Approaching the Subject

What appeared on the scene in the 1970s and '80s was the emergence into public discourse of a concern for dead children as actors in the world of the living, along with the rapidity with which this practice had spread and the strength of its popularity. In response, the Japanese media portrayed the practice of *mizuko kuyō* as a fad, dismissing it as another outmoded religious construction, a topic unsuitable for academic attention in Japan or elsewhere.

One's scholarly interest was aroused by the disjunction between the media's treatment of the practice, clergy responses to our inquiries, and the stories of lay participants whom we observed and with whom we spoke. *Mizuko kuyō* may be viewed as a complex phenomenon constituted by a variety of voices operating on many levels: some that were widely publicized, and others that remained private. If one regards these people—most of whom are women—as passive objects of social, mainly male manipulation, one is left to focus on the money spent in this practice as a pejorative way of interpreting this religious expression. On the other hand, if one chooses to view these individuals as acting subjects, one can interpret their participation as a *tactical* appropriation of religious elements in Japanese society addressing a central issue in their daily lives: the loss of a child.[4] As a result, one hears the voices of people who seek to create a relationship with their lost children despite the influence of those who shape the dominant social and religious discourse in other ways. Elizabeth Harrison has expressed this dilemma clearly:

> In contemporary Japanese society, the loss of a child, whether through abortion, miscarriage, or any other means, is such a personal and private experience that it is difficult for anyone outside those immediately involved to obtain personal accounts of that experience; perhaps this is the reason the media and clergy constructions of *mizuko kuyō* have gone virtually unchallenged in the public forum.
>
> Especially in the case of miscarriage, when in Japan there may be some question of the mother's responsibility for the loss, and of abortion, which always raises the issue of responsibility, few if any of those involved are willing to discuss their thoughts openly. Yet it is precisely the thoughts of lay practitioners of *mizuko kuyō*

that we need in order to uncover the complexity of the practice that has been flattened in the public constructions we have examined so far.[5]

Because of the many ways to interpret this "movement," *mizuko kuyō* remains a case study of how old and new forms of myth, symbol, doctrine, praxis, and organization combine and overlap. In the process, one is struck by the anguish expressed and the immense variety of religious responses to emotional and spiritual needs. The study of *mizuko kuyō* provides a fresh perspective upon the history of religions, Japanese Buddhist studies, and anthropological materials dealing with the religions of Japan. In particular, this inquiry sheds light on topics that are seldom examined together as ingredients in the relationship between Japanese religion and contemporary Japanese society. This includes the sociology of the family, the power of the medical profession, the economics of temples, the import of ancestral connections, the need for healing in both private and communal ways, and, perhaps above all, the place of women in modern Japanese religion.

It is not surprising that the feelings a woman might have, alone or together with a partner, would be considerable. Expressions of anger, self-recrimination, sadness, loneliness, and a sense of anxiety about the future were to be expected, frequently in combination with one another. Because the loss of a potential child through stillbirth or miscarriage can be devastating, it is important to know that roughly a quarter of *mizuko* fall within these categories. As for pregnancies terminated by abortion, the feelings on a woman's part may also be multiple. Due to the lack of effective procreative choice, though abortion has been legal in Japan since 1948, Japanese women often become pregnant against their wishes.

While this book is not about the pros and cons of abortion, it deals with the social and historical aspects of this subject in Japan as they relate to the major focus of this study. One surprisingly neglected issue that may lie at the base of the *mizuko* phenomenon is not the fact that the woman had an abortion but rather that she was often not empowered to *choose* whether to have it. While it is clear that many women do have residual issues in this area, this study does not imply that all women do or should or that access to abortion is anything other than a hard-earned and prized right permitting women to *choose* to control their bodies and destinies.

In effect, the phenomenon of *mizuko kuyō* provides another opportunity to examine ways organized religion responds to an important human and contemporary social problem. It also provides organizational, ritualistic, and cosmological contexts for addressing a sense of parental relationship with the child, however that relationship may be construed.

Among the Characteristics of Mizuko Kuyō

Prior to World War II a dead fetus was not regarded as a dead person and thus was not the subject of family religious rites. As to why *mizuko kuyō* began to appear in the 1950s and then develop into a significant movement by the mid-1960s, Takahashi Yoshinori, a sociologist at Kyoto University, rehearses a number of customary explanations: the recognition of the rights of children in the postwar Japanese Constitution in 1948; legalization of abortion in Japan since 1949 and hence the sizable increase in the number of abortions; the inadequacy of procreative choice and of comprehensive sex education; the trend toward seeing the aborted fetus as having its own individual identity; fascination of the media with the more ersatz features of these phenomena; the decline of traditional "family religion" practice, especially in the depersonalized anonymity of life in urban communities; and the uncertainty of how *mizuko kuyō* is to be understood in terms of religious teachings by most religious institutions.[6]

The formalized practice of offering memorial rites for aborted fetuses began roughly fifty years ago. Today such rites have become institutionalized in many forms of Japanese religion. The word *mizuko* literally means "water-child." By the late 1960s this word was used to denote the objects of the new practice of *mizuko kuyō*. The main focus is on "children" who died while very young or were stillborn (*shizan*), miscarried (*ryūzan*), or aborted (*ninshin chūzetsu*). Until this practice, these "children" had been left out of the usual Japanese Buddhist funeral and memorial services for the dead.[7] Because the question of whether a fetus is a child is not generally debated in Japan, the term *mizuko* can be translated as "dead," "lost," or, in another reading of *mizu*, "unseen" child or children.

By the mid-1980s, the word had been broadened to include any child who died "out of order," that is, before its parents. It has been questioned, and in my estimation rightly so, whether the word *mizuko* should be used for these different experiences of loss. On the other hand, it has become clear in this research that there may be a significant sense of pain or sorrow in each of these and that it would be difficult to make a judgment call in any individual case as to the impact upon another person or family. Nevertheless, it may be argued that reestablishing a mother–child relationship with one's *mizuko* is at the core of this new practice.

In any case, the current practice of this ritual is modeled on memorial services for ancestral spirits (*senzo kuyō*), which center on performance of a *kuyō* service by a member of the clergy. As the practice became increasingly visible, visitors encountered rows of carved or molded figurines hung with cloth bibs and hats, decorated with flowers or pinwheels, and surrounded by all manner of toys and food set within easy reach. These figures are associated with the bodhisattva Jizō, who in Japanese Buddhism has been regarded as the protector of children and to whom parents often address prayers for the care of their dead or unborn child. Through the performance of a *mizuko kuyō* service such children may be brought to the attention of a bodhisattva or other sacred figure and provided with forms of "nourishment" (the literal sense of *kuyō*) such as offerings of money, food, flowers, prayers, and incense. The reading of religious texts are included, with the hope that these children will not suffer wherever they are, that they will be reborn into a good life, and that they will refrain from creating problems for their living families, as this is sometimes perceived to be the case.

To ensure the well-being of their deceased children families are encouraged to take part in these services together. One may participate directly in the service, but this is not a requirement. Some people see this as a one-time experience; others intend the practice to be a lifelong commitment (*eidai kuyō*). While each site that performs this service has its own variations of practice, a *mizuko* may be given a Buddhist-style death name (*hōmyō* or *kaimyō*) signifying that the spirit is a follower of the Buddha. Much more often, however, *mizuko kuyō* involves the giving of an ordinary Japanese name, such as Yoshiko or Takashi, along with the family name. Many individuals involved in this practice, clergy as well as laypersons, have inferred that one reason unborn *mizuko* are so easily forgotten, as Harrison points out, is because they are unseen:

> Herein, I think, lies the heart of *mizuko kuyō*. It provides a formal, public, ritualized way to acknowledge the existence of a child—both its potential existence in this world as a result of its conception and its continuing existence somewhere else after death, to (re)establish a relationship with it, and to care for it wherever it may be. In this construction, although the child might be absent from this world, it nevertheless remains a child to its parents and a sibling to its living

brothers and sisters. This acknowledgement of the child's existence is implicit in the way many respondents expressed their reason for doing *mizuko kuyō.*[8]

The Public Debate about Mizuko Kuyō

As *mizuko kuyō* became a growing movement there was extensive discourse about this practice in the media, in which the emphasis was more on the occult features, such as the belief that harmful spirits of the dead will haunt the living if these spirits are not placated in one manner or another. At the outset of this research it was not apparent that *mizuko kuyō* enabled women to become agents in their own behalf or whether they were being manipulated by a variety of others. By seeking this memorial service to address their own emotional needs, in what sense were women taking control of their own lives? Or did these rituals confirm the fact that they were simply victims of a medical culture within which they seldom had effective procreative choice? Was their need to be consoled or reconciled to their condition but another instance of being dominated as women in a patriarchal society?

The critics of *mizuko kuyō* were numerous, and the shape of their opposition has been an essential part of this study. The primary features singled out include the following: (1) the perception that some religious groups are taking advantage of women and men at a vulnerable time in their life; (2) the commercialization of this practice by temples that charge exorbitant prices for the ritual and for items that participants are encouraged to buy; (3) the imputing of guilt to those who have lost a child; (4) the use of scare tactics about what will happen if the spirits of dead children are not memorialized; (5) the attributing of past (and future) bad luck, illness, and family tensions to the failure to attend to these spirits; and (6) the negligence of priests who fail to reach out to participants—especially women—in ways that would help them become stronger rather than more dependent. These criticisms have been voiced by the media, by Japanese feminists, by social critics in Japan, and by a variety of religious personnel and groups that are opposed to this ritual because they see it as non-Buddhist or un-Christian or superstitious.

While acknowledging the importance of taking these seriously, our experience led us to different views of *mizuko kuyō*, seeing it as a symptom of contemporary social issues and attitudes rather than as a central problem in itself. From the start it was clear that a gap existed in the public

debate about the practice of *mizuko* rituals. Despite extensive public discourse in Japan and elsewhere about *mizuko kuyō* little attention had been
paid to what the experience of losing a child means to an individual. There
were few attempts to include the voices of the women (or men) who participated, let alone how they felt about their own experiences of child loss,
why they went to religious sites in search of help, and what offering *kuyō*
for their *mizuko* meant to them. The principal intent in this research was
to highlight the words and the experiences of real people. Utilizing a similar approach in interviews with priests, one finds considerable differences
expressed about *mizuko kuyō* as a phenomenon, together with a wide
range of practices in response to individuals who sought their help.

These differences provided a warning to us, in part because the voices
of women are obviously plural, as are the voices of temple priests performing *mizuko kuyō*, in part because we were aware of our own limitation of
vision. And because other voices or interpretations (by the media, feminists, Japanese academics) are intrinsic to the overall picture they needed
to be included.[9] The point was not to "explain" *mizuko kuyō* but to examine
what made it so prominent a feature on the recent Japanese religious and
social landscape.

Unresolved Grief and the Process of Mourning

The ordeal of losing one's child is among life's most devastating experiences. Only in recent decades have we in the United States begun to be
more sensitive once again to what it may mean to a woman who has gone
through experiences of stillbirth, miscarriage, or at times even abortion.
This more recent attention to the issue of mourning comes after a long
period in which the social denial of death, including that of a child, was
pervasive, even though there is substantial evidence that child death in
past centuries was an agonizing experience for parents.[10] There is now
increased awareness of a woman's need to confront and acknowledge its
pain, to find ways of expressing grief, and, ironically, to cultivate one's
ability to mourn:

> For most of the last half of the twentieth century…grief was fully
> internalized. It was part of the individual's psychological processes.
> The theory was that the goal of grief was to cut the attachment with
> the dead so that the survivor could be free to make new attachments
> in the present… When a child dies [however] the parent experiences

an irreparable loss, because the child is an extension of the parent's self. When a child dies, a part of the self is cut off… How does one find a meaningful new identity when a central aspect of the self has been amputated? How can the task be accomplished in a culture that provides almost no guidelines?[11]

Unlike more painful types of child loss, such as early infant death, still-birth, and miscarriage, abortion is in most cases a voluntary action on the part of the woman. Even when the choice of terminating the pregnancy has been willed, it is clear, when listening to women discuss the context of their decision making, that many factors are involved in these decisions. Aside from her own potential ambivalence, the degree of a woman's own volition may be merged with the interests, advice, and stated desires of others. Obviously, the will of her husband or partner can be a factor. So too are economic circumstances, the number of children a couple may already have, a woman's age and health, and other considerations. The calculus behind a woman's choice to have the child or not is a complex affair. But, unless she is literally forced to make the decision, she normally assents to it, even if there are later regrets. In other words, behind the choice lies internal and external debate about what to do. Whatever her own reactions to the experience may be, they are personal and unique; it is not atypical for her feelings to be mixed.

In the case of Japanese mothers, there is substantial evidence that the decision to abort may entail contradictory feelings, deep sadness at the sense of loss, yet also a "sense of a continuing presence of the child" or fetus.[12] Evidence for this is expressed in several chapters. As the hope to reconnect with the *mizuko* one has relinquished is not an irrational one, so in Japan with the commonly sensed presence of the dead a woman may keep alive and nurture the existence of her unborn child long past the time when it had ceased to exist in this life. The extensive recourse to *mizuko kuyō* provides comparable evidence of Japanese women's need to mourn the loss of an aborted fetus no less than one lost involuntarily. A major factor contributing to this need is the manner in which Japanese women's sense of self-worth is merged to a large degree with the existence and well-being of their children.

To generalize about Japanese women's reactions either to unwanted pregnancies or to the experience of abortion can, of course, be misleading. A spectrum of this complexity is exceedingly diverse. The responses arising from feelings of anger, depression, guilt, loneliness, sorrow, and fear are as variegated as the women expressing them. Even if a woman favors having an abortion, it does not mean that she will go through this experience unbruised. Even with perfect concurrence, she may later encounter forms of unaddressed grieving, much to her surprise. To what degree such feelings are induced by cultural attitudes, specifically religious ones, vary with the particular woman and the many influences upon her life. In some cases, guilt may well be a factor, but it is by no means a constant variable. In fact, as Ueno Chizuko adroitly expressed it about the practice of *mizuko jizō* in the Edo period, the motivation for this practice (at that time it was the practice of infanticide) was "grief rather than guilt"[13]—so too about certain experiences of *mizuko kuyō*. More often, a woman may experience a sense of sadness, brought about by something deeper than hormonal adjustment. Immediate reactions to such an experience seem to be less common than those that may emerge later, even years later. Thoughts of "what might have been" surface in any life. While these can be laid to rest, they must first be encountered.

While most Japanese women favor the availability of choice, they may have misgivings after having made that decision themselves. In trying to reconcile their own decision with their sense of what being a woman and a mother mean, a woman may come to see abortion in the larger category of child loss. Whatever ambivalence may exist in the decision to abort, experiencing the need to mourn is acknowledgment that something of consequence has occurred. The following statement by a Japanese feminist reveals not only ambivalence but also social expectations and personal (often private) feelings:

> As to how one feels about the loss of a child, it depends on the age of the child at death. For the first child or the child that had been much hoped for, the parents may feel very mournful. In the case of an abortion, quite a few parents, especially with more than two experiences, may feel more at ease, taking the matter quite rationally. In my case, I was deeply depressed emotionally. It was not merely a sense of guilt; I had a strong feeling of being "sorry" for my "child." With the lapse of time, I recovered, but a friend of mine suffered a lot, physically and emotionally. By all means, the husband's support is needed, but actually it is too rarely given.[14]

A person learns to incorporate the memory of what has been lost and to live with the ongoing psychological presence of that specific loss. Mourning is not simply grieving the loss of one who has died; it may also be grieving the loss of one's own world of meaning. A major factor contributing to this need is the degree to which Japanese women's sense of self-worth is merged with the existence and well-being of their children. This social ideology of a woman's role as mother conditions her sense of self long before she marries and has a child and can be part of the pain a Japanese woman may experience when she loses a child. However socially constructed that may be, this ideology can affect a woman's self-image:

> From the parents' point of view, then, the bond with their child symbolizes their larger bond with transcendent reality in many ways. When a child dies, the parent loses that sacred connection; thus one of the spiritual tasks faced by bereaved parents is either to reestablish or to create a new connection. One of the ways parents accomplish that task is by the continuing bonds parents maintain with their dead children.[15]

"It Is Always in My Heart (kokoro)*"*

These words are a frequently voiced sentiment by one mother or another who seeks to find ways by which her aborted fetus or lost child may have an honored presence in her heart: not a presence that incriminates or a burden that weighs heavy but one that frees her to move on with her life and respond to the pain of others. Central to such an expression is the mother's wish for this experience to remain a part of herself, the hope that the *mizuko* will remain in her heart (*kokoro*). Her desire is for some kind of representational form, symbolizing the one she has lost, enabling her to keep alive that memory and in the process to experience genuine healing. In some sense, this is the core of *mizuko kuyō* in its most sincere form. It is illustrative of what women often write at the end of a questionnaire. The tenor and spirit of these comments reveal a mature strength and, for the most part, a sense of quiet resignation. There seem to be three qualities to this kind of aspiration.

The first is the yearning to find a place that is quiet in which she can experience a deeper form of herself, a place that is in some sense sacred, one that may be solitary but "where there is no loneliness." One woman identifies such a place in Kyoto: "There was something about Nenbutsuji. I don't know what it was, but I was extremely moved and began to cry. I was very grateful."[16]

A second ingredient in her yearning is to have the persons in her life to whom she feels closest join her in this experience of healing. Without this, loneliness deepens. "My sense of *tsumi* (committing some offense) is so strong; the man seems to feel nothing. I cannot understand how he can be so calm about it."[17] "There should be a place where not just the person with the *mizuko* alone but where the father, brothers, and others could also comfortably go."[18] "There is no need to feel guilty or to see it as related to difficulties. Nor is there any need to blame oneself."[19]

The third feature of a mature yearning is to act in behalf of another. It could be termed "vicarious *kuyō*." "My mother lost two children before I was born...I do not think she has done *kuyō*. I am coming in her stead. I dream of a happy family life, and this is why I hope to continue. *Mizuko kuyō* is not just something to ease one's mind."[20] For this woman, who may not even believe in *mizuko* or in the efficacy of *kuyō*, the goal may be to honor the unspoken presence in her mother's heart, a goal that may never be voiced in public.

A poignant example of this combination of sorrow and dignity appears in a well-known Japanese novel.[21] Eiko and Satsuki Nakanishi, close friends of Yoko Katei, are both forty-six years old and have not been able to conceive a child. With medical assistance, Eiko finally becomes pregnant, but because of her age her husband requests amniocentesis. The test reveals the near certainty of Down's syndrome, and the quandary over the next step begins. After being told the child has additional complications, they, crushed by the news, decide to terminate the pregnancy. To which Mrs. Nakanishi responds, "The truth is, I've given the child a name...when I knew it wouldn't be born and live. I call it Mio, meaning 'unborn'—it's neither a boy's nor a girl's name."[22]

In reply, their friend Yoko adds a dimension that responds to the deeper need of Eiko Nakanishi. Not only is it good to have a name for the child, she says, for it helps one think about and talk about this child, which was so wanted yet which was not to be born. It also helps to "pray for someone specific and clearly say the name Mio."[23] Yoko's next statement to the couple transforms their sense of what being Mio's parents means:

> The two of you are not a childless couple, you see. You had a child, but you lost it. You are really quite splendid, you know, very unusual people. Mio made you parents, and from now on you can speak of Mio and make Mio a part of your life.... It is surely no waste that Mio had half a year of life. Even a retarded child.... [You] have

been driven to the limits of human endurance, and [you] have been shown what extremes life can hold.... What kind of child can this be who not yet even born can give its parents a vision of such extremes of life and death?[24]

The wisdom of these words provides meaning to an otherwise devastating experience. After the pregnancy is terminated, the Nakanishi couple receives the remains and prepares a cemetery plot for their child, planning that they too would eventually be buried alongside Mio. In the meantime, they feel fulfilled, knowing both sadness and gratitude. Inseparable from the agony of their decision, the occasioning of human nobility is born.

A Cross-Cultural Perspective on Grief and Mourning

It is at this point that changes in Japanese society in recent decades have implications for the problems associated with abortion. This picture has been recognized by Hoshino Eiki and Takeda Dōshō. Among the principal assertions of their article on abortion and *mizuko kuyō* is that with the gradual devolution of the earlier family system in modern urban areas the responsibility for abortion, which used to be shared by the local community in Edo Japan, must now "be borne in secret completely by the individual."[25] In a society with a rich ancestral heritage this modern privatization of grief is ironic. Hoshino and Takeda are correct in identifying the erosion of past forms of grief sharing. The immense social changes since 1945 have meant that the Japanese family is rarely the place where birth and death occur, meaning that the family no longer plays a necessary role in these areas and that those "customs and practices that developed on the basis of [the] former family structure must be totally reconsidered."[26]

In today's society, it is common for women to secure abortions at clinics or hospitals where they are not known. If they seek out a Buddhist temple or some other place where memorial services are conducted for aborted fetuses, they do so anonymously and at temples where they have no family connection. While attended sometimes by a husband or sexual partner, they ordinarily come alone. And even when other women may be present at the same service, there is rarely communication between them about their reasons for coming. Unlike a normal funeral service in which there is often opportunity for sharing grief, the situation with regard to miscarriages and stillborn children may be ones in which there is no interchange at all. The same is even truer in cases of abortion.

Discussions about matters of this intimacy almost never happen, though a recent survey indicates that a majority of religious organizations in Japan say they are willing to provide "consultation," depending on the circumstances, to women interested in discussing matters connected with *mizuko*. The nature of these consultations, the training of religious personnel in the area of pastoral counseling, the willingness of women to be frank, and the follow-up to these meetings naturally affect their helpfulness. In general, the experience remains private, and a woman comes to it with mixed feelings and motivations. At the very least she wishes to be freed from fears and negative emotions. She hopes for a new beginning, yet she may also desire to maintain psychic and spiritual contact with her *mizuko*.

While this study is not comparative in nature, over the past twenty-five years there has been increasing evidence among American women, including feminists, about the feelings of loss a woman may experience after stillbirth and multiple miscarriages but also following an abortion. However one defines the embryo or fetus whose existence has been terminated, it is not uncommon for women to experience some sense of loss. Central to this issue is a woman's need to grieve whatever sense of loss she may be experiencing as well as the importance of particularizing this loss and of coming to terms with what this means in her life. With analysis of this kind increasingly more available, it is appropriate to examine some of the central differences as well as the similarities between various forms of memorial practices in Japan and in other cultural settings.

From a cross-cultural perspective dealing with instances in which women have played a dominant role, Susan Starr Sered, ethnographer and scholar of healing rituals, makes a number of observations that are relevant here. With regard to child death, including infanticide, she argues that the death of children "encourages women to ponder existential and theological questions" and prompts them "to organize and demand social change that will enhance maternal and infant health."[27] Sered's work suggests that for women this quest for meaning is carried out through the personalizing of suffering and death. "For many women, being the mother of a dead child remains a—or the—core element of personal identity; memories of the child do not fade; sorrow does not ebb; life does not 'go on.' For these reasons, women seem especially likely to seek religious interpretations of and responses to child death."[28]

In dimensions of religious experience influenced by women, Sered asserts that "suffering does not need to be passively accepted."[29] Women's concerns, commonly expressed in ritualistic form, tend to emphasize the existence of the sacred *within* the secular world, with a strong accent upon this-worldly blessings. Communication with the dead through prayer, ritual, and pilgrimage is central to a larger axial relationship and reciprocity "with ancestors, with descendants, [and] with unborn children" whose assistance is sought and whose well-being is attended to.[30]

Observations of this sort serve to highlight certain elements of *mizuko kuyō*. These include the necessity felt by large numbers of women to participate in ritualized practice as a way of helping them to grieve for the children they have lost. Also, the nature of this grieving tends to be highly personalized, enabling women to engage in one mode of communication or another with the child or ancestor who has died. While these modes of contact between the living and the dead vary from culture to culture, Sered's research reveals that women "use their relationship-focused concerns as a point of entry into the great tradition...[reinterpreting] aspects of the great tradition to meet their own relationship-focused religious needs. Domestic religion is not a particular subset of rituals, but a spiritual theme that pervades and organizes the religious lives of many human beings."[31] While possessing an awareness of two worlds that are bridged in this contact, the primary focus is upon locating the sacred *in* this world. The emphasis is practical, *down to earth*; it is on personal, this-worldly benefits and protection from one form of harm or another.

Through this kind of approach Susan Sered underscores the importance of communal support and rituals in helping a person to move from a deep sense of personal loss to an ability to mourn that loss and to discover a greater awareness of wholeness. As one considers child loss as part of a larger discourse about grief, mourning, and death ritual, one is examining ingredients of practice that, while personal, are inevitably social at the same time.

Society, Women, and Pregnancy Loss: Interactions of Discourse and Practice

The more one studies Japanese women and their experiences of child loss, especially but not only by induced abortion, the more one finds multiple ways to interpret the complexity of this subject. The initial method used in researching this subject was a field study approach that began in the mid-1980s when Harrison and Smith interviewed over a period of eighteen months a large number of Buddhist priests in Honshu and Kyushu and, with their permission, distributed questionnaires to laypeople who came to their temples for the *kuyō* service. Elizabeth Harrison has discussed this material in a number of published articles. A second approach, over a period of twenty more years (1990–2010), was to focus primarily on two Jōdoshū temples in the Kyoto area. The analyses of these sites and the people who came to them for *mizuko kuyō* are presented in Chapters 3 and 4. Primary attention throughout both phases of this research is given to the experiences of Japanese women and their reactions to one form of pregnancy loss or another.

In pursuing this field study approach, certain theoretical approaches have proven to be useful, and some of these are discussed throughout the book. Among the criteria for a theory's value is how it explores, frames, illuminates, and raises questions about the topic being researched. At its best, it also requires one to engage in self-criticism. While this study focuses on Japanese women and pregnancy loss, it includes how their experiences have been shaped by social values together with how women are able to find ways of gaining greater agency in a cultural setting where, to use Pierre Bourdieu's term, *symbolic domination* is a common experience.

In seeking for a balance between theory and primary material, Bourdieu seeks "to recover the practical side of theory as a *knowledge-producing activity*... [rather than utilizing] theory as a separate, self-enclosed, and self-referential realm of discourse."[32] Still more ambitious, he advocates "the *fusion* of theoretical construction and practical research operations... [causing them] *to interpenetrate each other* entirely."[33] Because changing situations prompt revisions in how a theory is interpreted, this is what he means by *interpenetrating* each other. In studying this topic, I have found this to be a common experience.

Among the theoretical approaches discussed in this study, three need identifying at the start. The first is how the study of *mizuko kuyō* and the experiences of women can be enriched initially by Michel de Certeau's familiar distinction between the producers of cultural systems and the users or consumers of those systems, but even more by his many visually perceived depictions of interactions between these two worlds.[34] The second is Pierre Bourdieu's perspective on the subject of *symbolic violence* or *symbolic domination*, which sheds light on the varied situations of Japanese women within a patriarchal setting in modern Japan and how women have for a long time bought into this frame of mind. Of greater interest, however, is how resourcefully women have countered this setting even while remaining in it. A third approach is an inquiry into what happens "when reproduction…is placed at the center of social theory." This approach is pertinent to ongoing theoretical discussions of the emerging politics of reproduction.[35] Among many illustrations of this is a recent scientific study of how Japanese women's narratives express their personal experiences with in vitro fertilization (IVF). This refinement of reproductive ethics resembles some of the social and cultural values found in the study of *mizuko kuyō.*

First, in *The Practice of Everyday Life* Michel de Certeau makes a basic distinction between producer elites who have access to techniques of sociocultural production, fashioning their own place from which to make use of *strategies,* and common people consumers who have no proper place and so make use of *tactics* as a way of practicing "an art of living in the other's field".[36] As Michèle Lamont has written, "De Certeau develops a theoretical framework for analyzing how the 'weak' make use of the 'strong' and create for themselves a sphere of autonomous action and self-determination within the constraints that are imposed on them…[and who thus use] tactics to manipulate events and turn them into opportunities."[37] For Lamont, the *theme of resistence* used by Certeau locates him "in the ongoing research in cultural anthropology, social history, and cultural studies."[38] The value of this starting point, intrinsically and in studying this topic, is what this distinction leads to.

While women can be construed as "unnamed and indistinguishable" users whose tactics are employed for their own survival, this would be to homogenize their efforts and, more important, would miss Certeau's cataloguing of the "infinitesimal procedures of resistance against apparatuses of control."[39] A tactic "operates in isolated actions, blow by blow. It takes advantages of 'opportunities' and depends on them, being without any base…It can be where it is least expected. It is a guileful ruse. In short, a tactic is an art of the weak."[40] Even this depiction is but a starting point. The principal contribution of Certeau's approach lies is how he finds in stories, dramatic performances, and architecture images of *frontiers* and *bridges* that open up new spaces, new ways of relating across boundaries. "By considering the role of stories in delimitation, one can see that the primary function is to *authorize* the establishment, displacement or transcendence of limits, and as a consequence, to set in opposition, within the closed field of discourse, two movements that intersect."[41] As in theater, a story "creates a field that authorizes dangerous and contingent social actions."[42]

The imaginary landscape of an inquiry [as of a theory]...keeps
before our eyes the structure of a social imagination in which the
problem constantly takes different forms and begins anew...The
landscape that represents these phenomena in an imaginary mode
thus has an overall corrective and therapeutic value in resisting
their reduction by a lateral examination.[43]

These newly created spaces are a surprise, a shock to the producers, giving
voice, agency, and new standing to consumers, providing images of newly
habitable space, opening up spaces that have not existed before. Part of
Certeau's insight lies in portraying the frontier, for example, as "a sort of
void" and how a transformed void becomes "a plentitude."[44] "Far from
expressing a void or describing a lack, [this paradox]...makes room for a
void. In that way, it opens up clearings; it 'allows' a certain play within a
system of defined places. It 'authorizes' the production of an area of free
play."[45] And, in his final two chapters he presents the inevitably human
task of contending with the *unthinkable* and the *unnamable* (namely, death)
and the *indeterminate* (namely, the unforeseen), the unknowable lying at
the core of what we think we know.

While this is not the place to dwell on what Certeau is stressing here,
it is fair to say that the heart of *mizuko* study has been to listen to stories
of persons who have encountered death and who have been altered as a
result. "Thus to eliminate the unforeseen or expel it from calculation as
an illegitimate accident and an obstacle to rationality is to interdict the
possibility of a living and 'mythical' practice of the city."[46] And hence he
utters the famous words, "Let us then return to the murmurings of everyday practices."[47]

It is precisely through practicing *mizuko kuyō* that the nameless, voiceless participants extend the boundaries of public discourse, realigning it
subtly with their own concerns in a type of production Certeau calls "quasi-
invisible."[48] This element he identifies as "surprising"; it has the potential of becoming subversive. By listening to Japanese women as acting
subjects who have chosen to participate, one assesses how lifelong "practice of everyday life" reveals itself. By paying attention to their stories, to
the authors themselves, one juxtaposes these with the public images and
reports of what *mizuko kuyō* is supposedly all about. Numerous examples
of these narratives are noted throughout this manuscript, perhaps starting
with images of *mizuko* themselves that proliferate in temple compounds
but even more with the construction of what it means to be a woman

and a woman-as-mother in particular. In effect, these stories are central to viewing pregnancy loss on a larger canvass while knowing these losses are experienced by women as individuals, though potentially with other women (and men) in forms of mutual support.

Second, in tension with Certeau's accent on the potential for voiceless members of society to become acting subjects, even to the point of being subversive, Bourdieu's insight suggests how easily the "dominated" can subscribe to predominant definitions of social roles and expectations yet how incorporating this point of view coexists with challenges to it. That sort of dual stance appears throughout this study of *mizuko kuyō*. A complex tension prevails, for instance, among the varied entries by women in the notebooks discussed in Chapter 3. Chapter 5 details more fully the history of how a woman's role as mother became her primary function in society and in subsequent chapters in which feminists argue against patriarchal positions, yet by their own personal reproductive experience may be transformed in the process.

Bourdieu's key term *symbolic violence* is "the violence which is exercised upon a social agent with his or her complicity."[49] Expressing this tension more lucidly, he writes, "Any symbolic domination presupposes on the part of those who are subjected to it a form of complicity which is *neither* a passive submission to an external constraint nor a free adherence to [its] values."[50] Essential to Bourdieu's task is the attempt "to unravel the logic of gender domination, which [to him] is the paradigmatic form of symbolic violence."[51] One comes to see the subtle interplay between prescribed social realities and how both men and women are actually affected in their interrelationships. Listening to individual women who share their experiences of pregnancy loss and of symbolic domination is a vital corrective to secondhand forms of discourse about this kind of experience. Bourdieu locates a classic example of such a corrective in Virginia Woolf's novel *To the Lighthouse* (1987):

We find in this novel an extraordinarily perceptive analysis of a paradoxical dimension of symbolic domination, and one almost always overlooked by feminist critique, namely the domination of the dominant by his domination: a feminine gaze upon the desperate and somewhat pathetic effort that any man must make, in his triumphant unconsciousness, to try to live up to the dominant idea of man. Furthermore, Virginia Wolff allows us to understand how, by ignoring the *illusio* that leads one to engage in the central games of society, women escape the *libido dominandi* that comes with this involvement, and are therefore socially inclined to gain a relatively lucid view of the male games in which they ordinarily partake only by proxy.[52]

A third theoretical approach is discussed by Faye Ginsburg and Rayna Rapp in the introduction to their edited volume *Conceiving the New World Order: The Global Politics of Reproduction*. For them, the emerging politics of reproduction "offers a new framework that allows us to explore what happens when reproduction—in both its biological and its sociological interpretations—is placed at the center of social theory."[53] It is clear how prominent the question of reproduction is in the phenomena of *mizuko kuyō*. In Chapter 5, for instance, the case is made that as Japanese society in the late 1890s begins to define the identity of women as grounded primarily in their role as mother, the subject of reproduction and childrearing assumes new dimensions in virtually every sector of society. Pregnancy loss in Japan is only now being examined in this wider context. By implication, the essays collected by Ginsburg and Rapp provide a theoretical perspective on the Japanese scene:

> Reproduction also provides a terrain for imagining new cultural futures and transformations, through personal struggle, generational mobility, social movements, and the contested claims of powerful religious and political ideologies. These imaginings and actions are often the subject of conflict, for they engage the deepest aspirations and the sense of survival of groups divided by differences of generation, ethnicity, nationality, class, and, of course, gender.[54]

Intrinsic to their thesis is that as reproduction is moved to the center of social theory one looks again at every area of social life, including the medical profession, the politics of birth control, reproductive technologies, family life, human sexuality, demographic shifts, life course perspectives, and all levels of education. Central to this study of pregnancy loss known as *mizuko kuyō*, whether through abortion, miscarriage, or stillbirth, is not only how this may impact a woman's experience, as well as a man's "participation in and concerns about reproduction," but also how it brings to light a host of factors that are rarely part of social discourse.[55]

> Institutions may intervene into areas such as birth control, abortion, and maternal and child health in the name of social need or

national priorities but fail to acknowledge the impact of these interventions on the lives of women and their communities . . . [As] when a woman's identity as a mother (or nonmother) is split off from her sexuality and broader social relations. [56]

A significant complement to this discussion can be found in a recently published analysis by Masae Kato and Margaret Sleeboom-Faulkner of the narratives of fourteen women and the husbands of four of them, all of whom produced embryos through in vitro fertilization in Japan from 2006 to 2008.[57] A prime focus of this research details the meaning that their embryo has to these individuals, as voiced in their narratives. Of central consideration is the importance placed on the narratives not only of these eighteen persons but also on forty other persons, likewise in their early to mid-thirties. This larger group, composed of twenty-four women and sixteen men who did not have an IVF experience, but their reproductive experiences did include miscarriage, abortion, and stillbirth.[58] The narratives of the larger group reveal cultural values "attached to a prospective child" similar to the cultural values of the eighteen individuals with IVF experience. The key factor in each group is the value of a close relationship of a "mother" to her "child," whether that be a stillborn child or a fetus or, one might say, *even* an embryo.

Beyond the value assigned to listening to the experiences of women and men, as expressed in their interviews and in their written communications, the authors of this study stress the importance of honoring personal feelings and the ways they reflect social values. "We argue that a lack of sufficient analysis of the socio-cultural meanings of the embryo result in a situation where the use of reproductive technologies in Japan advances without reflecting upon the voices of women and married couples that use them."[59] As a consequence, there are alternative worldviews in which Japanese scientists argue that the "cultural meanings attached to the embryo are insignificant" in contrast to vivid expressions by women about the significance of their experiences prior to, during, and following the implantation of an embryo. Before their study there had been no evidence of such narratives:

There are several explanations for the underrepresentation of some voices in Japanese society in the process of formulating regulations [for human embryonic stem cell research]. In IVF clinics in Japan clients can hardly bring themselves to express their thoughts

and feelings about embryos to doctors. Instead, women under
IVF treatment write anonymously of their feelings on Internet
blogs...[saying] that they have no other space to express their feelings. In a situation in which there is little communication about
the meaning of the embryo between clients and professionals, IVF
specialists admit that they do not know what women and couples
feel during IVF treatment. [60]

The importance of listening to these expressions is equivalent to the value
of heeding the voices of women in our study who have lost a *mizuko*. It
was unexpected that the cultural values felt by those having IVF experience would be comparable to the meaning of a "prospective child" felt by
those experiencing stillbirth, miscarriage, or induced abortion. "Not surprisingly, those children actually born are indeed valued more highly than
are embryos...[but this does not mean] that embryos are valued lightly
compared to foetuses or actual children. To those who do not yet have
children, embryos *are* their children. For them, losing an embryo is painful."[61] Neither in IVF fertilization nor in *mizuko kuyō* has there been a
public debate about the emotional implications of pregnancy loss of either
kind. A key discovery is that these sociocultural values regarding the bond
between a "mother" and a "child" would be present this early in the relationship. Such a bond would not have been discovered apart from what
women and men were communicating. While the experiences of women
who have lost an embryo are distinguishable from those who have lost a
child, one finds them to be comparable in many respects. In both, one
recognizes the strong influence of Japanese social values, as constructed
and reinforced over time.

Primary Sources and Resources for This Project

The Harrison–Smith research project began by conducting extended interviews with a number of priests and other religious personnel at numerous
sites on the islands of Honshu and Kyushu, with the largest concentration
in the areas around Kyoto and Tokyo. We interviewed intensively during
the period 1986–88, less intensively until 1996, and I have taken periodic
soundings up to 2010. In addition to these interviews with clergy, our study
included the following primary sources: (1) interviews with lay individuals
who came to religious sites to participate in *mizuko kuyō*; (2) observations
of *mizuko kuyō* rituals at a wide variety of sites across Japan; (3) responses

to questionnaires of several kinds, designed and administered by us; (4) popular and scholarly materials published in Japanese and in English that directly addressed the topic of *mizuko kuyō*; and (5) a variety of popular, scholarly, and literary materials dealing with Japanese religion and with Japanese women especially. All of these served to view the primary topic of women and child loss within a larger field of vision.

Contacts with individual clergy and lay officials were central to this field study of *mizuko kuyō*. Had it not been for these contacts, we would have had a more limited access to the laypeople who came to these temples for help in their grieving process. Through permission from our contacts with priests and other religious personnel copies of our questionnaire were made available at many *mizuko kuyō* sites for people to write about their experiences. Approximately three hundred of these completed questionnaires were either returned to the site's office or mailed directly to us. The most valuable part of these replies was the comments made by women about what they actually do in *mizuko kuyō* practice.

A second resource of major importance was discovered in the first months of our field research, during fall 1986, namely, the Sociological Research Group on Contemporary Religion (*Gendai shukyō shakaigaku kenkyūkai*), composed of eight colleagues from Kyoto University (Kyōdai) and Osaka University led by Takahashi Saburō at Kyoto University. As this project unfolded, *mizuko kuyō* was studied from the perspective of five different groups: (1) 209 officials at sectarian headquarters of religious organizations; (2) 152 temple and shrine priests, ministers, and individual religious leaders, including spiritualists (*reinosha* or *ogamiyasan*); (3) 284 Buddhist temples in Kyoto Prefecture that were specifically self-identified as performing *mizuko kuyō*; (4) 1,127 individuals who came for *mizuko kuyō* to Adashino Nenbutsuji, a Jōdoshū temple in Kyoto; and (5) 59 spiritualists (*reinosha*) who were known to be conducting *mizuko kuyō* or some other kind of healing ritual.

Some of the data obtained from these questionnaires are discussed and analyzed throughout the book, but especially in Chapter 4. The primary focus there is on the survey of individuals who came to Adashino Nenbutsuji for *mizuko kuyō* over the period 1983–86. This survey was supervised by scholars at the Tokyo Institute of Polytechnics, in consultation with the Kyōdai group. The volume published in 1999 by the Kyoto University group contains not only a large amount of quantitative data, including written comments to open-ended questions, but also, at my request, correlations of various data sets that proved to be of great value.

This study provides information and perspective about particular religious communities, their activities, and their attitudes regarding the phenomena of *mizuko kuyō*. As a whole, this material contains the most extensive information thus far available about the people and social contexts in which *mizuko kuyō* is offered.

A third body of material provides in detail personal reflections over three decades at Jikishian, a small yet well-known Pure Land Buddhist temple in the Arashiyama area of Kyoto. This primary material known in Japan as *omoidegusa* (literally, leaves of memory) is a genre of informal recollections or reminiscences anonymously handwritten into notebooks placed on small tables in this temple. While notebooks of this kind are conducive to reflecting on very personal relationships and may be found in some other settings, the collection at Jikishian is exceptional in providing a spectrum of feelings of pain and anger about issues of sexuality, including abortion, that have been expressed by both women and men. The anonymous writers fill these notebooks with the awareness that their inner thoughts will be read by those who come after them. In this sense, their observations are unique and, while highly individualized, present a rich tapestry of human reflections on life. We were given eight published volumes of these reminiscences by the head priest, Oda Hōryū, who had continued the practice of collecting these reminiscences, which had been started by his predecessor, a Buddhist nun. Selections from this material, including extensive comments from the head priest, are the principal focus in Chapter 3.

Finally, though the largest extent of secondary comments on various aspects of *mizuko kuyō* has been from Western scholars, a number of further studies in Japanese need mentioning. While some have been translated, as of now most have not. Mention of these materials is found in two basic resources. The first is CiNii, which describes its purpose as a valuable database available from the National Institute of Informatics (NII) that consists of articles and citations to articles from scholarly journals, magazines, and university bulletins published in Japan. The second is WorldCat (World's Largest Library Catalog). In the latter, only a few need to be mentioned. Of sixty items listed, a large number of these have been cited and discussed in this volume. The CiNii listing is of greater use, and several items have been included in my bibliography. Some that were originally written in Japanese have been translated; most others have a useful abstract in English. While the topics are of some interest, they do not amplify the picture beyond what was already familiar. For the most part, these discussions fall into three categories: (1) the psychological difficulties (ambivalence) that women have in deciding to have an induced abortion; (2) the care of women (by nurses, for instance) who have undergone this procedure; and (3) the analysis of trends in induced abortion in Japan, especially among adolescents, compared with trends in the United States.

Framing the Discussion

The book's nine chapters are informally grouped in three parts. In most field study approaches, there is a progression of discovery—moving from awareness of greater complexity to a growing sense of why this phenomenon has greater historical, social, and cultural implications than could have been imagined in the mid-1980s. The plural term *worlds* implies that many disciplines and methods of study were employed to locate the issues that are intrinsic to this subject. In the process, different theories of interpretation provided different frames of reference about what is inevitably a political discourse about issues of importance to individuals and society at large. As already mentioned, these theories are discussed at several points in the book.

Part 1: Approaching the Worlds of *Mizuko*: Temple Sites, Interviews, Notebooks, and Surveys

Chapter 1 looked in detail at the contemporary scene, with primary emphasis on the response of women to child loss, the child or fetus as *mizuko*, and the ritualization of a mother's grief, as these are portrayed by the three strands of primary material just cited. This approach looks beyond what one finds in the public discourse and recognizes the diversity of people whose voices were being listened to.

Chapter 2 introduces the reader to the architecture, iconography, and doctrine of Hasedera, a well-known Jōdoshū temple in Kamakura, as a way of illustrating how classic forms of Buddhist teaching and practice are interwoven with the ongoing human concerns in life. Central to the teaching and practice of this temple, as at most Buddhist sites in Japan, are the sacred figures of Kannon and Jizō, who have long been perceived as responding to the needs of women. In fact, from recent Tokugawa research there is evidence of protective and healing rituals that reveal the serious attention that had been paid to child loss and the experience of women long before the emergence of *mizuko kuyō*.

Chapter 3 discusses two Jōdoshū temples in the Kyoto area that serve as different models of memorial services for *mizuko*. This material was obtained through interviews over a period of twenty years with the respective priests who conduct these services. Together with the materials in the genre called *Omoidegusa* (Recollections), the chapter provides extended comments on this material by the head priest Oda Hōryū at Jikishian in his efforts both to counsel and to place *mizuko kuyō* within a Buddhist context. The comments by Oda-san are among the most wide-ranging discussions of its kind by a Japanese Buddhist priest.

Chapter 4 expands this picture by analyzing portions of five questionnaires conducted by the Kyoto University research team. Particular attention is paid to the detailed survey conducted at Adashino Nenbutsuji, a temple in Kyoto; more than a thousand people, for whom memorial services had been performed, responded. This research project on women and experiences of child loss in Japan is the largest survey of its kind and is the only scholarly book-length study in Japanese on *mizuko kuyō*. Beyond analyzing the results of these surveys, this chapter discusses one of the five essays in the book published in 1999 by the Sociological Research Group on Contemporary Religion, based at Kyoto University under the direction of Takahashi Saburō.

Part 2: Deciphering the Worlds of Pregnancy Loss: Women, Men, and the Unborn

This part consists of three chapters that position the contemporary phenomenon of *mizuko kuyō* in a historical framework that begins with the Meiji period (1868–1912) and continues to the present time. The intent in these chapters is to analyze the social and cultural influences on women-as-mothers, on the changing relationship of the living to the dead, and the newly emerging forms of feminist critique of social prescriptions for the role of women in modern Japan.

Chapter 5 discusses social and political history in modern Japan (1868–2010) as this reveals cultural changes in the depiction of women's status in society, concentrating on the evolving role of motherhood from the late nineteenth century. This is the background for raising questions about how the social paradigm of woman-as-mother has contributed heavily to the close relationship between mother and child in the past forty years and how this feature sheds light on the impact of child loss, including abortion, in recent decades. As a way of illustrating the resistance that has

always been a part of Japanese women's compliance with social expectation of them, the chapter uses diverse kinds of disciplinary approaches:
historical perspectives, anthropological materials, demographic and life
course studies, literary works, and gender studies.

Chapter 6 examines the concept of *mizuko* as an anomaly within the
ancestral chain that stretches the limits of what being an ancestor means.
The various *kuyō* used for these "children," these "unborn," are adapta-
tions of regular memorial services for adults. In this way, *mizuko kuyō*
raises questions about who constitute one's ancestors and how the living
and the dead relate to each other. In this vein one examines the deeply
grounded theme in Japanese religious and folk belief of how the unme-
morialized dead on an even larger scale can return to haunt the living.
Included in this same discourse is the Japanese feminist critique of the
ancestral system and its implications, especially for women.

Chapter 7 discusses social and cultural constructions of motherhood,
how these have impacted women's experiences in pregnancy loss, and
how feminist critique over the past twenty years has focused on the interrelationship of power, identity, and sexual liberation. One example is the
manner in which Meredith Underwood challenges earlier feminist discourse (Japanese as well as Western) to look beyond the perceived exploita-
tive nature of *tatari* and to ask how this relates to the contemporary sexual
culture of Japan. A second example is found in Ueno Chizuko's observations about the expanding forms of women's bonding, based on "free
and pluralistic interpersonal relationship in which people can choose one
another," in contrast to the sense of isolation experienced by "the average
urban housewife." A third example is the perspective of Hashimoto Yayoi,
who, as a clinical and social psychologist, views the concept of *mizuko*
not only as a lost child or fetus but also as the mother's own, more fundamental potential. Hashimoto's grasp of this larger truth makes graphic
the unexpected question, "Who is the *mizuko*?" In general, the chapter is
a challenging of conventional interpretations.

Part 3: Reconceiving the Worlds of Profound Loss

The core of Chapter 8 articulates further the pain of pregnancy loss and a
number of ways healing is sought. The discussion includes both Japanese
and other cultural settings, forms of ritual that are religious and those
that are ritual-like but more artistic in nature, those that are contemporary
and others that have a long history, and circumstances in which shared

healing includes but a small number of people and some in which the community of shared pain and healing is wide-ranging. Two examples of healing rituals, found together at Jikishian temple in Kyoto in 1990, are described at length by Oda-san in one case and by Yvonne Rand, an American Buddhist priest who has performed *kuyō*-type services for many years in North America.

After discussing how pregnancy loss is increasingly being addressed through the arts, especially the performing arts, the chapter concludes by looking at artistic forms in postmedieval Japan of how the living have sought continuing relationship to the dead. These are expressed within well-known contexts—the Noh play *Sumidagawa*, the popular devotional song (*wasan*), and a site in northern Japan (Osorezan) to which each year hundreds of people go to seek a connection with a recently deceased person. Each of these has ritualistic, social, and historical ingredients, yet each speaks to forms of profound loss in contemporary existence. The most moving expressions are often channeled through works of art, many having no direct religious connection but are possibly ritual-like in breaking open new sources of imagination.

The intent of Chapter 9 is to locate human experiences of pain, suffering, and death on a wider screen. Earlier chapters discuss specific temple sites to see how ritual practices respond to the larger phenomena represented by *mizuko kuyō*. Because the issues involving ancestors and the rituals surrounding death are typically couched in cosmological language that rarely have the same significance they once had, the question arises of what might replace these. What kind of inclusive vision of existence supplies a scope and framework that, while beyond customary social and psychological realms, does not exclude them? This final chapter examines rituals that confront the ongoing conflictive nature of the human condition yet asserts that transformation is possible only when conflict is taken seriously.

2

Architectural, Iconographic, and Doctrinal Features of Mizuko Kuyō

SITUATED HALFWAY UP Mount Kannon on a lovely site in Kamakura, a carefully planned arrangement of buildings compose one of Japan's older and more prominent temples, namely, Hasedera. However well-known in the past, this temple has been noted more recently for its early response to the problems of abortion by offering memorial services for *mizuko* and for the visibility of its hillside throngs of *Mizuko Jizō*. Hasedera has remained independent from the doctrine and control of other sects, though it loosely belongs to the Jōdo-shū (Pure Land) tradition. Legend associates the temple's establishment with the washing ashore in 736 of an image of Jūichimen Kannon, the eleven-faced bodhisattva, at a place near Kamakura. Historical records preserved at Hasedera indicate that the temple became a site of major proportions in the mid-thirteenth century, during the Kamakura period (1192–1333).

In such a religious complex one sees the architectural and iconographic interplay between doctrinal forms of Mahayana Buddhism and what is customarily identified as concerns for this-worldly benefits or forms of protection. Over the past few decades there has been a changing focus in scholarly understanding of the relationship between paths of enlightenment and human needs and desires. The focus in these studies is more how they relate to each other than seeing them as entirely separate.

It is important to an understanding of *mizuko kuyō* that it be viewed within the dialectic between the central teachings of Japanese Buddhism and the ordinary lives of human beings. One finds this interplay in the sermons of Buddhist priests as well as in the research of scholars who are attempting to understand the complexity of Japanese religions and the changing social values since the beginning of the Tokugawa period in the early seventeenth century. While *mizuko kuyō* is a recent phenomenon, emerging in the 1960s and still continuing, it incorporates a significant number of religious beliefs and practices that, in many instances, have a long history. It is also clear that in the minds of many critics this movement distorts and misuses what it borrows as well as invents new "traditions" to justify its own existence. The purpose of this and subsequent chapters is to discuss how this long tradition has been employed in the controversial and many-sided phenomena of *mizuko kuyō*.

Doctrines, Practices, and Cosmologies in Wood, Stone, and Plastic

Entering the temple compound through a gate at street level, one proceeds to climb the hill on which are located various buildings that compose the complex until one reaches the summit. There the main hall dedicated to Kannon stands; in it one finds the central image of that figure. As one enters the main gate at the bottom of the hill, one passes a small hall immediately on the left dedicated to Daikokuten, a prominent deity known also by its Shinto name Daikokujin who is sought for happiness and worldly success, especially in commercial endeavors (Figure 2.1).[1]

Before continuing up the hill, one may turn to the right, proceed over a small bridge, and enter an area called the Benzaiten Grotto in which is located an unpretentious shrine or hall erected to Benzaiten or Sarasvatī (the Indian river goddess of music, learning, eloquence, and wisdom). On the sides of this hall are engraved images of sixteen children who represent minor deities serving the goddess, each of whom presides over realms such as long life, learning, love, progeny, and other desiderata. In India, Sarasvatī is traditionally associated as consort to the Hindu creator god Brahma and is often supplicated by couples, seeking offspring, for the "flow of children."[2] In Japan, the deities Daikokuten and Benzaiten are incorporated as part of the highly popular Seven Gods of Fortune (*shichifukujin*), found singly or in combined form throughout the country and whose widespread presence testifies to the ubiquitous concerns for good luck, health and well-being, longevity, and commercial success.

It is no accident that these two shrines or halls exist within a religious compound dedicated to Kannon, the bodhisattva of compassion, or that they are placed where they are, near the entrance. Pilgrims and tourists alike come with desires or needs of one kind or another in body, mind, and spirit. In fact, the majority of shrines and temples in Japan, as with their counterparts elsewhere, acknowledge the universal concern for this-worldly benefits. The point here is that human needs are respected

FIGURE 2.1 Kaizōzan Jishō-in (diagrammatic sketch of Hasedera temple compound, Kamakura). (Reprinted with permission of Hasedera.) (1) *Kannon-dō* (Kannon Hall) The central image in this hall, Jūichimen (Eleven-face Kannon), carved late in the eleventh century, is approximately 30 feet high and is said to be the largest wooden sculpture in Japan. (2) *Amida-dō* (Amida Hall) The central image here is a seated Amida Nyorai (Tathāgata Amitabha), about 10 feet tall, is the Buddha of the Pure Land to the west who grants rebirth in the Pure Land to those who recite or chant the *nembutsu* or name of the Buddha. Popularly known as the *yakuyoke* or "good luck" Buddha. (3) *Jizō-dō* (Jizo Hall) The Bodhisattva Jizō stands "at the border of this life and the next" and "guides the souls of the dead on the way to salvation." In the last fifty years Jizō is seen as the one to whom women pray for the safety and guidance of their *mizuko*. (4) *Daikoku-dō* (Daikoku Hall) The original image of this figure was moved to the Treasure Hall. In its place is the present image known as Daikokuten, to whom people turn for "success in worldly endeavors." (5) *Kyōzō* (Sutra Repository) Installed here is the *Tripitaka*, or Three Baskets of Buddhist scriptures. Rotating the shelves on which these sit represents a symbolic reading of the Buddhist canon and is considered an act of great merit. (6) *Shōrō* (Bell Tower) The original bell dates back to 1264 and is a precious asset, as it indicates that this temple was flourishing in the Kamakura period (1192–1333). (7) *Benten Kutsu* (Benzaiten Grotto) is associated with Sarasvatī, goddess of eloquence, wealth, music, and learning, who is surrounded by sixteen minor gods who serve her and preside over the previous areas. (8) *Hōmotsu-kan* (Treasure Hall) was built in the Meiji Period (1868–1912) and is the repository of many cultural treasures belong to Hasedera.

and, in spatial, architectural, mythic, symbolic, iconographic and ritualistic form, are observed within a temple complex that is dedicated to leading its visitors further along a religious path. While the deeper quest for liberation attracts those who sense their spiritual needs to be even greater, the basic concerns of men and women have never been foreign to the Buddhist path. In fact, in the worship of Kannon one finds paths toward enlightenment (awakening) side by side with concerns for protection and worldly benefits. This nonseparation, each element of which is carefully distinguishable, exists at the core of Japanese religious life and thought.

Continuing up the hill, one climbs stone steps en route to the *Jizō-dō* or hall in honor of the bodhisattva revered today especially for his concern for *mizuko*. Among the images that stand out in *mizuko* shrines, none is more dominant than the bodhisattva Jizō. Every student of Japanese religions recognizes the omnipresence of this figure, whose assistance is sought in numerous situations of need. Besides Jizō, two other figures from Japanese religious cosmology are of importance in how *mizuko kuyō* is constructed by various religious groups: the bodhisattva Kannon and the lesser known deity Hārītī from early Hindu and Buddhist pantheons, known in Japan as Kishibojin. Both of these figures are seen as female.

But the principal actor upon the *mizuko* stage is unquestionably Jizō. Before reaching that hall, one passes two areas set aside as visual reminders of Jizō's role in caring for the spirits of dead children. One is a large rectangular wall against which is set a depiction of a typical *sai-no-kawara* scene with its legend about children piling up pagodas of small stones on a dry riverbed, serving as a liminal zone between this world and that of the dead. It is sometimes said that each stone represents a prayer for parents who mourn the loss of their child. Along come *oni* or demons that knock down each pile of stones with equal regularity. The scene repeats itself day after day in Sisyphus-like fashion. Onto this scene, portrayed in deeply emotional hues, descends Jizō, savior of dead or endangered children, rescuing them from the implacability of this fate (Figures 2.2 and 2.3).

Conversation with the head priest of Hasedera at that time provided an ingenious way of interpreting this mythic story in popular Buddhism, a story often retold but rarely explored. The question I posed was how to interpret this story. Did most laypeople tend to take this story literally or not? His response was, "Probably many do; others may not." What about most Buddhist priests? He answered, "Some may, but most may not." "And you, sir, how do you interpret this story?" Without intending to be

FIGURE 2.2 Kannon and Jizō, located at entrance to Hasedera temple.

evasive, he said, "No, I think it is too important to be taken literally." The significance of that comment is threaded throughout this study.

Not far from this illustrated legend and farther along toward the Jizō Hall lies a meadow of small *Mizuko Jizō* figures, in plastic, bamboo, and stone, virtually mushrooming from the ground. These red, white, or pink-bibbed statues, some with knitted caps and others with rosary-like prayer beads (*juzu*) atop the shoulders of Jizō, provide in their vast numbers some sense of the legions of children who have been memorialized at Hasedera year after year, and, even more interesting, some feeling for the overlapping congruity of the Jizō and *mizuko* figures. While the statues are plainly of Jizō, each one represents a particular donor's belief that Jizō

FIGURE 2.3 Benten (Japanese name for Hindu goddess of the arts, eloquence, and wisdom) at Hasedera.

does for the dead child what the child (or its parents) cannot do for himself or herself.

Beyond these preparatory "stations" one reaches Jizō Hall, at which the ceremony of *kuyō* is normally conducted. Here one enters the doctrinally familiar worlds of Mahayana Buddhism, but reminders are everywhere that the worlds of so-called folk religion and canonical tradition are interfused. As the temple brochure comments, "Jizō has spread through Japanese popular religion in various forms, such as Jizō of longevity (*enmei Jizō*), Jizō of rearing children (*kosodate Jizō*), Jizō of vicarious suffering (*migawari Jizō*), Jizō of pulling thorns (*togenuki Jizō*), and Jizō of stillborn and miscarried or aborted children (*mizuko Jizō*)."[3] The principal, perhaps only remnant at this place from Jizō's

FIGURE 2.4 Jizō and cascading mountain of *mizuko* figures at Hasedera.

origins in India resides in the Sanskrit name *Kshitigarbha* (from which the Chinese Ti-ts'ang or Dizang and the Japanese Jizō derive), meaning *Earth womb* or *Earth repository* bodhisattva. Jizō's prominence originates in his unending vow to rescue all suffering beings, attesting to his resourcefulness and to the virtually infinite forms in which he may be found.

As one passes the Bell Tower (*shōrō*) and reaches the summit, one faces Hasedera's largest structure, three interconnected buildings with the prominent Kannon-dō in the center flanked by the hall for Amida Nyorai (Skt. *tathāgata*) on the right and a sizable Treasure Hall (*hōmotsu-kan*) on the left. Next to the Treasure Hall is the Sutra Repository (*kyōzō*) in which the "Three Baskets" (*Tipitaka*) are stored. This combines a locus for early Buddhist doctrine with symbolic readings of the canon in a form of prayer wheel practice. Even as one approaches the two cosmic symbols—the Buddha of the Pure Land (Amida) and his most revered bodhisattva (Kannon)—one catches the worldly juxtaposed with images of universal reality. The central image of Amida located here was constructed, for example, at the behest of the great Minamoto Yoritomo (1147–1199), the first shogun of the Kamakura period, as he approached his forty-second birthday, popularly feared as an unlucky year for males. Today, the image is still called the "good luck" or *yakuyoke* Buddha, drawing worshipers especially during the times of spring and autumn equinox.

In this juxtaposition of insurance against harm alongside a cosmic symbol for the lofty path of nonattachment, the worshipper is provided a visual sense of the connections between Buddhism's infinite levels of existence and its numberless means of deliverance. As Stephen Teiser comments, "Scholars working at the intersection of art, architecture, and Buddhist studies have long grappled with questions of representation, ritual, and meaning...A reading of temple architecture, then, does not lead straightforwardly to the discovery of an empirical audience. Rather, the layout of sacred space tells us as much about the implied ritual participant as it does about actual visitors to the site."[4]

Jizō and Kannon: Saviors from Hell, Bestowers of Blessings, and Guides to Paradise

In contemporary forms of myth and cosmology in *mizuko kuyō* one finds the omnipresence of Jizō and Kannon. As soon as one enters the precincts of any temple that offers memorial services for *mizuko*, one is aware of one or both of these bodhisattvas. Whether one comes as pilgrim, devotee, tourist, or student of religious studies, one enters a scene that is redolent with religious symbols in which the ancient past and contemporary life coexist in ways that each visitor discovers in her own manner. The quest for worldly blessings of one sort or another is typically part of visits to such a place; these may or may not be a cover for more spiritual forms of need. The power of the Hasedera site lies in its abundant depictions of how in Buddhist teaching and practice the paths of awareness and compassion are one yet manifold. In earliest Buddhist teachings they were sometimes called the "two wings of a bird." The rich symbolism of this temple's offerings connects these two, though in each visitor they resonate in different ways.

Because the present scene is in some sense contemporaneous with the past it seems appropriate early in this study to identify specific elements within *mizuko kuyō* beliefs and practices that in the past have been associated with Jizō and Kannon. This is not to say that the practice of *mizuko kuyō* as we know it today existed prior to 1960. Instead, it is to claim that the same deeper needs of people in centuries past are as present now as ever before. Coming to terms with suffering of one sort or another and the fragility of all existence provides a thread linking people across boundaries of time and place. While the worlds of Buddhism are peopled with bodhisattvas, some of these figures have remained prominent.

To examine their roles in "time past" is to understand more clearly why they continue to appeal. The average person who comes to a Buddhist temple for *mizuko kuyō* may be unaware of how Jizō and Kannon have been sought for one reason or another and how these have always included specific prayers for healing, long life, safe childbirth, and help in countless forms of unrest. At the deepest level the need may be spiritual, but along the way all forms of need are honored. The perceived nature of bodhisattvas, in this case Jizō and Kannon, is to be present in each circumstance.

Within *setsuwa* or narrative literature, in the *Lotus Sutra,* and in the *Sutra of Jizō's Original Vow* (*Hongan-kyō*) there are different strands of a worldview that opens up the middle ground. It is the substance of a bodhisattva's vow to connect this world with its cosmic ground of "miraculous power," yet this middle ground represents the possibility of transformation *within* the world as we know it. In this kind of cosmology, Jizō and Kannon become paradigms that provide the ordinary human world with a cosmic dimension, a dimension that is no less within this world than beyond it.

It is no accident that, when theories about the final age of the dharma (*mappō*) began to characterize Buddhist worldviews in Heian Japan (794–1185), cults dedicated to salvific figures such as Amida, Kannon, and Jizō emerged. In some cases, salvation was deemed possible only through rebirth in the Pure Land; in other cases, ultimate transformation occurs *within* the world. That is, Amida's grace transforms human obstacles, and worldly blessings are bestowed on devotees of Kannon or Jizō. The greater the sense of personal and social dilemma, the stronger became religious yearning. The bodhisattvas Jizō and Kannon emerge as parallel expressions of belief in the power of compassion extended to all social classes. Because each figures prominently in *mizuko kuyō*, it is appropriate to underscore their historic role over the centuries in meeting the needs of both women and children.

Among the many examples of this literature two are central: Tales of
Times Now Past (*Konjaku monogatarishū*), ca. 1120; and *Miraculous Stories
about the Bodhisattva Jizō*, attributed to the mid-eleventh century.[5] Each set
of narrative tales sparked Buddhist imagination with a sense of hope in the
midst of dismal settings. *Tales of Times Now Past* presents materials that
combine two equally strong accents in late Heian Buddhism: one is world
affirming, with emphasis upon worldly benefits (*genze riyaku*); the other
preaches deliverance from attachment, with accent on the world to come.[6]
If human effort is of no avail, human beings need help not only to attain
salvation but also to live in this existence without constant sorrow, danger,
or fear. These collections of tales provided signs of hope by grounding
human needs within a cosmology that saw no separation between this
world and the larger cosmos. Signs of miraculous cures and personal protection show up repeatedly in *setsuwa* literature where one might expect
petitions for worldly blessings, but these signs are also within texts like
the Lotus Sutra where the ultimate goal is rebirth in the Pure Land.

Stephen Teiser emphasizes this dual concern about Chinese Buddhism
in the medieval period: namely, there are more ways so-called orthodox forms of religion intermingle with so-called folk elements or popular religious expression than there are ways these exist separately.[7] This
is certainly true in the areas of myth, symbol, ritual, pilgrimage, artistic
expression, and religious biography in Japan as well. In this sense, the
Konjaku is encyclopedic, seeking to help its readers deal with the threatening and bewildering complexity of everyday existence.[8]

Around the mid-eleventh century another collection of *setsuwa*
appeared: *Tales of the Miraculous Virtue of Jizō Bodhisattva* (*Jizō bosatsu
reigenki*, Ch. *Dizang pusa xiang lingyan ji*). With twenty-five tales devoted
entirely to Jizō, these compilations provide a varied sense of Jizō's role
in the late Heian period. The image and function of Jizō as guide (*Indō
Jizō*) from the worlds of suffering to the realm of Amida were increasingly
prominent in the Kamakura period, with the founding of Pure Land sects,
when the dwelling place of bliss (*Sukhāvatī*) became the goal of those who
were devoted to Amida. In this way, the cults of Amida and Jizō were
frequently in tandem. The traits of Jizō as savior were seen as parallel to
those of Kannon, for both had become symbolic links in this expanding
cosmology.[9] As connective links, both were guiding spirits in the transition from one circumstance to another.

In her extensive study of Dizang (Jizō) in medieval China Zhiru Ng
makes the important point that the "Pure Land connection appears

often in the history of Dizang worship." It is precisely in this age without a buddha that Dizang emerges as a soteriological figure. In fact, one finds a "range of soteriologies, especially crafted to suit the exigencies of that period."[10] This distinction in medieval China between two salvific figures—Amitābha (J. Amida) Buddha and Dizang Bodhisattva—had its counterpart in Japan and may be found today in architectural and liturgical forms, as illustrated in the Hasedera temple in Kamakura. To note the origins of such differentiation centuries ago helps one to understand how Jizō continues today to combine the bodhisattva ideal of liberation with his role of alleviating suffering in the everyday world.[11] It is also true that through myth, symbol, and ritual Jizō is still viewed as part of a larger cosmology, even as cosmological renderings may have less heuristic significance to the ordinary person.

Faith in Jizō as Savior Figure within the Everyday World

Starting in the Heian period, a number of Chinese Buddhist writings dealing with Jizō were available in Japan. The most central of these was the *Sūtra on the Original Vow of Jizō Bodhisattva* (J. *Jizō bosatsu hongankyō*, Ch. *Dizang pusa benyuan jing*).[12] Copied in Japan in the mid-eighth century and often referred to simply as *Hongankyō*, this text presents Jizō as a savior figure, with mysterious powers, who appears in countless forms during the extended eons between the death of Shakyamuni and the advent of Maitreya (J. *Miroku*), the Buddha to come. This is the principal sutra dealing with Jizō's vow to save especially those trapped in hell or those undergoing excruciating suffering in this life: "I vow to establish many expedient devices in response to living beings who are suffering for offenses."[13] This sutra is an encomium in praise of Jizō's compassion for all living beings and is said to be the first Buddhist text in East Asia to introduce the possibility of salvation for women.[14]

Faith in Jizō (*Jizō shinkō*) was part of a late Heian syndrome that included belief in repeated rebirths for sentient beings within the six realms of existence. Though his emerging prominence in Japan was akin to that of Kannon, Jizō is regarded as more accessible to common folk. With the advent of dynamically construed depictions of human suffering, as one finds in *sai-no-kawara* legends and in pictorial form at Hasedera, one comes to understand better the extent of the pain that this figure addresses and the forms with which adversity is portrayed. The perception of Jizō's omnipresence makes graphic the continuing expression of his vow. Dotting the landscape, the figures of Jizō signify imagined cosmologies within the world of ordinary existence. Statues of Jizō may still be found throughout Japan, from deserted but once used mountain trails to crossroads around the land to tiny neighborhood shrines to chapels and main altars in larger temples.

Over time Jizō becomes the central figure in the drama of young children, infants, and the unborn in Japanese Buddhist cosmology and in related ritual. This is clearly the case in *mizuko kuyō*. As the Jizō cult grew, it found resonance among Japanese women who sought this figure in various conditions of adversity. There is evidence that, at least a thousand years ago, women desirous of conceiving a child turned to Jizō or Kannon in supplication. This was also true where the incidence of early infant death and women's death in childbirth were high. From the Kamakura period (1186–1333), evidence exists of *Jizō-kō* or lay associations at which "elderly women prayed for their future deliverance, while younger ones asked for easy childbirth or the well-being of their newborn babies."[15] These meetings, held on the twenty-fourth of each month, were traditionally an observance of Jizō's festival day (*ennichi*). Jizō's role as protector of children grew out of his association with the special needs expressed by women. As early as the ninth century there is evidence that prayers and amulets for fertility, easy childbirth (*koyasu*), safe delivery (*anzan*), good health, child rearing (*kosodate*), and life prolonging (*enmei*) became central features of how women especially related to Jizō over the centuries.[16]

The *Hongankyō* establishes the legitimacy of Jizō as a bodhisattva of major importance in East Asia. As with Kannon, Jizō is revered for purposes of meditation, liturgy, and cosmology as well as for reasons of benefit and protection. Among the features of this sutra is one of manifesting these coequal forms of devotion to Jizō: a quest for deliverance and salvation; and a plea for help in coping with everyday life. In a genuine sense, the path and the goal are inseparable. The intent is to alert persons to their buddha nature but in the meantime to help them through a variety of means to encounter and overcome inner and outer obstacles that becloud their vision and constrain their will.[17] In her study of Buddhism in medieval China Zhiru identifies how the unfolding success of Dizang lay in his ability to embody this twofold approach, thus undermining categories "such as elite versus folk, doctrine versus practice, canonical versus noncanonical, textual versus visual."[18]

It is typical of the *Hongankyō* that these two levels of devotion to Jizō are virtually in juxtaposition. In the sutra's final chapter, the Buddha, responding to questions about the benefits of paying homage to Jizō, mentions twenty-eight kinds of blessings, adding that these will accrue to all "good men or women in the future who... hear this sutra or read or recite it; who use incense, flowers, food and drink, clothing, or gems as offerings; or if they praise, behold, and worship him."[19] While no blessing is too inconsequential to be sought, the final blessing is to realize one's interdependence with other beings, to express this reality to those in intense suffering, and to be reborn in the Pure Land of Amida. While the classical statement on "skillful means" (*upāya*) is within the Lotus Sutra, Buddhism itself is the practicing of skillful means. Its cosmologies, teachings, symbols, rituals, and forms of meditation are of this order. Hell and heaven, the three so-called ages of the dharma, the six realms of sentient existence, the infinite vows and blessings of the buddhas and bodhisattvas are but means by which people awake to the reality from which they actually start: "emptiness" and "interdependent co-origination."

In any event, the worldly needs and yearnings of human beings are seen not just as starting points along the path to enlightenment but also as dominant expressions of need to which a bodhisattva responds in wisdom and compassion. As one reviews the shapes of myth and cosmology that were prevalent in Japan beginning with the tenth century, it is clear that considerable overlapping exists among the various religious worldviews. Bodhisattvas like Kannon and Jizō serve as guides, intermediaries, and workers of miracles to meet the needs of suffering beings by using infinite forms of protection, healing, and salvation on all levels of existence. This last worldview dominating the scene in early medieval Japan remains the substratum for many forms of devotional piety even in the present day and is often central to the belief and practice in *mizuko kuyō*.

Expanded Perspectives on Buddhism in Tokugawa Japan

Due to an enormous uncovering of new source materials over the past forty years dealing with the Tokugawa period, it became possible to examine in detail the social contexts in which temple Buddhism existed and how these temples interacted with one another and their own members. "Beginning in the 1970s, in every region of Japan down to the smallest of villages, local governments established historical archives for the purpose of publishing local history."[20] In the process, temples also created their own archives of manuscripts and records. The result was a "complex interplay of customs, beliefs and rituals shared across the spectrum of Japanese religions, such as healing or funerary rituals, [which] often served as the common denominator that bound priest to layperson, as well as members of different sects in the same village."[21]

In spelling out the complexity of this picture, Duncan Williams uses the term "management of the dead" to identify ways everyday, practical Buddhism offering this-worldly benefits coexisted with funerary Buddhism offering benefits for the world beyond. Utilizing these new sources, he and others have provided a rich sense of the ordinary or common life of both priests and laypeople. Accenting "the other side of Zen" creates a picture of how the "lived religion" and the "elite tradition" within Buddhism "shared a seamless reality...[in which] most of its priests ignored contradictions and lived in multiple universes of praxis without ever having to explain or integrate the whole."[22]

Nam-lin Hur makes a similar point about the commingling of Buddhist belief and practice with popular ideas and customs in the Edo period, though this commingling may be found throughout Buddhist history:

> Nevertheless, it should be noted that these Buddhist rituals are not strictly "Buddhist" in either content or structure. Traditional ideas and customs related to death pollution, purification, temporary lodges of deities, deification processes, ancestors, calendars, the other world, grudge-bearing spirits, and so forth were all inseparable from the context within which these "Buddhist" rituals were practiced. This was the religious context of Buddhist death, which contributed to the merging of funerary Buddhism and the *ie* society of Tokugawa Japan.[23]

Within these new source materials, there is evidence of both protective and healing rituals that reveal the serious attention paid to child loss and the experiences of women long before the emergence of *mizuko kuyō*. It is common knowledge that rituals of protection against various kinds of "hungry ghosts" (*gaki*) for which ceremonies (*segaki-e*) have existed for centuries. Rituals of this kind were intended to offset possible recrimination by spirits who were not given proper *kuyō* or by those who died without relatives (*muenbotoke*), or for women and children who died in childbirth as well as for children who died at a young age.[24]

To Williams, these kinds of practices had the impact of "universalizing funerary Buddhism in Japan by the seventeenth century."[25] The task of rituals was not only to protect the living against the angry dead but also to purify the spirits of those who had died in some unsettled condition and to make it possible for them to join the "collective ancestral body of the household."[26] While it was not customary for deceased children before they had reached a certain age to receive normal funeral rites, there was growing belief during the Tokugawa period that, because children also had spirits, special kinds of funeral rites and separate graves were appropriate for them.[27] Fabian Drixler in his study of infanticide in Eastern Japan during the Tokugawa period mentions that *"mizuko kuyō* (rites in behalf of water-children) were not unknown in the eighteen century. In 1756, a *mizuko kuyō* stone was erected in Shōgenji in Mamurokawa (in Dewa), just after a terrible famine in the area."[28] He cites also a *mabiki jizō* and a *kosodate jizō* being raised and dedicated elsewhere in the region during that period, arguably serving "a similar purpose of appeasing the wronged spirits of fetuses and infants."[29]

It would not be appropriate, however, to claim that these rituals in Tokugawa Japan were a foreshadowing, let alone a precursor, of what emerged centuries later in *mizuko kuyō*. On the other hand, death rituals, some informal in nature, were observed centuries before, "especially for women who had died in childbirth and for miscarried or aborted children."[30] Many of these would fall into the larger category of violent deaths, the kind that augur ill fortune if their "needs" go unattended. Even if no discernible link exists between what Williams describes and the phenomenon of *mizuko kuyō*, there is a shared train of thought that the welfare of the living depends to no small degree upon the perceived well-being of the deceased. The remnant of such a belief, while ordinarily now appearing in psychological garb, retains a strong motivating power.

In the introduction to their edited volume *The Buddhist Dead*, Bryan Cuevas and Jacqueline Stone provide a summary of how over the past twenty years in Buddhist studies, and religious studies generally, there has been an increasing shift to "claim as legitimate topics for study a range of hitherto marginalized areas, including Buddhist funerary and mortuary culture."[31]

> Once dominated chiefly by textual, philological, and doctrinal concerns, Buddhist studies has expanded in recent decades to include the methods of history, anthropology, and sociology, as well as

literary criticism, cultural studies, gender studies, and other disciplines... Buddhologists are increasingly expected to be familiar with the historical and social specifics of particular Buddhists
cultures.[32]

This is nowhere more prominent than "with beliefs and practices surrounding death." In this sense, death studies and Buddhist studies came
into a new kind of alignment. As one learns about the extent of these
practices, it becomes more evident that the feelings and experiences
being addressed by the performance of *mizuko kuyō* are universal, personal, and deeply human ones—even as the ritual itself is idiosyncratically
Japanese.

A parallel but strikingly different sort of evidence, also from the Tokugawa
period, provides expressions of bereavement experienced in the life and
death of family members. Indications of such personal grief are rarely if
ever found in the kinds of sources we have just discussed. For this reason,
the translations by Harold Bolitho of three separate accounts in journal
form by Japanese men who describe their loss of a child, a father, and a
wife provide perspectives on the emotions of grief to which there is seldom
access in premodern Japan. In fact, it is the contrast between the "wealth
of documentation" now available about this period and the relative silence
about the expressions of grief from individuals that include the emotions
of "fear, anger, joy, love, sorrow" that make these accounts extraordinary.[33]
"Even discounting their most uncommon feature, their emotional freight,
they earn their status simply because they record the ordinary deaths of
ordinary people."[34] At the same time, by providing the reader not simply
with depictions of loss and bereavement but also with a full spectrum of
domestic life, these accounts constitute "an entry into a world still largely
unknown."[35]

One learns almost in passing that the three men whose accounts of
bereavement are portrayed in these testimonies from Tokugawa Japan had
"fathered eighteen children, only to bury twelve of them."[36] In the face of
such loss and with the evidence that parents "wanted their children, felt
responsible for them, took pleasure in them, loved them, worried franti-
cally when they took sick, and mourned them when they died," it is natural to ask how they faced such sadness.[37] In what ways did the cultural
beliefs of their day provide consolation? How might the doctrines and rituals of Buddhism have made solace available?

If young children were not usually considered important enough to be given formal funerals, or graves, or offered memorial services, as has been claimed, that news had certainly reached none of these men, who did all those things for the children they had lost. If any of the three thought that young children were either expendable or interchangeable, or at best might be returned to the Buddha...they gave no sign of it in their writings. If they believed in some kind of afterlife, where the dead could be contacted perhaps at the cemetery or the household shrine, or welcomed at the annual *Urabon* reunion, might be in Paradise patiently waiting the arrival of other family members, they failed to suggest that this in any way eased their grief.[38]

This discovery by Bolitho implies there seems to have been no "uniquely Japanese defense against grief," no consolation that is adequate, no solace in the promise of a future dispensation.[39] Having to live with this lack of assurance constrains a person to cope with the indelible factor of finitude, of death in the midst of life; also, the source of dignity in a person's life is that she becomes able to dwell in the coexistence of these two realities. It is intrinsic to the attempt to understand how a woman or a man faces the extent of a loss whose bereavement and consolation remain often in some kind of unsettled tension that is both unique and universal. At its best, in any account of how people face child loss in its individualized forms one may discover in expressions of deep grief not only instances of human dignity but even more the nature and source of human community. This discovery is the process of healing. At its best, analyzing *mizuko kuyō* can provide glimpses of these realities.

Contemporary Mizuko Kuyō *at Hasedera*

In that initial conversation with the head priest of Hasedera Kannon, we learned of the agony felt by many women soon after World War II.[40] As Japanese people were returning to their earlier ways of life, women especially began to think of all the children who had died during the war or were left behind in Manchuria, which had been occupied by Japan since 1931. Even at that time there was fear that the spirits of these children who died such unhappy deaths would return to haunt the living, inflicting a curse or *tatari* upon the living.

According to this priest, a particular woman came to his temple to dedicate a *mizuko* statue, presumably of the bodhisattva Jizō (guardian and protector of children), about 1945 or 1946. This small statue aroused considerable attention among other women who shared similar grief and sorrow. Soon the practice of dedicating statues became widespread at this temple. Technically, this was not the beginning of *mizuko kuyō*, as the practice described by him did not yet include a memorial service. However, it was the earliest known forerunner at his temple of the ritual that began to take shape about the mid-1960s.

One of the points stressed by this priest is that the practice of *mizuko kuyō* became, for the first time in the 1980s, a major factor in drawing younger women into temple life, normally participated in primarily by much older women. In his words, "You need some kind of *en* (an intimate, karma-like connection) to be very close to the temple. For these young people, *mizuko kuyō* is the biggest *en*, and after their first *kuyō* the relationship between the young generation and the temple starts. The more often they visit the temple, the stronger and steadier their bond becomes."[41] At that time there were meetings twice a month with an average attendance of about seventy people, mostly women, 80 percent of whom had memorial services performed for their *mizuko*. (The priest added, "and also for the women themselves.") This community of women became an active group, a nucleus among a less active membership of nearly one thousand women whose names were listed in the temple register. According to this priest, the members of this core group remain deeply bonded to one another, having similar kinds of feelings with respect to loss, sorrow, and sometimes guilt. Most of these women were in their early forties to late fifties. It was his guess that women in their twenties or thirties were perhaps still too close to experiences of abortion to be willing to share these with others.

Our initial purpose to meeting with the head priest was to inform him of our research project, with the hope that he might invite people attending *mizuko kuyō* services at Hasedera to respond anonymously to our questionnaire. Over a period of two months (December 1988 to February 1989) we received twenty-six responses from this temple.[42] Four of the following six statements are drawn from those collected at Hasedera; the other two are from elsewhere. All but one were written by women. Each provides variety yet represents themes that appear frequently throughout Japan. Each has an unaffected quality, seemingly unscripted by religious doctrine, by fear of *tatari*, or by commercial pressure. What characterizes them is an experience of loss and a sincere effort to comprehend the meaning of this, untrammeled by the judgment of others. These reflections are presented here as a fore-taste of a larger sample of what follows in subsequent chapters:

I had a miscarriage when I was two months pregnant... The doctor said there was no particular reason for this miscarriage. From my point of view the fetus was my child from the time of conception. During the week I was in the hospital I frequently talked to the fetus, saying, "We'll make it! I want to hear the sound of your first voice." From the bottom of my heart I prayed. Even if it didn't come into being it remains a member of my family. I requested the temple for a *kuyō*, offering both candles (*rōsoku*) and incense. I felt relieved by doing this, and will continue to give *kuyō* for this lost soul.

KANAGAWA-KEN, age 28

For me, *mizuko kuyō* has many meanings. I have heard that some temples perform this as a profit-making scheme. Despite this, I believe it is good that one wants to give *kuyō* for a *mizuko*... Every month on the day of abortion I cry, and in my mind I pray. Three years have passed, and I've now decided to request *kuyō* and to express my feelings in a certain form. I came to Hasedera in part because it is not far from my house, and because it is in a beautiful and quiet environment facing the sea... While I do not think that performing kuyō will free me from feelings of guilt, I wanted to discipline myself by continuing to give *kuyō*. I will try never to forget this child who could not be born.

KANAGAWA-KEN, age 30

Twice, I have gone through abortion. For the first one, I had a service given at this temple [Hasedera] as well. I was determined then not to go through this again, but, unfortunately, I had another abortion after I married. At that time my husband asked me to give up having the baby. While it was hard on me and I felt more guilt than the first time, I obeyed my husband, but came here to pray for these two lost souls. Fortunately, my husband came with me both times; this was my only relief. I bought a Jizō statue, putting my name on it, and went to the *Jizō-dō* and the *Kannon-dō* to pray and offer incense to *Jizō*. I want to respect the tiny life that could not be born into this world, whether because of stillbirth or miscarriage or abortion, and to treat a *mizuko* as a person, not simply as a medical reality. Whatever happens, I won't keep worrying about this and will live my life as fully as I can. This will be the best *kuyō*.

JŌDOSHIN-SHU, Tokyo, age 25

I am hoping there may be some consolation (*nagusame*) for the child I was not able to bear…I gave the child a name. And, when various things happen, I share them with the child in my heart. I think the best *kuyō* is to remember it, not forget it. Responding to this survey is another way of confessing that I have sinned, and as such it is part of *kuyō*. No matter how much *kuyō* is done, it does not mean that suffering goes away (*ki ga sumu*). Because I am [still] keeping it secret from others, it isn't possible to get it out of my system. Aren't there times where telling someone else of something unpleasant is a release? But such release is not possible for me. Even with kuyō there is still bitterness (*nigai*) [in my heart]. After a year and a half of kuyō I am now more able to think about the child with calmness (*odayaka*). At the time of the event I was full of hate (*nikumi*) for the people who did not allow me to give birth (i.e., my mother, his parents, and others). I will continue doing *kuyō*. In spring of the year after next, I will probably marry the father of the child. When that happens, I would like to establish a *mizuko Jizō*, even if it's small, and to do *kuyō*.

YOSHIZU, KYOTO-FU, age 22

A number of features in these comments are frequently found in responses to the questionnaires we left at approximately twenty Buddhist temples and other religious sites in Honshu and Kyushu.[43] One feature is how often a woman talks to her *mizuko*, whether the loss was through voluntary abortion (*chūzetsu*) or due to miscarriage (*ryūzan*). In many cases, there is a personalization of the experience, an imagined conversation, an establishing of a relationship. Another common ingredient is a woman's expression of her own feelings, whether of guilt, regret, sadness, or some resolve about the future. Often mentioned as well is the importance of communication between the so-called parents of the *mizuko*, though just as often there is the absence of openness between them. As there is no one depiction of this experience, there is the expressed need for some means of coming to terms with the sense of loss, of which *mizuko kuyō* is one but not the only one. It is significant that the first four comments were written by people between the ages of twenty-two and thirty, while the last two are from persons who are forty-four and sixty years of age, respectively. The following two instances are more complex and call for extended comment:

I am 44 years old, and my husband is 48. We have an 18-year-old daughter and a son who is 16. We are a typical Japanese nuclear family. My last pregnancy was six years ago when my daughter was 12 (in junior high) and my son was 9 (in fourth grade). It was coming to the time when I was almost finished raising my children, and so I was hesitant to have another baby. Besides, we had just built our new house, which we could barely afford and which put us in some financial difficulty. Therefore, I started to think about getting a job to help meet these expenses. With all this in mind, at the age of 38, I decided to have an abortion, for the first time. I discussed this with my husband, and he agreed. At that time, I did not take abortion seriously. To me, it was just letting it [the *mizuko*] flow away like water (*mizu ni nagasu*). Since then, we did not have anything performed such as mizuko kuyō.

Now, however, after six years I was abruptly reminded of *mizuko kuyō*, perhaps because I had failed in raising my son. At such times of distress one turns to *kami* for help. I am deeply ashamed and disappointed with myself for being so selfish; I do not think I deserved to ask the *kami* for help. It started last spring, when my son who used to be such a good and honest boy seemed to change drastically about the time he entered high school when he was 15. He became rebellious. He started to smoke, wore clothes sloppily, getting to school late or leaving school before classes were over or escaping from school altogether. His behavior became worse and worse and he ended up getting involved in a case of violence.

This whole series of events was devastating, as if the whole life I had created, my belief, my strength, and my enthusiasm had been completely destroyed. For the next six months our whole life was topsy-turvy. However, although we admit that our way of raising children was not perfect, we didn't think it was far from the norm. We were not extravagant nor too poor, not too strict or too indulgent. We were just ordinary parents; we came to think this was just a trick of fate.

One day while shopping, I happened to see a fortuneteller (*uranai*) and, for the first time in my life, had my fortune told. As expected, I was told that the *mizuko* was jealous of my son and was therefore disturbing him. [On the other hand] I felt that the problems we were facing were the result of what we had done in the past. In other words, even if we were [conscientious] in how we had raised our son, we were wrong at the root, in our heart (*kokorogake*) as parents or rather as human beings. I cannot forget the fortune-teller's words: "Because it is your child just like your son." Thinking that I would not be pardoned with thousands of "forgive me" (*gomen nasai*), I was urged to pray. To speak of praying, this humble attitude of praying was what I had neglected. I began to reflect about myself (*hansei suru*). I used to regard kuyō or visiting a shrine (*miyamairi*) as a nuisance or as superstition or something out of fashion, pretending that I was an intellectual. How conceited I was. While I do not expect ever to be completely pardoned by performing this kuyō, what else can I do? This is at least a start.

KANAGAWA-KEN, no religion, age 44

In such a statement, many features draw one's attention. The first is the devastating sense of failure that can arise when one's child at whatever age seems, often suddenly, to rebel against family, school, and established norms. As will be discussed in Chapters 5 and 7, this is not an uncommon experience, and, because child rearing has for generations been viewed as a mother's responsibility, it is she who bears the weight of such behavior. The term *kyōiku mama*, while a descriptive stereotype, remains normative all too often. And, when taken seriously, this role becomes her *ikigai*, her raison d'être. The counterpart of the previous point is the question about the father's role in child rearing. In this particular instance, there seems to have been communication, but in another statement she adds, "I blamed myself, and my husband and I blamed each other. For the next six months our whole life was topsy-turvy."

A third aspect of such a quandary is obviously, "What constitutes good child rearing?" This may be the single most important ingredient. With this assorted puzzlement, not really knowing the cause of their son's revolt against authority, she is vulnerable to suggestions and finds herself consulting a fortuneteller (*uranai-shi*) "for the first time in [her] life." Even though she was told what she expected, namely, that all of this is attributable to her having an abortion six years ago, an all-too-common diagnosis of unresolved problems in the world of *mizuko*, the surprising element here is that she did not stop pursuing the real source of her family's predicament. Her sustained quest for understanding is in sharp contrast to attributing the unrest of a jealous *mizuko* to an abortion. In the end, one recognizes the maturity of this woman who, through a process of self-reflection (*hansei suru*), comes to detect a kind of conceit in her own makeup that she had not detected before. This is quite remarkable, as are the following comments from a sixty-year old man:

> Visits to the graves are made at *obon* and *ohigan*. Large cemeteries have been built in the suburbs of large cities, but I am surprised by the number of *mizuko Jizō* everywhere, and [even] the existence of graves for cats and dogs. It is taught that *Jizō-sama* is a wonderful (*arigatai*) bosatsu who travels between hell and this world to save the sufferings of all beings (*shūsei*). The sight of a smiling Jizō, standing at desolate roads or corners, with a soiled bib, as the "*hotoke-sama*" of common people, brings back many memories. However, recently in the new (*shinkō*) cemeteries, small and similar images have begun to proliferate under the name of *mizuko Jizō*. What is a *mizuko*? In *Kojien* it says it is a child very recently born—*akago*. But now the concept of *mizuko* has expanded to include aborted fetuses.
>
> According to a survey, the proportion of middle to senior age couples who have experienced an abortion is over 82%. When specialists are asked what current *mizuko* are, they cannot give a clear answer. This is because differing opinions are held regarding the issue of when life begins. We are warned that trying to decide on a particular point in time is a political issue. However, to become pregnant is to conceive a fetus, so it is a fact that a life has come into being at this point. Even if an abortion is not legally considered murder, it is to be expected that [many people] might have a religious awareness of sin (*tsumi*), or [at least a sense of] blame.
>
> Even if the practice is widely accepted, when a person involved experiences an awareness of *tsumi* through a feeling of regret, some means of atonement and repentance must be found. To repent and atone from the heart is to accompany the physical "purging" with a spiritual cleansing. However, this is not done through the erection of *mizuko Jizō*. Nor is it done through the worshipping of *Jizō-sama* in the heart, nor will erecting a Jizō save the parents, or the child.
>
> While I do not have a *mizuko*, many of my friends and acquaintances have had *mizuko* and there are occasions when we discuss *mizuko*,

but people often end up bemoaning the poor fate of their children. If good works do not accompany such feelings, the weight just becomes heavier…To feel sorry for one's child is natural for a parent, but to take that heart and extend it to others is the way of creating virtue (*kōtoku*)…When such a *kokoro* of serving the world and others in some way arises, then both self and others are saved.

ZENSHŪ, HYOGO-KEN, male, age 60

In a reflective approach similar to that of the forty-four-year-old woman just discussed, one finds in this sixty-year-old man an attempt to understand the phenomenon of child loss, specifically from an abortion. It seems extraordinary for an elderly man to be engaged in this kind of endeavor, which also lends historical perspective to the changes that have taken place in recent decades. In the process of thinking his way through such a decision he grants there may be legitimate afterthoughts of regret and that it is only reasonable to seek some kind of resolution of whatever mixed feelings one may have. Thus far, his is a rational approach to what may remain a moral dilemma. Recognizing that "feelings" may weigh heavy on the shoulders especially of a woman, his tack is gender inclusive in that there are inevitably two parties involved in this decision as there are in the conception of a *mizuko*. The gist of his argument is that genuine resolution comes by the combination of virtuous behavior (*kōtoku*) and reaching out to others in compassion, with sensitive feelings. As he says, "If good works do not accompany such feelings, the weight just becomes heavier." In this vein, he argues for a form of self-reflection that reaches out to others that goes beyond self-preoccupation or doing "religious works" to justify one's behavior. In other words, true cleansing of one's spirit may have nothing to do with "erecting a Jizō statue" or even with performing a *kuyō* in memory of a *mizuko* without a basic amendment of life.

From Kamakura and Hasedera on the slopes of Mount Kannon we move to two other Jōdoshū temples in the western part of Kyoto. As in the case of Hasedera, these temples have existed in one form or another for centuries, and both have also been active in reaching out to individuals who come with needs of a personal nature, including that of pregnancy loss or induced abortion. Chapter 3 looks at each temple and how its ministry has evolved in recent decades, often relating to those who are not *danka* or regular members but who come for *mizuko kuyō*, maybe once, maybe many times. Conversations with the priest at each temple have provided a perspective of almost two decades in one case and twenty-five years in the other from the mid-1980s to 2010. In each instance one has the impression of a person who has responded with sensitivity to those who come seeking help. This chapter provides a detailed sense of the concerns that women especially bring to such temples and how these reflect or are congruent with the wider social and cultural anxiety that exists in contemporary life.

3

Situating the Rites of Mourning

TWO TEMPLES AND A VARIETY OF VISITORS

In the middle of the novel Beauty and Sadness (*Utsukushisa to kanashimi to*) by Kawabata Yasunari (1899–1972), a mother and daughter visit Adashino Nenbutsu-ji in the hills of Sagano in Kyoto. It is the season for Bon, the Festival of the Dead, at which time custom calls for welcoming home one's ancestors, entertaining and feeding them, and sending the sated spirits back to their realm (*yomi no kuni*)...[In this case] the two fictionalized visitors to Adashino are drawn to this ancient burial ground by a solemn ritual of mourning constituting the temple's most important annual ceremony: the *sentō kuyō*. At dusk on 23 and 24 August a thousand candles are lit and placed at the old gravestones rendered anonymous by wind and rain. Mother and daughter participate in this memorial rite for the unaffiliated and unmourned dead (muenbotoke) in the sacred grounds of "'the children's limbo"' (*sai-in no kawara*).[1]

AT THE HILLTOP temple of Adashino Nenbutsuji one's initial sight is an extraordinary field of 8,000 roughly carved stone Buddhas (*sekibutsu*), who are said to honor the spirits of the dead whose bodies had been brought here since the Heian period (794–1185). For centuries, the destitute of the Adashino area have lain their dead on the sloping mountainside behind what is now the temple, leaving these unclaimed dead exposed to the elements. Receiving no gravestone or proper burial, these spirits are now honored as ancestors without family designation. They are the unmourned dead, the unaffiliated ancestors, left here in repose as *muenbotoke,* the dead with no known bond to the living. As is often mentioned, the sight is evocative in the late afternoon, as the shadows beneath the figures lengthen. This is especially the case when large numbers of people gather at nightfall for the "Service of a Thousand Lights" (*sentō kuyō*) and light votive candles, "illuminating a path home," as they say, for the anonymous spirits of the dead. It is a sight that serves as one image of the unborn dead (*mizuko*) as well, a being that lingers between light and shadow and at the boundaries of life and death, which is the focus of this study.[2]

The first part of this chapter concentrates on interviews with the late Hara Satoshi, a priest at Adashino Nenbutsuji, over a period of sixteen years (1986–2002) on topics that were of central importance in his ministry to those who visited his temple. These topics included his role as counselor to those seeking advice; discussions about birth control, abortion, and *mizuko kuyō*; and his assessment of the expanding commercialization of this ritual in recent years. It is of considerable interest that Hara-san chose in this first interview to draw attention to the topic of *sexual culture* in Japan. It is a topic to which this book returns with some frequency.

The chapter's second part concentrates on the *Omoidegusa* notebooks (of reminiscences, recollections) that play a significant role in the appeal, especially among young people, that Jikishian has had for a long time. Selected entries from the collected eight volumes of these published notebooks are included, along with discussions by the nun Hirose Zenjun in the first four volumes and at greater length by Oda Hōryū, who succeeded her as head priest (*jūshoku*), drawing from several conversations with him and especially from the last four volumes.

Conversations at Adashino Nenbutsuji

Hara Satoshi began this particular conversation by discussing a social phenomenon known as *furin* (literally "affair" or "illicit love") that became popularized in the 1980s.[3] It referred to the impression that women (ages thirty to thirty-five) were having affairs with younger men (college age through ages twenty-three to twenty-five). Hara-san called this kind of relationship *futsuriai* ("out of proportion," "incongruous" or "unbecoming" because the woman is older). On the other hand, the slang term *tsubame* ("swallow" or young lover) connotes a little bird (a younger man) kept by an older woman. As Hara-san said, while this kind of relationship has existed since olden times, it was less out in the open then. It was "taboo." Until recently, should one of the couple come for *mizuko kuyō*, it would be the woman, but now they occasionally come together.

Since this interview was conducted in 1988, it was only five years after the movie *To the Friday Wives* (*Kinyōbi no tsuma tachi e*) that dramatized the term *furin* with its focus on affairs between married people (in contrast to the more traditional style of men playing around with women, mostly unmarried women). A Wikipedia entry referring to this movie, which was released in 1983 by TBS and Kinoshita productions, discusses a TV drama series whose theme was the relationship between "nuclear families" and *furin* (affairs) that occur among these families.[4]

Reflections on Counseling

In recent years the numbers of people ages eighteen to twenty or younger coming to Nenbutsuji for *mizuko kuyō* have increased. As to the question of whether it is easier these days to talk openly about birth control, Hara-san responded that thirty years ago discussions about sex almost never occurred. During the past ten years (in the 1980s), according to him, this had changed markedly. At one point he called *mizuko kuyō* a *ryūkō* (fashion/fad) but suggests now that the growing openness about sex may actually be a side effect of the ritual of *mizuko kuyō*.

He had therefore begun to talk with people (especially young women) about the importance of not making the same mistake again. Even though men are equally responsible for causing pregnancy, because men do not experience abortion directly, in their own body (*dansei wa amari kankei nai n desu ga*), Hara-san believed it had less or no aftereffect on them. In his view, however, women of high school age (sixteen to eighteen) who have one or more abortions do damage to their body and their spirit or psyche (*kokoro*), saying that this will haunt them by the time they reach menopause. If women want to grow old "beautifully" (he used this word several times), they need to be attentive to the damage they may be doing to their body and psyche at this point in their young life. He called the effects of abortion on body and mind *kōishō* (lingering effects of disease). Before this trend (among younger visitors and mismatched couples), he purposefully refrained from giving such advice, realizing the need to tailor his words (*hanashi*) to the age of the listener and not to talk only about religion.

In responding to women who seek help in breaking up with their partner, he told them that they already have a wonderful family and husband, that right now because they are a fully mature woman or man in their own right they should return to their family. In discussing this whole phenomenon, he used some expressions multiple times: (1) *rippa na* (wonderful, fine, splendid, magnificent) in reference to family and husband and to the women themselves (in which case it means "mature or responsible"); (2) *tsumetai* (coldhearted) used often to signal his refusal to sympathize with them and to tell them to return to their family; and (3) *tsuki-hanasu* (to push away) used more than once to indicate that he wanted them to solve their own problems, such as talking with her husband or partner.

According to Hara-san, the mother is the mainstay of the family; the father is like a *hojoyaku* (assistant) who steps in when needed. Most men are so busy with work they tend to neglect their wives, though in recent years men have obtained a small amount of time off on Sundays. In general, because she is neglected, the wife is lonely; her children are older and she is less busy, with free time on her hands. In the years while her children are young, she has little or no time to pursue her own interests and thus grows out of touch with once familiar pastimes. She has a space (of time, in her heart) that she is seeking to fill. This may explain the psychology of women who get involved in affairs, particularly with younger men. He reminds women of their central place in the family and encourages them to understand their husband's situation (*otto ni taisuru rikai*): "It's not that he hates you; he is just busy."

Hara-san emphasized the importance of solving these sorts of problems by oneself. Though one may regret the past, one must move ahead. Only as one suffers through resolving the problem does one refrain from making the same mistake again (*jibun de kaiketsu shita kurushimi dewa, nido to ayamachi o okosanai*). In contrast to women who are thirty to thirty-five, young women have a life ahead of them (with a new partner), but with women who are older he stressed that they "already have a wonderful family and husband." He reiterated the importance of returning to the family (*katei to iu mono ni kaette iku*).

When asked whether there were surprising results from the questionnaires recently filled out by the hundreds of women coming to his temple for *mizuko kuyō*, he said there were many more cases where women had "2, 3, 4, even up to 7 or 9" abortions than he would have suspected, even though one abortion remains the norm. This unexpected incidence of multiple abortions prompted him to think about *ningen no morosa, yowasa* (human fragility and weakness). On the other hand, he joked that a woman who has had multiple abortions might say *mata onaji shippai shita wa* (Oh dear, I've gone and made the same mistake again). Rhetorically, he wondered, "Why do they repeat the damage to themselves?" "In this sense," he added, "the human heart hasn't changed since primitive times."

With respect to the overall data from the questionnaire, Hara-san's main comments were as follows: Women's feelings can't be expressed just by numerical data; human emotions are complex and cannot be made to fit the data; and it is difficult to see overarching patterns when there are so many influences upon each person's life, behavior, and thought, hence the importance of their varied responses to these questions. In the future, he had planned to inquire further about *nihonjin no shūkyō ishiki* (the Japanese consciousness or way of regarding religion).

Discussion about Birth Control, Abortion, *and* Mizuko Kuyō

Actively participating in this next interview, conducted in fall 1990, were Bardwell Smith, Shinji Kazue, and three American students (Amy Dreyer, Karen Matta, and Dawn Ollila), who were enrolled in a year-long intensive Japanese language and homestay program for college juniors known as the Associated Kyoto Program (AKP) that began in 1972. They were part of a class doing a field study approach to several forms of Japanese religions in the Kansai area, and it was their choice to focus on *mizuko kuyō* at both Adashino Nenbutsuji and Jikishian.⁵

BARDWELL SMITH (HEREAFTER BLS): How do Buddhist groups in Japan educate their adherents about birth control?

HARA SATOSHI: While abortion [actually *mabiki* or infanticide] may have been unavoidable due to severe famine in times past, Buddhism teaches that the fetus is considered to be a human being from conception. Because of this, abortion is regarded [by many Buddhists] as homicide; that is why we tell women not to have abortions. As stated in the Eugenics Protection Act (*Yūseihōhō*) of 1948, in the case of rape, abortion is legally allowed, which means that we do not say that all abortions are wrong.

While Hara did not talk much about birth control, he supported sex education and often referred women to a doctor to discuss contraceptive methods. When asked what particular methods are most commonly recommended, he cited *hinin-yaku* (birth control medicine) for men and women, condoms, and vasectomy, which he called "pipe cut." [This produced much laughter.] He acknowledged that birth control is not infallible; it may work for some but not for others. Besides providing rudimentary medical advice, he taught that they should regard sex as a sacred act and that their mental and spiritual attitude (*kokoro no mochikata*) is essential. Both men and women should take the responsibilities of sex seriously, men no less than women.

Couples who already have a sexual relationship are apt to hide this from parents, even from close friends. They do not want to be seen as wild or crazy (*tonda*). They are often willing, however, to discuss these matters freely with Hara-san. Many who come for consultation talk seriously about their relationship, including marriage. Some return more than once, and at times he is invited to their weddings. In many cases, he is the counselor who helps them to focus on the "goal" of marriage.

BLS: It seems as though the high rate of abortions is because the most common method of birth control (the condom) depends upon a responsible use by males. Would the rate of abortion be less if the pill were more extensively approved and available?

HARA SATOSHI: Yes, this is true. And because so many in Japan continue to favor *dansei-jōi*, with the male in a higher position (of authority), women remain submissive. The male ego is deep-seated. Therefore, the kind of birth control still practiced today in Japan remains in its infancy. Even young people, despite their wild (*tonda*) and rebellious ideas, behave according to older traditions. Additional factors exist. Large numbers of Japanese boys and girls have only a high school education; many have grown up in small villages and may thus be ignorant about how to use birth control effectively. Even more important, young people nowadays live in nuclear families, or alone, and therefore have fewer if any members of an extended family with whom they might consult. Finally, increasing numbers of young people who have abortions are unemployed, or are part-time workers, students, or who work at home. Next in number would be those who work in small companies (for instance, *kaisha-in* and office ladies).

BLS: Japan's birth control methods seem to be primarily controlled by males (for instance, the condom or withdrawal). Why is this so?

HARA SATOSHI: One factor may be that gynecologists make considerable money on abortions. While this is not true of well-known doctors in hospitals, it is perhaps the case with those who have their own clinics and who may specialize in abortion. If there were more women gynecologists, more serious attention would be given to women's perspectives. For about ten years there has been discussion about the pill becoming available in drugstores. Actually, it is relatively easy to get a prescription. It is unclear, however, how much Japanese women know about the pill's effectiveness. There are rumors that it is ineffective, and therefore some do not trust it.

In conversations with women or couples, Hara-san stressed that it is the woman who will be hurt by having an abortion and that they must be careful. While one can talk about birth control, Japanese people often have a sense of uneasiness, even lack of trust (*fushinkan*), regarding new (Western) medicines that they know little about, the pill in particular. Hence, they are reluctant to take that step.

BLS: When you enjoin women to take their experience seriously, are you implying that they do not?

HARA SATOSHI: The main reason women (sometimes with their boyfriends) come for consultation is to ask how they can avoid being in a situation where they are apt to have a *mizuko*. That is when it is important to talk seriously with them about what they are doing.

BLS: Regarding the memorial service (*kuyō*), have all participating women had a *mizuko*? And are they embarrassed?

HARA SATOSHI: There are different kinds of feelings; there is no one pattern. Some are worried about *tatari* (revenge by angry spirits) and also feel sad for their baby's spirit; some have feelings of guilt (*tsumi*). One of the goals of *kuyō* is to alleviate the feelings of guilt. Probably ninety percent do feel some guilt, and the service helps to alleviate this.

BLS: Won't telling them not to take a life increase their feelings of guilt?

HARA SATOSHI: Since artificial abortion (*chūzetsu*) has already taken place, there is nothing they can do about it. Part of what occurs in counseling is to help them deal with the regret that follows, but they are also told not to repeat the same mistake.

BLS: How do you respond to charges about the commercialization of *mizuko kuyō*?

HARA SATOSHI: Those who come to this temple for *kuyō* are discouraged from making expensive gifts. Rather, they are instructed to keep the *mizuko* in their hearts and minds, perhaps offering little remembrances like snacks, as if their child had actually been born. This will keep them conscious of the spirit of the *mizuko*, but does not cost money. It is true that at some places these services cost lots of money; that's when *mizuko kuyō* becomes commercialized. For example, one woman reported going to a fortune-teller (*uranai-shi*) who told her to spend tens of thousands of dollars on a statue for her *mizuko*. This is clearly irresponsible behavior.

BLS: Does the ceremony you perform differ depending on whether it's an abortion or a miscarriage?

HARA SATOSHI: No, the ceremony remains the same, but the feelings people have may differ considerably. The majority of women who come to this temple for *mizuko kuyō* are not married, and about 10 percent are engaged in extramarital relationships. Those who come are worried about their own responsibility. When young couples come together, it is the woman who is more *sekkyokuteki* (talkative, participating actively) in the conversation, possibly because women are more hurt physically and mentally by the act. When they come as a couple, they are often thinking seriously about marriage (Figures 3.1 and 3.2).

Hara-san added that it is sometimes difficult to understand young people's ways of thinking; the current generation seems to be "testing" each other's feelings by means of their sexual relationship. They worry that even if they love each other they might not be compatible sexually. Hara-san and his generation call these people *shin-jin-rui* (a new race of human beings). The very idea of loving someone but "not being sexually compatible" is difficult for his generation to fathom. Once more, he used the term *tonde iru* (fly away, strange or weird).

BLS: What sort of cases do you see the most?

HARA SATOSHI: Some have already had an abortion; some come before taking that step and ask what would happen if they had to have an abortion. But 70 to 80 percent have had an abortion (as distinguished from miscarriage or stillbirth). A small number (10 to 20 percent) may have lost a child or fetus due to some kind of accident.

BLS: How long has this ritual been around?

HARA SATOSHI: No one knows; it probably evolved from the Buddhist practice of doing "wakes" (*tsuya*) for the departed. As for the word *mizuko*, it may date back to the Kamakura period. At that time, there would have been no abortion. First, what is "*mizuko*"? Originally, "water," which here means drinking water. Like water, the fetus washes away completely (*nagarete shimau*), "easily slips away." It doesn't become a living being; it simply flows away.

FIGURE 3.1 An artist's rendition of a small *mizuko* shrine, using an old style sign with kanji reversed, by Dale Haworth.

It also may mean *mizu*—to not see, because the child dies without seeing the face of its parents. It doesn't see the "light" of the world. This doesn't imply only aborted children. In the middle part of the Tokugawa Period (1603–1867) when there are too many children and not enough food, they would often put the child to death as soon as it was born (*mabiki*).

Another meaning for *mizuko* relates to the word *ubuyu*, the water used for washing the newborn. In cases of *mabiki*, sometimes the midwife and family would drown them in the *ubuyu* and therefore they would become *mizuko*. Another method would be to soak a piece of rice paper and cover the baby's mouth and nose. Rice paper, once wet, is hard to tear, so the baby is suffocated. Again, the method is related to water.

So the word *mizuko* has lots of dark connotations. It was only in the postwar period that the term *mizuko kuyō* began to be used. Before that, the wakes (*tsuya*) for aborted fetuses or killed children were held

FIGURE 3.2 Three AKP students and Shinji Kazue, at Adajino Nenbutsuji, Kyoto.

out of the public eye and never talked about. So the practice of abortion and *mizuko kuyō* has been in the background throughout the years.

In conclusion, Hara-san talked about *kakochō* or records (death registries) of the history of a temple, of "the past." These records include things that happened to the *danka* (congregation), including children who died. In the Edo (or Tokugawa) Period there was the well-known Tenmei Famine (1780s) during which time there are records of wakes performed for nameless children (who must have died or been killed as infants). The detailed records of Nenbutsuji go back at least 300 years. Records were kept when the temple first opened, about a thousand years ago, but they were all destroyed when the temple was occupied by thieves and was burned. We know that the main temple hall was built in 1712 and contains a medieval sculpture of the Amida Buddha created by Tankei (1173–1256) in the Kamakura Era. The details of the old stones in front of the temple are unknown, but they are gravestones. Some of them still have names, though these are not famous names.

Assessing the Commercialization of Mizuko Kuyō

(Participating in this interview on October 3, 1992, were Hara Satoshi, Bardwell Smith, and Shinji Kazue.)[6]

BLS: What kinds of changes in the practice of *mizuko kuyō* have you seen within the past few years?

HARA SATOSHI: In the past, *mizuko kuyō* was focused on *kokoro no sōdan* (consultation about matters of the heart), but recently money has entered further into the picture. Now women come after being cheated because of a new business called *reikan shōhō* or *reishi shōhō*. For instance, a spiritual advisor tells them that because they wish to confer with the dead they need to buy expensive products or conduct costly rituals to protect themselves. Some women come here for the first time to complain about this, and some have seen such a person before.

The current trend is to use a person's desire to believe as a way of extracting money from them. Because women who perform *mizuko kuyō* want to keep their abortion a secret, predators use this fact also to make money off of them. For example, one woman was fooled into buying expensive things for *mizuko kuyō*. She was about to turn on the gas and was prepared to die. I said to her, "Okay, go ahead." Later, she called back, and after talking with her for more than an hour she did not commit suicide.

Yes, some temples are involved in these schemes. The approach of *reikan shōhō* is completely different from that of *mizuko kuyō*, but there is a new kind of *mizuko kuyō* that combines elements of *reikan shōhō*. When they sell charms, *mamori* (protection amulets), statues, etc., they claim that these objects will have a magical effect. They then inflate the price for a rosary (*juzu*), for example, from one or two thousand yen to 100,000 or 200,000 yen.

BLS: Does criticism of this phenomenon affect the general perception about *mizuko kuyō*?

HARA SATOSHI: No, but the critics imply that those who benefit from this kind of scam must be rich.

BLS: Who are the main critics of this practice?

HARA SATOSHI: In general, women are the most critical. At Nenbutsuji, the basic principle is *jiyū* (free-form). Women are told to use the talents they have to make *sonae* (offerings) for the fetus, such as sewing a kimono, or making a flower arrangement. They are told not to spend a lot of money. When people say they were told that for a proper *kuyō* one should spend large sums of money, we tell them that a large, one-time payment is not the way to do *kuyō*. Had the child lived, a woman would have provided care for it day after day, so she should do something on a regular basis every month or every year in remembrance, some little thing that a parent would do for or give to their actual child. This might even continue until the child reaches the age of leaving its parents (*seijin no hi*, age 20).

To Hara-san, the commitment to remember the *mizuko* was the important thing, not the act of giving money. They can buy prayers and incense burners if they like, but they are not required to do so. He thought this emphasis on spending money might reflect the growing wealth of Japanese society (as it was until the early 1990s). Even young women can afford a large outlay. These new religious groups work together to extract sizable amounts of money.

BLS: Do women write about this phenomenon in responding to the questionnaires?

Hara-san replied that he stopped handing out these questionnaires around two years ago. He still had 2,000 or so that had been completed earlier and was then considering a new survey that would be more appropriate to the current situation. For instance, he would add questions about money, such as how much they can afford. He would also ask them about *reikan shōhō* and warn them how to avoid it.[7] (In fact, he died before doing that.)

BLS: Have other temples done such studies?

HARA SATOSHI: This may perhaps be true, but they do not communicate with one another. Not that this is secret, only that there is no custom of exchanging such information.

BLS: How about the headquarters of the Pure Land sect (Jōdoshū)?

HARA SATOSHI: They are not currently doing this kind of research.[8]

BLS: Do they teach priests who are interested?

HARA SATOSHI: No. They want to avoid criticism for appearing to encourage abortions. For instance, they hope the phenomenon will become less established, so that women will not think that having a *kuyō* justifies abortion. Also, they do not want to be associated in any way with a *reikan shōhō* type of *kuyō*, one in which people are pressured to pay high prices for services or religious objects. As to which people are especially vulnerable to such practices, since 60 to 70 percent of Japanese women have had an abortion, stillbirth, or miscarriage, the "crooks" usually target single women, twenty-eight to thirty years of age, who are sometimes called *hai misu* (misses of a high age). Some of these "con people" are priests; actually a larger number are women.

They find women in their twenties or thirties in their workplaces or on the street, pressure them to conduct *kuyō*, and sell them expensive implements. They say that the spirit of the *mizuko* is watching them 'behind their back,' and that they need to get rid of such a spirit in order to be happy.

BLS: Are more women coming for counseling?

HARA SATOSHI: The visits seem to have leveled off. Recently we have come to realize that those who are recruited into the business of *reikan shōhō* are often women. The bosses are men, but the women who work for them prey on the weaknesses of their own gender. Of those who do the actual canvassing, many are insurance saleswomen who try to get other women to buy *kuyō* on the side. Women running such a scam can use information from these questions for insurance purposes, such as, "Have you had an abortion?" Even if the victim appeals to the police, the perpetrator frames it as an *extra service* they offer. There are many cases in which women lament about having been tricked. When they call the insurance company to complain, the company denies the existence of such salesladies.

BLS: Are there other changes in recent years?

HARA SATOSHI: *Mizuko kuyō* is not decreasing. Worshippers who come to our temple fill out the form, get a candle, and an incense burner and pay their respects (*omairi*), but they are told they do not need to do it that way. Some come every holiday and buy miniature dolls, *koi-nobori*, boots filled with Santa Claus candy [and so forth] for *sonae* (sacrifices). There are also women who come for *kage-mairi/ kakure-mairi* (shadow or hidden visitation without letting the temple know), so it's hard to gauge the exact numbers. When one totals all the pages in the record book, it is a sizable number, but judging from the even larger number of candles and incense offered it's possible there are three times as many worshippers.

Nenbutsuji has a *mizuko* service on the twenty-fourth day of every month. Some visitors do *kankuyō* or regular visits every year. In that case, the name of the *mizuko* is read aloud at the service, even if the woman or family does not attend each time. One set of the candle (*kyogi*) and incense burner costs 1,000 yen, but the one-year package costs 12,000 yen. One can also pay for three months or for six. These women come from all over Japan, although Kyoto, Osaka, and Shiga are the most numerous. The temple opens at 9:00, and from 9:30 until 4:00 there are numerous visitors. Many who come to Nenbutsuji just for *mizuko kuyō* are not of the Jōdo-shū sect.

Generally, one pays a fee to visit Nenbutsuji, but those who come for *kuyō* are given a special card so that they do not have to pay each time they visit. About 700 to 1,000 of these are issued a year, or approximately three cards per day. On average, there are two or three people each day who come and, of course, there are more on holidays (*kodomo no hi* or *higan*). There might also be one or two telephone calls daily from people who want to come for *kuyō*. It is suggested that they come for the first time, buy the package, and then the next time to let him know. If they keep coming two or three times, they are given a card. The people at the gate notice when women come multiple times and in these cases also we recommend that they be given a card.

The toys people bring for *kuyō* are collected and kept in a special place in the temple; on June 24 every year they conduct a service and burn them. Hara-san once noticed that someone had left an 18 liter jar of saké during Golden Week. He speculated that this woman's *mizuko* may by then have become twenty years old and that she may be giving (the fetus) the saké as a sign that her *mizuko* had now grown up (*seijin suru*). With that gesture she was completing the cycle of *kuyō*.

BLS: Has there been any TV documentary on *mizuko kuyō*?
HARA SATOSHI: A crew from a TV station did come last year [1991] and made a film about a particular woman's situation and how our temple responded. It was broadcast on MBS [Mainichi Broadcasting System] in Osaka; Hata Megumi was the woman who directed the documentary. It

covered one woman's experience: first how she came to know the man, then her experience of pregnancy, followed by an abortion (*chūzetsu*), and eventually *mizuko kuyō*. They followed her thought process. The TV show showed only her back and changed her voice so that she would remain anonymous. We would recommend this documentary as a good example of *mizuko kuyō* as a social phenomenon. It was part of a series focusing on various social phenomena such as the stock market crash, the rising price of land, *juku* (cram schools), and *reikan shōhō*. Each film is only a short news segment. This was a typical visit and was actually not that interesting. One sees more extreme cases at many temples. Recently, occult programs have been popular on TV. Every summer there are lots of ghost stories. To Japanese, abortion is a *nichijo-sahanji* (everyday matter), a matter of common knowledge.

Hara-san's father was at that time the head priest at Nenbutsuji. Hara-san himself had two daughters, the older of whom was a sophomore in high school. She had learned the sutras, and he hoped that in seven or eight years she would marry a *yōshi*, a man who would take over the temple. At that point, Hara-san had planned to retire young (*waka-inkyo*) and to continue listening to concerns about *mizuko*, and other issues involved in male and female relationships. After all, because it's embarrassing for people to talk about these things with their family and intimate friends, there are many who desire their worries to be heard, and they seem to feel comfortable discussing these matters with him, even if it's the woman who does most of the talking.[9] While he had other duties in the morning, he usually begins counseling about 12:30 p.m. and continues on into the evening.

Omoidegusa *Notebooks: The Expression of Muted Voices*

While the small temple known as Jikishian belongs to the same Jōdoshū (Pure Land) sect and is only a short distance from Adashino Nenbutsuji, it is strikingly different in many respects.[10] Its much smaller temple is located in a quiet, somewhat isolated part of the Sagano area of Kyoto. This location is inherent in its appeal. Situated as it is in a gently forested bamboo area with skillfully pruned azalea bushes surrounding a modest temple building, the beauty of the setting and the simplicity of the structures are conducive to visitors lingering longer than they ordinarily might at most temples. In the words of one visitor, this place "invites contemplation and introspection." The central appeal of Jikishian lies, however, in its long tradition of receptivity especially to young women (and men) who are drawn to the notebooks in which hundreds of people have revealed, anonymously, the deepest feelings of their heart. There is a kind of dialectical process—what they read from the entries of others seems to stimulate their own desire to express themselves. It is an invitation not just to unburden what they are feeling but also to join an invisible community of others whose muted expression is finding their voice.

Accompanied by my friend Shinji Kazue on September 5, 1990, I met with Oda Hōryū, priest in charge (*jūshoku*) of this temple, to request permission for three of my AKP students that fall to have direct exposure to his temple's approach to *mizuko kuyō*. Outlining the nature of my course, we discussed how Jikishian might be included in this. We talked about how these students would attend the monthly *kuyō* performed on each of three months that fall. Meeting with him as a group on at least two occasions, as well as being allowed to do some work around the temple, would provide them with a sense of daily life at Jikishian. We also discussed the value to them of going slowly through a typical *kuyō* service with him, to understand the structure, the content, the significance, and the interrelationship between the various parts of the ritual. During the semester the students would be reading materials in Japanese from the *Omoidegusa* volumes to get a feeling for the variety of personal concerns that people bring to this temple, as reported in the notebooks.

It is possible to read the life experiences expressed in the *Omoidegusa* notebooks collected over the past forty years at Jikishian and dwell principally on the personal circumstances of individual women. It is clear, however, how profoundly social and cultural forces influence individual experiences and how they impact each one's sense of identity. Even in the small selection of statements from the eight published volumes in Japanese that have been chosen for this study, one quickly detects the "real-life" turmoil endured by women and men who find themselves caught in relationships that are destructive. Each of these entries contains threads of deep sadness and is an expression of the sexual culture that often characterizes gender relationships in contemporary Japan. These feelings are poignant in large part because those who express them have been unable to communicate these openly with other people. Their words in these notebooks are an attempt to fill a void, to articulate the unspoken, as expressed by the Buddhist nun Hirose Zenjun, who originated the practice of these notebooks at this temple:

When I see almost ten people sitting in this little room facing the notebooks, I start to wonder whether this is a Jōdoshū temple or the Temple of the Notebooks. I once thought of burying the notebooks in the temple garden and performing *kuyō* for them...but this May I decided to make a storage space for them and preserve them above ground. These records were not easily written...They are the "testimony" of an era, and I consider it my mission to keep them carefully preserved. Every time I think of these notebooks, which are like a long tapestry, and of the countless people who have woven a part of themselves into the tapestry and then moved on, for some reason I feel a desire to bow deeply in prayer [deeply joining my hands in prayer (*gasshō*)].[11]

NOVEMBER 1977

History of the Omoidegusa Tradition at Jikishian[12]

Beginning around the mid-1960s, when the Sagano area was developing into a more interesting tourist area, a larger number of people began to visit Jikishian than before. Among the visitors at that time were some who wrote graffiti on the walls. This was at the same time when many protest movements existed, when lots of young people especially were rebelling against society. The nun Hirose Zenjun decided to put notebooks on the table partly to allow them to express their feelings there instead of by graffiti. Originally, these notebooks were designed for visitors to register donations to the temple (*hōkachō*) by listing their names and addresses. As time went on, people began to express whatever feelings they had in their heart (*kokoro ni aru koto*), whether it was their pain (*kurushimi*), their sadness (*kanashimi*), or their worries (*nayami*). This has been the custom ever since.

As to confessional writings about abortion and *mizuko*, these appeared in the mid-1970s (Showa 40) and gradually increased, so that by the mid-1980s there were maybe 120–130 people who had written in each notebook. By that time there were eight published notebooks. Oda-san surmised that in each notebook there are perhaps six to eight people on average who expressed their feelings about abortion. Over time the age of people in this category became younger, and most appeared to be teenagers. In his judgment this represents a societal trend. While he knows one can find notebooks somewhat like this in other places—love hotels, coffee shops, *minshuku*—what makes Jikishian different is that after writing their various confessions people invariably express feelings of repentance or maybe just remorse by saying, *Akachan, gomennasai* (Baby, I am sorry, or, I'm sorry I did such a thing. I am deeply aware of what a grievous sin I've committed; I promise never to do such a thing again.)

To Oda Hōryū, this is what makes these notebooks different. As he began to detect instances of genuine regret (*zange*) or soul searching (*hansei*), he came to take these writings more seriously. At that point he set aside the twenty-third of each month as a time when people could come for *mizuko kuyō*, during which he would give a sermon whose intent was to put this experience into a Buddhist perspective. He would explain that the word *kuyō* is similar in meaning to the word *sonae* (offering) and that the word *yashinau* has the connotation of nurturing when written in Chinese characters. It is common for worshippers to bring all sorts of offerings to such a service—flowers, incense, or (with children in mind) toys and dolls. The implication is that as one gives offerings one is nurturing the heart. But whose heart? It is not the baby's heart; it is the heart of the person making the offering. While whatever is given may be offered to the *mizuko*, the real purpose is that one's own heart be nurtured.

Oda-san's perceptions serve to illuminate the *raw* nature of the feelings that have been recorded. Whatever offerings a person might bring, what is actually being offered is the expression of powerful emotions—of agony, grief, and alienation, and, even more basic, an inability to trust oneself or others. Through these notebooks the reader becomes privy to the experiences of persons who in most cases have not disclosed these feelings before. Reading large numbers of these generates a cumulative sense of being at the temple and coming closer to meeting the women whose voices yearn to be heard. As one senses the raw emotions of those who are at the core of this narrative, the question arises of how this journey through dark and wrenched feelings may find resolution. Only at that point do rituals such as *mizuko kuyō* come into play or even seem viable. In this sense, the nun Hirose Zenjun and the priest Oda-san emerge as unexpected role models through their growing sensitivity to what is entailed in the journey of those visiting Jikishian in sorrow and painful confusion.

Recollections from the Notebooks

The phenomenon of *mizuko kuyō* needs to be viewed in connection with the many concerns felt by younger Japanese women today. Though only 10 percent of the entries in these notebooks may deal directly with issues relating to *mizuko*, by framing *mizuko* within the wider elements of Japan's *sexual culture* one begins to understand this form of child loss more clearly. In addition, the very range of situations represented throughout these notebooks challenges stereotypes of passive Japanese women, even when women continue to define themselves primarily in relationship to men. For this reason, the importance of acknowledging feelings of conflict, pain, and brokenness is obvious. Expressions of pain may represent the beginnings of healing; they are at least the start of confronting conflict. Each of the statements in this chapter represents voices that began to move beyond silence; their variety provides contrasts with the monochromatic depictions of *mizuko kuyō* that one finds in media accounts. For this reason, it is important to accent the heterogeneity that actually exists.

In the person of Hirose Zenjun, the nun who preceded Oda-san in taking care of Jikishian for many years, one observes a person widely known for her sensitivity to the women who came to this temple for counsel. Typical of her compassion are these words: "There are many who visit this temple, and each seems to have her own worries (*nayami*), her own deep resentment (*wadakamari*). Most write in the *Omoidegusa* notebooks and then leave, but some talk with me directly. People seem to feel better after they open up; it is also true that they help to expand the capacity of my heart... It has now been thirteen years. Many people have woven their hearts into these notebooks. Each year reflects the social climate and also portrays the seasons of Sagano. As time goes by, a large, colorful tapestry is in process of being made. It seems as if those who visit Jikishian wish to add their own bit of color to this [tapestry]."[13]

An initial example involves a woman who has been married for twenty-six years and who is visiting Jikishian for the first time. While there is no *mizuko* in the picture, she conveys the emptiness, the death-like nature of their marriage. On the surface she and her husband may seem like a typical Japanese couple of their age. Their son and daughter, however, have been exposed to the truth of their parents' relationship. The wife-mother writes:

> I can forgive the fact that men have affairs, but you [her husband] are different. Your way of having affairs: you got together with my younger sister and made me live with her. You fell in love with one of the workers [in our business] and made me live with her. Of course, I suffered.[14]

Her husband's parade of affairs became a source of traumatic anxiety for this woman. Looking back on her life, she wonders what went wrong and whether she will ever understand. Though no child has been conceived out of wedlock from her husband's affairs, she is clearly mourning the death of a relationship that produced two children but no enduring love. The issue here, as so often, is how one encounters experiences of suffering and by what means one expresses feelings that are repressed. In a sense, the fabric of her worldview had been rent. A scenario of this kind tends to perpetuate "the submissive women" idea within Japanese culture. Large ingredients of the culture, religion, and tradition continue to depict women in this same way. As Hara Satoshi indicated earlier, because Japanese men still assert that men and women are not on equal ground, it is no wonder that so many Japanese women absorb the blame and deal with their pain alone.

A second example involves a younger married woman who also has come to Jikishian for the first time. She has temporarily left her husband following a serious argument, a month after she experienced her second miscarriage. Following each of these miscarriages, her mother-in-law yells at her as if she had killed the child: "You're a wife who cannot even bear a child...It doesn't matter how many times you have miscarried; you are useless if you don't have at least one child." (In the face of these tirades her husband was silent.) The wife writes in the notebook:

I felt so lonely, I wanted to cry in your arms, but you gave me the look of a stranger.

After reporting another of his mother's comments, her husband protested: "My mother would never say such a thing." For over a year, lacking all sensitivity to her feelings, he kept saying, "It doesn't matter how many times you have a miscarriage. Just bear one." Commenting on his callousness, she writes:

Those cold words. There was not a word of concern for my body. I didn't even cry. Without shedding a tear, I just continued to hate him...This time, though, I don't want to hide anything with tears. I don't know if we'll get a divorce, but starting from this December we are planning to live with my mother-in-law. I want to think things through, taking this into account...[I wonder if] my bitterness is a sign that I still love him. I'm going to become a strong woman, a strong human being. [And then, to her absent husband:] I don't care if it's only pretense, but from now on please protect me in front of your mother. Just a word, one word would do: Mother, don't say such a thing.[15]

One can understand why this woman would choose to come to Jikishian right after she left home. This piece reveals an old way of thinking—of women being useless if they are unable to bear children. People often come to Jikishian mourning the death of their child, and those who do so tend to fall into two different categories: those who come out of guilt for terminating a young life; and those who were unable to have a child despite their strong desires (e.g., miscarriage, financial reasons, family pressure). Theirs is a grief that is seldom reflected upon in a conscious, let alone outspoken, manner. Personal experiences of this kind not only are instances of individual loss but also reveal how society fails to help its members encounter deep loss and to move to greater self-respect and healthier relationships with others. The depth of disenchantment toward males expressed by women of various ages, but particularly by younger women, is wide-ranging and sobering. The following statements illustrate similar feelings by many women, of which these two are striking examples:

At the end of January I failed in an attempted suicide. I couldn't keep living, but neither could I die. Now here I am at Jikishian...Even while I write this, my heart is filled with nothing but guilt toward those I've made suffer, and a feeling of emptiness! The first person that I loved was married, with a child. To end the pain, I broke off our four-year long love affair, but then I jumped into the arms of another married man with a child. To make things worse, he's my uncle. How often I've resented the fact that the same blood runs through our bodies.[16]

BEAUTIFUL FLOWERS—I hope that what I write here catches someone's eye. For twelve years, ever since I was a little girl, I attended an all-girls school and grew up knowing only the gentleness and purity of girls. I am a woman now, and I can love only women—I will love only women...When I was a child, I was molested by a weird man. When men look at women, that's all they think of! I can't forgive him. There's no way I can forgive a man (a pervert, *yatsu*) who would hurt an innocent child like that!...Right now, Masako is my emotional support. She loves me as a mother...as a lover. I will continue to love what is beautiful. I will continue to love only beautiful flowers. I will steal all the women away from the men![17]

These selections reveal a good deal about Japanese society. Communication about problems within families (especially between mothers and daughters) is a common issue. As a result, many important problems go unaddressed. This last person cannot even discuss this with her best friend. In particular, it is uncommon for most Japanese to talk about issues relating to sexuality. At this point, we turn to two entries that stem from different experiences with males. The first is a statement by Hirose Zenjun, the nun at Jikishian, about a conversation she had with a man who came hoping to locate news about his sister who, apparently, paid a visit to this temple:

Soon after *Please Give Me One Cycle of Love* [*Ichirin no ai o kudasai*] was published, a man in his thirties came to visit me [Hirose Zenjun]. With a nervous expression on his face, he looked into my eyes and started the conversation by saying, "My younger sister seems to have written a certain piece in the book." As I listened to his story, the writing that he was referring to was by a person who was then working as a high school teacher. She appeared to be involved in a hopeless love affair...The man believed that the writing in the book was by his sister and asked to see the original notebooks. Because hundreds of notebooks are filled up each year, it would be like searching for a bird in the middle of the night. I had to decline his request. Instead, I had him pray for her well-being in the afterworld and perform *kuyō* for her with all his heart, because I could understand how he felt on seeing what amounted to her hidden will [in the published excerpts from the notebook]. He quietly left, leaving me with the words, "Even so, I'm glad that through your book I was able to understand my sister's state of mind, even just a little."[18]

(In fact, his sister had taken her own life.)

The following comment is by a caring male from Osaka, who accepts his part of the responsibility for these two abortions:

I am here at Jikishian with my girlfriend, in order to cleanse myself from a certain sin (*tsumi*). Last November 29th and this March

29th, the two of us made a mistake. The two lives we created have left this world. I don't know what I can say to make up for this. But, I'm going to love her enough to make up for the two lives that were lost…I am not asking for forgiveness for my sin by simply coming here. But deep inside my heart, I probably do feel that my sin will somewhat be atoned for by coming here. I never want to do this again, not ever. And I want to do all I can for her. With all my might, I want to make her happy…One of these days, when she and I are more calm, mentally and physically, we will visit Jikishian again. A. K., April 29[19]

Oda Hōryū's Approach to Experiences of Mizuko Kuyō

At this point we turn to the four volumes collected and edited by Oda Hōryū, who became the priest in charge of Jikishian in his early thirties. The first chapter of Volume 6 is devoted to the subject of abortion, from his perspective. He seems to be addressing himself mainly to women on the issue of *mizuko*, but he sees situations of this kind as involving both parties in a relationship. The following incident is an appropriate place to begin. Oda-san starts by discussing the visit of a young couple who come to his temple at the end of a day and are greeted somewhat impatiently by the priest who is about to close the gates for the night. An interesting conversation ensues, somewhat one-sided, in which it is clear that this couple was shaken by what they have just done and seem to the priest to be confused about what it means to be responsible either to themselves as distinct persons or to each other as a couple.

By retaining his own negative reaction to these two persons in the note-books, Oda-san is being unusually honest, yet at the same time it is clear that over time his reflections become more sensitive and more under-standing. One can see a kind of evolution taking place in his perspective as he focuses on the sacredness of life, together with the peril of uncon-trolled sexual desire, the ignorance that so many people have about con-traception, and the all-important need to love oneself.

As he seeks to understand the complexities of dysfunctional emotional relationships that make up the experience of so many young couples, he comes to the conclusion that there is a deep sincerity and honesty at work in the feelings that are often present in these *mizuko* experiences. This is not where Oda-san started, and he does not come to this observation through any kind of naïveté. Instead, as his sensitivity unfolds, it creates a kind of nonjudgmental stance enabling him to see these "reminiscences" as authentic and hopeful. Only after interviewing a large number of priests who are involved in performing memorial services for *mizuko*, in particular through abortion, does one come to see how relatively uncommon Oda-san's approach is to these matters. He describes his encounter with this couple:

> The other day, a young couple came to visit me at Jikishian. It was a full hour since I had closed the gates, and I went to the main hall to perform my last duty of the day. That was when I saw them standing in the place where you take off your shoes...When I informed them, 'We are closed for the day,' the man looked at me and suddenly said, "We just aborted a baby..." The woman was standing in his shadow, shaking. I invited them inside and listened to their story in the temple office. "And why did you have an abortion?" I asked. They answered, "We are both students. Even if it were born, we couldn't have raised it..."
>
> They were probably in their second year of college. The man's face still had traces of childishness about it. When I asked, "Why didn't you take precautions beforehand so you wouldn't have a baby?" on hearing my question they both hung their heads in silence. The woman's face was slightly pale. With those two in front of me, I thought to myself: When a baby is born from a woman's body and the father sees it for the first time, most fathers must think for an instant, "Wow, so this is my child." Then as the child grows, it begins to smile back when its parents smile at it. If they speak to the child, it responds by saying, *Ahhh*. Through experiences like these, parents begin to understand what it's like to have a child—and they come to learn what it means to be a parent. At that time, is there a single parent in the world who could wring [his] own baby's neck? Far from it. The parent will fight furiously anyone who tries to harm the infant, even at the cost of his own life...So how can one just say, "We had no choice but to abort it." Where does this conclusion come from?
>
> As I was observing these two with their heads hanging, I had the feeling they were not seeing the fetus...as their child, as a being with a life of its own. They did not comprehend that the fetus, the

child, was the result of their relationship, their act. She may have
been pregnant, but it wasn't showing yet. It [the fetus] wasn't something that could be seen clearly with the eye, something with form.
I even had the feeling that they thought of it as just a passing sickness. Even though the two of them were students and wouldn't
actually be out in society for some time, I couldn't help thinking
of them as spiritually impoverished... Of course, young people are
so caught up in their own life, and perhaps don't have the time to
think about things from a long-range point of view.

Confronted with a situation they had never faced before, they
tend to fall into panic and confusion, to flee from [such a] reality
as quickly as possible. Even though they were "going out together,"
which is just a superficial kind of tie, [with] no deep tie between
their souls, they were unable to think deeply about the "life" that
is born into this world as a "soul"... That is, they have no sense of
moral responsibility for [such an] act.

As I viewed these two [sitting there] in silence with their heads
hanging down, I couldn't help feeling that in reality they are very
much alone. They seemed to be living for the sake of [their own]
selfish desire. Is my way of speaking too arrogant?... The two were
listening to me, but once the sun set and the room was getting dark,
the man looked at me and asked a question: "I heard that you have
mizuko Jizō here at Jikishian. What should we do if we aborted a
child?"[20]

I told them, "As parents, you must perform ekō [memorial service for the well-being of the mizuko]. That is the only thing you can
do." And that they should also pay a visit (o-mairi-suru) on the anniversary day of their child's death...

In conclusion, Oda-san reflects, "It seems as though this area where
Jikishian and Adashino Nenbutsuji are located, there has been for a long,
long time a continuing relationship with the dead. Many women come
here specifically to perform kuyō for their child. This pattern is clearly
apparent in Omoidegusa."[21]

The Yearning To Be Held

Oda-san's comments are grounded in his sense of the preciousness and
sacredness of life. There are scores of entries about life and death. They

help to explain how desperate many young people are. For them, Japan is such a high-pressure country for young people—especially relating to school and success. Because these aspects of life are so stressful, it seems that important issues go unaddressed. This comes across in the following entries by three very different people:

> Today will be the last day, and I will separate my heart from him. A year ago, I was held by him and believed that my body and soul were his. But it is now the end; this is not right. He has a very cute wife and children and has said that he cannot get a divorce. Though he wants the two of us to live together in a place where no one knows us, that is impossible. I cannot really trust him, nor can I believe in a love that is held together with words alone. I am going to abort the child that is inside my stomach.[22]

The fact that *dakareru* (to be held) is often used by women and that *daku* (to hold) is normally used by men is revealing. When referring to sexual relations, this symbolic distinction is of considerable importance. In this case and in the next quote, women are the ones being held, desiring to be held, instead of holding someone else. It is perfectly reasonable for a male also to desire to be held. When it is *only* the woman who has this desire, then the notion of "being held" suggests not strength within vulnerability but passivity compared with a male's proclivity toward dominance. In contrast to both of these is the verb *dakiau* that suggests mutuality in holding and being held. It means to embrace each other. That is not what is suggested in either this or the following entry. The fact that the woman in the previous quote made the decision to leave this man, however, reveals a person who has taken the stand to move beyond what she once desired to what she realizes she must do. This is not passivity; it is strength. In the following quote, on the other hand, one sees a person, indeed two people, who are trapped in a kind of combined subservience, in what has been called a folie à deux:[23]

> Morita-san, it has been three years since we met. Though I am a wife, I cannot stop thinking about you; this causes me a lot of pain...When I think of losing you, I am pursued by a loneliness that is like death. You are young, and I am near forty. I realize it is useless for me to expect you to soothe my soul, you who are ten years younger and may not even love me. Why is there so much

senselessness (fugōri) within love [relationships]?...If you were to marry someone else, that would be the hardest thing for me. [24]

It's been almost five years since he and I began to go out. He is a wonderfully kind, dependable person. I am now twenty-two years old, and am getting a little nervous. Already I have had four abortions, but we have always said that we won't make babies until we are financially stable. To tell the truth, I can no longer have babies. As of now he does not know this, and I cannot bring myself to tell him, for he would leave me at once if he found out. Why would anyone love a woman who is not really a woman? Every month, he and I come to Jikishian to pray. Right now, there is nothing on my mind or in my heart; I just want to see him, to be held in his arms, to cry in his chest...I want to be happy (shiawase), to be content.[25]

Four abortions by the age of twenty-two is an extreme case, but it is part of a larger social and cultural pattern of seeking integrity outside oneself. This is equally true of men as of women. It shows that (1) Oda-san views this issue as important; (2) that many more people are writing about it; and (3) that it remains a large problem in Japan.

In discussing these issues, Oda-san's use of fire as an analogy is interesting:

Once you reach a certain age, it is natural to have that kind of desire. And it is also the case that in order to satisfy that desire, human beings [engage in] sex, but it is imperative that they think more seriously and carefully about the sexual act itself. Having an abortion is painful, and it leaves both physical and mental scars. I wish that people would [regard] the sacredness of human life more carefully. I often say that sexual desire is like fire. If used properly, fire can warm us and cook our food...However, fire is a terrifying thing: one false step and it can blaze up uncontrollably and reduce everything to ashes. Sexual desire is like that. If used wisely, it can produce descendents and bring prosperity, but if misdirected, one can wound oneself and end up causing irreparable damage. Your body is not only yours. I may sound repetitious, but I wish our youth would think more about the importance and sacredness of life.[26]

The following example is a case in point.

Sex as a Precondition of Intimacy

The man I was dating wanted me to have sex. But when I hesitated, he said it was a sign that I did not care for him and he left me. I have now begun to see another man; he too has expressed his interest [in having sex]. I am afraid that if I say no again he too will leave me. I cared for my old boyfriend. Also, I really like my present boyfriend. What should I do?[27]

It's not just that such a person is playing with sex but more that she is being controlled by sex. While she may say, "I really care for him. It's not just a game; I am very serious." When one examines [this kind of] situation, it is clear that is indeed a "game," though the woman involved fails to realize this. Only after experiencing several abortions, when the game is over, does she realize for the first time that it was a game. Once [stricken] with the illness of love, a person becomes blind. They cannot stop [their emotions] by force of will, so in effect, they just keep rolling out of control... This seems to be a common phenomenon.[28]

Oda-san believes that a sizable proportion of entries deal with dysfunctional relations between men and women. It is in these expressions that one finds the seedbed for affairs in which abortion is often the decision of choice.

The women I used to see years ago were usually under twenty, a year or two younger than the woman now sitting before me with her boyfriend/partner. I still remember how their eyes were open wide, and how those wide-open eyes were full of worry. Whenever a woman came to me with this kind of problem, I invariably replied in the same way...If a man really loves a woman, he would never say that to her [pressuring her to have sex]. These women knew the importance of self-esteem (*jibun o taisetsu ni suru*), as opposed to selfish desire (*gay-oku*). They had enough self-restraint to reflect on their actions, to question their behavior...I felt that these women were protecting their deep, rare love as if they were protecting themselves, but it is extremely difficult to attain passion (*koi*) or love (*ai*) without getting hurt.[29]

Ever since the various incidents of coin locker babies [beginning in 1971] that received so much media attention around Showa 50

[1975], when a fetus might be wrapped and put in a paper bag and placed in a locker at a train station, more women have written about their stories and the sorrows related to child loss. Before that, very few made such confessions; there would not be even one in any of these notebooks. Since 1975 the number of entries has increased. At this point in time, out of the 150 or so people who write in each of the *Omoidegusa* notebooks, there are as many as fifteen entries relating to child loss. Leaving aside the reasons for this change, what is clear is that, while the few examples that existed before the mid-'70s were written by working women in their twenties who were of marriage-able age, now in [addition to those] it is not uncommon to see notes by high school girls of sixteen and seventeen. Moreover, there are three distinctive categories in which these women fall: affairs with a married man; sexual experiments [between two youths with no intention of marriage]; and couples who intend to marry eventually but are forced to abort the baby because they are too young.[30]

Apart from what people tell others, aren't most abortions today due to reason number 3 rather than to the physical condition of the mother or the financial situation of the family? Many examples of this reason can be found in the notebooks. Let us look at some that I found from randomly paging through *Omoidegusa*... No matter what people tell others, it seems that the real reason is one of con-venience... Let's examine two instances, including one from the time of the former *jūshoku* [the nun].[31]

I wonder how many times I've taken a journey to Kyoto. Every time it's with different emotions in my heart... But now a new love is beginning. I can never be satisfied with just one person and am always with three or four others. I realize how lame an excuse that is, but I am so lonely and cannot help it. Relationships with the married man, with the one in Tokyo... They mean a lot to me. I care for all of them. There is a saying that one cannot love two people at once. While this may be true, I still love them. Perhaps I am living without knowing what real happiness means.

SHIHO[32]

June 6th last year was the day I will never forget. On that day, due to my selfishness, I buried a precious life from this life on earth. Now, I am here to practice *kuyō* at a temple where there is a Mizuko Jizō. The person who was to be the father is here with me. When

I sit on the veranda and look out at the curves of the green azalea
bushes in this garden, my soul feels cleansed. When I think about it
now, how immature and selfish I was...While this crime can never
be erased, I intend to continue doing *kuyō* with sincerity...As I visit
this temple and let the pen run on, I feel comfort and have found
a reason for living. My life will be long, and no doubt there will be
other painful things. But I intend to be strong and live through it all,
while remembering those painful and sad days last year. This is the
least I can do for my child [that I aborted]. When I feel sad, lonely and
helpless, I shall return here. For those who have had similar experiences and are visiting here please never forget about your child.

AN EIGHTEEN-YEAR-OLD GIRL FROM TOKUSHIMA[33]

For a Buddhist priest like me there is only one way to approach
the issue of abortion: through the belief in *sesshō kai*, namely, that
one must avoid the act of killing...The act of sex should be a ceremony between two healthy parents for building a proper family. "I have fallen in love with a married man and am pregnant.
What should I do?" That type of question is not asked by a [healthy]
human being. Even under those circumstances people should be
responsible enough to have and raise the child.[34]

Women who have affairs with married men and who get pregnant tend to blame themselves so much that they don't hesitate to
abort [self-inflicted punishment]. When I read that, I wonder why
they are not more careful about contraception and I become angry
about their carelessness.[35] We who are a generation older were not
taught about contraception either, nor do I recall anyone formally
attempting to educate me about sex. I came to learn about sex
through experience and out of necessity. When I look back on it,
my mind and body seemed to have balanced out the knowledge and
the technique subconsciously. Just because one knows about contraception, however, does not mean one can have sex with anyone
and everyone. If that were the case, one would be a slave to sex.[36]

Oda-san agrees there is lack of adequate sex education and also of easy
access to birth control. This situation is still not discussed openly in most
homes. Condoms may be more available in Japan, especially now when
more people are aware of AIDS. While some forms of sex education in
schools are beginning at an earlier age, widespread counseling and inex-
pensive (as well as confidential) gynecological service are rarely accessible

to young people in Japan. The consequences of all this include a high probability of unprotected sex, plus the fact that many young people seem to regard abortion as an easy option, and the rarity of open and honest communication about these matters between sexual partners.

The Preciousness of Self: The Need to Love Oneself

It is easy to criticize the actions and words of these women. Actually, these young women know their own faults more than anyone. When I read the confessions and prayers of these women, I always wish that they would take better care of themselves. When I speak this way, am I criticizing them? [His question is obviously rhetorical.] These women have no sense of "self." Or rather, they do not understand what the self is. Some may say, "But isn't that what being young means?" and I cannot deny that. However, I reply that there is only one "I" (*watashi*) in the world, and that is myself. While there are plenty of twenty-two-year-olds, they are all special and different from other twenty-two-year-olds. There is only one "I" who is that particular twenty-two-year-old. Let me cite just one case from *Omoidegusa*—a woman who did not know who she was. While getting hurt along the way, she struggled to grasp and eventually attain her sense of self, all the time trying to grasp the truth [about other things] and to face [more clearly] those around her.[37]

One may say, "If I am not a burden to anyone, then I should be able to do whatever I want." But is this true? Does your life belong only to you? Does not love begin by loving yourself? If you are unable to love yourself, then you are unable to love others ... Understand yourself and take good care of it.—I say this seriously to all. Shaka said, "If you understand yourself, then you are a sacred being." And Hōnen Shōnin said that by understanding yourself, your path to salvation becomes clear.[38]

If you were to act only by your own instinctive desires (in Buddhist terms, *bonnō*), then you will lack knowledge as a human being. The great thing about human wisdom is its ability to illuminate what one learns with sunlight and make it shine. In addition, humans should have compassion (*jō*) and goodwill (*i*). I will say [to them] again, that I want you to become an irreplaceable "I" (*watashi*) who possesses knowledge (*chi*), compassion (*jō*), and will (*i*).

In these *Omoidegusa* entries it is clear that people don't think it is right to abort a child. Many seem to have the desire to reflect about themselves, and they come to Jikishian to start over. I understand that feeling well, but it is not clear that they understand the negative weight of their actions. Human beings are the only ones who can confess (*zange*), who have spirituality, and who can pray to the Buddha. In order for aborted spirits to rest in peace, we, the priests, pray by chanting the sutra. It does not matter, however, how much a priest prays and chants if the people lack awareness of any sense of *tsumi* [feelings of regret for one's actions] and have no intention of *kuyō*.[39]

The Essence of Nenbutsu: Sincerity and Honesty

In *Omoidegusa* I read all these entries of people in despair over their love affairs with a married man, over triangle relationships, or over abortion. Often I read the words of young women who write, "I am sorry." Compared with other words that have been carefully selected and written out, this expression "I am sorry" comes out as if it were naturally and honestly falling out of their mind. There are many different ways of expressing I'm sorry, from almost screaming and yelling to [saying it] quietly, like a single tear falling, but all of [these ways of saying] I'm sorry are *sunao* [honest, unaffected, sincere]. It is that delicate and subtle, though there are millions of differences. Still, it does not take away from the fact that they are sincere. And when I see that, I think to myself, *Namu amida butsu* is being said in a different word.[40]

The women who come to Jikishian are sincere (*sunao*) as they sit with the notebook before them. They are trying to reflect on themselves, to understand their inner pain and anxiety, and to arrive at some sort of closure. As they write, they keep wishing to leave their precious self behind and, starting tomorrow, to become a new self. When one's sense of repentance is genuine, the ultimate intent is to live a genuinely humane life. Though Jikishian is just a small temple, the women who come here have come to Kyoto not to see the famous shrines, temples, and ancient ruins, but to try to look within themselves. They take a day off from work or school, come to this other-worldly place, and make a resolve.[41]

This issue appears continuously in the notebooks. The following two entries by women are examples:

Today is the 49th day [after the abortion]. This was our very first child. I went to the *Mizuko Jizō* shrine [Jikishian], with its candle-lights, and the smoke of the incense. While I was gazing at the lights, my [sense of] *tsumi* felt as though it were electricity running through my body. While I was praying to O-Jizō-sama, I faded in and out of consciousness. The only thing I could say was "I am sorry." When I think of it now, the tears flow. Sadly, however, they now seem to have dried up and there is nothing left for me now. I am sorry; I am very sorry. My baby. No matter how much I apologize, it is not something for which I can ever be forgiven...I am very sorry.

SHIZUKO[42]

I pray that when they return to everyday life, whether it be in Tokyo, their hometowns, or wherever, they will continue to keep the resolve that they made while facing *Omoidegusa* upon returning to their workplace, school, or family and upon resuming everyday life their resolve may weaken. Since they came all the way to Jikishian and resolved to endure, I hope they will stand strong; I hope that they feel like praying with each step they take. In Buddhism we teach that if one continues to maintain a feeling of "I am sorry" toward the Buddha, one can free oneself [from the bonds of this world and] and be free of [their] suffering. To give form to one's various feelings—"I don't want to be the person I was yesterday"; "Starting tomorrow, I want to be a new person"; "I want to find a new life for myself"; "I want to be happy"—one must apply oneself diligently [and] cultivate one's character. No one else can do that for you. Someone said, "We are searching for something as if it were distant, when actually it is right in front of us." I couldn't agree more. It is essential to believe in oneself and to remain strong.[43]

Central to Oda-san's reflections is his reaffirmation about the deeper meaning of *mizuko kuyō*. As usual, he is candid about how some people (some priests and many *ogamiya-san*) are responsible for emphasizing guilt and fear, capitalizing on ancient anxieties about *tatari*. When asked whether this appears more in older women than younger, he believes it is more present in younger women who have no traditional religious upbringing and are not as regularly exposed to Buddhist teachings as older women have been. In his counseling and in his *hōwa* (Buddhist sermons), he seeks to begin where individuals are and to lead them to an understanding of basic Buddhist teaching. As one examines oneself in front of Buddha, what is manifested is a more thoughtful examining of oneself.

Final Interview with Oda Hōryū, November 10, 2010

I expressed my appreciation to Oda Hōryū for the opportunity of meeting with him again. The first meeting was twenty-six years ago in fall 1984, and there have been four times since (1986, 1990, 2002, and 2010). On one of those occasions he mentioned his plan of having meetings (*sōdankai*) with various people from different walks of life to discuss the issues involved in *mizuko kuyō*. I was therefore interested in what kinds of meetings had taken place, how helpful they were, and how people might better have understood the whole phenomenon of *mizuko kuyō* as a result. Also attending the most recent meeting (2010) was my longtime friend Sakakibara Yasuo and my wife, Charlotte Smith.

ODA HŌRYŪ: There is a group called the *Jōdoshū Seinenkai* [young priests of the Jōdo sect], of which I served as leader. Those young men gathered to discuss how we should spread the Buddhist teaching to laypersons, and what form that teaching should take. I conducted that kind of meeting last year. It did not focus particularly on *mizuko kuyō*, but on the spreading of Buddhist teachings. It was a so-called *iken kōkan kai* (meeting to exchange opinions), a *benkyōkai* (study group). I often do those kinds of meetings.

BLS: What issues have been most central?

ODA HŌRYŪ: Today's young priests in particular have a sense of crisis regarding religion, especially Buddhism. The laypeople have become extremely removed from Buddhism. Back in the Meiji Period, when foreigners came to Japan they were surprised by our culture's religiousness. Shrines, priests, the household would all worship the *hotoke* (Buddha) together; they respected their parents; they cherished their grandparents. But nowadays, none of that is left. Because we priests are caught up in the trends of the larger society, we thus feel a deep sense of crisis.

A major cause of this is the sloppiness of us priests. In the old days, priests would carefully explain the Buddhist teachings. They would say, "This is the teaching of *Oshakasama*," and they would preach the dharma. But today's priests just chant the sutras and don't preach or explain the teachings. That is a big factor. So we older priests have an enormous sense of crisis about this as well, and we encourage young priests to promulgate Buddhist teachings. The young priests have now internalized this sense of crisis, and they also are going out to preach and explain the dharma. Currently, I spend from 100 to 120 days of each year preaching (spreading the teachings). The more I do this, the more effective it is, and the bigger response I get. So it is important for us to do this...

BLS: Are these talks given at Jikishian, or in a variety of places?

ODA HŌRYŪ: Here at Jikishian I give talks on the twenty-third of each month, and I also make trips to locations throughout Japan, from Hokkaido to Kyushu. Usually I talk to the same audience over a five-day period of time, fifteen to eighteen hours (per day), to audiences of laypeople, different talks each time. And why do I do this? I raise questions like: What about your life? Why were you born? Where have you come from? When your life is over, where will you go? What is the purpose of your life? What is true happiness (these people are all looking for happiness)? Well, then, what is true happiness? Buddha teaches that happiness is this... By means of asking these questions, I lead them to thinking about why religion is necessary.

BLS: Do you also speak at universities? And, if so, what are the principal questions that keep coming up?

ODA HŌRYŪ: As you'd expect, they also ask about life: What is life? Where did my life come from? They take these things for granted, but when I question them further, they begin to have doubts. Certainly, they begin to question, What is life, anyway? While they truly want to know about these questions, they usually repress that desire and forget about it in the business of daily life. But when I talk to them they are reminded of it afresh. Without helping them discover this, they cannot understand the preciousness of life—indeed, the preciousness and nobility of their own life.

BLS: Because one is always living with the central issue of one's mortality, the conversations you describe get to the central point, the meaning of life. What other questions emerge from those who are listening to your talk?

ODA HŌRYŪ: They ask what happens to us after death! Contemporary laypeople think that when you die, that's it. So they believe they can just enjoy life as much as possible, do exactly what they like, and then just drop over dead. But one can't die like that. Humans are under the delusion that when "the fun is over" they can drop over dead and that will take care of it, but...[they all laugh] Oshakasama says that the soul (*tamashii*) continues to live forever, although the body (*gotai*) is buried in the grave, buried and becomes ashes, but the *tamashii*, I guess you'd call it, continues forever. So when people ask, "Where does the soul continue on," I mention Hōnen Shōnin, who said "It is reborn [even while alive]; it is reborn."

The Buddha teaches that the purpose of our human lives is *jōbutsu*, becoming a Buddha. Becoming a Buddha through one's own power is the best way, but because buddhahood through one's own power [*jiriki*] is incredibly difficult Hōnen Shōnin told us to chant the *nenbutsu* and be reborn (*ōjō*) through the power of Amida. That way you can get to the land beyond, to the Pure Land.

BLS: Though people may agree to that, they may not know how to practice this in their regular life?

ODA HŌRYŪ: In Jōdoshū there is something called *Gojū Sōden*. This is when I talk about the teaching of the *nenbutsu* for fifteen hours, sometimes at times as much as twenty-four or twenty-five hours. When it's a five-day session [*itsuka gojū*] I talk for fifteen hours; when it's seven days [*nanoka gojū*] I talk for about thirty hours. The first day, one can hardly hear the participants chanting the *nenbutsu*, but when we get to the fourth and fifth days then the voices of people chanting the *nenbutsu* reverberate throughout the temple, so that the *hondō* [main hall] is filled to overflowing. When the participants take this block of time from their everyday lives to chant the *nenbutsu*, then one receives responses like those.

BLS: Is this similar, in some way, to the intensity of what happens in a Zen Buddhist *sesshin* [intensive meditation]?

ODA HŌRYŪ: In intensity, yes, though *zazen* and *nenbutsu* practice are completely different. The *nenbutsu* is chanting the Buddha's name, *namu amida butsu*—homage to Amida. When one hears the *nenbutsu* we and the Buddha are one. The heart of the *hotoke* and our hearts are one. The body of the *hotoke* and our bodies cannot be separated. This is called *myōtai furi*. So, for us humans, when we are one with the Buddha our hearts become pure, we trust in Amida, but when we do something bad, that's when our hearts (*kokoro*) are dark. When our hearts are dark, who knows what humans will do? But when they call out Buddha's name, when they and the Buddha are one, their hearts become purified. When their hearts are pure, humans are incapable of doing bad deeds. That is why Hōnen Shōnin says we should chant the *nenbutsu*.

BLS: And the natural response of that sense of oneness is to reach out with compassion to others, who may not yet realize that they and the Buddha are one. Helping others thus becomes a *natural* reaction.

ODA HŌRYŪ: Yes, that is the important point. Like that, it happens naturally. Even when we don't try to make it happen, it happens naturally. We humans want to do good, but we cannot. So, Hōnen Shōnin teaches us that if we chant the *nenbutsu* we will find it possible to be kind; we will find it impossible to do bad things.

BLS: In reading some of the writings in the notebooks (*Omoidegusa*), it was clear that most people had not realized their oneness with all reality, and therefore were struggling against themselves and others. Oda-san's responses, on the other hand, brought them back to another view of themselves and of others. Without this response, the writings in the *Omoidegusa* by themselves would mean very little. There would still be evidence of people who were expressing their anger, frustration, but it is your response that makes this material so valuable.

ODA HŌRYŪ: Yes, because I am in possession of these comments in the notebooks I am able to understand the turns of phrase they use to express their direct, frank emotions.

BLS: The difference between your approach and the responses to the Kyoto University surveys reveals how minimal is the discussion normally provided to those who come to most temples for *mizuko kuyō*. There are some priests who offer consultation, but what you are talking about is a more thorough, more sensitive kind of response.

ODA HŌRYŪ: You're right. Most temples do *mizuko kuyō*, but they just chant the sutras. And that's the end of it.

BLS: Because situations do not remain static, what do you think has happened to *mizuko kuyō* over the past twenty to thirty years? In some respects, of course, it has become institutionalized; it has spread. On the other hand, there were reasons for its beginnings and for its continuing. It reflects many things about society and about the needs of people. What is it that a person who is learning about this *mizuko kuyō* phenomenon should know, beyond what we have already discussed?

ODA HŌRYŪ: Well, there was a period when there was a *mizuko* boom, about twenty-five years ago. Before then, there *was* no Jizō who was known as *mizuko jizō.* But starting with that boom, there began to be such a Jizō, and that took on a certain form. One had to perform *kuyō* for the fetus. There was *kuyō* before that, in the old days, but since the boom it has become much more than that. On the other hand, sexual mores have become very loose. Young people are having sexual relationships from a very young age, and when the girl gets pregnant they deal with it by relying on *kuyō.* There is the inverse of this as well—those women who visit the temple and repent with all of their heart, who vow that they'll never repeat it, that is, having an abortion. Regarding those who come here for *mizuko kuyō*, there are fewer than before, but the ones who do come are truly in search of the dharma. Not just *kuyō;* they want to hear sermons (*hanashi*) as well.

BLS: One wonders why at this point in time, since the role of a woman seems to be primarily that of being a mother, the one who for the most part brings up her children, with little help from her husband, whether the burden of this may influence her decision to have few or no children, perhaps not even to get married. What is the effect of these tendencies?

ODA HŌRYŪ: Hmm, that's a difficult question. Certainly, it's true that for the Japanese of the past, it was the grandparents, rather than the wife, who raised the children. The grandparents retired from their [original] jobs and so they educated the children. Because of this, the children were incredibly well disciplined. The mother and father were, of course, very busy, so they didn't have much time to spend with the children. In any case, they often had many children. So it was the grandparents who went all out to bring up the children. But with today's nuclear families, the presence of grandparents has been radically reduced, and while the mother does her best to raise the child, she may actually pay less attention to them [because of her many social engagements]. The result is that the child receives no real discipline. That is certainly true.

SAKAKIBARA YASUO: Yes, throughout Japan it was the grandparents who not only raised the grandchildren, they also taught the children the rules. But now with predominance of the nuclear family it is the mother who has to spend more time with the children. Also, in the older days there were many children, but now there are few, so the mother tends to intervene in a child's life too much. Nowadays the parents are getting busier, but there is often nobody who helps young children to cope with life in the complex modern world.

BLS: In America in recent years while most women feel it is important for them to have free choice about aborting a child, an increasing number express the need to deal with the psychological aftereffects of an abortion. One understands why women might have these feelings after *shizan* (stillbirth) or *ryūzan* (miscarriage), but many, including feminists, seek the need for something like a *kuyō* as a means of dealing with the often-unanticipated impact of their decision to abort.

ODA HŌRYŪ: That's also the case with most Japanese. Rather than being conscious of it as a sin (*tsumi*), they feel *kanashimi* (*grieving*) over having lost a child. The reason why Japanese have become insensitive, I believe, is that so few people nowadays feel or reflect upon the nature of what they have done (Figure 3.3).

FIGURE 3.3 Oda Hōryū and Sakakibara Yasuo at Jikishi-an Temple.

Reading Omoidegusa *within Its Social Context*

As a way of moving beyond the cosmologies and worldviews that characterized the social and religious climate of pre-modern Japan, we began our discussion in this chapter by examining the written expressions of contemporary Japanese women who experienced pain but who did not know how to handle this and who saw little relationship of their plight to any larger social scene. It is possible to read these expressions drawn from the *Omoidegusa* notebooks and to dwell only on the personal circumstances of individual women. It is clear, however, how deeply social and cultural forces condition what persons experience and how they look at themselves and the world around them.

The selections from the eight volumes of these notebooks that have been chosen here illustrate the "real-life" hell endured by women (and some men) who find themselves caught in relationships that have become a form of imprisonment. While there is considerable variety expressed in these notebooks, there are threads of deep sadness that characterizes so many of them. And in many instances, one finds expressions of the current sexual climate that dominates gender relationships in contemporary Japan.

These feelings are poignant in part because those who write have been unable to communicate openly with other people. Their words are an attempt to fill a void and to articulate the unspoken. Jikishian's reputation as a temple with a history of receptivity to hearing such expressions of pain and confusion make it a kind of magnet for those who have repressed their feelings but can do so no longer. In general, Jikishian is an exception to most Buddhist temples in Japan that, while offering memorial services for children or fetuses lost through stillbirth, miscarriage, or abortion, rarely provide outlets for the kind of counseling or instruction about issues that women in these surveys have expressed a desire for. Except for a small number of religious organizations that have steadfastly opposed abortion, there has been little general opposition within Japanese Buddhism to the existence of abortion since it was legalized in 1948.

Though abortion has been condemned by Buddhists as the taking of a human life, there has been little systematic discussion of its ethical implications by mainstream Buddhist organizations. Rarely do Buddhist communities provide guidance to their followers about how to make responsible decisions in these areas, other than the generalized teaching that abortion is the taking of human life. While temple priests and organizational headquarters often voice negative feelings about abortion, it is reluctantly accepted as a given feature of modern society. Specifically, in a questionnaire sent to religious leaders in Japan, while approximately 15 percent said abortion should not be allowed *(zettai ni yurusareru beki de wa nai)*, 78 percent felt that induced abortion cannot be avoided in certain circumstances *(jijo ni yotte wa yamu o enai)*, and another 8 percent did not answer this question.[44] At this point, the conversation is apt to stop, and the problems remain.

As mentioned earlier, *mizuko kuyō* is interesting in part as a symptom of various social problems and as a means of helping people deal with particular needs that have surfaced dramatically in recent decades. Analogous to this is society's reluctance to grant women greater agency in the area of procreative choice. Providing the option of abortion without encouraging effective sex education or more positive kinds of family planning virtually guarantees a high incidence of abortion. One cannot comprehend the plight of individual women without paying attention to the cultural and social context in which they exist.

Again, the range of experiences represented in these pages challenge stereotypes of passive Japanese women, though, for the most part, they continue to define themselves in relationship to men. The sort of pain registered here is widespread; it is in no sense anomalous, though each instance is unique. For this reason, there is need to stress the importance of acknowledging and confronting conflict, pain, and brokenness and to examine examples of what this may entail. Contemporary experiences of pain and loneliness, for the most part, contain no images of karmic retribution, no literalized portrayals of fearsome hells, no longing for a pure land. In fact, there is often no evidence of a religious worldview as such, yet these experiences are deeply spiritual in nature. They are central to what many women are undergoing in child loss today, though theirs is a personal grief that is seldom addressed in a conscious and effective manner or in ways by which a society may help or fail to help its members encounter deep loss, and to move beyond this to greater self-respect and healthy relationships with others.

From this discussion of two temples in the Kyoto area that have performed rituals for women who had experienced some form of child loss, the following chapter provides different sets of evidence. During the mid-1980s a group of social scientists at Kyoto University, supplemented by colleagues at Tokyo Kōgei University, collaborated in a research project dealing with the complex sociological and psychological phenomena of *mizuko kuyō*. In the process, six questionnaires were constructed and circulated, four of which contain data and comments that are directly pertinent to this study. The criteria for selecting material to be discussed in this chapter are based on how they inform the principal subjects of this book, namely, how women react to their experiences of pregnancy loss, what they think has happened to their *mizuko*, and how they have responded to the ritual of *mizuko kuyō*.

4

The Phenomena of Mizuko Kuyō

RESPONSES TO PREGNANCY LOSS

*Matsuyama no ie...mizuko rei...*Facing the altar, the Pure Land Buddhist priest intoned the family name as he conducted a memorial service requested by the Matsuyama family for the spirit of a *mizuko* aborted ten years earlier. Behind the priest, also facing the altar, sat the family of three—Noriko, her husband Masao, and their four-year-old daughter Masako. Noriko could feel the cool tatami on her feet and knees as she listened intently to the chanted words of the service. The hollow, steady rhythm of the *mokugyō* (fish-shaped wooden drum) struck by the priest framed her attention upon what was taking place. A thin trail of incense smoke rising from the burner upon the altar helped to focus her mind on the sutras being chanted in her behalf and for the *mizuko* fixed in her memory.[1]

IF ONE VIEWS this hypothetical scene as a prelude to whatever in the service may evolve next, one finds that each person's reason for seeking a memorial service is distinct and that every *mizuko kuyō* is experienced differently. The nature of pregnancy loss—by induced abortion, miscarriage, or stillbirth—is obviously important. The social circumstances surrounding the loss vary with each person or family. The manner in which the priest handles each situation is of great significance. Above all, the state of mind of the woman and that of her partner or husband will condition how profound or how devoid of meaning are their experiences of loss and the means of dealing with them.

The point here is to set the stage for examining some of these differences and, by implication, to suggest how difficult it is to probe into what is essentially private and what remains elusive to statistics. Yet by analyzing data obtained through a major research project the variety of these experiences becomes evident. The material discussed in this chapter is based on five questionnaires conducted by the Sociological Research

Group on Contemporary Religion (*Gendai shūkyō shakaigaku kenkyūkai*), a group composed of eight colleagues from Kyoto University and Osaka University, hereafter referred to as the Kyōdai project.[2] The statistical information secured by this project provides a wealth of evidence about Japanese religious institutions and their practices of *mizuko kuyō* and of individuals who frequent these sites for these services.

For the purposes of this chapter, the most important findings deal with how women react to their experiences of pregnancy loss, whether by induced abortion or otherwise, what they think has happened to their *mizuko*, how they have responded to the ritual of *mizuko kuyō*, and whether they sustain a relationship to their *mizuko*.[3] This particular material is contained in the results of a questionnaire made available to individuals participating in *mizuko kuyō* services at Adashino Nenbutsuji in Kyoto. This survey, administered during the years 1983–86 by the Tokyo Polytechnic University Collaborative Research Group (Tokyo kōgei daigaku kyōdō kenkyū han), is hereafter referred to as the Kōgei survey.

At my request, Takahashi Saburō, director of the Kyōdai project, provided computerized correlations, drawn from a variety of responses to several of these questionnaires. These correlations highlight the complexities that characterize the experiences and feelings of women and also locate the results of this survey within wider social, religious, and cultural contexts. These correlations, selected principally from the survey completed by individuals for whom memorial services were conducted at Adashino Nenbutsuji, added many useful perspectives. None of these correlations have been published before. The fact that the extent of responses (1,127) to this questionnaire was so large contributes to the representative nature of these findings. The return rate was high, in part because the priest at this temple (Hara Satoshi) urged participants to complete the surveys so that his temple might respond more adequately to the expressed needs and suggestions of those who attend the service.

The first part of this chapter examines tabulated responses to a variety of questions, including correlations with other parts of the questionnaire. The following section explores detailed comments written by individuals at the end of their completed survey. The third section combines an interpretive discussion by one member of the Kyoto University team of social scientists about the roles of revenge (*tatari*) and of guilt (*tsumi*) in the experiences of *mizuko kuyō* along with my own overall assessment of this material. The chapter concludes with a summary of statements by a wide range of Japanese religious institutions about the differences and the shared beliefs about *mizuko kuyō*, as these appeared in the institutional responses to the Kyōdai project.

Examining the Responses

Who were the 1,127 respondents to this particular questionnaire supervised by Tokyo Kōgei University?[4] While women far outnumber men in seeking memorial services for their *mizuko* as well as in responding to this questionnaire, it became more common by the late 1980s for men to accompany women to these services. More than seven of every ten respondents were between twenty and thirty-nine years of age, but when the age range is extended to forty-nine the percentage increases to 82 percent. Less than 15 percent were younger than twenty or older than fifty. The completed levels of education were as follows: junior high, 11 percent; high school, 44 percent; a specialty school, women's junior college, or university, 40 percent. Roughly 40 percent of the respondents were single; 49 percent were married or remarried; and 6 percent were divorced, separated, or widowed. Of all the respondents, 45 percent had living children, while 52 percent did not.

With children now being seen in Japan as full-fledged human beings more commonly than sixty years ago, there has been a growing tendency to regard and treat their death in a certain sense as one's ancestor. In the words of one woman responding to the Kōgei survey: "Instead of dwelling on its being a *mizuko*, each person should do *kuyō* in the same manner as for an ancestor. Whether a *mizuko* who was never born into this world, or a person who dies of an illness at fifty, or a person who lives a full life until one hundred, they are all the same in being *hotoke-sama* [on the way to Buddhahood]."[5] In the minds of some, if one neglects *mizuko* spirits (*mizuko rei*) this may bring about retribution, a fear that has been associated with the spirits of "neglected" ancestors for centuries. While not a prevailing belief, *mizuko kuyō* in its most alarmist forms does tap into fears and anxieties about what may come from neglecting one's ancestors. These feelings may well arise from a variety of unaddressed needs felt by large numbers of women and bear little or no relationship to ancestral spirits of any kind.

An initial question is whether the respondent had lost either a child or a fetus. Of those responding to this question (1,046), 86 percent (896) said yes, while 14 percent (150) had not experienced this kind of loss. Though it was uncommon for priests to ask a woman how her *mizuko* was lost, from responses to other questions it is clear that the causes of pregnancy loss are as follows: induced abortion (*chūzetsu*), 76 percent; miscarriage, (*ryūzan*) 19 percent; and stillbirth (*shizan*), 3 percent. Since the literature on *mizuko kuyō* tends to highlight induced abortion to the virtual exclusion of other reasons for child or fetal loss, it bears emphasizing that almost 25 percent of loss had been experienced by means other than induced abortion. Because the term *mizuko* has been used for various forms of reproductive loss, it is objected by some that the general term *mizuko* should not be used for these different forms of loss.

Thus far, no detailed study has examined the differences a Japanese woman might have following an induced abortion in contrast to one or more kinds of involuntary pregnancy or reproductive loss, let alone psychological studies that contrast the personal experiences of women at various stages of miscarriage, stillbirth, or early infant death. The richness of human responses to pregnancy loss of whatever form is, however, essential to note, for they give voices to a large spectrum of women who have experienced some form of pregnancy loss.

How Women React to Experiences of Pregnancy Loss

By correlating how a *mizuko* was lost with marital status, it is clear that abortion is the dominant cause for single persons (96 percent), though even for married persons the abortion figure is nearly 80 percent. Almost 90 percent of all miscarriages and stillbirths are by married or previously married women. This information highlights the connection between marital status and the incidence of abortion but also that a significant number of married women have lost a child or fetus involuntarily. As to whether the emotional consequences of such pregnancy loss are as severe for single women as for those who are married, there is insufficient evidence in this material to draw on.

As one might expect, the cause of death has a stronger impact on those who believe that *tatari* will result. While these differences may seem predictable, the actual proportions are striking. In the cases of abortion, 90 percent believe that *tatari* will result, with much smaller numbers in cases of miscarriage (19 percent) and stillbirth (4 percent). With some frequency many women ask for instruction about how to understand and deal with their situation. While temples often expressed a willingness to provide such instruction, it is not clear that many actually do this unless they are specifically asked.

By means of the Tokyo Kōgei questionnaire, at the end of which there is opportunity to add comments, one encounters different, even conflicting, levels of apprehension about *tatari* as expressed by individual women seeking *mizuko kuyō*. The following comments from three women provide examples of diversity:

1. "In scientific terms it is clear that curses do not exist, but there is something I cannot completely dismiss emotionally."
2. "I was told by a religious organization that a *mizuko* was cursing my eldest son."
3. "Whenever something unfortunate, unhappy, or difficult occurs, I see it as *mizuko*'s *tatari*... Since I killed four, it is only to be expected. Whenever I encounter something bad I take it as the *mizuko*'s retribution. No matter how much I suffer I take it as fate."[6]

The close connection that exists between the decision to abort a pregnancy and the belief that *tatari* will result, *especially* if *mizuko kuyō* is not performed, suggests the importance of assessing how this sort of memorial service may contribute to some kind of healing or at least help an individual "come to terms with" the experience of pregnancy loss. Toward the latter part of this twenty-five year project, especially over the past ten years with the help of multicultural evidence in ritual studies, it has become more useful to view the Japanese context, despite its distinguishable features, within a larger frame of reference. Chapters 7–9 expand on this topic by examining in detail varieties of ritual, including developments in the United States.

How Feelings for Their Mizuko *Vary with the Causes of* Mizuko *Death*

How women react to their experiences of pregnancy loss is obviously a fundamental question. In replies from nearly 1,100 individuals, the most commonly used term for these feelings is *tsumi,* a word connoting a sense of deep regret, sometimes self-blame, a desire to make amends, and at times profound guilt. The hundreds of personal statements, however, reveal that no single term is adequate for such an experience. One might therefore object to using this term, as it could imply the respondent *should* feel a sense of *tsumi*. On the other hand, the term *tsumi* somehow captures, or at least suggests, what many women actually express in their responses. In any case, the following discussion serves as a starting point (Table 4.1).

Table 4.1 **What kinds of feelings do you have with respect to your *mizuko*?**

Number of responses	1,097 (97.3 percent)
I feel a sense of *tsumi* (offense, blame).	826 (73.3 percent)
Sometimes I feel a sense of *tsumi*.	134 (11.9 percent)
I do not feel a sense of *tsumi*, but my heart is heavy.	90 (8.0 percent)
I do not feel any sense of *tsumi*.	10 (0.9 percent)
Other	37 (3.3 percent)

Source: *Mizuko kuyō: gendai shakai no fuan to iyashi* (Mizuko Kuyō: Anxiety and Healing in Contemporary Society), ed. by Takahashi Saburō (Kyoto: Kōrosha, 1999). 251.

The implications of the word *tsumi* are complex and subtle. In a general sense, *tsumi* does convey a notion of "blame" or offense" or "guilt" and is sometimes translated as "sin." As one woman writes, "I keep blaming myself for understanding the value of life only *after* losing my own child. Right now I feel guilty, and do not know what to do about my pitiful self. I hope to learn how to make even limited amends."[7] As the figures in Table 4.1 indicate, whatever has caused a *mizuko* the proportion of women who have a sustained experience of *tsumi* (85 percent), including those who sometimes have these feelings, these numbers are surprisingly high. If one adds to that another 8 percent who may have no sense of *tsumi* but who acknowledge having a "heavy heart," this amounts to an extraordinarily high proportion.

But of all who have some sense of *tsumi*, regularly or even sometimes, the largest share by far (93 percent) had at least one abortion. This formidable link between *tsumi* and abortion is similar to the connection between abortion and the belief in *tatari*. And the fact that so many who had miscarriages (54 percent) and stillbirths (57 percent) had some feelings of *tsumi* suggests social and cultural factors that need to be explored. It is also clear that some women have undergone pregnancy loss in more than one way. Because these connections are seldom recognized, they are virtually absent in scholarly, let alone popular discussions of *mizuko kuyō*. Another appropriate question is how one relates on a daily basis to one's *mizuko* whether one chose to abort the fetus or lost it involuntarily (Table 4.2).

While 40 percent of respondents indicated that their *mizuko* lives always "in [my] heart," these feelings depend on what she thinks has happened to her *mizuko*. The most common feelings are that this child has gone to the world of the spirits or exists now as a reborn spirit in this world

Table 4.2 How do you relate to your *mizuko* on a daily basis? Choose as many as are appropriate. Number of choices selected: 1604

I have feelings of *mizuko* every day.	448 (39.8 percent)
There is no day when I don't remember it.	213 (18.9 percent)
Since it weighs on my heart, I try not to remember.	202 (17.9 percent)
I'm so busy I don't have time to think about it.	169 (15.0 percent)
When having trouble, I consult my *mizuko* or ask it for help.	152 (13.5 percent)
I have no substitute for my *mizuko*, but I would like one.	129 (11.4 percent)
I live with a substitute for my *mizuko* (e.g., doll, picture).	115 (10.2 percent)
Other	176 (15.6 percent)
Number of responses	1042 (92.5 percent)

Source: *Mizuko kuyō: gendai shakai no fuan to iyashi* (Mizuko Kuyō: Anxiety and Healing in Contemporary Society), ed. by Takahashi Saburō (Kyoto: Kōrosha, 1999). 253.

or has gone to the place of the ancestors. Whatever the specific belief, women actively *image* the whereabouts of their *mizuko*. This is made graphic in the following statement:

> I go to the temple, join my hands, and whisper, "I'm sorry. I'm sorry." This is what I find myself doing each time. When at home, I talk to the *mizuko* every morning and night. I have given it a name myself, and say, "Sleep peacefully. Please forgive your mother." But its lack of form makes it harder. I think about how happy it might be if I could only hold it in my arms.[8]

The process of imaging is clearly important to women, whatever their age. When asked whether they carry around daily feelings of *kuyō* in their hearts, 43 percent of women of all ages answered that they do. There is considerable variance, however, at different age levels: 36 percent (ages twenty to twenty-nine); 43 percent (ages thirty to thirty-nine); 59 percent (ages forty to forty-nine); and 68 percent (ages fifty-plus). In general, the older a woman gets, the more she carries this child around in her heart. In the words of one woman, "I would like to have an *ihai* [spirit tablet representing *mizuko*] and to do *kuyō* properly on each anniversary and at vernal and autumnal equinoxes [*higan*]...It would be helpful to have something I could keep by my side, something that no one else would know about."[9]

If the sense of *tsumi* declines somewhat with age, why would a woman carry a *mizuko* increasingly in her heart as she became older? Is this *because* she was older or because she grew up in a more "traditional" Japan or because she had less education? Other possibilities? One needs to know more about a woman's experience when it is free of any sense of *tsumi* but in which she still lives with a "heart that is heavy." Living with a "sense of *tsumi*" is living with a heavy heart, but presumably it may include some sense of guilt, whereas living with a heavy heart may not. At this point, whatever overlap exists between such experiences can be only speculated. As one woman put it, "It takes courage to visit a temple and do *kuyō*, because as a woman one is forced to come face to face with something very painful both spiritually and physically. I hope *kuyō* will be a means of gently reaching out to such women and give them strength to face tomorrow with courage."[10] This woman had four abortions (Table 4.3).

On the other hand, 89 percent of women whose sustained experiences of *tsumi* have been stressful believe that *kuyō* provides a sense of atonement for *tsumi*. Similar experiences are mentioned when *tsumi* is *sometimes* but not always felt as well as for those who mention having "heaviness of heart." In general, there is a sense that *kuyō* brings feelings of serenity, that it is natural to do *kuyō*, that it brings support

Table 4.3 Which of the following describes *kuyō*? Choose as many as are appropriate.

It redresses *tsumi*.	833	(73.9 percent)
It brings serenity.	503	(44.6 percent)
It is a natural behavior arising from natural feelings.	450	(39.9 percent)
It gives consolation or support so that one can go on living.	356	(31.6 percent)
It lightens the weight in one's heart.	294	(26.1 percent)
It brings good fortune (*shiawase*).	229	(20.3 percent)
It addresses turning points in one's life.	147	(13.0 percent)
Others	118	(10.5 percent)

Source: Mizuko kuyō: gendai shakai no fuan to iyashi (Mizuko Kuyō: Anxiety and Healing in Contemporary Society), ed. by Takahashi Saburō (Kyoto: Kōrosha, 1999). 257.

and comfort, lightens one's emotional burdens, and brings happiness or good fortune, and that it helps to straighten out one's priorities. To understand the subtle though important dissimilarities between these different and perhaps overlapping sets of feelings would require further study.

Of those believing that *tatari* will result if *kuyō* is not performed, 90 percent attribute the cause to abortion, while only 19 percent would attribute it to miscarriage. In responses to the effect of having a *kuyō* performed, one can observe that this practice has many connotations and that its impact is not simply the alleviation (or "atonement") of guilt. Whatever "definitions" of these terms apply, respondents were asked to locate their experiences of *tatari* within the following circumstances: affects me physically; illness or injury in the family; unhappiness, misfortune, calamity; appears in my dreams; inability to have children; unusual circumstances; children doing poorly in school; domestic disharmony; and assorted others. While each was cited frequently, the first three were particularly prominent when viewed together with personal comments expressed at the end of the questionnaire. One way to assess how *tatari* affects a person is to ask those who believe in *tatari* what they pray for when they participate in a *kuyō* service or when they are alone (Table 4.4).

By associating how pregnancy loss occurs with what is prayed for when doing *mizuko kuyō*, one finds some expected results. When miscarriage and stillbirth are the causes, the major concerns are *kanai anzen* or good health and good fortune for present children. When the cause is abortion, the concerns are the same, with the addition of prayers to forestall *tatari*

Table 4.4 What kinds of things do you pray for through *kuyō*? Choose as many responses as are appropriate.

Good health and fortune for me and my family.	480 (42.6 percent)
That disaster and bad fortune go away.	430 (38.2 percent)
Safety in the home (*kanai anzen*).	427 (37.9 percent)
Good fortune (*shiawase*) for my living children.	370 (32.8 percent)
That there be no *tatari* from now on.	355 (31.5 percent)
For a good [or happy] married life (*shiawase na*).	326 (28.9 percent)
For birth of a child.	289 (25.6 percent)
Others	258 (22.9 percent)

Source: Mizuko kuyō: gendai shakai no fuan to iyashi (Mizuko Kuyō: Anxiety and Healing in Contemporary Society), ed. by Takahashi Saburō (Kyoto: Kōrosha, 1999). 252–253.

(34 percent) and for marital good luck (that is, for single persons seeking for a suitable spouse, 31 percent). As to whether *kuyō* should be continued for a lifetime (*eidai kuyō*), there is a virtual consensus between respondents who say that it *should* be continued for a lifetime (37 percent) and those who want to continue it for their lifetime (49 percent). Only 1 percent do not regard this practice as a lifelong obligation. The more positive responses may indicate how influential this ritual has been to those who have requested it, but this is only a supposition.

Responses from a Thousand Points of View

At the end of each questionnaire, there was space for respondents to reflect on their experiences of having *kuyō* performed for them and their *mizuko*. Comments from over a thousand people naturally vary in length, in topics discussed, in their personal perspectives, and perhaps with the spirit of the temple they visited. As a way of trying to make sense of this sizable amount of material, four categories are presented here, each of which is familiar but which is rarely discussed in relationship to one another: (1) the perception of *mizuko kuyō* as a form of business (*shōbai*); (2) the extent to which this practice may be related to fears of *tatari* (revenge by a *mizuko* on its "mother" and wider family); (3) the sense of guilt or blame (*tsumi*) a woman may feel; and (4) the degree to which counseling is available in religious circles and the expression of need for this, especially by those who have induced an abortion.

Reexamining the Commercial Features of *Mizuko Kuyō*

Among the commonly vocalized complaints about *mizuko kuyō* are the considerable prices that some temples charge for this service, making them, in effect, a form of business (*shōbai*). These allegations may be based more on the reputation of certain temples that are renowned for extravagant fees than on the practices of the average temple. *Mizuko kuyō* has also been construed as another search for protection and blessing— protection against curses invoked by the unhappy spirits of *mizuko* not properly memorialized and blessings for women and their families who request services in behalf of these spirits. While it cannot be denied that many forms of *mizuko kuyō* include various elements of this practice, in a more revealing sense *mizuko kuyō* is a window to a host of unaddressed issues in Japanese society. In fact, the study of *mizuko kuyō* prompts one to reconsider the ways one understands the practice of Japanese religions more broadly.

As is commonly known, within the diversity of Japanese religions the concerns for good fortune and protection from adversity abound. Those of enduring nature include desires for a child, a healthy pregnancy and safe childbirth (*anzan*), and a good upbringing of children (*kosodate*). In addition, hopes are expressed for the healing of illness, the overall well-being of mind and body; concerns for prosperity and wealth (*shindai*); good fortune in general (*kaiun*); and protection from all manner of danger (*yakuyoke*). Newer forms include anxiety about doing well in school (*gakugyō jōju*), worries over traffic safety (*kōtsū anzen*), safety in the home (*kanai anzen*), success in business (*shōbai hanjō*), coping with new kinds of illness (HIV), and finally generalized wishes for the "successful completion of all requests" (*shōgan jōju*).

In times of personal or social uncertainty there is heightened anxiety about the future, stimulating the wish to know what the future may hold. It is this anxiety that drives the widespread resorting to fortune-telling or divination in Japan.[11] Because people are emotionally vulnerable at times of severe loss, some expressions of *mizuko kuyō* amount to a commercialization of human suffering generated by those who take advantage of the fear and guilt of others. If one were to study this aspect in all of its complexity, one would also need to analyze the lavish prices charged by commercial companies for statues of Kannon, Jizō, and *mizuko* themselves; the income garnered by temples who sell these to those requesting memorial services; as well as the profit made through the sale of amulets, charms, and talismans for the innumerable kinds of blessings or protection (*omamori*).[12] To study the economics of *mizuko kuyō* in any serious sense, however, a more apt place to start would be with the overall economic needs of religious institutions and the current means by which they seek to meet these needs. We look briefly at this complex issue in Chapter 6, but it is a subject that would benefit by more detailed study in the future.

If memorial services for *mizuko* are seen as but another instance of desires for protection or for worldly blessings, then it is ironic that in virtually all Buddhist sects, as well as in many of the new religions, the practice of *mizuko kuyō* exists. Though Jōdo Shinshū (True Pure Land sect) is theoretically an exception to this, officially protesting against this practice, many of its priests conduct this kind of *kuyō* when it is requested by laypersons. That is, without promoting it they do permit it. It is even more true that large numbers of Shinshū adherents visit temples of other sects to have this service provided. One may, therefore, see the practice of *mizuko kuyō* along a wide continuum from commercialization and the promotion of guilt feelings (these are not necessarily combined) to a reluctance, if not a refusal, by priests to offer these services at all. In between these extremes lies a varied middle ground, in which temples may offer this service but do not accentuate or even advertise the fact. In numerous remunerative ways religious institutions combine the tension or paradox between "folk religion" and "established belief." In discussing this dialectic, Shinno Toshikazu writes:

> Here we see the double-layered structure of these religious organizations. They have some sort of affiliation with "established" religious organizations, but they also have a side to them that deviates from the boundaries of the traditional teachings and doctrines of the established organizations. In fact, it is precisely this aspect that tends to attract followers. This is an important point to keep in mind in discussing the questions of orthodoxy and heresy, or in considering the dialectic between religious creativity and the continuity of traditional doctrines and organizations.[13]

Fears of *Mizuko* Revenge (*Tatari*)

Of greater importance to this study than the issue of *shōbai* is the fear in some circles that if a *mizuko* has been intentionally aborted (*chūzetsu*) but has not been properly memorialized it will return to haunt the living, especially its mother and her family. This oft-debated subject deserves extended study. While different approaches to the issue of *tatari* are discussed in several chapters, we discuss here responses from the Tokyo Kōgei questionnaires. As mentioned earlier, a large proportion of respondents (72 percent) said that *tatari* will or sometimes might result if a *kuyō* is not performed, while only 11 percent said that it will not. By far the largest share of those who believe *tatari* will result are from persons who have had abortions (93 percent). The same issue may be approached in another manner, as, for example, when the question is posed to Buddhist priests who advertise the fact that they offer *kuyō* as to whether people coming to their temple believe that "*mizuko* can harm the living" (*mizuko no tatari ishiki*). Of these priests 18 percent think that the majority of laypeople coming for *kuyō* believe that this kind of harm can happen; another 45 percent of the priests think that "a considerable number" share this view.[14]

By analyzing responses to the Kōgei questionnaire, one sees that attitudes about whether *tatari* exists are more complex than what the media have presented. In the words of one respondent, "Newspapers and advertisements often claim that 'If you pay X, then we will take over the responsibility for *kuyō*.' This does not take *mizuko kuyō* seriously." Comparably critical responses about the media from most temple priests may also be found. For instance, in response to a question addressed to religious personnel of how television programs and magazine articles present *mizuko kuyō*, 52 percent stated that they "distort the original meaning" of this practice. Most others are mixed in their reply.[15]

If one connects feelings of this sort with the emotions a woman might have in contemplating an abortion, particularly in situations where there is little if any understanding or support, it would be no surprise if she found it difficult living with the negative, even destructive thoughts of becoming a mother for the second or third time. It is not surprising that a woman may live uncomfortably with or in denial about her own negative thoughts. As one woman commented, "No matter how often I do *kuyō* I cannot escape the despair I feel...I would like to have a clear feeling of resolution from *kuyō*, but that is not the case. If this is a curse I would like to know what to do."[16] To this woman the so-called curse may be nothing but her own mixed feelings: of affirmation about children in the abstract but negative feelings about bearing another child or, if not yet a mother, of bearing a child at this time in her life. The ambiguity with which she may live might itself be a curse, but the curse may exist as well in already having a child or also in the experience of not being able to have a child.

The variety of reactions expressed in these questionnaires is considerable, including self-pity, feelings of guilt, thoughtful self-reflection, and genuine compassion for others. Such a spectrum serves to personalize the reactions one discovers as one listens to women discuss their experiences or reads their comments on questionnaires. If one ignores this spread of responses, it is easy to settle for the fear of *tatari* as being the driving factor in their emotional outlook toward their own experience. Statements of this sort also suggest how social problems aggravate personal decision making or how they may minimize the importance of expressing one's feelings.

While fears of *tatari* have been associated with having a sense of *tsumi*, self-blame, or feelings of personal responsibility over the decision to abort, the reverse is not necessarily true. That is, feelings of self-blame are not inevitably accompanied by fears of angry spirits. While younger women are more vulnerable to such rhetoric, they also represent a portion of the population in which the incidence of abortion remains high. For older women, years after the event, it is not uncommon for them to attribute problems of bad health or poor family relations to a *mizuko* that was not properly memorialized. At this point in their life there is often little sense of *tsumi*. In fact, they may never have had self-condemnatory feelings about the decision, since during the first two decades after the war when Japan was still recovering from social and economic devastation, women could more easily justify having an abortion. If feelings of this sort exist years afterward, they may not stem from the decision to abort. They may be based more on the belief that the spirit of the aborted child has been neglected. In these situations, fears of *tatari* may or may not be a factor. On the other hand, a statement like the following one keeps alive the larger question of how people react to unexplained suffering, a topic that is addressed at length in Chapter 6:

> Whenever I encounter something bad I take it as *mizuko* retribution. No matter how much I suffer, I take it as fate... Although I have such a strong sense of *tsumi*, the man seems to feel nothing. I cannot understand how he can be so calm about it. The sin belongs to both the man and woman, but why is it that the woman has to carry the full weight of this?[17]

Tsumi—A Sense of Guilt, Blame, Offense

It is important to emphasize again that feelings of *tsumi* do not necessarily lead to or stem from a sense of *tatari*. When the question, "Why do you think people come to your temple to do *mizuko kuyo?*" was put to priests in the Kyōdai survey sent to Buddhist temples that perform this *kuyō*, the results were revealing: (1) "from an awareness of *tsumi*" (50 percent); (2) "looking for a solution to a variety of types of distress" (30 percent); (3) "for future happiness" (16 percent); (4) "fear of a curse" (12 percent); and "other" (13 percent). Because of the claim that a feeling of having committed some deep offense is linked to the promotion of fears about *tatari*, one searches for detailed evidence about this. As one seeks to understand the ingredients of both *tatari* and *tsumi*, one becomes skeptical about automatic links between them. Instead, one may begin with the hypothesis that the feeling of *tsumi* does not necessarily lead to or result from a sense of *tatari*. Support for such a position was seen in the observations of Oda Hōryū at

Jikishian, discussed in the preceding chapter, in which he refrains from attributing the cause of *tsumi* to fears about *tatari*.

A further clue may be found in discovering that when asked whether they carry around daily feelings of *kuyō* in their hearts, 43 percent of women of all ages answered in the affirmative. As a woman grows in her ability to live with her lost *mizuko*, however, she is not driven by fears that this departed spirit will seek revenge on her as a mother (causing her to blame herself) or on the wider family of husband and siblings. Indeed, as she begins to live with this *mizuko*, its "presence" in her life is more real to her than its "absence." Her feelings of *tsumi* may well subside. When one correlates the ages of respondents and their feelings of sustained *tsumi*, there is evidence of a decline in feelings of *tsumi* with age: 89 percent (twenty to twenty-four); 77 percent (twenty-five to twenty-nine); 63 percent (thirty to thirty-nine); 65 percent (forty to forty-nine); 57 percent (fifty and above). To grasp the meaning of this, one comes to intuit the importance of ritual in helping the woman to sustain an image of its "presence." At this point, there is a steady decline in the fear of *tatari* and of attachment to one's earlier feelings of guilt or any other sense of "offense." Instead, she may experience a kind of fullness, a sense of well-being that could not have been predicted beforehand.

Another way of assessing variations in an experience of *tsumi* is to ask what effect the performing of *mizuko kuyō* may have on women coming to a temple for this service who may have a sustained sense of *tsumi*. The following multiple responses are at least suggestive: (1) doing *mizuko kuyō* is an atonement for sin (*tsumi*) (89 percent); (2) it brings feelings of serenity (44 percent); (3) it is natural to do it (39 percent); (4) it brings support and comfort (33 percent); (5) it lightens one's emotional burdens (29 percent); (6) it brings happiness (22 percent); and (7) it straightens out one's priorities (12 percent). The same experiences are mentioned when one says that *tsumi* is sometimes but not always felt and also for those who mention experiencing a "heaviness of heart." While this range of responses may be difficult to interpret, it at least indicates that the sense neither of *tsumi* nor of how *kuyō* may affect it is in any sense uniform. It is even possible that a person may start with a sense of *tsumi*, but with time she may come to have other, less negative feelings about herself and about any sense of recrimination. Instead, the experience may be viewed as an unfolding, dynamic process, not something that remains static. Also, it suggests that most temples are not prescriptive about what this sense of offense or blame means or should mean.

A further element to introduce here, but not developed until later in the narrative, are the ways a woman discovers how to cope on a daily basis with feelings about her *mizuko* and how these feelings seem to vary with what she thinks has happened to her *mizuko*. To repeat, the daily experiencing of a *mizuko* in a woman's heart stands out among all age groups. In terms of a woman's concern over what happens to her *mizuko* (checking as many as apply), the most common feelings expressed by women are that " it is always in my heart" (45 percent), "it is a spirit (*reikon*) in the other world or *ano yo*" (34 percent), "it returns to where our ancestors are" (26 percent), "it is in Paradise or Heaven" (21 percent), "it exists now as a reborn spirit in this world" (20 percent), or that it returns to some form of the natural world and its life force (16 percent), among other possibilities. What exists here amounts to informal "cosmologies" in the minds of laypeople, however religious or secular they may be.

From these sets of replies one gets at least two impressions—that a sizable number of people have many things about which they feel threatened and that their prayers are principally for a successful and healthy family life. Correlating this more positive sense of what performing *mizuko kuyō* accomplishes with feelings of *tsumi* one finds an even greater connection, namely, that doing *mizuko kuyō* helps one to redress one's sense of *tsumi*. In the process of experiencing this kind of consolation, women especially express their hopes for the future. When one asks what they pray for (checking as many items as apply), one finds again this kind of range: wishes for good health for family members; requests for safety in the home; prayers that disaster and bad fortune go away; hopes for good fortune for their living children; prayers that there will be no *tatari* from here on; the desire to have a good married life; and prayers that they may be blessed by having children. These are clearly expressions of hope for a sound and happy family life and marriage. Having lost a child or aborted a fetus has the effect frequently, not so much of guilt and fear but of contributing to one's desires for a life that is filled with promise.

Whatever the specific beliefs, and they can be innumerable, women actively image the whereabouts of their *mizuko*. It is the transposing of one experience onto another, as one sees in the following comment by a woman who appears to be moving from profound sadness and heaviness of heart to their very opposite: "I hope to continue with an annual *kuyō* for the rest of my life, but I question the tendency to think of it as a burden that torments oneself excessively. It may be unavoidable that one keeps carrying it as a burden in one's heart, but in a positive sense this sad experience should be turned into a 'plus' for one's future."[18] Similar expressions are as follows:

> For a woman, the decision to [abort] a *mizuko* is spiritually unbearable.[19]
>
> As the years pass, I feel more strongly repentant toward *my mizuko*.[20]
>
> I am full of guilt. I feel as if I may ruin myself. I do not know what to do. *Kuyō* is the only answer. Perhaps after tens of years this feeling will lessen.[21]
>
> How can a person such as I make amends? I'd like to find someone who could listen to my heavy thoughts. Every time I think about it, tears come to my eyes.[22]

In one woman's voice, "I feel as if I am always doing *kuyō* in my heart. Is this acceptable?" Among those who seek *mizuko kuyō* there is a tendency to harbor feelings of culpability. As mentioned earlier, *tsumi* carries the connotation of responsibility (*tsumi o okasu* means to commit an offense). This term has many ramifications. While guilt and *tsumi* are not equivalent terms, they sometimes suggest similar responses. As one woman phrased it:

> The *tsumi* of having killed children through abortions is not something that lessens over time. I live with the feeling of being pierced in the heart. When others betray me, the thought of *mizuko* crosses my mind. Spending tens of millions of yen will not erase the *tsumi*. Rather, reaching out to [such a person] and offering her forgiveness and answering her wish for *jōbutsu* [to die in peace and go to heaven] is true *kuyō*.[23]

To review, when one correlates sustained feelings of *tsumi* with the ages of the respondents, one finds a steady decline from a high of 83 percent for women in their early twenties to 57 percent for women fifty years old and above. On the other hand, more than 60 percent of women beyond the age of thirty admitted experiencing sustained feelings of *tsumi*, and another 18 percent felt this way at times. In other words, one has here a sense of more than regret.

In their article on the detailed reactions of six women to their experiences with *mizuko kuyō* at a Nichiren temple in Tokyo, Richard W. Anderson and Elaine Martin argue that a sense of sadness and regret is more the norm than expressions of guilt or fear.[24] They add that, when *mizuko kuyō* is performed at temples that do not specialize in this ritual, one finds that guilt is much less present than sadness. This is probably a valid assumption, yet, as one widens the scope of one's research, the expression of *tsumi* is quite common. In fact, there are many kinds of responses, and it is certainly true that the factor of guilt will vary with how much this is accented by the priest in charge or with the religious background of the person who comes for help. One woman expressed it this way: "I think a sense of guilt (*tsumi*) should be avoided. Instead of feeling badly toward the *mizuko* and apologizing, one should think about life, and strive to live with enough happiness for oneself and the *mizuko*."[25]

There is substantial evidence that feelings of sadness and neglect are more common than those of fear and guilt, that frequently a man or a woman may request *kuyō* for another person in the family, that a large number of women express the need to know what to do to address their feelings, that the negative feelings a woman may have after an abortion or a miscarriage may be more metaphoric than literal and may arise out of their own feelings of ambivalence about having a child, and that, whatever feelings of anxiety women may have in the realm of conception and pregnancy, these may be related to a larger climate of fear and unease that exists at many points within the larger social context.

While statistics of this kind do not capture the richness of individual experience, they do indicate how prevalent is the belief that the spirits of dead children or fetuses continue to exist. As to whether these spirits present a threat to the living, the responses are varied. In any case, the ritual of *mizuko kuyō* is sought for all kinds of reasons. While some forms of *mizuko kuyō* may be found in the category of fear promotion, the evidence from temples and from the experiences of most women who have been interviewed or have responded to questionnaires is not that simple. The irony is that guidance is so seldom sought by women or directly offered by priests. Nevertheless, it has become convenient in recent years to put fears and anxieties about *mizuko* into the frequently used category of *joseiteki fuan* or "feminine anxiety or troubles." The result is often to trivialize the experiences of women who have either gone through an abortion or have literally lost a child and to marginalize situations of women whose problems do not arise in a vacuum but are grounded in the society as a whole.

Need for Counseling, Discussion, Instruction (*Sōdan*)

The question in the Kōgei survey that relates directly to the matter of angry spirits asks: "If *mizuko kuyō* is not performed, do you think that *tatari* [often or sometimes] will ensue?" Three-quarters of those replying answered affirmatively, often, or sometimes, with 12 percent saying they did not know (*wakaranai*) but would like to be instructed. In fact, many asked for instruction about how they might proceed both to understand and to deal with their situation. While temples often express a willingness to provide such instruction, it is not clear that many actually do this unless specifically asked.

Another concept familiar in discussions about *mizuko kuyō* but not widely discussed is *mizuko rei*, the spirit of the departed child or fetus. While not addressed in the Kyōdai survey sent to "parent religious groups" or to "independent religious groups," it was a prominent question in the survey sent to religious groups that do perform *mizuko kuyō*. The specific question was, "Does your group acknowledge (*mitomeru*) the existence of *mizuko* spirits (*rei*)?" In response to this question, 76 percent acknowledged the existence of *mizuko rei*, with only 11 percent answering they did not. Among Buddhist priests as well, about two-thirds indicated their belief in the existence of *mizuko rei*.[26] Unfortunately, there were no follow-up questions, nor was any attempt made to assess what this means. While the concept of *mizuko rei* may receive attention in Buddhist sermons, it does not seem to be clearly understood among laypeople.

> I would like a clear feeling of resolution from *kuyō*, but that is not the case. If this is a curse, I would like to know what to do...My husband reminds me that dwelling on it accomplishes nothing, but I still cannot forget. I had been feeling the need for *kuyō* for a long time. After thirty-one years of marriage I was finally able to do so on Showa 61 (1986), January 25. I feel now as if I have found some peace. Do *mizuko* become dust in the universe? Do they go underground? Do they continue to live in our hearts?[27]

This relative lack of adequate counseling and instruction about a full range of issues arising out of the experience of pregnancy loss and how religious groups deal with these issues, both formally and informally, is a virtually untouched subject in scholarly research about *mizuko kuyo*. With respect to another form of religious instruction, from a question addressed to "parent religious groups" and to "independent religious groups" as to whether they provide any "special guidance or make public/official statements regarding the right or wrong of *mizuko kuyo*" to member groups or organizations, one learns surprisingly that 78 percent indicate they do not, and only 14 percent answer that they make these available.[28] In the area of counseling and instruction, this was the most striking disclosure.

Except for a small number of religious organizations that have steadfastly opposed abortion, there has been little general opposition within Japanese Buddhism to the existence of abortion since it was legalized in 1948. Though abortion has been condemned by Buddhists as the taking of human life, there has been little systematic discussion of its ethical implications by mainstream Buddhist organizations. Nor have Buddhist communities provided extensive guidance to their followers about how one makes responsible decisions in these areas, other than the generalized teaching that abortion is the taking of human life. In a questionnaire sent by the Kyōdai research group to religious leaders in Japan, approximately 15 percent said it should not be allowed *(zettai ni yurusareru beki de wa nai)*, whereas 78 percent felt that induced abortion cannot be avoided in certain circumstances *(jijo ni yotte wa yamu o enai)*, and another 8 percent did not respond to this question. At this point, the conversation is apt to stop.

The fact that these questions were sent to a representative sample of religious groups in Japan reveals that, at least when the Kyōdai study was published (1999), there was almost no formal instruction on the subject of *mizuko kuyō* provided by three-quarters of religious institutions to their suborganizations or to local temples or shrines. This also raises questions about how parent religious groups relate to their member organizations as well as how religious officials within "independent religious groups" relate to their lay membership. Chapter 5 of the Kyōdai study on *mizuko kuyō* addresses this topic, but because of the complexity of these issues the specific role that institutional polity of religious groups plays in doctrinal matters remains inconclusive.

The topic of *mizuko rei* and what this may mean is but one example of what often goes unaddressed. The terms conventionally used for ways temples may reach out to people who are seeking for help are *shidō* (guidance), *jogen* (advice, suggestions), and *sōdan* (advice, counsel). Through responses to various Kyōdai surveys, one is informed that 47 percent of religious groups that perform *mizuko kuyo* "actively offer" counseling or consultation (*sōdan*) and 42 percent offer it "when needed." The picture is similar in Buddhist temples that either proactively (29 percent) offer counseling to those who wish to do *mizuko kuyō* or do so in cases "depending on the situation" (52 percent). The most common problems for which people seek counseling in temple situations are those that are essentially personal in nature: illness or injury of self and family, a child's education and delinquency, problems in a marriage or in another relationship, among others.

> I have been married for half a year, but I lost the child conceived with my husband to an ectopic pregnancy, which is why we came here. Because it was our child, we both wrote our names and did *kuyo*. But the previous time is what concerns me; I aborted a child conceived by someone I was seeing before my marriage. So this is my second child. Because of the nature of this current pregnancy everyone understands my sorrow in losing this child, but I continue to be bothered about the child that no one (including my husband) knows about. This was a child conceived in my twenties; if it were still living it would now be four or five years old. I remain troubled by this earlier loss.[29]

While these are familiar subjects in most forms of counseling, what seems to be missing or at least is not often talked about in counseling or consultation is how religious teaching is brought to bear upon the whole topic of *mizuko kuyō*.[30] While this does not mean that temple priests fail to provide teaching in their *hōwa* or Buddhist sermons or in counseling, it ironically appears as a neglected topic in the public discourse about this subject. From responses in surveys sent to a variety of religious groups as well as to Buddhist temples that perform *mizuko kuyō*, we know that those who perceive a natural connection between their religious teachings and *mizuko kuyō* (60 percent) do more counseling than others and that those who perform this *kuyō* from a sense of duty more than because of doctrine (52 percent) provide counseling depending on the situation.

When clergy or other officials at sites that perform *mizuko kuyō* were asked about the connections between the specific organization's teaching and this *kuyō*, an equal number (41 percent) responded by saying that it accords with their teaching and that while there is no direct doctrinal relationship it is part of one's religious duty. Few oppose the practice of *mizuko kuyō*, but because almost 60 percent of those who were sent questionnaires did not respond to this question, one suspects that considerable uncertainty exists on this matter.

As one woman stated, it would comfort me to know that there was a *kannushi* (priest) always present at Nenbutsu-ji to instruct and work for the *ekō* (transfer of merit) of each person instead of each of us doing our own thing. It seems lacking to just do what one sees fit.[31]

As to when temples and other religious groups began to do *mizuko kuyō*, it is clear that the initial growth came in the years 1966–75 (14 percent), while the largest single growth occurred during the years 1976–85 (42 percent). As to why religious groups began this practice, several factors were central: because of requests from individuals (47 percent) and either for doctrinal reasons or because of directions from parent organizations or from earlier personal experience (31 percent). Whatever other factors were involved, only 6 percent attribute the reason to the popularity of this practice (the "boom" factor), and only 5 percent claim they began doing it for its monetary value. This conflicts with the widespread perception that this *kuyō* is largely for financial reasons. The small numbers may well be accounted for by the reluctance here to admit these kinds of motivations.

On the other hand, when Buddhist temples advertising the fact that they offer *mizuko kuyō* were asked why they began this practice, the reasons were as follows: (1) "people requested it" (73 percent); (2) "reflecting on my own experience" it "seemed the natural thing to do" (26 percent); (3) from our sect's doctrine, it seemed natural to do this (24 percent); (4) because "the previous chief priest had done so" (17 percent); (5) because it is a "boom" and is popular, (3 percent); (6) for "financial reasons" (1 percent); (7) other reasons (16 percent).[32] The differences among these reasons are of genuine interest, both those that are the principal motivating factors and those identified by priests as having virtually no interest. The most conspicuously unchecked item was about any financial incentive. Since it is widely known that temples need income to survive and that they charge for all manner of services, one naturally asks what lies behind the claim that there is no financial incentive to performing this *kuyō*. It would take considerable honesty to acknowledge this motive publicly.

Finally, when Buddhist priests whose temples perform *mizuko kuyō* were asked for their own thoughts about the basis in doctrine for *mizuko kuyō*, the replies are as follows: (1) conducting *mizuko kuyō* is "natural in terms of doctrine" (34 percent); (2) there is "no direct link with doctrine, but it is a natural religious activity" (57 percent); and (3) as to doctrine, "it is problematic, but we have no choice but to do it" (5 percent). This range of why Buddhist priests perform *mizuko kuyō* suggests that it is neither firmly rejected nor wholeheartedly endorsed by Buddhist doctrine. This strikes one as an important revelation and raises a number of questions that will be addressed in subsequent chapters.

Locating Mizuko *in Social Contexts*

Chapter 3 of the Kyōdai volume steps back from statistical tabulations and seeks to understand alternative approaches to the subject. Titled *Futatsu no mizuko kuyō* (Two Types of *Mizuko Kuyō*), the chapter explores two hypotheses: one from the standpoint of "uneasiness" or anxiety about the threat of *tatari*; and the other from "guilt" (the sense of *tsumi*). As mentioned before, prior to World War II a stillborn or miscarried fetus was not the subject of family religious rites. As to why *mizuko kuyō* began to appear in the 1950s and then to develop into a significant movement by the mid-1960s, Takahashi Yoshinori, the author of this chapter, rehearses a number of customary explanations: the trend toward seeing the aborted fetus as having its own individual identity; increase of interest in spirits and the occult; growth in the practice of religious rites for *mizuko*, along with awareness by temples of its money-making prospects; the decline of traditional "family religion" practice, especially in the depersonalized anonymity of life in urban communities; and the uncertainty of how *mizuko kuyō* is to be understood in terms of religious teachings by most religious institutions.[33]

From these circumstances a "gap [emerged] between the traditional religious system that still perceives a dead fetus as not being an individual, and the way that [many other] people perceive fetuses and feel about them."[34] Because belief in the individual identity of a fetus, living or dead, had become widespread in modern Japan, Takahashi examines the existence of two distinct types of *mizuko kuyō* with their different motivations behind the decision to seek a rite for an aborted fetus. He acknowledges he is not addressing the issue of pregnancy loss through miscarriage or stillbirth, though, as we have seen, not factoring in the experiences of miscarriage and stillbirth, especially when we know from questionnaires that these represent 20–25 percent of pregnancy loss, raises some questions that are difficult to answer.

The first kind of motivation arises when a woman decides to abort but later becomes concerned lest this result in one form of imagined retribution or another. Negative experiences of this sort may "explain" unfortunate experiences in the past, or they may occasion anxiety or "uneasiness" (*fuan*) about the future. This unexplained consequence is interpreted as a violent form of revenge by the victim in response to the other person's act of violence through abortion. To Takahashi *kuyō* becomes a means of self-defense. While deciding to have a *kuyō* is to offset the prospect of another's retaliation, it also helps to explain other causes of misfortune that have gone unexplained in the past. Even if a *kuyō* is intended to heal a broken relationship, it is first and foremost a shield against revenge. In Takahashi's terminology, this is "*Mizuko Kuyō* from Uneasiness."

Within Japanese historical frames of reference, but not limited to these, he views this defense against revenge as constitutive of the larger relationship between the living and the dead. As one considers this apprehension about the power of the dead historically in Japanese society, one recognizes these cautious responses to *mizuko* by the living today. We have already cited a number of examples, similar to the following one:

> In the thirteenth year of our marriage my husband stopped going to work. There seemed to be no reason for this, but the one thing that came to mind was my *mizuko* incident. When I asked older people, they said that such things do happen.[35]

Takahashi acknowledges that this "leap of logic" is not the only explanation possible.

> In reality, all around us are many things that offer explanations...[One doesn't] have to adopt the explanation of *Mizuko Kuyō* from Uneasiness. However, for people under these conditions, and for people thinking uneasily about the future, if they are people who have experienced abortion, there is a strong possibility that they will accept [this explanation] as something real.[36]

To Takahashi, the puzzle is why "from the position of realism...this sort of explanation, which seems to be nothing but [a work of] fiction, is accepted as having specific reality?"[37] Turning to the forms of *mizuko kuyō* that proceed from feelings of guilt, one comes to what Takahashi describes as not something "to avoid a future 'undesirable situation', or to eliminate an existing one...[but] to bring out the feelings of 'I am sorry' or 'I am remorseful'...[and whose] purpose is to fully give oneself to the abundance of these emotions, and this is for oneself."[38] He then asks where these feelings come from. To be sure, one may encounter the same manipulative tendencies that project fears similar to those about *tatari* on vulnerable women, usually but not always younger women. In this case, however, the implication would be that one *should* feel guilty.

Without encountering this expectation directly, he undertakes a sophisticated yet still undeveloped approach. What he suggests is that if a woman feels guilty it is because she believes she has violated an ethical commandment. The violation is not to a set of rules or abstract ethical principles but to what he calls a "we relationship." Acknowledging that this sense exists in some form in every society and is culturally conditioned, he wonders why the "relative weight of the 'we' relationship [is] so high in Japanese society." In fact, this sense of *weight* is analogous to what we discussed earlier in terms of how frequently women who while not having any sense of *tsumi* (blame) have feelings which they call a *heavy heart*.

Without answering that question, Takahashi follows it with another: "Why are the people involved in *mizuko kuyō* (unlike those involved in other deprivations of life) wrapped in feelings of guilt about another person?" This too is a question for which there could be multiple responses, many of which could expand one's understanding of guilt and of a we relationship. At this point it is best to quote him on the subject of the twofold identity of the fetus or *mizuko*.

> Certainly, [while] the fetus is an individual identity that forms part of a "we" relationship…it cannot be said to have a completely independent individual identity. This is because all of us are dependent on our mother's body for our existence. From the mother's point of view, the fetus is another person (who has an independent individual identity) but at the same time is a part of her. The fetus is outside her, but at the same time inside her…[From] the mother's point of view, the existence of the fetus is positioned on the border between herself and others, internal and external. The act of fetal life deprivation is, at the same time, an act of self-damage…When there is a sense of reality about the rapport and a strong feeling for the mother/child unit, the reaction of "crying" occurs…[It is] the deep experience of this unity that [brings about] the sense of guilt about another person. [This is what] causes the crying.[39]

At this point it makes sense to locate within larger frames of reference the extraordinary sense of guilt or blame that so many, but certainly not all Japanese women have felt about aborting a fetus. While it is important to distinguish between voluntary abortion (*chūzetsu*) and pregnancy loss through miscarriage and stillbirth, it is just as important to ask what common factors might exist. Though there is wide disparagement about religious personnel who promote a climate of fear, there is also a long history of uncertainty, even cultural anxiety about how the living interact with the dead.

The spectrum of reactions expressed in hundreds of responses to these questionnaires is considerable, including self-pity, feelings of guilt, thoughtful self-reflection, and genuine compassion for others. Such a spectrum serves to personalize the reactions one discovers in listening to women discuss their experiences or reading their comments on questionnaires. If one neglects this spread of responses, it is easy to settle for the fear of *tatari* as the driving factor in their emotional outlook toward their experience. On the other hand, while the phenomenon of *tatari* is exceedingly dramatic and is promoted by some religious groups and individuals and is highlighted by the media, it is less a factor in the average women's psyche than is the sense of *tsumi*. Because these two factors are often seen as coordinates of each other they should be carefully distinguished. It would be more accurate to say that the fear of *tatari*'s causing misfortune in the future is much less common than is the tendency to blame *tatari* for past or present unexplained aches and pains in a person's life or for the troubles that plague her family. In other words, it serves to explain something that has already taken place or is currently a factor.

For these reasons, it is essential not to dismiss the negative experiences that large numbers of Japanese women have in their roles as wives and mothers especially in a society that continues to highlight their status as housekeeper and mother. While becoming a mother remains an important value for the vast majority of women, there is increased resentment about the demands placed upon wives and mothers who exercise their roles in virtual isolation and who are provided little child care help from others. Combined with the common reality of a shaky self-esteem, one finds much anguish among young mothers today.

Summation of Statements from Religious Institutions

As a counterpart to the voices of women discussed in this chapter, the following views are summaries of those held in virtually all major religious groups, listed here, that have responded to the questionnaires sent out by the Kyoto University survey project: Shinto, Shingon-shū, Jōdo-shū, Zen-shū, Catholic Christian, Jōdo Shinshū, Protestant Christian, and several new religions. Beyond the areas in which there is extensive agreement, there are important differences among and within these various religious groups.

- All of them expressed strong opposition to using *mizuko kuyō* in commercialized ways, that is, for profit seeking. Likewise, there is a similar opposition to using the practice of *mizuko kuyō* as a means of taking advantage of a woman's vulnerability, including her feelings of guilt, her fears of retribution, and her loneliness. In any case, there are recently increasing statements about the need for both parents to be part of the process of taking responsibility for *mizuko kuyō*.
- The central issue for many groups, primarily in cases of abortion, is mainly one of repentance and amendment of life rather than the stimulation of guilt, though feelings of guilt may themselves lead to the desire to change one's pattern of life. Nevertheless, there is recognition that the fear element (fear of *tatari*) is part of a larger climate of fear stimulation in Japanese society, and recognition that many, but not all, approaches to *mizuko kuyō* are driven by the fear of being cursed by the angry spirits of *mizuko*.
- To a large degree, the belief exists that a human life begins at the moment of conception and that interruption of this life process is fundamentally against Buddhist, Shinto, and most Japanese Christian teachings about human existence. A clear distinction is made, however, between abortion and miscarriage or stillbirth, though the word *mizuko* may refer to all three. Many, though not all groups distinguish between necessary abortions (health of the mother, rape, incest) and so-called abortions of convenience.
- There is widespread recognition of how the current sexual culture contributes to considerable confusion about sexual morality and how it promotes lack of respect for one's own sexuality and that of another as well as furthering the ease of getting abortions, the absence of significant sexual education, the lack of reliable procreative choice, and the breakup of family values. In other words, one is dealing not simply with isolated individuals but with a context in which abortion has become a pervasive recourse within sexual affairs.
- Regardless of different attitudes toward *mizuko kuyō*, there is substantial agreement among most but not all groups that its practice should be seen within the larger practice of ancestor *kuyō*. While not identical, these different forms of ancestral *kuyō* are often viewed as analogous, as ways of paying respect to the spirits of the dead. This paralleling does

not blur the differences. Instead, it provides evidence of how many religious groups have grounded *mizuko kuyō* within a widely accepted practice of paying respect to all ancestors and of acknowledging the sacredness of life itself.

Considerable similarity exists between most Buddhist and Catholic practices of saying prayers for the well-being of the dead. While the Catholic stance against abortion is more negative, it is not unlike Buddhist teaching that human life begins at the moment of conception. Several features that exist in this form of Christianity also may be found in Jōdoshū and Shingon Buddhism: (1) reverence for the sacredness of life; (2) the importance of consoling those who have suffered death in their family, including a *mizuko*; (3) prayers for the dead but not fears about the dead or their impact upon the living; (4) the importance of repentance in dealing with experiences of guilt; and (5) the sense of a genuine and ongoing relationship between the living and the dead—as seen in the ancestral lineage in most forms of Buddhist tradition and in a somewhat parallel sense of the community of saints in Catholic Christianity.[40]

From this focus in both the previous and the present chapter on the activity of temples in the Kyoto area that have been engaged in performing rituals for women who have experienced some form of child loss or who have chosen to terminate a pregnancy a shift is made in the following chapter to an examination of the larger historical and social scene over more than a century. Whatever the relationship may be between a woman who is deeply affected by pregnancy loss, regardless of the cause, and the social role that society has constructed for most women, her role as mother is bound to be a point of focus.

Beginning with the Meiji period (1868–1912), there were newly emerging definitions of what it meant to be a Japanese woman, how her principal roles began to be defined, how she came to fulfill and shape these roles, and how in the process she both conformed to and wrestled with these circumstances. She was both active and acted upon. Of importance to this study is the task of understanding these unfolding definitions. The overall picture is exceedingly rich and complex; its relationship to *mizuko kuyō* has not previously been explored by any study. Because the central characterization of Japanese women during this long period became— and largely remains—that of mother, one asks how and in what ways this strong emphasis upon woman-as-mother contributed to and helps one to understand some of the ingredients that gained prominence in *mizuko kuyō*. This is the subject matter of the following chapter.

PART TWO

Deciphering the Worlds of Pregnancy Loss

Women, Men, and the Unborn

5

Japanese Woman as Housewife, Mother, and Worker

PATTERNS OF CHANGE AND CONTINUITY (1868–2010)

THE PURPOSE OF this chapter is to outline how the roles of modern Japanese women as housewives, mothers, and workers have been shaped and reshaped within the last 140 years and to discuss how women have responded to these circumstances. Its principal focus is on a woman's role as mother, for this is how what being a woman had been socially defined to most Japanese women in the twentieth century and is also central to their participation in the social phenomenon known as *mizuko kuyō*. To be understood in its complexity, however, a mother's role has also been linked to her other functions within the structures and dynamics of modern Japanese society. While it may be useful to speak of an overarching image of what it means to be a woman and mother in Japan, such an image can block recognition of how differently individual women have patterned their lives to fulfill that role. Just as ideological constructions of women's roles have varied in modern Japanese history, women's responses have been shaped not only by their specific circumstances but by their own choices as well. Women are not only acted upon; they also need to be viewed as actors.

The sections in this chapter are arranged chronologically to expose the differing emphases placed on Japanese women's roles as wives, mothers, and workers, especially during the past 100 years. After reviewing briefly women's place in the family during Tokugawa times (1603–1868), we examine the Meiji period (1868–1912) when the nation was being molded by social and political forces that brought women's roles to the forefront of political discussion for the first time in Japanese history. The political construction of a woman's principal role as mother is a prominent focal point. This section considers the tension between that role and the state's need for women workers in the decades leading up to World War II as well as the desire among women beginning in the 1920s to be employed (full or part time) and to be involved in issues of social change. The latter is important, since it would be a mistake to portray Japanese women as silent or passive objects, though, to be sure, social and cultural forces have tended to constrain them to passivity.

Beyond that depiction, the following section, with its focus on the husband–wife relationship, underscores the developments in Japanese society from 1945 to the present, for these have opened new directions for women while they have remained tied to earlier norms. Two central issues in this sixty-year period are the nature of the complex interrelationship of women with their husbands and children and how a woman's activities beyond the home affect her roles as wife and mother. Contrasts between ideological-turned-cultural images of woman as wife and mother and how women have felt about themselves become apparent in this discussion. Finally, through examples drawn from Japanese literature as well as from historical and social scientific studies, Japanese women's tactics of response are examined, whether of compliance, resistance, or subversion to the social forces to which they are exposed. This final section serves as a springboard to subsequent chapters that deal with the breadth of women's responses to child loss through *mizuko kuyō* and as a means of addressing other issues raised initially in this chapter.

Early Discourses about Womanhood: Social Forces and Normative Images (1868–1945)

Although the Japanese equivalent for the term "motherhood" (*bosei*) was first used in 1904, the meaning of motherhood in Japanese society has been discussed in governmental, educational, and literary circles since the 1870s when it became a controversial subject. Prior to the Meiji Restoration in 1868 one finds a rather tentative picture of women's roles, one that differed among the four archetypal "classes" of pre-industrial Japanese society (samurai, farmers, artisans, and merchants). It also varied by local tradition, custom, and practice. Focusing on the division of labor in the household, we can see at least two different models of womanhood in Tokugawa Japan (1603–1868). Neither of these emphasized women's role as mother.

In one, the reproductive roles were shared within the household. When the farm population composed 80 percent of the nation, peasant and village women were more involved in productive work connected with the economy of the whole household than with the reproductive tasks of motherhood, child rearing, and household chores.[1] Women worked in support of the household economy, and children were raised by all members of the household. Since both productive and reproductive work in farm families took place in or near the home, men also had the possibility of a close relationship with their children and a high stake in their upbringing.[2] Of course, children were also significant contributors to much of the farm work. In the other model, characteristic of the samurai (warrior) class principally, mothers were referred to as "borrowed wombs" who were to produce heirs to carry on the family line, to be instruments toward this larger familial and societal end. They had few responsibilities outside the home and only limited authority within. The authority for child-rearing decisions rested with the father, though they were actually carried out by various people in the household or extended family.[3]

The dominant ideology of the Tokugawa period regarding the role of women had been formalized in different versions of the textual genre known as *Great Learning for Women* (*Onna daigaku*) that began to appear in the late seventeenth and early eighteenth centuries and was rooted in Confucian ethics. These texts upheld the ideal of *danson johi*, men's superiority over women, used to characterize the norms of Edo society, and because of their supposed inferior qualities women were deemed unsuited to rear children.[4] Written for more literate women among the samurai class, these teachings made their impact upon ordinary people in both rural and urban Japan as literacy spread through sermons and other popular performance media. Recognizing the distinction between ideology and actual practice, there is little doubt that motherhood was not yet regarded as the "natural" responsibility of women of any class in preindustrial Japan.

In the Meiji era this earlier ideology gave way to another that constructed women's role as predominantly maternal. After the Meiji Restoration of 1868 in which the Emperor was returned to the center of political power, the new government opened Japan to foreigners from the West who had been seeking entry for years. This move was treated with ambivalence by political leaders, intellectuals, educators, and those involved in trade. Controversy raged over how to balance older Japanese values with new ways of thinking and new styles of life coming from the West. The debate between liberals and conservatives about what constituted family life and the role of wives and mothers was a sizable part of this controversy. The

overall scene revealed the beginnings of female education, the involvement of large numbers of women in Japan's emerging textile industry,
and continuing influences from abroad.

Early in the Meiji age there were strong critiques of the old *Great
Learning for Women* prescriptions. Many saw women's central task to be
not only giving birth to children but also caring for them.[5] For a while,
this altered view of women's social importance stimulated belief in the
value of equal education for males and females, a position influenced by
Japan's growing knowledge of educational systems in the West. The new
Ministry of Education's 1872 document "The Current Blueprint of the
Compulsory Educational System" has the appearance of being a genuine
concern for women. The purpose of female education, however, was not
to benefit women for their own sake but to outfit or, at least, prepare them
in their new role as mothers and caretakers whose influence on children was now regarded as paramount in the creation of a strong polity.
Education for women was presented as a way to produce "good wives and
wise mothers" (*ryōsai kenbo*) who would stay at home and were entrusted
with the future of the nation in the form of its children.[6] Kathleen Uno,
among others, stressed the socially constructed nature of this modern
Japanese conception of motherhood, arguing that as new opportunities
became available to women by the turn of the century women's political,
legal, and educational rights were severely confined within their newly
(re)defined role.[7]

Prominent among the voices advocating new opportunities and a
higher status for women was the group called Meirokusha (Meiji Six
Society), established in 1873, with its own journal, *Meiroku zasshi*. Among
its members, the one most notable for our purposes was Fukuzawa Yukichi
(1835–1901), whose writings on women were extensive. Through his trav-
els abroad Fukuzawa was embarrassed by the differences between conditions of women in the West relative to those in Japan.[8] Singling out one
version of *Great Learning for Women,* he argued that, with this inequality of
power in relationship to men, wives and mothers had no means by which
to become responsible or acquire a sense of their own dignity.[9] Wives were
accused of causing tensions within the home; they were counseled to be
patient, gentle, and forbearing. Easily divorced by their husbands and
taken advantage of by in-laws, wives were treated as disposable tools, without regard to deeper human qualities they might possess or needs they
might have.[10] Fukuzawa believed that Japan could never be strong and
modern if its women remained in this condition.[11] For him, this meant

that education for women was as important as for men, that they needed to have a sufficient degree of economic independence, that the marriage relationship of wives and husbands should be an equal partnership based upon love and respect, and that a mother's child-rearing role should be given social weight equal to the work performed by men.

The concept of "good wife, wise mother" (*ryōsai kenbo*) was central to this construction. Early Meiji formulations, inspired by Western examples, expressed concern that if Japanese women were to be good wives and wise mothers they must receive an education that equips them properly, and the term *ryōsai kenbo* initially argued for the "creation of a new woman-hood suitable for Japan's modern society."[12] Rather than being Confucian and thus carried over from earlier, "unenlightened" times, it was heralded as the "Japanese version of the nineteenth-century Western cult of female domesticity."[13] Implicit was the idea of separate spheres for men and women, with emphasis on the importance and power of women's con-tributions in the domestic sphere. A woman was to be judged by the suc-cess with which she raised a child, investing her guardianship and with consequences for both mother and child. This position is, in some ways, the opposite of *Great Learning for Women* formulations in which women are portrayed as unworthy of educating their children or of exercising any influence in the home, let alone in society.[14] Providing women with a role perceived as important to society, this new construction narrowed the scope of what being a woman meant by linking her daily existence to that of her children. As the debate in the 1880s and 1890s about the nature and purpose of this education proceeded, reactions against Western influences were strong, particularly against those urging women's involvement in social and political issues. As conservative forces became dominant, wom-en's education was viewed "as a pillar of the state: from patriotic mothers come patriotic children."[15]

Central to the dynamics of the Meiji period and to understanding their meaning for women was the transformation of Japan from a preindus-trial, agrarian, feudal economy to a modern industrialized nation. This evolution corresponded with the Meiji era itself, beginning in the 1880s. While farming occupied the main share of workers during this time, increasing numbers of men and women were employed in textile mills, factories, and mines. By 1902 those working in agriculture had dropped to 67 percent. That same year industrial workers numbered 499,000, ris-ing to 863,000 in 1912.[16] In silk factories women were 94 percent of the labor force in 1902.[17] The proportion of women in the cotton mills was 83 percent in 1909.[18] Most textile workers were unmarried girls from poor farm backgrounds helping their families to make ends meet; it was not until the 1960s that married women entered the work force in significant numbers.

While the numbers of people working in these sectors were small compared with the farm population, the significance of these industries was high because of the revenue that textiles brought Japan on the world market and because of the changes they brought to patterns of social organization and to the lives of women. Industrial development stimulated migration toward the cities, with both men and women repositioning themselves in the host of new jobs that began to appear there. Family patterns revealed remarkable changes, including increased separation of the spheres in which husband and wife spent their time. The pattern of males working outside their homes expanded, and by the end of the nineteenth century married women in nonfarm families were more identified by their roles as wife and mother in the home at the same time that young women were still being called on to work in factories.

The state's involvement in formulating the home's role, hence the woman's role, was an added element. In Meiji Japan there was fierce debate between social reformers who believed in better education for the future wife and mother as the "moral center of her home" and those who argued for greater state control of "women's proper roles" and the family as "a bulwark against social chaos."[19] One finds in the Civil Code of 1898 a culmination of intense controversy over an appropriate family structure for Japan as a modernizing state.[20] This Code established the *ie* or corporate extended family as the basic familial unit, thereby sanctioning patterns harking back to the earlier samurai family: "the concentration of authority in the household head, the centrality of the parent–child relationship in view of the importance of continuing the lineage, and the primacy of the *ie* over the individual family member."[21] A wife's role was again seen as submissiveness to the authority of her husband in addition to his being the head of the *ie*, this time in legally binding forms that had not been part of the earlier *Great Learning for Women* texts. Yet the Meiji Code was not simply a reversion to Tokugawa norms; instead, it affirmed the civic responsibility of women to contribute to the well-being of the nation in her position as good wife.[22] In the context of these changes women's role was radically limited in scope, even while being ideologically inflated. The consequences for women and for the rest of society were immense.

With the 1898 Civil Code the state's strategy was to use women to bolster a society it sought to manage.[23] Early Meiji discussions claimed that if the separation of home and workplace dissolved, if women moved outside of the home for reasons other than caring for their children, there would be no basis left for genuine Japanese identity. In fact, it was fear of losing that identity that ignited political xenophobia. By the late Meiji, however, revisionist versions of the new ideal of women as mothers in the home responsibly managing their children and their households began to appear. In the context of Japan's involvement in wars with China and Russia (and later in World Wars I and II) governmental compromises with the "good wife, wise mother" adage encouraged women's active support of the war effort both in the home and outside. "The orthodox 'good wife' was one who pursued whatever employment and education would serve her family and society. Despite rhetoric about filial piety, frugality, and feminine modesty, these policies were not simply the preservation of past ways."[24] There was a clear recruitment of women for nationalistic purposes: a good wife was one who served her nation in whatever capacity was needed.

In less critical times during the late Meiji and early Taishō (1912–26), the government continued to promote its more restrictive, nationalistic image of women's role in society by affirming a virtual separation of public and private spheres in which men and women played out their respective roles.[25] Even private schools were pressured to promote women's homebound role by offering courses that would serve women when they became homemakers. On the other hand, achievement of this ideal was limited by increasing employment opportunities for women in Japan's growing economy. Either the need to help her family survive in inflationary times or her own desire to work for its intrinsic appeal created conditions that ran counter to the state's plans for keeping women at home.

Questions about conflicting roles for women, as wife and mother or as working woman in the public sphere, revealed a society "struggling to reconcile changes wrought by modernization and urbanization with the early twentieth century's construction of women as good wives and wise mothers"[26] who preserved Japanese identity in the face of foreign influences by correctly raising their children. From the state's point of view increased numbers of working women were seen as eroding the *ie* system and its redefined principle of good wife, wise mother. At the same time that working women threatened current social goals, however, they were helping the state to reach its economic objectives.

What emerged was a "cult of productivity" where women's efforts in the home and outside were both construed as support for the nation. In terms of women's reproductive capacity, whenever the need of the state was for more births to man the army, farm the fields, or work in industry, government policy became pro-natalist. But with Japan's defeat in 1945 and the resultant economic emergency the critical need was for fewer mouths to feed, hence the government support for abortion in the final form of the 1948 Eugenics Protection Law (*Yūsei Hogo Hō*). In the decades since the war governmental policy has viewed women as a fortuitous labor force in times of insufficient workers in both the industrial and the white-collar sectors. Yet the image of the ideal Japanese woman as one who best serves her nation by staying home to raise her children and manage her household, in a subservient role to that of her husband, remained dominant. In other words, there was a continuing clash between the ideology of what a woman's role should be and the actual need at certain times for women to be part of the nation's labor force.

By the 1950s the Meiji definition of woman as mother, now easily identified as the "traditional" role for women, remained, as did the reality of a growing female work force. Two tacit solutions to this dissonance were reached in the later postwar era. At an ideological level woman-as-mother continued to be the ideal, with girls being socialized and educated into that role but allowed to work until they married. At a practical level, nevertheless, it was understood that women working outside the home were still held responsible for the reproductive work expected of them as wives in the home. It must also be stressed that an increasing number of women's groups beginning in the 1920s were established and that involved many women with social, economic, and political issues in a unprecedented manner. Their involvement carried an agenda of its own, namely, to advance the cause of women's issues. It was not simply a case of women being used by the state to advance state interests; in many cases women were utilizing governmental influence to further their own causes. As Sheldon Garon makes clear, instead of opposing intervention by the state "these Japanese groups more often urged the government to play an active role in the 'social education' of women and girls. Women leaders and educators also shared with the bureaucrats a commitment to modernizing the mores and habits of ordinary women."[27] In the period from 1920 to 1945 women's groups were "more successful in influencing the official agenda when they embraced the modern state's ideology of separate spheres for men and women."[28]

Japanese Women in Postwar Japan: New Possibilities and Old Realities

With the defeat of Japan's militaristic state in 1945 came the American Occupation, the new constitution, and the end of legalized inequality because of gender, religion, class, or family origin. Among the earliest measures enacted by the Japanese government was the Revised Election Law, granting women equal voting rights and electoral privileges. By means of the new Constitution (1947) and the Revised Civil Code (1948), the 1898 Code was dismantled. Replacing the *ie* or corporate extended family system, at least as a legal entity, the nuclear family became the basic familial unit. Women were granted equal rights of inheritance, as were all children in each family. In a legal sense, primogeniture disappeared. The new code ruled out preferential treatment for men in cases of adultery. Wives and husbands were given equal access rights to divorce, while the custody of children was to be adjudicated rather than having the children automatically remain with the father as had been the case since 1898. Arranged marriages could no longer be legally forced upon either women or men. Furthermore, with the right to vote and participate in political organizations and causes women's organizations expressed their views on matters of public policy.[29] In legal terms women now had opportunities that had not existed before.

Kathleen Uno raises the question of why in this new climate motherhood remained "the dominant image of Japanese womanhood" when in fact large numbers of women were employed in the workforce. The key to this apparent contradiction was that state and corporate policies sought to have it both ways. They were designed to tap a ready supply of women for the labor force when this was needed but not to undermine the "traditional" nationalistic construction of the Japanese woman's primary role in the home. It became important to the state to strengthen the ideology of woman as mother precisely when large numbers of women were involved in work. Continuing subscription to a division of function between men and women, between those who worked outside the home and those who served as mother and wife in the home, remained the dominant ideology as it had been since the late nineteenth century.[30]

It took more than a decade for postwar changes in the legal status of women to be woven into the fabric of a society in the throes of uncertain transformation. One gets a vivid sense of the immediate postwar continuity with earlier Japanese society through anthropological, ethnographic, and sociological studies done in the 1950s. Such connections are evident in accounts of work routines, household hierarchy, and life cycle patterns as well as in inheritance and succession customs. *Village Japan*, a seven-year interdisciplinary study (1950–57) of a rice-growing community of 130 people in rural Okayama, is one example.[31] The involvement of women in farm work as well as in the house remained common practice. For both genders the work was long and hard; farm rhythms were set by the seasons. Three-generational households were the norm, each generation having responsibilities according to status and ability. Included in this study's materials are letters from two grandmothers, still in their fifties, that testify to the tough existence eked out on small farms in prewar Japan, to the tragedy of losing children in their early months or years, and to the severe hardships of the war years. These letters show how rice planting was as difficult after the war as before and that farm women were intensely involved in this work.

Though long-established customs enable a household to function in a harmonious, productive fashion, in practice they may institutionalize harsh forms of relationship.[32] The picture conveyed in *Village Japan* is of a society shaped by old ways, though moving uncertainly into a new world. When a young woman married into a family, her name was crossed off her birth family register; in effect, she became the property of her husband's family. Her common misfortune in this setting is well documented: The "duration of a marriage depends mainly on the bride's relation to her mother-in-law."[33] The multigenerational farm family was still organized around the authority of the head of the family, usually the eldest male and, by association, his wife. The stakes were high for a new wife to have a child as soon as possible, especially a son. Only then did she ensure continuity for the household and validate her own existence in this new family. Here we see the conjoining of the older samurai values that portrayed women as borrowed wombs with those of farming families in which women participated in both production and reproduction. This compound image of womanhood offered postwar rural Japanese women a balance of sorts, between the narrow restrictions of married life within the *ie* system and the more creative productive responsibilities that fell to them as wives in farming families.

In discussing Japanese rural society and its *ie* family system before the war, Tadashi Fukutake maintained that "Japanese farm families have still not reached the point at which the final dissolution of the *ie* is in sight."[34] This simultaneous "dissolution and survival" of the *ie* system is of major interest, as one realizes that the *ie* system was not simply a legal entity. It was a frame of mind, a pattern of relationships, a nexus of institutions, a system of ethical judgments, even a certain view of the world. Although the nuclear family replaced the *ie* system as the legal family unit immediately after the war, in social and cultural terms there was never (until the advent of feminism) any clear and sustained denial of the *ie* and the relationships it fostered.[35]

The collaboratively constructed record, *The Women of Suye Mura*, by Robert J. Smith and Ella Lury Wiswell, published in 1982 from material gathered earlier in a small village in central Kyushu, shows another view of women's lives in rural Japan.[36] Aside from the salty nature of the largely uninhibited village women and their sheer vitality, one sees another of the many faces of male–female relationships in Japan. It is the face of a richly colored, often conflictive world in which childhood deaths are common, gossip about adulterous trysts is constant, and women are not basically submissive. It is a world in which quarrels are frequent, daily work is hard, and the average life span of adults is below fifty. Wiswell details the sharing that took place among these women and how even as outsiders to the community into which they had married they formed economic ties, shared labor, and forged bonds of friendship entirely on their own. This study "shows that women can be submissive without being controlled by men, and also that the life course of women can depend on that of men without losing its distinctive pattern."[37] Women's resourcefulness within a world they could not control is a perceptive understanding of how women can and do create their own patterns within that world. This is a theme to which this study returns in several chapters.

Today there are differing interpretations of what this way of thinking afforded those within it—particularly women, who had little authority or voice. A traditional anthropological point of view (both Japanese and Western) holds that the *ie* system created an ethos in which the potential for harmony rests upon sensitivity to reciprocal relationships within the extended family, mutually held responsibilities and expectations, and a high valuation of family interdependence. As units within this structure, women were forced to take on the corporate family goals as their own but in many ways found that kind of commitment fulfilling.

In the last several decades, however, Japanese feminists have begun to portray the *ie* system in an entirely different and less salutary way. To many feminists, prewar women were seen as trapped within a family (*ie*) system that depends on their existence but devalues their contributions at every turn. Even with the legal changes after World War II, the *ie* system's patterns of behavior continue to underpin the social and cultural structures within which women fashion their lives. Statistics suggest that the growing number of women who view marriage as only one among several possible choices of lifestyle may feel constrained by social attitudes and legal realities such as the lack of support for unwed mothers and their children into choosing marriage regardless of their personal resistance to it.[38]

Each of these interpretations is tied to the context from which it emerged. In focusing on rural communities that maintained some continuity with their prewar predecessors, postwar anthropological studies took their cue from those earlier Japanese folklorists (*minzokugakusha*) who sought the essence of "Japaneseness" in rural village life as well as from a contemporary Western anthropology engaged in an essentialist search for authentic lifestyles. What made this project believable was that for most Japanese until the postwar era daily life was measured against a rural fabric. In contrast, Japanese feminist views, discussed later in this chapter, emerged from urban experience and a greater integration of legal changes in the status of women into the patterns of daily life. Indeed, this is the change from largely rural to largely urban experience over the past 100 years. While there was a postwar shift in conceptual paradigm from village to urban life, there were lingering traces of nostalgia for earlier rural styles.[39]

Changes of this sort in the Japanese context are made vivid in a study over a twenty-five year period of Kurusu, a village twelve miles from Takamatsu in Shikoku. The Kurusu of 1975 "presents a picture drained of some of its earlier beauty. The consumer revolution has hit with a vengeance."[40] Within the space of two decades (1955–75), rural Japan becomes a kind of oxbow, with the action moving toward urban complexes. This was essentially a one-way street, with occasional returns in the form of school children on tour or as family members to some fading hometown or as modern-day pilgrims on buses to sacred sites. Of particular importance for our study is what this means for family life, especially for a woman's relationship to her husband, her children, her home, and her life outside the home. Understanding this shift helps one to put the phenomenon of *mizuko kuyō* into an enormously changed social, political, and economic context than had ever existed in Japan before.

Continued migration to the cities, increased employment of women, and new ways of thinking put greater value on individual enterprise. As more young families moved to urban areas, household size decreased, the incidence of small conjugal families relative to extended families grew from 54 percent in 1920 to 63 percent in 1980, and the average number of children in each home dropped from 5.2 in 1920 to 1.8 by 1978.[41] The diminished sharing of productive daily life in postwar urban Japan has been depicted for decades in films, the media, and academic studies. This has posed many questions about the high incidence of dissatisfaction in marriage, the extent of both male and female loneliness, and the attempt to find in work outside the home the personal satisfaction that is not found at home. To what degree a husband–wife relationship, now the center of home life, can flourish without the shared responsibility experienced in farm marriages is a question that remains significant.[42]

Susan Ophett Long, in her monograph on life course perspectives, provides data and commentary about what directions the Japanese family system has taken in recent decades.[43] Some of these data need to be recalled as they have immense import in the changing construction of the roles of Japanese women, including the relationship of mothers to their children and, potentially, to their *mizuko*. For instance, the fact that the average number of children in a family declined from over five in 1920 to less than two in 1980 carries all sorts of implications. Not only having fewer children but also having them closer together would appear to decrease the time that close child care by the mother is needed. On the other hand, with the increasing prominence of the educational establishment in Japan, women were now kept busy as mothers attending to and assisting in the academic success of their children..[44] Indeed, the expense of tutoring and *juku* (or cram schools), deemed necessary to get children into the best schools, it became important for many women to work outside the home, usually part-time so that they might also continue to fulfill their duties in the home. The demands of being an "education mother" (*kyōiku mama*) became a postwar addition to what it means to be a mother in Japan.

At the other end of the time scale, the approximate life expectancy (at birth) rose from forty-five for females (forty-four for males) by 1904 to seventy for females (sixty-five for males) in 1960 to eighty for females (seventy-four for males) in 1983. A significant consequence here is the longer time a husband and wife will live together. In 1940 the average marriage lasted twenty-two years before one spouse died; by 1972 the figure was forty-four years. This extraordinary increase in time span combined with fewer children at home and fewer years of child rearing meant a more extended time in which "the conjugal relationship is primary."[45] Having spent most of the first half of their married lives almost singlehandedly raising and seeing to the education of their children while their husbands focused on work outside the home, Japanese women came regularly to ask how their later lives alone with their husbands can become more satisfying than they often are to both husbands and wives.

Increasing life expectancy also dramatizes the problems of caring for the aged. For males who were sixty-five in 1983, there was an average expectancy of fifteen more years; for women, it was eighteen more years. Especially striking is the growing proportion of elderly (above sixty-five) in the total population. In 1900 the proportion was 5 percent; in 1990 it was 11 percent, with an estimate of 14 percent early in the new millennium. The socioeconomic, political, and psychological implications are clear: A decreasing number of the young and middle-aged have the responsibility of caring for an increasing number of the elderly. The import of this was not lost to the national and prefectural governments, though they have yet to respond adequately. Families remained the principal social and financial resource. The nation was awakened to the problem of caring for the elderly in strikingly personal terms by Ariyoshi Sawako's 1972 novel *Kōkotsu no hito* (The Twilight Years).[46] The novel's impact lay in personalizing what many were becoming aware of at a societal level: that caring for elderly members of the family in the home was fast becoming an added responsibility of women already burdened with child rearing, household management, and, increasingly, work outside the home.

How does evidence of this sort translate into concrete family experience? One way to explore that question is to look at two types of family life in Japanese society over the past thirty or more years. In a sense, these two types are worlds apart, yet they overlap. One of these portrays an urban housewife whose primary concern is the household and its children, a world virtually separated except by the paycheck from the outside, workaday world of her husband. By the 1960s the image of the *salaryman,* commuting long distances to and from work, leaving early and returning late, with scant time for wife and children, became the stereotypical image of men in the corporate world. To the contrary, this has not been the case for families working in agriculture or those operating small businesses in which both parents and children are often cooperatively involved or for women working part-time in urban factories who for economic reasons combine the responsibilities of both family and work.[47] In contrast to this urban image is the example of a woman in rural Japan whose existence is justified not primarily by her children's success but by her own work. While these two types cannot represent all Japanese women, they provide commonly discussed images of women reaching for sources of fulfillment outside the husband–wife relationship that is, legally at least, the center of a postwar marriage. These contrasting depictions make graphic the social and psychological climates within which the phenomenon of *mizuko kuyō* needs to be addressed.[48]

An Urban Housewife

As the postwar Japanese economy began to flourish in the 1960s, many families in the urban context experienced pronounced separation between the worlds of men and those of women. This separation had been stimulated by industrial development, by an evolving political ideology, and by early forms of social management in the late nineteenth century. The conventional image of a woman's role in urban middle-class Japan became that of housewife and mother, responsible for household chores, family finances, and her main role of serving the needs of husband and children. To be a woman meant to be a wife and mother; to be a wife and mother meant to stay home and take care of the household. The husband's center of gravity was his own work, with its considerable demands upon his time and energy. These separate sets of responsibilities were to a great degree mutually exclusive; the worlds rarely overlapped. As the children began their schooling, the wife-mother was alone at home for much of each day. While many found interests in and beyond the home and were kept busy supporting their children through their education, a sense of isolation was commonplace. A women's communal world had shrunk to her small household of one or two children. She found herself separated, even isolated from her extended family and childhood friends.[49]

This ideologically prompted withdrawal of women into the home is a conspicuous characteristic of the "postwar family" in Japan. The sociologist Ochiai Emiko reminds us that the "birth of the housewife" occurred during modern times in the West as well, as did other changes in Japanese women's role in family and society: the separation of public and private (home) spheres and the accompanying division of household labor along gender lines, the new prominence of the nuclear family, and the focus on children.[50] These changes were not generalized across class lines until after the war. At that time the preoccupation with economic recovery together with a demographic shift (the baby boom) served to push women into the home in an urban setting (to produce and raise children) and then to push them out again into the work world (to help support them).

Although Ochiai argues that demographics rather than culture generated this trend, she herself demonstrates that the older *ie* structure remains in place conceptually; "family" still conjures up the image of the extended network of family connections in the *ie*. The new urban frame for daily life, however, could not maintain the centrality of the extended family in more than nostalgic form. In its place emerged a focus on the husband–wife relationship. Yet this substitution seems to remain metonymic rather than complete. For all the attention it received in the media in Japan, the husband–wife relationship remains a conceptual stand-in for the more complex and well-established relationships within the *ie* structure.

Over time, many a young Japanese wife has suffered disenchantment not only with the isolation of the nuclear family but also with the lack of communication with her husband, frazzled as he was from a workaholic pace, and with his infrequently demonstrated interest in her or even in spending time with the children. Whether the marriage was a "love marriage" or one that had been arranged, there was an increasing desire by the woman for a relationship of intimacy. The constant heralding of "romantic love" in recent decades had elevated expectations for companionship beyond what most situations could deliver. The result was often frustration, loneliness, and a growing sense of separate existences. There were exceptions, but experiences of disillusionment were common.

This situation is extensively documented in Muriel Jolivet's book on the crisis of motherhood in contemporary Japan, especially young mothers who frequently "admit that they find motherhood tedious, exhausting and exasperating."[51] Many of Jolivet's findings came from a study group composed of Japanese women with whom she met on many occasions. In this context, women openly discussed not only the problems experienced by working mothers, the absence of help with childcare and housework, and the lack of intimacy in their marital relations but also self-doubt about their competence as a mother, the constant state of exhaustion that often attends the caring for children, along with fears of harming their children. While a woman's plight is mitigated if her husband shares with some of the child care and the household work and while the incidence of this sharing is increasing, it is still not common.

The problem becomes more acute if the woman works part-time outside the home, with the need to juggle a frenzied schedule and to find proper child care. Her predicament is especially galling when she is made to feel by other women that she should be a full-time mother. In living with her own ambivalence, which sometimes takes the form of wishing they had never given birth, a woman can easily generate her own set of psychological demons. "Women do admit the inadmissible, namely that they do not find their children lovable—a euphemism to express their difficulty to grow attached to them," in fact a wish that they did not exist.[52]

At the core of a contemporary urban, middle-class Japanese woman's responsibility is being caregiver to her husband and children in the home. While "advice, education, and consultation are easily obtainable, emotional support or comfort may be less available" to such women.[53] She and her husband complement each other functionally in what they contribute to the home, but emotional comfort is seldom shared between them. The discussion of what constitutes a woman's raison d'être (*ikigai*) is found in most societies; in Japan the dominant response in the twentieth century and still today has been her role as mother: "Japanese housewives get more emotional gratification from their children than from any other relationship."[54] Herein lies her purpose in life, supposedly the means by which she finds her deepest sense of self-worth. The downside of this is preoccupation with her child's success or non-success as judged by society. With the child's success the mother's self-esteem blossoms; with something below "success" her persona is diminished.

In *Japanese Women: Constraint and Fulfillment*, Takie Sugiyama Lebra provides extensive discussion of the personal implications of motherhood as an "intensely filiocentric" condition signifies that it is common for a mother to have a sense of inseparability from her child. Hence, a "child's death is the most unforgettable experience of separation." Quoting one of her informants, "The death of your parent or your husband is nothing by comparison. Your child's death, that's the worst."[55] In this conception, an "unbreakable bond" exists between mother and child. Lebra speculates that the breakup of the legal status of the *ie* family system and the "general decline of communal solidarity in postwar Japan" may have intensified the "exclusive nature of the mother-child bond."[56] This is an important observation and is pertinent to discussions about mothers and *mizuko*. One may reason further that with the decline in the number of children a mother chooses to have, compounded by the fact that in a nuclear family she is their primary, if not exclusive caregiver, one understands more clearly why her sense of self-worth is so deeply tied to her offspring.

Motherhood [in Japan] captures the depth of complexity inherent in a woman's self-fulfillment. On the one hand, it is mothering itself that constitutes *ikigai* for her; it is the child's growth and achievement that fulfills her life goal. On the other hand, it is as a mother that she loses her autonomy, enslaved by the tyranny of her child, who seeks her attention and care insatiably; motherhood is thus identical to sacrifice and selflessness. Japanese women today have begun to question whether motherhood is the surest road to a woman's fulfillment, whether or not they should look for other alternatives.[57]

A Rural Wife

A second example displays another kind of world, in which a woman's work, as much as a child's success, is her driving force. One need not look far for examples of women whose sense of self-esteem is less tied to their children's success, women who love their children but whose world is not filiocentric—in other words, women whose commitments, pleasures, hardships, and involvements are multiple. In *Haruko's World*, Gail Bernstein studies social dynamics as these are manifested in the microcosm of a particular family. Of importance to understanding this family in the changing circumstances of social, economic, and political life is the fact that her study and observations stretch over twenty years (1974–95).[58]

The world of Haruko Utsunomiya includes her husband, Shō-ichi; daughter, Yōko; son, Hisashi; Obāsan (her husband's mother); and a community of others with whom they interact in the hamlet of Bessho and the township of Uwa in western Shikoku. Haruko, the farm woman, housewife, daughter-in-law, mother, and part-time construction and textile worker, is portrayed as a central actor in this combined farming and residential community, now peppered with small industries. Similar to Japanese farm women over centuries, Haruko (born in 1932) grew up to work alongside other women and men in the farm fields. As a young woman, she moved from her family of kinship and intimacy to the family of her husband and to the status of being daughter-in-law to her husband's more "traditional" mother. At the same time, Haruko embodies the emerging values of postwar Japan. In her own person she combines the life experience with which she grew up in the 1930s, the world of rural Japan, with a time beginning twenty years later in which the center of gravity was being shaped more by urban, industrialized patterns of life. As a consequence, her sense of identity combines worldviews that appear at odds with one another. The manner in which she conceives herself does not fit neatly into the categories of good wife, wise mother, obedient daughter-in-law, or the lonely wife of an urban commuting businessman.

The strength of Haruko's prewar roots, with its emphasis on hard work and the identification of personal and communal well-being, is clear. As with other farm women of this period between the ages of thirty and sixty, Haruko took on outside jobs alongside what she did on the family farm. The drawback of this demanding existence lies in the ease with which one becomes addicted to work for its own sake, yet this work provides meaning to her life and a more multivalent sense to her identity. Her work was "a source of power. The price she paid, however, was a frenzied daily pace."[59] When Bernstein visits again in 1993, one gets a sense of the deepening consequences of Haruko's plight.

Haruko is not caricatured in this study. Portrayed as a complex, remarkable human being, she is bright, assertive, opinionated, generous to a fault, bossy, resourceful, strong. As a field of energy, she likes to manage her environment. Strong but not invulnerable, her deepest needs were not being met. Among the book's values is its frank presentation of conflictive relations within the home, whether between Haruko and her husband, Shō-ichi, or between Haruko and her mother-in-law. Similar to the worlds of wives and husbands throughout Japan, the worlds of Haruko and Shō-ichi overlapped and intersected, but in social and public ways they were often apart. His concerns were clearly outside the home; hers were central to the home, yet she was deeply involved in activities outside the home. There were threads of communication between them, however. Through the willingness of Haruko and Shō-ichi to air their grievances openly, they became more comfortable with each other. In his words, "In your fifties you are finally resigned to each other. And in your sixties you feel *kansha*, gratitude, which is the expression of love."[60]

Though her relationship with Shō-ichi intersected at points, Haruko's ties with her children, while they were still at home, suffered through "lack of communication."[61] The children of this generation were no longer involved with the basic work of their farm family. Yōko's and Hisashi's worlds were school and home; little connection existed between their daily lives and those of their busy parents. This is Haruko's double bind: She yearns for a close home life yet thrives on her work outside the home. The price she has paid is one her daughter does not wish upon herself. Young women like Yōko are rarely interested in marrying into a farm family because of the hard work entailed, yet these young women face a no less problematic existence. Indeed, Haruko's generation, like the middle-aged and older women depicted in *Village Japan*, see today's children as somewhat spoiled, unacquainted with adversity, and unprepared for life's problems. Yet the value put upon having children and being parents remains exceedingly high in contemporary Japan.

When Bernstein returns in 1993, the distance between Haruko and Shō-ichi had increased. By this time their children had married and lived away. Obāsan had finally been placed in a nursing home, but the long years of caring for her, with its "sense of obligation," the ambivalence of relief and guilt that plagued Haruko for placing her mother-in-law in this home, and the resentment that she had never been fully appreciated for these years of care weighed heavily upon Haruko. In her sixties now, no longer employed as she had been for years, she is bogged down with asthma, depression (*utsubyō*), and insomnia. Shō-ichi, on the other hand, is regularly reelected mayor of Uwa township. The reader is left with the impression, nevertheless, that with the death of Shō-ichi's mother in 1995 Haruko is beginning to emerge from this endless albatross of being a daughter-in-law. She is hopeful that when Shō-ichi finally retires they may have a life together, freed from social expectations.

The contrast just sketched between an urban middle-class housewife whose emotional rewards often stem from caring for her children and a wife in a rural setting whose self-image is more based on work on the family farm or employment in small industry is a contrast that has its parallels as well. While both are ways of finding one's own worth and fulfillment, it is also true that overinvestment in either causes problems. When a woman's essential function and ultimate worth are believed to exist in being a mother or in her role as a wife who is also a daughter-in-law, whether working outside the home or not, her sense of self-esteem is grounded in what others expect of her. That these expectations remain operative in contemporary Japan is central to this chapter, though, as Bernstein suggests in her portrayal of Haruko's married children and their spouses, there are also signs that increasing numbers of young couples are sharing parenthood and are placing greater value upon their relationship with each other.

Continuing Forms of Ryōsai Kenbo *and Its Modern Critics*

Beginning in the 1970s there was greater understanding of how Japanese society was coordinated and managed by forces in government, business, and the media with implications that were restrictive to women.[62] It was clear that women's entry into the labor force (full-time work before marriage and part-time work for married women when their children were in school) was intrinsic to a carefully planned political and economic strategy. The policies of Japanese industry played a determining role in this strategy, contributing to the marginalization of women in the labor force. This pattern became more complex in the 1980s as increasing numbers of housewives in their forties sought not only full-time employment but also more interesting jobs with better pay and improved opportunities. The tradition of separate "gender roles [has] supported Japanese economic performance, which has made Japan a company-centered society in which companies have enormous power and authority over individuals and private family life."[63] The issue was whether household and child-care obligations were being met and to what degree women were willing to assume a double burden because of this dual role.[64] It was increasingly perceived by feminist scholars and other women activists that this development was at the expense of women's creativity and energy in Japan and was therefore unhealthy for society at large.

A second area of debate was over women's education. As originally conceived in the 1890s, "women were perceived as having not a right to equal education but an obligation to undertake what was defined as 'women's education' in order satisfactorily to fulfill a dual role of wife and mother. In this sense women's education constituted a form of vocational training."[65] While this philosophy was less publicly promoted in the 1980s, the curriculum in girls' schools remained unequal to that of boys, with implications for young women who might wish to attend major universities. "The underlying premise of education for females did not significantly move beyond the concept of *ryōsai kenbo*."[66] In terms of what students were taught, what courses they were obliged to take, and what paths they were encouraged to aim for, the differences by gender remained striking. This engendered difference was far from being limited to classroom education. It was promoted also by the "media industry, from women's magazine publishers to the producers of children's television, soap operas, and educational programming."[67]

In a study of Japanese women who took part in political activities, Susan Pharr compares prewar women's roles with contemporary positions she identifies as neotraditional, new women, and radical egalitarian.[68] While research for her study was completed in 1980, it shows how greatly ideas about women had evolved from the immediate postwar years. The dominant group among these was depicted as neotraditionalist, those who believed that a woman's role should not be confined to being a good wife and wise mother or that a status difference is appropriate between men and women or that sex-role specialization is natural and right. Instead, the content of one's education should be as open to women as to men, one's marriage partner should be one's own choice, and work opportunities, part-time and full-time, should be available to women at times when they desire it, not just when corporate Japan allows. As one perceives changing Japanese concepts of motherhood within a larger social context, one realizes that some women experience a greater conflict between these roles than others. The more a woman participates in ways that are significant to her outside her own home, the less she is prone to defining her identity in terms of motherhood alone. To many women, these worlds are not in conflict, but in terms of how society rewards these roles they may in fact collide.

The so-called new women in Pharr's study were even more independently minded; theirs was a stronger desire for access to multiple roles. While they were often unclear about what they were searching for, these women desired flexible definitions. Thirty years ago, in the 1980s, they had begun to register dissatisfaction with the housebound role of Japanese women, both as wives and mothers, and to involve themselves in social, civic, and educational ventures. Unlike the women Pharr calls radical egalitarians, they did not place themselves in adversarial relationships to society. To Sumiko Iwao, writing in the late '80s, the core of this new women generation, born in the main between 1946 and 1955, was now engaged in a "quiet revolution," preferring stances that are nonconfrontational, pragmatic, and having a long-term perspective.

In contrast to both of these groups, the radical egalitarians of the mid-1970s were countercultural in lifestyle, sexual mores, political orientation, and their disillusionment with conventional life. While no longer a major player in Japan by the 1990s, this group's disenchantment with Japanese society cannot be dismissed. In some respects, they voiced what others refused to admit but could not finally deny. In commenting on Japanese family life one of the more radical women stressed, "The war destroyed the [former] family system in Japan, but the basic problems remain. Marriage in this society involves a relationship between possessor and possessed, not between two individuals who think of each other as equals."[69]

To the majority of middle-class, educated Japanese women, the "quiet revolution" is bringing about results that could not have been imagined thirty years before. There is deep concern among Japanese women about the meaning of their own lives beyond, but not necessarily excluding, their roles as wife or as mother. While not minimized, these roles do not exhaust a woman's potential. This paradigm shift is a major, perhaps irreversible one. Japanese women began to discover they have more independence than Japanese men, who are often encased in a company that expects long hours and complete dedication. Some men have begun to discover this as well. While there are professional women climbing the corporate ladder, becoming trapped in similar ways, most working women seem to value job satisfaction more than future rewards. These women also have higher standards for a compatible relationship in marriage, even if this is not widely experienced. Though they do not represent all Japanese women, they suggest the shape of things to come.

Woman as Idealized Mother, Respected Companion, Sexual Object

No matter how improved women's chances for satisfying employment become, according to various feminist positions there is a more basic issue affecting the modern Japanese family: namely, the dynamic of gender and sexuality. The lineaments of this family system include disparate conceptualizations of female gender: of womanhood as idealized mother, as respected companion, and as sexual object. Ironically, these are partial remnants of the *ie* tradition; each is a socially scripted, essentially male way of viewing women. While different expressions of these appeared over the past hundred years, there is clear continuity between the earlier sense of what "wise mother" (*kenbo*) meant and the more contemporary forms of womanhood as idealized mother, whose most significant role remains the bearing and nurturing of children. Similar connections exist between Meiji perceptions of woman as "good wife" (*ryōsai*) and the widely accepted role of woman as respected companion, one who shares a life not only with her children but also with her husband and who maintains the home as a locus of security in a rapidly changing society.

A third expression of womanhood exists in severe tension with the first two but in a real sense is the product of a society that sees women in these carefully orchestrated ways as mother and wife. The idealized and limited nature of these abstractions fosters images of woman in the home as the paragon of nonsexuality, with the consequence that men frequently sought sexual relief outside the home in the more "invisible" world of prostitutes and mistresses and through the thriving culture of pornography. The consequences of fleeing from the burdens of mutual respect and companionship are that "wife," "mother," and "sexual object" are each treated as commodities: for the semblance of domestic security and reproduction, for sexual pleasure, and for distraction from ordinary life. This is the underbelly of what Helen Hardacre in her book on *mizuko* calls the "sexual culture" of Japan. This cultural bifurcation has been prominent in Japanese society since at least the Meiji Restoration. In that era there was a common saying that sexual women should not be mothers and that mothers should not be sexual women. "This idealization of motherhood and confining of mothers strictly to the sphere of reproduction and children is certainly a protection of the order of the patriarchal family-based society."[70] Persistently, one hears expressions of disillusionment along the following lines:

> The modern nuclear family contained within itself the fantasy that it could fulfill the desire for individuality, the desire for a couple relationship, and the desire for community...[We Japanese] are thoroughly entrapped by this fantasy. Our feelings of love and hatred, our buried desires and the models for our sexualities—all are formed and developed by the family and are dependent on the family in everyday life.[71]

An influential and often critiqued essay, published in 1989, by Nancy Chodorow, "The Fantasy of the Perfect Mother," examines American feminist literature on motherhood over the previous thirty years and identified themes that have created unrealistic expectations for both men and women. Her observations have striking relevance for Japanese society. According to Chodorow, "Belief in the all-powerful mother spawns a recurrent tendency to blame the mother on the one hand, and to create a fantasy of maternal perfectibility on the other."[72] In modern America and Japan alike there has been a propensity to absolutize the child's needs, making the mother's task impossible. In both cultures, if the child turns out well her efforts were vindicated; if not, she was a ready target for blame. Or, when internalized, there can be self-reproach. This is the *filiocentric* mother whose life revolves around that of her child.

The other side of the "wise mother" in Japan is, of course, woman as "good wife" who serves her husband (and his family) well by taking appropriate care of him and by being a good mother to his children. However, this is a distanced sort of relationship. The historic bond between husbands and wives in which they worked side by side on the family farm in a predominately rural setting is a familiar one, though it was not the typical experience of young housewives coming into their husband's family world. *Haruko's World* portrays a relationship between spouses that is more complicated, in part because they live in a transitional economic community where their many involvements draw them away from family matters but where they may eventually come to realize the importance of their relationship.

Also, within larger towns and cities there remains the common situation of husbands, wives, children, and grandparents who as a unit work cooperatively in their own small family retail or convenience store, neighborhood restaurant, cleaning establishment, or the like. In these situations men and women live and work in a more interdependent, mutually reinforcing situation, although for wives these family–work responsibilities are added to all that she must do in the home. Dorinne Kondo's study of a small, family-owned confectionery factory in an industrial area of Tokyo in the 1980s reveals yet another urban example. In this work environment women enact their "conventional gendered identities" in a variety of ways that, while not fitting the stereotypes of passive Japanese women, contribute to the burden of combining their work identities in part-time jobs, often involving eight hours a day, with their household roles as wives and mothers.[73]

Kondo reminds us of the ideal image of middle-class women, unlike those with whom she worked and lived, as seen in the "Professional Housewife who commits herself wholeheartedly to the betterment of her *uchi*." In this case, *uchi* is the domestic domain with which wives are identified. Along with such practical duties as child bearing, housework, repairs, and family finances, this image requires women to exhibit culturally defined feminine and middle-class qualities such as gentility, politesse, skill at cooking and traditional arts, graciousness, cosmopolitanism, and an aesthetic sense.[74] These qualities not only should be shown to the outside world (*soto*) but ideally also structure the wife's relationship to her husband within the home by providing vocabularies (linguistic, aesthetic, behavioral) for her role as respected companion.

These roles, however, do not normally allow wives to express their sexuality in more than sublimated form. The idealized mother focuses almost exclusively on her children, and the respected companion on providing an aesthetically pleasing environment for her husband (as a working wife she is still expected to provide a functional environment for her husband). In either role there is little place for overt sexuality. Unable to envision his wife as an intimate sexual partner, the husband may look outside his marriage for sexual satisfaction, thereby objectifying other women as sexual objects. Within such a lack of mutuality one may expect disillusionment, resentment, rage, and sexual violence in one form or another.

In a 1988 documentary film on the Japanese family, *The Yamaguchi Story*, this conflict illustrates less abstractly what happens when varied interpretations of gender are at odds with one another.[75] The Yamaguchi family live in an affluent suburb, thirty minutes outside Tokyo. Husband Ichirō and wife, Hiroko, live together with daughter, Masako. The wife-mother and husband-father are conventional Japanese figures, living out the stereotypes of an upwardly mobile middle-class family, with the standard pattern of home and workplace surgically separated—two worlds in perfect disconnection. Ichirō is a firm believer that economic success is the path to happiness. In his own words, he lives only for his work. With little else to fill her life, Hiroko pursues interests in flower arrangement and tea ceremony, dreaming of eating once a week with her husband. "But he was never around." She thinks of how he gambled on the stock market and lost all and of his frequent bad health and wonders about spending her whole life with such a man. Coming from a large family that does not live nearby, she feels her loneliness. Every night her husband arrives home late, after drinking with office cohorts, and expects her to wait up for him and have dinner ready. She obliges, but with growing despair, wondering if something is wrong with her. Having been brought up not to complain, she begins to lose all hope for the future.

Both figures have their "expected personalities."[76] His is the hardworking, strong-willed company man, always on the run, wedded to his company and colleagues. Hers is the stereotypical obedient, dutiful, submissive, loyal wife who looks after the needs of others. Her self-image stems from her upbringing, deriving her worth from playing a role. She cannot give what she has not gotten, namely, a sense of her own dignity. Raised to please, even when Ichirō returns home night after night in his demanding, besotted condition, Hiroko plays out her role as perfect wife—helping him to stumble out of his clothes into a kimono, serving up his dinner, and heating his bath. The ritual repeats itself day-in, day-out, year after year. Essentially, he takes her for granted, expecting her to meet his needs, using the home as a pied-à-terre, a location and possession that society expects him to have. Each assumes the well-learned role as familiarly as they don their clothes: he the demanding spoiled-boy-turned-successful-spoiled-man; she the obliging wife-mother to a man accustomed to being mothered. On the surface, all goes as socially scripted, until the bubble bursts: she discovers he is having an affair.

After twenty-two years of marriage her world collapses. "He broke my trust." Since infidelity is not uncommon, she may subconsciously have expected it. But when it comes, her mask of self-esteem dissolves into self-contempt, internalized rage, and profound despair, carved into a new mask of resentful dejection. Internally, she flails out in all directions, loses twenty pounds, and locks herself in a dark room for days on end. The husband thinks, "Usually she gets angry, but my wife sits dejected, wasting away." She goes out to the ocean, feeling like a discarded cigarette butt, wanting to leave him, but in her mind she "hears" the voice of Mrs. Abe, an older family friend to whom she then turns for help. Mrs. Abe and others in the new religion Shinnyōen talk of karmic connections, urging her not to blame her husband or hate his mistress but to create a climate of gratitude and to work out her own bad karma by joining Shinnyōen volunteers who clean up dirty train stations, parks, and other public places. At first, Ichirō complains about all the time she spends with her new religion, but gradually he is so unnerved by his wife's lack of recrimination over his affair that he begins to examine his own life and to show interest in Hiroko's religion.[77] A five-year process commences. With counseling and instruction, he too joins Shinnyōen, and the relationship begins on new terms.

One suspects that what Hiroko craved from the start was companionship with her husband. And what was it that he sought in another woman? Was it an intimacy that he did not seek with his wife, the all-obedient Japanese woman? Both husband and wife craved companionship but didn't know what they sought or where it might be found. The sexual intimacy he pursued was a substitute for what he needed, which was first to be freed from treating his wife as his mother. What she lacked was self-respect coming from within, not something bestowed upon her by the canons of domesticity. It is not a mother that he needs at this point in his life or a sexual object that substitutes for both wife and mother. And her need is to break out of the culturally fashioned mode that she has accepted *if* she is to discover her own capacity for relationship.

The fact that sexual intimacy of a satisfying sort is often suppressed in the Japanese husband wife relationship puts added weight on the mother son tie in ways that may or may not have overt sexual implications. Among Japanese feminists there has been extensive discussion of this. A commonly used term for this phenomenon is *mazākon* (mother complex), for what is viewed "as an excessive level of emotional investment and dependency on the part of Japanese mothers in relation to their children—in particular, their sons."[78] This is not in opposition to the *maternal function* of women, only to preoccupation with it as a woman's defining role. Many see this preoccupation as a central consequence of "the general sexual division of labor, by which child rearing [at least in the modern era] is assigned to the mother almost exclusively."[79] That this can issue in a mutual dependence between mother and child continuing throughout the life of both is a commonly stated assertion. It is argued that this bond linking mother and son is often characterized by "unresolved sexuality."[80] Out of a mother's longing for companionship and intimacy springs profound ambivalence on the part of the son as well, for being male he is both "an expression of and a cure for her narcissistic wounds."[81]

Needing but unable to achieve a close relationship with his father to offset excessive maternal love, a son may be destined to spend his life seeking for the perfect alternative to what he recalls, what he has experienced with his mother—an alternative sought in one person after another. *Substitution* becomes a repeated pattern, undermining discovery of an integrated selfhood. The dangers of substitution are familiar in the experience of both Japanese men and women and are manifested frequently in Japanese literature. The mistress becomes the substitute less for the wife than for the mother. It is a sexuality that neglects the requirements of genuine intimacy. While the mistress takes on the sexual side of his imagined relationship with his mother, the wife performs the mother's mothering role, which further distances her from having an intimate and satisfying relationship with her husband. In this process, the deeper meaning of motherhood is lost as well, for the fuller function of parenthood is to encourage strength in one's offspring and to further their capacity to engage in reciprocal relationships. The result has been a misconstruing of family, motherhood, the father son relationship (indeed, of what it can mean to be a father), companionship between the genders, and the deeper connotations of the relationship between sexuality and respect.

The collection of essays *Japanese Women* (1995), edited by Fujimura-Faselow and Kameda, deals in part with the many perversions of genuine sexuality in Japan from a feminist perspective. These include forms of pornography, gender-based violence, and the employment of Asian migrant women in Japan's sex industry. As Kuniko Funabashi puts it, "Pornography does not stop at presenting familiar erroneous images of women, such as that 'women are sexually passive,' 'women are men's possession,' or 'women want to be raped'... Pornography destroys [a woman's] dignity as a human being and does injury to her identity and self-respect; it represents violence committed against her."[82] Funabashi details the several groups of women in Japan are beginning to protest these forms of sexual violence but acknowledges that this movement has a long way to go. Implicit but not developed is a critique of any form of sexual exploitation by Japanese males, within marriage or not. This would include a man's refusal to wear a condom, increasing a woman's chance of becoming pregnant and thereby necessitating the recourse to abortion. The other side of the story, as many feminists urge, is the importance of women's taking greater control of their own bodies and of their own sexual life.[83]

Funabashi's position has been argued more forcefully by Matsui Yayori, a senior staff writer for the *Asahi shinbun* who, in part because she had been posted for four years (1981–85) in Singapore, came to link the structure of sexual politics in Japanese family life with the extent of "illegal Southeast Asian women workers seeking jobs in Japan's sex industry and [with] the flow of Japanese men on organized sex tours" in some of the same countries.[84] She sees Japan as a "prostitution culture" in which Japanese women as well are complicit in an economic system that exploits other societies, that ignores the sexual needs of married Japanese women, and that amounts to acquiescence in the male proclivity of pursuing sexual pleasures beyond the home. In these ways she draws connections where they are often neglected. As a Japanese feminist making these connections graphic, Matsui asserts that the "fundamental problems in the traditional husband-wife relationship—for that matter, the very nature of the Japanese family—contribute directly to the existence and vastness of the sex industry."[85]

One finds an analogous form of protest, without the same social analysis but with a powerful metaphoric impact, in the writings of Amino Kiku

(1900–1978). While her works received literary acclaim during her lifetime, she was never included in the canon of Japanese women writers, a canon controlled by male writers and critics.[86] In an essay examining the reasons for this omission, Chieko Ariga depicts Amino's virtually unique style of representing women. Throughout her fiction she portrays women in ways that have no relationship to men, women whose nonidealized bodies subvert the cultural parodies of a woman's body that has for generations been "tamed and appropriated by the dominant ideology of patriarchy."[87]

> Amino's women assert the otherness of their existence through their bodies, which produce excess, blood, and defecation, having nothing to do with the seducer or the container of penis....Their "grotesque bodies" exist for the benefit not of men but, rather, of themselves. This body demystifies and degrades the idealized femininity prescribed by the patriarchal symbology. As the entity outside the system, it cuts through male codes and rules and therefore has a destabilizing power.[88]

To Amino, the principal category of excluded others is that of the single woman. We have seen how womanhood and motherhood have for the past hundred years in Japan been virtually synonymous. If not literally, at least in symbolically powerful ways, the pressures to get married levied upon women have been immense. To be a complete woman is to be married, and to be married is to become a mother. The conventional sense of identity for women is derived from their relationships with males (with father, husband, and son, as the "three obediences" of Confucianism were conceived long ago). Single women in Amino's world are, to the contrary, "unattached to men; they have no romantic expectations about men; they are disillusioned and disappointed by marriage; they do not want to live with the husband's family; and they have no children...These women are self-representations from inside the marginal woman's territory."[89] Her representations of women are a direct challenge to worldviews that attribute a woman's identity and self-respect only to her association with men. In contrast to portrayals of women in most twentieth-century Japanese prose, even by the most influential women writers, that typically locate women in the context of a male-centered family system, Amino's strategy is to create a world in which women discover their own potential—independent of conscripted norms. It serves as a catalyst to redefining what relationships can become once they are freed from conventional strictures.

Japanese Feminism and the Social Constructions of Motherhood

As the discourse on women's roles became outspoken and as alternate networks of communication between Japanese women's groups materialized, a "spectrum of alternative media [evolved to] oppose the popular image of women in the mass media and offer a forum for political debate and the dissemination of information on a range of issues from international defense to consumer rights and contraception."[90] This effort was stimulated by women's journals, large numbers of newsletters and multiple channels for informing subscribers about discriminatory practices or misleading advertising in the media, and the efforts of teachers and groups of feminists working to encourage nondiscriminatory education in the schools.[91]

One example of effective political action is the manner in which coalitions of women were mobilized to defeat four efforts in the 1970s and 1980s to undermine the clause within the Eugenics Protection Law that permits abortion for economic reasons. These proposed amendments would have made it difficult to obtain abortions legally; this was the goal of antiabortion groups within Japan. But while the current abortion law (enacted in 1948 and amended in 1952 to include the so-called economic clause) may be liberal by some standards, it also is evidence of how women continue to be constrained by state policy. In large part because they are not provided adequate sex education, women choose to have abortions with great frequency. While proposed amendments have failed, the present law still "does not allow women control of their own bodies."[92] This dilemma exemplifies how motherhood continues to be promoted by a constructed ideology dating back to the late nineteenth century.

The many accounts of women's disenchantment with this ideology indicate that no clear consensus exists among feminists in Japan, not to mention Japanese women at large, about the meaning of motherhood. While being a mother can add value to whatever other roles a woman may play, the reverse remains true; other roles and experiences can enhance their ability to become a better mother. The premium put on motherhood may become a burden on those who cannot conceive a child as well as on those who experience multiple miscarriages. It may also cast aspersions on those who prefer to remain single. As long as motherhood is the raison d'être of a woman, the parenting roles of both genders are not taken seriously. Some feminists argue that "women [can] be liberated only through the creation of new value systems and that feminist debate in the 1980s did not take the desired path because it remains rooted in existing value systems."[93] In fact, by the 1980s and 1990s the women's movement in Japan started to recognize that diversity in this movement can be a source of new thinking and more effective strategies by which resistance to change, among women as well as men, is overcome.[94]

The current issues about day care, access to the labor market, educational opportunities, health-care availability (including procreative choice, sex education, and modern forms of family planning), attitudes toward adoption, shared parenthood, and many other issues are specific instances of a larger question, namely, how the lack of social power affects the forms in which mothering occurs. This point is of exceptional importance if one is to understand much of women's experience in the phenomena of *mizuko kuyō*. The process of analyzing the politics of mothering, which has only begun, is a crucial feature of understanding what it means to be a woman *and* a man in Japan, what parenting does and can mean, and what society's responsibilities are to those who parent and those who are its children. Acquiring sufficient power to be one's own agent is central to this theme. In a suggestive manner Takie Sugiyama Lebra responds to this question. As she points out, the issue ranges from those who are aware that the social views of motherhood are, in fact, *constructed* to those who argue that motherhood is therefore not *natural,* that "the family is a cultural construction having nothing to do with the natural, biological givens of life."[95]

> By and large, motherhood is denigrated or condemned in some feminist writings as the ultimate source of oppression and danger to women...Motherhood in this view is nothing but men's appropriation of women's bodies to reproduce patriarchy and therefore should be totally relinquished by women....Inspired but confused by these debates current in Western academia, I propose to interject another viewpoint drawn from a non-Western case...What stands out in the Japanese history of feminism is the centrality and persistence of the motherhood issue...Nevertheless, motherhood, like womanhood, is far from being unitary but is variable and multifarious and has changed historically, as historians have amply documented.[96]

In a parallel but different fashion, Kanai Yoshiko sees a clear-cut distinction between "housewife feminism," which has been issue oriented, and "radical feminism," which concentrates on the structures of society as its main focus. "As a result, feminist critiques of the sexist division of roles have not been able to confront the internal and subjective problems of sexual discrimination or to see the structural background of sexual discrimination as something shared by all women."[97] As an antidote to settling for a diversity of lifestyles, even for expanded forms of sexual freedom, Kanai argues for a radical feminist social theory to explain the "invisible and internalized" forms of oppression that all women share. An area to which she keeps returning is the importance of "a new subjective identity for reproductive rights"[98] As Kanai indicates, it has finally become more common in the 1990s for Japanese women to see "sexuality [that is, equality of sexual power] as a human right of women and sexual violence against women as a violation of human rights."[99] The task of translating such a perception into common social practice is for Kanai among the principal issues that Japanese feminists need to pursue. Achieving greater self-determination here would be a catalyst in a woman's life toward becoming a more empowered agent in other areas of her life. In the long run, agency and empowerment are indivisible; growth in one area of one's life helps to engender growth in other areas.

Japanese Women and the Rhetorics of Everyday Practice

This final section presents three separate instances of tactics used by Japanese women in response to how their lives have been shaped by prevailing values, institutions, and circumstances. From Michel de Certeau's perspective, as mentioned in Chapter 1, these tactics are the *rhetorics of practice*. Whether expressed in thought, word, or action, they are "manipulations of language relative to [specific] occasions and are intended to seduce, captivate, or invert the linguistic position of the addressee."[100] In essence, they are "ways of speaking." His distinction between strategies and tactics illuminates how Japanese women have responded with effectiveness to patriarchal forms of society and culture. A strategy is the calculus and utilization of power available to those in positions of dominance, whereas a tactic "takes advantage of 'opportunities'...where it is least expected. It is a guileful ruse. In short, a tactic is an art of the weak."[101]

It is a form of "weakness," however, that serves to transform or upend traditional expectations through ridicule, surprise, irony, and even apology. It appears in *The Yamaguchi Story*, where Hiroko was counseled not to blame her husband for his infidelity or hate his mistress but to work out her own bad karma. From many Western points of view this may seem counterintuitive, but in this instance the consequences were the reverse. And, in Enchi Fumiko's novel *The Waiting Years*, discussed at the end of this chapter, one observes an even more devastating use of irony. No tactic is all-purpose; it must arise from the occasions of everyday life. In fact, instances of "muted protest" send signals of distress and may have an impact on a sizable number of people.

Because the phenomena of *mizuko kuyō* may seem less intentional, it may not strike one as a tactic of resistance. It may be more a signal of distress, a sign of something profoundly personal but more than personal. Jolivet uses the term "gentle resistance" for the ways Japanese women have been manifesting their "silent little revolution" against earlier and persisting social patterns of treating women.[102] As a differentiated phenomenon experienced idiosyncratically, it serves to illuminate troublesome features of modern existence. Viewing these examples of resistance takes one into the following chapter that examines the reactions of women (and men), after experiences of abortion, miscarriage, stillbirth, or early infant death, there is the decision to have memorial services done for themselves and their children or *mizuko*. Whether the experience of *mizuko kuyō* becomes a tactic of resistance by some women or not, its influence stems from the fact that it highlights and may address an important need felt by large numbers of women, often by men as well.

Medicalization of Distress: Protests of the Good Wife and Wise Mother

Convinced that the medicalization of life in Japan today is rampant, Margaret Lock has focused her research on culture-bound medical symptoms, especially in women, symptoms that telegraph the presence of issues that, while personal, are not simply personal but have broader social and cultural implications. She deals with illnesses of women that reflect inner discord over their role as wives and mothers and in their relationships with various members of their family.[103] The fact that these physical symptoms so regularly end up as forms of self-aggression where anger or frustration or guilt is absorbed, with consequences to the body, means that these symptoms are themselves insignia of protest. Lock discusses strategies of resistance that are used by Japanese in situations of potential conflict. *Somatization* is a common form of self-aggression, particularly in societies where direct accusation and confrontational methods of approach are discouraged; strong emotions are internalized with great impact upon a person's physical and psychological health.

Lock also discusses the common practice among Japanese physicians to identify the root problem behind the many symptoms that beleaguer Japanese women in mid-life as "nonspecific complaints." This generalized, reductive diagnosis is widely used, inducing those involved to avoid deeper issues that may be triggering the actual distress behind women's aches and pains. Medical treatment is "applied entirely at the physiological level, and the patients are returned to their former lives and situations" without serious consultation about the psychosocial etiology of their condition.[104] The result is to deflect both patient and physician away from the "social origins of distress." In Lock's judgment, while women often draw connections between their physical ailments and tensions within the home they rarely associate these with the "structure of society at large [or] female subordination in general."[105] Physicians avoid this topic as well, though in individual cases they write books about the pressures of modern society, sometimes blaming both mother and father for neglecting their children, and tend to look back nostalgically to times when being a wise mother was the accepted ideal.

Lock's research on the *somatization* of protest in Japan has its counterparts in Western feminist studies on the body as a medium of cultural distress among women. Realizing that differences exist across class, racial, and religious lines, Susan Bordo's words echo those of Lock: "It is as though these bodies are speaking to us of the pathology and violence that lurks just around the edge, waiting at the horizon of 'normal' femininity. It is no wonder, then, that a steady motif in the feminist literature on female disorder is that of pathology as embodied *protest*—unconscious, inchoate, and counterproductive protest without effective language, voice, or politics—but protest nonetheless."[106] Bordo stresses the typically counterproductive nature of this protest, seeing it as an expression of *voicelessness* that reinforces the social ideal of the "silent, uncomplaining woman." Yet the bodily symptoms may be seen as a clear-cut signal of distress, and of muted protest.

In Critique of Gender Ideology: Different Metaphors of Sexuality

The worlds of fiction are equally able to reveal strategies of resistance to women's experience of objectification. One contemporary example, reaching millions of Japanese women, exists in the New Romance genre in Japan, a spinoff created two decades ago by Japanese women authors from Harlequin novels in England and the United States.[107] Published by the Sanrio Company of Tokyo, these novels may appear on the surface to be either subordination of women by sexually aggressive males or as fantasies of revenge in a woman's search for control. In fact, Japanese romance writers have created a world that is more complex, for they depict gender relations in which qualities of *aggression and yielding* on the part of both sexes intermingle. It is a path that points beyond bipolarities. As Chieko Irie Mulhern maintains, Sanrio women are defined less by their relationships to parents, in-laws, husbands, or other men than by "their own social accomplishments or careers."[108] It is a milieu of engagement, beyond submission, but still within the gendered contexts of social reality.

This strength of women in a male-oriented society is vulnerable not only to male violence but just as much also to the instincts of conventional heroes for protecting women. In response to these ambivalent feelings of strength and weakness, the objective in these narratives is to undermine male power and to reinforce a woman's sense of self-control. While the Japanese woman has a strong sense of her power and authority within the home, in these novels she reveals a newfound "autonomy, competence, and career option." In romance literature the quest lies *beyond* issues of social justice. Her goal is to erase persistent images and experiences of bifurcation, whether idealized mother versus sexual object or domesticated wife versus career woman. Complementary levels of interpretation are evident.[109]

If one interprets this undermining of male power on a literal plane, the intent could easily appear as a perverted expression of strength through weakness or of turning vulnerability into dubious advantage, a skill that Japanese women have already honed to perfection. As one seeks for the import behind the metaphor of mutilation suggested by these women writers, one is induced to go beyond sadomasochistic impulses, beyond simple revenge, beyond death wishes. The symbolic intent of this dramatized violence, referred to as *mutilation,* is to underscore the diseased nature of typical gendered relations and to challenge standard portrayals of what being male and what being female mean. In this case, mutilation of male power becomes the impairment of what is already vitiated. Ultimately, mutilation stands not simply as diagnosis but also as a catalyst for healing, for transforming the entire basis of gender relations, and for providing a vision of sexuality beyond ideology. Through metaphoric language, mutilation partakes of the transformative process. Sanrio romances envision a world of reciprocal relations between equals, in which neither gender treats the other as commodity.

Unleashing the Suppressed Energies of Women: The Literary Quest of Enchi Fumiko (1905–1986)

While the visions of transformation one finds in the Sanrio heroines are authentic forms of resistance, another twentieth-century writer, Enchi Fumiko, envisions a world that is more conflictive, a world painted with images of reality that are dark, subterranean, and frequently Vesuvian. The constructed world of Enchi's fiction draws upon perspectives of Japanese literature and society that reflect the convolutions and turmoil of the human spirit. Past and present eras inform, challenge, and threaten each other. Psychological, social, and spiritual realities intertwine in a characteristically complex, ambiguous fashion. Her short stories and novels portray the wrestling of supernatural forces set in recognizable social contexts, giving the reader endlessly interconnected levels of meaning.

Among the most compelling of her portrayals are the circumstances of Japanese women caught for centuries in states of suppressed power and energy by the forces of culture and society to which they have become accustomed and to which they respond in an oblique fashion. Enchi's genius for portraying these dilemmas provides copious examples of women whose capacity for resistance, seemingly abortive and suppressed, nonetheless endures. In the midst of delineating patriarchal culture, she creates modes of human response, particularly those of women, that reveal agonistically creative forces at work, no matter how unchanged society remains. Hers is a world akin to that of Greek tragedy where circumstances may not change but in which a wider spectrum of human potential for both treachery and nobility is portrayed. Hers is less a social message than a deeper exploration into the resourcefulness of the human creature, especially when caught in intractable situations.

This means there is no release from struggle; there are only endless ways to confront it. Her works of literature, though troubling, are not expressions of despair. While the writings of Enchi Fumiko portray the suffering and self-sacrifice endured by women, they also manifest the intricacies of a social system that generates this suffering. If the strategies of resistance exhibited by some of the women in her stories appear picayune, they may be viewed in symbolic terms that are devastating to an order that assumes its own rectitude.

An elegant example of this may be found in *Onnazaka*, translated as *The Waiting Years*.[110] This novel has sometimes been cast as perpetuating the image of women subservient to Meiji codes of conventionalized morality (*tsūzoku dōtoku*). In fact, Enchi sets the reader up for that kind of predictable reaction. Her sustained picture of Yukitomo Shirakawa, a prefectural official first in Fukushima and then with the Metropolitan Police Agency in Tokyo, reinforces this image. He is a man infatuated with budding young girls whom he serially shapes as concubines within his own home. At the age of thirty, his wife, Tomo, twelve years his junior, is sent by Yukitomo from their home in Kyushu to Tokyo to choose for him a fresh young girl, "good-looking" and from a "respectable family," ostensibly to enter the Shirakawa family service. Married since she was fourteen herself, Tomo over the years has come to realize that her husband "with whom even in the past she had never been able to effect real contact was moving still further away."[111] Even so, after selecting Suga from alternative prospects, Tomo is suddenly overwhelmed by the implications of her action:

> The pain of having publicly to hand over her husband to another gnawed at her within. To Tomo, a husband who would quite happily cause his wife such suffering was a monster of callousness. Yet since to serve her husband was the creed around which her life revolved, to rebel against his outrages would have been to destroy herself as well; besides there was the love that was still stronger than the creed.[112]

Longing, jealousy, hatred toward her husband, and pity for the objects of his lust fueled her repressed passion. With her two children cared for by others and her husband's sexual needs being met by concubines, known as his "adopted daughters," and later even by his daughter-in-law, Miya, with whom he has a twenty-year incestuous relationship, Tomo's role as the good wife, wise mother is reduced to managing the Shirakawa household affairs. In this sense, the novel is, indeed, a truer-than-life portrait of Meiji ideology.

The vulnerability of her husband, and of the world that he represents, gradually comes into focus. In times of trauma Yukitomo returns to Tomo, as a young child to its mother, for solace and sexual oblivion, especially when his world is threatened, as when he was confronted by a political adversary, whom he assumed had died in jail. This man, appearing like a ghost from the dead, taunts him that his days of political privilege are coming to an end, that the new Constitution with its National Assembly will throw out the lackeys of bureaucracy. That night Yukitomo "wanted to place his daunted spirit in Tomo's protective arms." As he thought about the various women he had loved, he fought "against the loneliness that swept through him like a chill, dark wind."[113] Relentlessly, the novel catalogs the signs of his aging. His personal needs still attended by Suga and his sexual appetites now met by Miya, Yukitomo finds consolation primarily in his grandchildren, one of whom he may have fathered through Miya, their son's wife.

As her husband declines into indulgent self-preoccupation, Tomo questions more acutely the mere acceptance of her fate. The impact of Yukitomo's illicit relationship with Miya, which violates all that Meiji codes permit, shakes Tomo to the core. Concerned as always about the family's reputation, she is outraged not only by her husband's incestuous union with Miya but also by the seeds of similar patterns within the generation of her grandchildren. She begins to see her life situation as part of a larger pattern of inexorable destiny thrust upon women. She feels "revulsion against her own complicity in the four-way relationship of husband, son, mistress, and daughter-in-law."[114] Trapped as others in an endless cycle of human births and deaths, she asks herself why "should she be obliged to spend all her life entangled with such distasteful affairs?"[115]

Toward the novel's end, as she trudges wearily through the snow up the slope leading to the Shirakawa homestead, Tomo experiences conflicting feelings of happiness for the harmony that must exist in the small houses she passes on the way and "a sudden, futile despair" for the life she has known with Yukitomo, "where the darkness seemed to stretch endlessly ahead."[116] With customary resolve, she refuses to surrender to this despair, vowing to seek for light within the darkness she has known. In this sense, it is a rejection of cynicism.

Shortly after this episode she comes down with an illness that proves to be fatal. As Yukitomo comes to her bedside, she asks him to retrieve her will from the cabinet drawer. "Through all the past decades she had never looked at her husband with such a direct and unwavering gaze. The approach of death had set her free" from having to play a role any longer.[117] As Yukitomo reads the will, he finds "himself reeling before a force more powerful than himself. There was not a word of complaint from Tomo against the outrageous way he had oppressed her: nothing but apology for not having trusted him...yet the words of apology bore down on his heart more heavily than the strongest protest."[118] Yukitomo tells her not to worry, that he understands her feelings. And she replies, "So you forgive me? I'm so grateful."[119]

That scene becomes even more powerful when reinforced by the final scene when Tomo sends a message to Yukitomo through a niece who watches by her bedside. The end is near. Now free to be frank, Tomo, as if in a kind of trance, says to Toyoko: "Tell [your uncle] that when I die I want no funeral. Tell him that all he need do is to take my body out to sea at Shinagawa and dump it in the water."[120] When Yukitomo receives this message, "fear stirred as though he had seen a ghost"; his body "suffered the full force of the emotions that his wife had struggled to repress for forty years past. The shock was enough to split his arrogant ego in two."[121] With these words, the novel ends.[122]

Enchi Fumiko's genius lies in her ability to arrest the reader's imagination and to conjure multivalent imagery. One gradually comprehends the power these concluding episodes have, not simply on the fictional Yukitomo but on what they imply about the world of gender and family relations in Meiji Japan. Beyond this, what Enchi sees not just in that culture and society but also in her own takes on universal implications. She has created a world that transcends its immediate context. In a political sense, some might fault her novel for reproducing a world we believe we have gone beyond, for not providing role models of strong women, and for seeming to reinforce traditional images of the ideal Japanese woman. In actuality, rather than settling for the self-sacrificial woman, she creates a character who, while groomed to play that part, concludes her life by turning upside down the hallowed canons of how to treat the dead. Since she has been discarded throughout her life, it would seem magnificent symmetry to dump her body at the end into the sea.

This denouement sets Yukitomo shivering in fear, "as though he'd seen a ghost," for it is the dead who have been wronged in life that return to haunt the living. It was as though he had created his own *tatari*, his own self-retribution. In this manner, Enchi punctuates her story about women who have been wronged throughout their lives by a *symbolic inversion*. One does not simply dump another's body. This powerful gesture serves to negate the facade of official power and status and underscores its implications for those who like Tomo felt discarded like worn-out slippers. This image of being dumped symbolizes the degree to which a woman's sense of self-worth has been linked to her social utility. The reader is presented here with a form of distilled power that, when unleashed through Tomo's request, reveals the force of a person possessed. This distillation of power underscores the tensions felt by women as wives, mothers, and sexual objects in the Meiji period and beyond.[123] This scene underscores the question of why women in the modern period have such an investment in their role as mother and therefore why child loss, even in the form of abortion, can become so traumatic to so many.

Looking back at several instances described in this chapter in which the factors of *symbolic domination* and *symbolic violence,* as depicted by Pierre Bourdieu, are pervasive in the social milieu, it is also evident that Japanese women can be skilled in crafting countermeasures that expose male vulnerability to their own dominance. As Bourdieu puts it, referring to Virginia Wolff's insight, "namely the domination of the dominant by his domination." This is an important theme in any culture, any society in which dominance goes unchallenged in direct and ongoing ways. This is discussed further in the next two chapters.

The following chapter examines how the constructed practices of *mizuko kuyō* raise questions about who constitutes one's ancestors and how the living and the dead relate. The chapter initially discusses conventional forms of ancestor belief and practice in their classical Indian and Chinese expressions and more fully in Japan. Beginning with more or less standard expressions of what constitutes the ancestor–descendent relationship, we discuss its perceived benefits to the dead and to their living descendants. The chapter then looks at the opposite end of the spectrum, at situations where individuals and communities probe for the causes behind unexplained suffering.

6

Ancestors, Angry Spirits, and the Unborn

CARING FOR THE DEAD ON PATH TO ANCESTORHOOD

WE HAVE VIEWED *mizuko kuyō* in relationship to abortion, issues of gender, and the personal lives of women in contemporary Japan. Chapters 4 and 5 focus on the ways women especially have faced the grieving process and how this relates to the social constructs that have both formed and influenced these issues. *Mizuko kuyō* needs also to be seen in tension with the Japanese practice of caring for ancestors (*senzo kuyō*). A *mizuko* becomes identified with or at least homologous to ancestors in one's family lineage, though for many Japanese this sense of ancestral lineage has become increasingly attenuated. Whatever it means for a people to experience dislocation from their past, however, it is a past remembered and reconstructed that continues to influence society, culture, and personal identity.

Throughout much of Japanese history there has been a strong belief in the existence of angry spirits. The fear of being cursed by angry *mizuko* has been discussed in Chapter 4. Here we suggest that modern fears of unhappy *mizuko* are similar to the sustained belief in Japanese history about discontented ancestral spirits. Further evidence of this fear of angry spirits may be seen in the cult of the war dead in modern Japan, in which the spirits of the war dead have been manipulated by political ideology and ultraconservative forces. In effect, this is a powerful instance of how this cult has been used to impose and maintain social structures and the subordination of women. In opposition to this is the case of an "ordinary woman" who resists the attempts of nationalistic forces to impose the status of a potentially angry spirit on her deceased husband. The chapter also includes an example from one of the newer religions that approach the ancestral relationship in a different manner than one finds in the older, clerically governed Buddhist sects.

Through historical, religious, ethnographic, and anthropological analysis one sees how ancestral lineage manifests a society's sense of a continuum from remote and recent ancestors to an ongoing line of descendants. The present is called into being by the living hand of the past, a past that is continually being reconstructed. Care for the well-being of the dead is the consummate task of the living. To default this care exposes the living to a variety of perceived consequences: sustained misfortune, deracination from one's social matrix, and the prospect of indifference toward the dead as shown by one's own descendants. In writing about East Asian societies, Meyer Fortes points out that there is "acute anxiety lest this breaking of the chain of descendents should occur. This has to do with their belief that the dead cannot rest in peace if there is no one to care for their worship after death. This brings up...[an] abhorrence of the possibility of a person's total extinction by death," that extends to the group as a whole.[1] Ancestors *are* the past. In this sense, relationship to one's lineage, personal and communal, is an ambidextrous reality, with the capacity to stifle and threaten as well as to inspire and nurture.

In the earliest strands of Confucian thought and practice in China the concept of filial piety was institutionalized as the epitome of parent–child relations. Unlike bonds that can be reciprocal, like those of marriage and intimate friendship, the bond between parents and children is the embodiment of what filiality signifies. Reverence toward one's ancestors conveys the ideal of how the living should address the dead as a whole *as well as* the social past that the dead represent.

As Buddhism became rooted in China, even more dramatic models of filial piety evolved. In the many Chinese marvelous tales about the filial devotion of Buddhist monks and nuns toward their parents, one finds counterparts to those recorded in Confucian literature. In fact, those claimed by Buddhist partisans exceeded those that were previously conceived by Chinese society.[2] Kenneth Ch'en implies that the Buddhism that entered China from India had not emphasized the practice of filial piety but had begun this practice only after being *sinicized* over centuries in Chinese society. Ch'en was unaware, however, of how common this practice had been among Buddhist monks and laypeople in India long before Buddhism entered China.

In a well-documented discussion of the early and widespread practice of filial piety engaged in by Buddhist monks and laypeople in India, Gregory Schopen presents a different picture from that of Ch'en: "We have come to see that 'filial piety' was an old, an integral, and a pervasive part of the practice of Indian Buddhism from the earliest periods of which we have any definite knowledge."[3] These findings document the long-standing relationship between Buddhist practice and concerns for the well-being of ancestors on the part of both monks and laypeople. Evidence of this practice validates for Chinese Buddhism, as it had for Indian Buddhism, the belief that merit accrues from making religious donations to one's parents, whether living or dead.

The emotion engendered from acts of kindness shown by filial children to their parents, alongside the power transmitted from the *sangha* to those in suffering, were repeatedly attested by Buddhist communities in India and Sri Lanka.[4] Within Theravada Buddhism a tension exists between the popular belief that ancestors who are reborn among the *petas* (world of the departed ones) benefit from offerings dedicated to them and the view that while ancestors do not benefit by these gifts they are perceived to enjoy the generous deeds of their descendants.[5] Early visions of such kindness and spiritual power took root throughout the Buddhist world, with particular resonance in China, Korea, and Japan.[6]

This tension between so-called orthodox teaching and popular practice has been central to Buddhism throughout its history. Stephen Teiser's study of the ghost festival (*yü-lan-p'en*) in China focuses principally on its development during the T'ang dynasty (618–907). Drawing on primary sources from texts out of diffused religious sources as well as from materials from the literati tradition, Teiser shows (1) how this festival and its ritual (observed during three days in the seventh lunar month) combined the cycle of ancestral sacrifices, the seasonal rhythms of monastic life, and the fertility rites of agriculture; (2) how it became part of the Chinese state religion during the T'ang dynasty; and (3) how it incorporated elements of a Taoist festival, tantric Buddhist features, and cosmological aspects of popular religion.[7] Teiser's work contributes to the understanding of how Buddhism in China appropriated in this festival a variety of indigenous social and religious features, including the Confucian phenomenon of filial piety. His analysis is crucial to appreciating the Chinese background to what appeared for the first time in Japan within court Buddhism of the early seventh century.[8]

We move now to the Japanese counterpart of these ancestral beliefs and practices. Later we return to what this ghost festival meant in T'ang China and ask what implications it has for Buddhist teachings and practice in Japan. Through an understanding of this, one perceives how newly created symbolic and ritualistic aspects found in the practice of *mizuko kuyō* have been integrated into the more widely held elements of the ancestral connection in Japan and in the process have responded to the expression of newly arising needs.

Ancestral Relationships in Japan: Reinforcing the Social and Cosmic Order

While considerable distance exists between the ideal image and many forms of actual experience, the influence of norms associated with ancestral relations remains powerful in Japan. The typical forms of ritual observance provide structure and a sense of continuity in which the transition from life to death occurs within the immediate and extended family and its close friends. As the status of individuals is inseparable from their identity within a familial context, so the reasons given by participants for their practice of ancestor worship (*senzo kuyō*) are as differentiated as one might expect. Robert Smith's depiction of this heterogeneity is as accurate today as it was a generation ago, and one may find a comparable spectrum among the practices of *mizuko kuyō* in contemporary Japan.

> Some people seek to benefit the spirits of the dead by comforting or pleasing them or by helping them to enter Paradise. Some share this concern but appear also to fear retribution if rites are neglected. Others say that they seek from the ancestors both personal protection and health and happiness for all family members. More commonly, people report that they simply wish to express gratitude to the ancestors for their past favors and for their continuing protection.[9]

A purpose of memorial services is to promote the deceased person's safe and orderly passage to the next world, a practice that represents the fact and value of continuity. This transition is believed to occur in intense forms over the first several weeks following death and more gradually over a number of years. "Life in this world is growth to full adulthood. Life in the other world is growth to full ancestorhood."[10] This latter growth is thought to be in process over a thirty-three-year span, with frequent variations in practice. This long sequence is designed to keep alive the memory of the dead, to engage in a process of remembering, and to begin moving the deceased to the status of ancestorhood. Gradually, the person is "expunged from the memories of the living" to the point years later where they are literally forgotten, meaning that "in time the living will let go of, will indeed forget, the dead."[11] Strictly speaking, the deceased as a whole are not forgotten. Ancestors remain part of a life–death continuum that lends greater significance to life and to experiencing the familial continuity than would otherwise be felt.

In analyzing ingredients of ancestor worship in Japan, Fortes provides an overview of the "affective and structural ambivalence" found in the relationship between the living and the dead.[12] He draws attention to the regular "care and feeding" of ancestors that are intrinsic to the process of remembrance. As one cares for someone who is dependent—an infant or small child, a very sick person, the old and infirm—the process of caring tends to *foster* in the caregiver feelings of kindness and compassion. This is precisely what can occur in remembering the dead, one's ancestors. In the case of the dead it can evolve from simple obligation and indebtedness to an awareness of benefits received from countless other, still existing sources as well.

The basic term for memorial service, *kuyō*, combines the character for *sonaeru* (to offer or dedicate) with the character for *yashinau* (to feed or nourish). One is not offering something separate from one's self; one is offering oneself through whatever offerings one may bring. When this occurs, dedication (that is, self-dedication) is an apposite concept. Performing *kuyō* when there has been a close relationship between the living and the dead activates the memory of having been cared for and includes the realization of one's own continuing need for such care. Research on women whose pregnancy has been terminated or whose children have been stillborn or died in infancy reveals frequent expressions of the need to *feed* in some way the lost child and equally the need to *be fed* in the midst of an experience of loss. The expected succession in one's life is to lose someone who gave one life; the unnatural course is to lose a child to whom one has given life.

When ritual becomes intentional, it is designed to keep ancestors and the living in a web of reciprocity. Ancestors are more than symbols; they are reaffirmations of actual living connections with the past. The most intimate expression of this relationship is before the family altar at home. Tu Wei-ming expresses this well: "Indeed, memory of the dead intensifies the care for the living."[13] The past becomes grafted into present existence. This memory may be kept alive from day to day over many years, especially when it is of those with whom the bond has been close. For some, there may exist an ongoing conversation with the spirit of the deceased, particularly but not only in times of need. A central feature of commemorating the death of an adult especially is also to face the inevitability of one's own death, which lends a note of sobriety and realism. As Herman Ooms writes, "Thus ancestor worship in its religious aspect provides man with a frame through which he is able to face [his own] mortal existence...everybody is destined to become an ancestor."[14] Ironically, the unpredictability-yet-inevitability of death may bring one closer in spirit to one's ancestors. While the deceased remain dead literally, they live symbolically as human beings open themselves to the past and its impact upon them.

On the other hand, the practice of *sosen-kuyō* (memorializing one's forebears) has undergone important modifications in recent decades, in part because the Japanese family system has changed from what it was prior to 1945. With a stronger accent now put upon personal identity and with fewer family constraints, the question is often raised whether this idealized pattern of reverencing ancestors is doomed to perish or whether its fundamental sense of the inseparability of life and death will take on new forms. In either case, it prompts one to examine what is at stake in the observance of *kuyō* independent of whatever forms it may take or whatever social values it may espouse.

In his research in Nagasawa, a part of Kawasaki City near Tokyo, in the mid-1960s, Herman Ooms found that the deceased children, even infants, were included among *muenbotoke* (those who died but lacked connection with living relatives). He notes that most kinds of *muenbotoke* at that point were not considered harmful.[15] In updating his research on ancestor worship republished in 1987, he looked at the *mizuko kuyō* phenomenon, which had arisen since his earlier study, and asked new questions.[16] Since ties with the traditional *ie* family system had become less of the norm, he wondered whether revering one's ancestors would continue to be observed in urbanized nuclear families? If so, in what form? Because ancestral rites are being performed in fresh ways by lay believers in the newer religions and because radically simplified, often secularized expressions of ancestral belief and practice are on the rise, one asks how much continuity with older forms of *senzo kuyō* or *sosen sūhai* will remain even in the near future? Can new definitions of what *mizuko* means fit into the old category of *muenbotoke*?

Singling out the guilt factor often present in women who have had abortions as well as the emotional tensions associated with this feeling, Ooms connects these with the fears some women have of being cursed by the spirits of aborted fetuses. Of considerable interest is his suggestion that because children are being seen differently in Japanese society and have a transformed legal and economic status than before the war, the *mizuko* phenomenon may be parallel to current Japanese movements that advocate the rights of the physically handicapped, persons of mixed blood, those of Korean ancestry, and the outcaste class known as *burakumin*.[17] This creates an expanded context within which any focus upon *mizuko* as well needs to be placed. Ooms is perceptive in suggesting a relationship between the changed status of children over the past two generations and the heightened emotional degree with which women especially experience child loss, even abortion.

As suggested in Chapter 2, one finds the beginnings of an earlier discourse of fertility control and changing concepts about children back in the Tokugawa period. However one interprets fragmentary evidence from premodern Japan, it contributes to a recognition of the varied social and cultural attitudes toward children over the past three centuries and how a woman's consciousness of herself as a mother has been modified in recent decades. In premodern Japan, since young children who died were not regarded separately from their family and the larger community, there were no ways of conceiving them as autonomous beings in either a social or religious sense. What one finds in contemporary Japan is some combination of relative autonomy alongside a continuing sense of connection with one's family. With the current religious attention given to *mizuko* there are newer implications for how one treats the death of a child. There is clear evidence about how the practice of *mizuko kuyō* confirms the existence of new ways of looking at the death of children, even aborted fetuses, and the difficulties that some women may experience in child loss.

While one may wonder how ancestor worship can survive the changes that have occurred in the Japanese family structure, an even more interesting question is whether the gradual move toward social inclusiveness, together with the increased numbers of people living into old age who may tend to become more religious with the years, carries the possibility that reverence for ancestors might continue in *new forms*. What Obon's welcoming of the dead's return once a year is to Japanese society, the Day of the Dead is to Mexican life and culture. Both are remembrances of All Souls who have departed but who keep returning. Each affirms a sense of the life–death continuum.[18] But when the living are out of touch with the presence of the dead, as is more common in highly commercialized, secular society, the living may ironically become more vulnerable to anxiety about death. It is ironic, but not surprising, that an age that has a diminished sense of its ancestral connections is a time when the so-called hungry ghosts (*gaki*) of Buddhist cosmology make their presence known once more, albeit in new guises. We turn now from images of mutually supportive ancestral relations to perceptions of what can happen when these relations go awry.

Mizuko, Muenbotoke, *and Other Angry Spirits:* *Anomalies in the Ancestral Chain*

In Japanese culture there has been sustained belief that angry spirits of the dead are a potent force with which the living have to reckon. Since the resort to *mizuko kuyō* is criticized for promoting such a belief, it is important to recognize the long history of this belief. For centuries it has been held that the anger of neglected spirits stems from their having been ignored or removed from human concern. As such, angry spirits, coming in infinite forms, may be seen as the unresolved demons of personal and communal brokenness. Clues to understanding how a society deals with unexplained suffering are often expressed in newly interpreted mythic forms, associating life experiences of the present with what happened in the past.

By providing examples of this in Japanese history, Robert Smith and Herman Ooms devote considerable attention to the Japanese belief in *muenbotoke*, those spirits of the dead, especially but not only the newly dead (*shirei*), who wander endlessly in search of food and comfort. These spirits either lack connection with the living or whose death has not been commemorated. This category of the dead represents those believed to have died *unnatural deaths*—either those who are "in a state of jealousy, rage, resentment, or melancholy" or those who died an early death (as a child or an unmarried young adult) and thus were left without heirs.[19] The category of *muenbotoke* helps one to understand the symbolic significance of ancestor worship. The newly deceased presents a threat, the assumption being that this soul becomes harmful to the family and to itself when the dead are not provided proper rites. With the offering of memorial rites the commemorated soul becomes a link between the living and the dead. [20]

For the unfortunate ones, particularly those thought to be malevolent, various Buddhist sects in Japan have from at least the fifteenth century conducted a ceremony called *segaki-e* (feeding the hungry ghosts) that acts as a kind of exorcistic prelude to Obon.[21] It is intended to offset difficulties and to quiet the spirits of hungry ghosts. Generally, Obon is observed for those spirits of the dead considered to be benign, while *segaki-e* is for the potentially dangerous spirits.[22] Because life is capricious and cannot be subsumed into some ideal and enduring order, provisions for anomalies such as *muenbotoke* are thought to be required. This sort of enigma feeds the belief in harm being wreaked upon the living by the angry dead. The obvious question is how one understands the many levels of belief in the angry spirits of the dead, whether spirits of the war dead who have not been properly memorialized, spirits of dead children (*mizuko rei*), or spirits of ancestors in a more conventional sense.

Ancestors are present to their living descendants in ways that are often agonistic or threatening. One looks especially at spirits who died a violent death in one form or another. The process of trying to identify the causes behind unexplained misfortune commonly regards angry spirits of the dead as serious threats to the living. While such a perception may not be shared by most in Japan today, there is a substratum of anxiety about angry spirits (*onryō*) that still exists and whose history in Japan is long. To put another face on this phenomenon it is helpful to examine several cultural instances of the problem of coping with unexplained suffering and the belief in angry spirits of the dead. This fear of vengeful ghosts from whatever source is thus a seedbed for contemporary anxiety, often referred to as *fuan* (apprehension or unrest), out of which beliefs about unhappy spirits of *mizuko* may also spring. One needs to ask how these spirits of *mizuko* resemble yet differ from the older anomalous category known as *muenbotoke*, the dead who threaten because they remain disconnected from their ancestral chain.

Ancestors and the Continuing Problem of Unexplained Suffering

The difficulty of living with unexplained suffering is a classic problem in every culture. The very surfeit of explanations contributes to the confusion. In the West the archetypal example is found in the Book of Job. Seemingly a paragon of virtue, Job is afflicted with chronic illness, deaths in the family, financial devastation—in unending succession. Of torment to him is the issue of *why* he is being afflicted. Convinced of his own goodness and shattered by the possibility that God is neither good nor almighty, Job's quandary is one that has hounded Western cultures for centuries, namely, the question of theodicy.

While religious traditions arising in Asia deal with a similar dilemma, they formulate the problem differently: Unless the dead are memorialized and their needs are properly respected, living relatives will be haunted by spirits returning in angry form. The literature on this in South, Southeast, and East Asia is extensive. Indeed, it is a dominant explanation for most people, though it is not the canonical Buddhist position on why people are afflicted with adversity. In Buddhist teaching, misfortune stems from one's personal karma, one's addictions to the transient, one's own angry spirit, and one's self-deception about the nature of reality. Because orthodox teaching may not be persuasive when one is in the midst of such entrapment, at the opposite extreme lies a more literal belief in angry spirits, especially those of neglected ancestors. Today it seems easy to disregard the theory of angry spirits as explanation for misfortune or calamity, though formerly such a belief flourished. As a theoretical answer to the causes for suffering or evil these notions can readily be dismissed. What cannot be dismissed is the problem itself or that *belief* in angry spirits lingers as a living phenomenon for many in Japan, as elsewhere.

Among many discussions of this issue within modern Japanese religions, Winston Davis's study of the religious group Sōkyō Mahikari in Nakayama City suggests how this community associates persisting misfortune with being possessed by vengeful spirits (*onryō*) and how it views exorcism of these spirits as a ritualistic necessity.[23] Davis explores what he calls the problem of theodicy, construed as "the symbolic resources mobilized by a group or a whole society to deal with the ultimate frustrations of life: misfortune, sickness, and death."[24] Relationships between ancestors and descendants in Japanese religions are positive or negative, depending upon filial responsiveness. "When mistakes are found in their [attendance to the] *butsudan* people are expected to apologize to their ancestors."[25] The ritualized process of apologizing acts as a cathartic restoring of reciprocity as well as a reconciliation of bad relations. Misfortune can thus be transformed into renewed energy, health, and good fortune.

Elaborating on this thesis, Davis discusses how multiple causes for misfortune may amount to what he calls a "laminated theodicy." Unable to conceive a child, a woman may seek a variety of solutions—medical, social, and religious. If successful, she may attribute "her previous inability to become pregnant to a tipped uterus, and at a deeper level, both to possession by a grudging spirit and to her own lack of religious zeal."[26] What happens when all explanations fail? Herein lies the problem of theodicy. For members of Mahikari, the sufferings and adversities of the world are caused by both the "sins and pollutions" of individual karma and the pollutions of modern technology, greed, political strife, and other factors, including modern medicine. It is of considerable significance that a social dimension is seen to exist in the law of karma, as consequence and as cause. When problems go unattended, angry spirits begin to stir.[27]

While many in Mahikari find the roots of their ailments and a means of being healed in body, mind, and spirit, large numbers who try this path leave dissatisfied, doubtlessly searching elsewhere. This community represents one among scores of spiritual paths found in Japanese religions that face the uncertainty of the human condition, each practicing its own versions of theodicy, its own "dike against chaos," as Davis puts it. The fear of so-called curses inflicted on the living by neglected and vengeful spirits of the dead can be recognized as one way people may identify the causes behind otherwise unexplained suffering. We now explore some of the ways this fear of the unrequited dead have appeared in modern Japanese society as a backdrop for seeing how this has contributed to a similar anxiety about angry spirits found in some forms of *mizuko kuyō*.

Ancestor Religion, Yasukuni Shrine, and the Cult of the War Dead

By looking at the cult of the war dead in modern Japan one sees clear evidence of how a climate of fear in a society can be manipulated by political ideology and ultraconservative forces. Because some elements of *mizuko kuyō* have been influenced by this same climate, it is important to assess how the culture's view of ancestors has been linked to a nationalistic ideology, a reactionary definition of social order, a religiously controlled legitimization of power, and an uncritical loyalty to national goals. With rapid social changes threatening Japan's sense of identity from the 1890s to 1945, the appeal to reactionary ideology was frequently resorted to, even cultivated.[28] This included emphasis upon the family–state ideology, with its visions of an overarching collective family construed as Japan.

Religious institutions have thus been used to honor the war dead as a means of celebrating the spiritual dimensions of political power. There has also been promotion by political forces to graft the family tradition of ancestor worship into a national family and to utilize a major Shinto shrine for maintaining a cult of the war dead. As Franziska Seraphim shows in *War Memory and Social Politics in Japan, 1945–2005*, one needs to locate this tendency within a complex cluster of interest groups, in which nationalist right-wing interest groups have been in contention with other groups along the political spectrum with regard to specific issues.[29]

> The social politics of war memory remained tied to issues of bureaucratic control of school curricula and textbook approval, attempts to revive official celebrations of the war dead at Yasukuni Shrine, the public use of the national flag and anthem, and the restoration of wartime public holidays. Yet these controversies also revealed the shifting parameters of the memory debate...[as] the landscape of contentious political activism changed significantly [over these five decades].[30]

These nationalistic tendencies occurred not just in prewar Japan but also throughout the twentieth century in the cult of honoring the war dead who, having suffered violent deaths, could harm the living unless they were properly cared for. Not to honor these ancestors of the nation was thought to incur their fury. With celebration of their honor come protection and blessing. Their enshrinement throughout the land serves to transmute the horrors of war into the glories of peace. This message was transparent— no sacrifice was too great to pay for ensuring this destiny. Those who died in warfare had made the supreme sacrifice; they had given themselves for their emperor and their country. While veneration of the war dead is not unique to Japan, its support there has kept alive the ancient conviction that by honoring the dead for their sacrifice to the nation one activates the ancestral presence as protective *kami*. Protection against harm and benefit for the living are complementary sides of the same belief.

The most famous institutional example promoting this theme remains Yasukuni Jinja, a Shinto shrine transferred from Kyoto to Tokyo in the early Meiji period. Commandeered as the principal shrine to honor the spirits of those who had lost their lives fighting for Japan, beginning in the mid-1890s Yasukuni became the pivotal point in a network of shrines throughout Japan. This shrine's basic role began with and continues to ensure the pacification of the souls of the war dead. When not memorialized, these spirits become vengeful gods (*onryōgami*) or wandering, homeless spirits of the dead (*muenbotoke*).[31] In the early twentieth century, with the engendering of patriotism in the Russo-Japanese War of 1904–5, there was an activating of Yasukuni as a national shrine, with its network of prefectural branches helping to underscore the public's sense of national identity and the state's need for unquestioning unity.[32] Shrines dedicated to the war dead from this conflict and from Japan's military exploits in East Asia between 1931 and 1945 were prominent in glorifying warfare, especially through honoring its dead heroes. Indeed, the highest honor for any member of the imperial armed forces killed in battle was to be enshrined at Yasukuni.

Following Japan's defeat in 1945 and with the new constitution that altered the status of the emperor and created a legal separation of religion and the state, Yasukuni could no longer be legally supported by public funds. With the constitutionally guaranteed freedom of religion and the disestablishment of State Shinto came the emergence of a legally recognized and protected religious pluralism. While these factors created unprecedented forms of countervailing power within Japanese society, right-wing forces persistently seek to reestablish connections between Shinto religion and elements in the government. Through legal measures in the national Diet and in local constituencies as well as through covert action, ultranationalistic forces have promoted ties between the state and the shrine, despite strong resistance from other elements in society.[33] At issue has been the continued use of Yasukuni especially to appease the spirits of the dead.

In this state-erected creation of *ancestor religion* one finds an uneasy tension between ancestor and descendant. It can be argued that the same social climate that kept alive the fear of angry ancestors has given rise to a similar anxiety that the spirits of unplacated *mizuko* will return in one form of curse (*tatari*) or another. While clearly distinguishable, these two instances of anxiety about dead spirits derive from a common social matrix. In Chapter 2 we saw how the earliest foreshadowing of *mizuko* may have begun soon after World War II with concern over the large number of dead babies born to the wives and mistresses of Japanese soldiers in Manchuria and Korea during the years 1931–45. In a real sense, these were war babies, and in this fact one has an ironic interweaving of these two phenomena.

We turn now to a specific example of how the power of ideological stances represented by Yasukuni Shrine affects the lives of individuals who oppose its implications. In this example one sees a graphic instance of how conservative politics, using religious means and tapping into the widespread fear of unrequited spirits, is able to ride roughshod repeatedly over the legal rights of common citizens. It also shows how ordinary individuals can be successful in garnering public support even while losing their case in court and how women in particular are able to claim agency for their own lives when they become resolved to do so and when they are supported by others. As in the chapter as a whole, we see different perceptions of the ancestral relationship and how there can be social policy implications to many of these perceptions.

An "Ordinary Woman" versus the Practice of Enshrining the War Dead

Starting with the Meiji period, Norma Field provides evidence in her book *In the Realm of a Dying Emperor* of the roots underlying contemporary forms of nationalism, which she labels as "atavism."[34] She discusses the case of a Japanese woman, Nakaya Yasuko, who spent fifteen years resisting the attempts of nationalistic forces to impose the status of a divine spirit upon her deceased husband. This woman brought suit against the Yamaguchi Prefectural Branch of the Self-Defense Forces (SDF) and the Veterans' Association for violating constitutional provisions for separation of religion and the state and for infringing on her own religious rights as a Christian. At issue was the enshrining of the spirit of her husband as a *kami* by the prefectural Defense-of-the-Nation Shrine following his death in a traffic accident while on duty in 1968 with the SDF.

Though her case had been upheld by two lower courts, it was overturned by the Japanese Supreme Court on June 1, 1988 in a historic 14–1 verdict. For an *ordinary woman* to take on the powers of local and national authority was unheard of in Japan. Her persistence led to a large number of supporters, but it also evoked "a barrage of threats and vituperation" from others. To some, she symbolized the importance of standing up for rights guaranteed in the constitution, and she represented the burden and very existence of minorities in Japan. To her detractors, she stood in the way of forces advocating public support for Yasukuni Shrine and the other Defense-of-the-Nation Shrines. While her legal brief was in defense of religious rights guaranteed in Article 20 of the constitution, the battle had a larger scope:

The significance of the suit brought by Mrs. Nakaya Yasuko lies beyond, the merely legal: the case reflects the incommensurateness of judicial capability and judicial will with the challenges she issued to Japanese militarism, to the Japanese treatment of religious minorities, and to the situation of women in Japanese society.[35]

This case is another instance of how the forces of ideology and state power employ age-old beliefs in potentially angry ancestral spirits. It also displays how those who resist these forces are challenging a whole way of life. While the legal structure changed radically sixty years ago, it still retains its grip, not just in governmental circles but also on large segments of the population. Few would have guessed that an ordinary Japanese woman might have engaged in a sustained fashion such forces and against such odds. Nevertheless, it signals the presence of a cynical attitude toward women and their status on the part of many who exercise power and authority at local and national levels. For our purposes, it reveals continuing reinterpretations that surround the concept of ancestor.

To some, ancestors are potential benefactors, but when not properly attended to they are disturbers of the peace. To others, who take the ancestral connection a step further, the noblest of ancestors are those who lay down their lives for the country and, unless otherwise stated, are uncritical supporters of state policy. As Prime Minister Nakasone, the most prominent recent supporter of Yasukuni Shrine, declared in 1985: "It is fitting that the people express their gratitude to the nation's martyrs, else who would offer his life for his country?"[36] As a subtle political concept, it can be used to whip those who challenge entrenched mores. In this sense Nakaya Yasuko heard her critics call out: "Have you no feeling for those of us who lost husbands, brothers, and sons, whose only consolation lies in the knowledge that they will be honored in perpetuity by the nation?"[37] As if she had not also lost her husband.

In her willingness to persist against reproaches this ordinary person is an unlikely hero. Her life reveals the extent to which Japanese women have been subordinated to age-old patterns of male domination, though women as well may become complicit in and reinforce these same patterns. The fact that most women refused to confront their own constraints made Nakaya as "wary of matriarchy as of patriarchy." Associating her own "childhood privations with state intrusion into her widowhood," she saw how the state appropriates self-legitimating political and religious forms. Even more disturbing to her was how the state's ideology of compliance was accepted by her relatives and in-laws and by coworkers and strangers who are "baffled or even angered by an ordinary Japanese widow objecting to what are evidently commonsensical Japanese propositions."[38] The case of Nakaya Yasuko reveals the Yasukuni Shrine controversy in graphic terms. We move now to a concerted critique by Japanese feminists of the ancestral system as it was constructed in mid-Meiji Japan and expressed as a central part of the *ie* or stem-family system.

Feminist Critique of the Ancestral System and Its Legacy

In times of rapid social change it is not unusual for people to revert psychologically to an era and its values when life seemed simple, less threatening, more secure. This form of nostalgia, this yearning for *traditional* Japanese society, is linked to reverence for ancestors and is what feminists view as rationalization for the continued subordinating of women. Having discussed aspects of this ideology in Chapter 5, we examine here features of the *ie* system that retain their impact in contemporary Japan, relating this to an idealized ancestral system and to the perception by many feminists that *mizuko kuyō* is a reinforcement of that ideology.

From the outset of the Tokugawa period (1603–1867) there has been an ongoing discourse about women's roles, not only what they should and should not do but also what roles they have in fact played. During the Meiji era (1868–1912), a young woman was often regarded as having an inferior position in the *ie* or family system. Recent scholarship, however, reveals that in preindustrial times men could be involved in both housework and child rearing and that women as well as men did heavy labor in the fields.[39] By the mid-Meiji period, however, the dichotomizing of life into private and public spheres was a development that occurred in many segments of society. With this came a subordination of women in legislative form, in patterns of household responsibility, and in definitive statements about a woman's primary role as good wife and wise mother (*ryōsai kenbo*). In reaction to this ideological development, feminist critique has been most pointed.

Of special interest here are some aspects of the relationship of women to the ancestral system. Ancestor religion may be seen as an emotive force not only for each family's sense of lineage but for the Meiji concept of the nation-state. Devotion to ancestors deepened loyalty to the emperor and to the religious and social system that he represented. Cementing this system was loyalty, obedience, and gratitude to those previously mentioned. "The love and respect towards the (family) ancestors is the central concept that unites the family."[40] Defined by their roles as mothers, women often experienced contrasting loyalties to her family and to the imperial system.[41] Part of the Japanese feminist agenda during the past forty years has been to challenge this social and cultural definition of women and their roles in society. The ideology that defined the Japanese *ie* family system was symbolically embedded in the practice of ancestor worship. It is this family system, which in many respects continues to exist, that contemporary feminists have been seeking to deconstruct.[42]

While the 1948 Constitution extended the political, legal, and economic rights of women in Japan, including the discontinuance of the *ie* as the defining factor of Japanese households, many of the values identified with the *ie* system retained their impact. Examples include the importance of producing a male heir, of taking ritualistic care of her husband's ancestors (not to mention his parents in their elderly years), and of regarding her own children as *atotsugi* (heirs in the same lineage). Examined here are four ways the position of women in Japanese society has been constrained by the ancestral system, how each of them has been the object of ongoing critique by Japanese feminists, and, even more importantly, how changes are gradually occurring in each.

First, reverence for ancestors, when seen as the glue that holds families together, may still be viewed as binding women into a patriarchal structure from which there is no normal escape. While women may exercise their own forms of influence and power, they are still commonly seen as having a patrilineally conceived religious identity in which they share a household with their husband's parents who become their own future ancestors. In cases where the wife's parents have moved in with the family rather than the husband's, however, the situation can be considerably modified. As she is the principal caregiver in the home and as she is the one who maintains and prays before the family *butsudan*, perpetuating the family's spiritual contact with its forebears, her ancestral line may now include both sides of the family.

Second, feminists have claimed that, because ancestor system has been grounded in the *ie* system, a woman lost her original identity. One sees this manifested clearly itself in the family register (*koseki*) in which the woman's name was removed from her own family register and entered into her husband's. Assuming her husband's surname, his ancestors became hers, she left her own family, and for all practical purposes she received a new identity in the family of her husband. On the other hand, with changes in family law in the late 1980s her legal identity no longer need be severed from that of her original family. Because her primary family ties may still remain linked to those of her husband, it has become more common for her contacts with her parental family to be no less vital than those with her husband's. Obviously, this depends on propinquity of residence and a variety of personal factors.

We saw a fictionalized example of this in *The Yamaguchi Story* where the loneliness of a wife whose husband's work was his preoccupation and where her contacts with her original family were distant and less available. In such a situation a woman is between identities, with no meaningful family ties. This particular wife comes into her own only as she finds personal meaning through one of the new religions. Paradoxically, the husband in this story also comes to find a deeper significance to his life, beyond that of devotion to his company, in this same religious community and thus in his household family as well.

Third, among the most painful experiences of a wife can be her relationship with her husband's mother. Despite the many exceptions to this the basic perception may still endure. Again, with changing circumstances brought about by greater affluence, increasing nuclear family households, more educational opportunities for women and extended work options, a younger wife's environment and her self-identity depends much less today on her relationship with her husband's mother. Yet, psychologically, old patterns of loyalty often persist, causing family strain. The previous chapter discusses how *Haruko's World*, where the husband's mother placed expectations on Haruko, provides an example of the resentment that may follow. As this occurs, women feel marginalized and are often left to deal with these feelings on their own.

Fourth, the identity that a woman acquires upon marriage is nowhere more powerfully symbolized than in the ancestral grave. In almost all cases she continues to share this with her husband and his ancestors. Side by side in life, they lie juxtaposed in death. As other aspects of ancestral connections are in flux, so is this custom acquiring new forms. For their own good reasons some wives prefer to have separate graves. For instance, when a couple is divorced or when the relationship has been a destructive one, she may decide, after her husband's death, not to share the same grave site with him and his family.[43] While this is becoming more common, it is far from being the standard choice.

Assessing the survival of *ie* ideology from a fresh perspective, Kathleen Uno indicates how recent studies have shifted from concentrating on patrilineality and primogeniture to an increased emphasis on coresidence, continuity, and economic and ritual functions.[44] In the process, she provides the feminist critique with a significantly different perspective and opens up a new space in which to assess the social and cultural contexts in which *mizuko kuyō* takes place. Uno has found evidence that "early modern merchants and peasants regarded marriage as a partner-ship (in work more than in leisure); that women headed households; that women earned income, managed businesses, and headed enterprises; that women inherited property; that women represented the household to outsiders; and that women held public office."[45] In other words, the house-wife in pre-Meiji times often possessed considerable authority within the *ie* household.

This sort of evidence is a major challenge to stereotypes about Japanese women as traditionally and naturally passive. Furthermore, it has impli-cations for the meaning of agency, both before and after the Meiji period in which the roles of women became tightly defined. It also questions the perceived existence of patrilineality as an ongoing pattern in Japanese society since the seventeenth century, and even its existence prior to the early modern period. Just as important, it highlights the character of the *ie* system as a time-bound, evolving, socially and culturally constructed insti-tution. Viewing the ancestral legacy of the *ie* system in other than static terms prompts questions about what gave shape to the *ie* as it evolved in early modern and modern Japanese society.

Uno's approach widened the scope by which one conceptualizes the *ie* system and its counterpart ideology about the reverencing of ancestors. Central to her point is the importance of exploring in detail "the early modern regulations, values, and behavioral patterns concerning gender, households, and larger associations" that made their impact on the emerg-ing features of the *ie*, not only as a system but also as a surviving ide-ological reality.[46] In many respects her analysis is a challenge to earlier critiques by some feminists. The way this system has affected attitudes toward the dead, especially one's own ancestors, has been central to our focus in this section.

Ritual Care for Ancestors: Feeding the Economics of Temples

Among the indictments of *mizuko kuyō* practice is its reputed commercial-ism. However valid this criticism may be, little attention has been given to whether this practice is important to the economic viability of Japanese Buddhist temples. Helen Hardacre's assessment is an apt place to start. "*Mizuko kuyō*'s economic contribution to such temples is usually far over-shadowed by funerals and ancestral memorial rites. When [the practice of *mizuko kuyō*] assumes a larger role, it is generally because the temple is unable, for some reason, to sustain itself by traditional means."[47] It is well-known that the average temple in the modern period faces economic hardship for many reasons. Assessing this situation requires examining the economics of temples within a broader historical and institutional framework. In the process, one sees how deeply ritual care for ancestors feeds the economics of temples. The most important context with which to start is the Tokugawa or Edo period (1603–1867) during which the *danka* system (*danka seido*) came into being and to which Buddhist temples were linked and on which they became dependent for financial survival.

Briefly put, this system has been described as the "enduring relationship between a Buddhist temple and its funerary patron household, cemented from generation to generation through recurring rites and services related to death and ancestral veneration."[48] Among the driving concerns of the Tokugawa shogunate was to secure and maintain stability throughout the social and political order.[49] Prominent among the government's original motivations for instituting such controls were its apprehensions about the perceived threat of Christianity with its primary loyalty to a power above and beyond the political.[50] Determined both to control and reinforce the influence of the temples specifically, the central government (*bakufu*) established "strict edicts mandating parish temple membership for every Japanese."[51]

Besides their function as ritual centers in the Edo period, temples played other roles. "They were local market centers, pilgrimage sites, festival sites, pharmacies, and schools."[52] Temples were woven into most aspects of ordinary life. Before Japan became increasingly urbanized in the nineteenth century most temples were located in rural areas; agriculture was central to everyday life; and income from temple lands was important to a temple's financial survival. Because people tended to live in the same village generation after generation and to be part of the same temple, there were ongoing threads of continuity between the living and the dead. The dead became ancestors, and their remains were located in the temple's graveyard. Because "the temple's role in ritual care for the ancestors helped to ensure the continuation of the *danka* membership system,"[53] there was a natural fit between the overall value of the temple to its members and the degree to which they were willing to help meet its expenses.[54]

The economic and organizational implications of the Tokugawa system served not only to extend governmental supervision into local areas but to empower temples in the major Buddhist sects in their function as *ritual centers*. Central to how parishioners related to the temple was the fact that affiliation was based on household (*ie*), not on individual membership. Intrinsic to this relationship was the obligation upon parishioners to support the temple's maintenance and its priest financially, satisfying its need for a more stable economic condition.[55] This mandate required parishioners to participate regularly in the temple's ritualistic life. The income generated from ongoing services for the dead became the lifeblood for Buddhist temples throughout the long Tokugawa period. This was especially the case while Japan remained essentially a rural society, when household ties to particular temples were the common experience. As the household was the unit of religious affiliation, there was the stipulation that successive generations of this unit were obligated to safeguard the household's link with the wellbeing of the dead, thereby guaranteeing continuing economic support of the temple. Continued ritual observances of one sort or another were deemed mandatory. While the income varied considerably from temple to temple and from household to household, there was, in a general sense, guaranteed support from these sources, whether in *danna* fees, offerings, or as a result of special fundraising campaigns (*kanjin*).[56]

Because famines occurred with some frequency during these times and because of burdensome taxes, temples had to compete with other needs. As a way of ensuring fulfillment of religious observances, temples devised a widely recognized pattern of social and religious penalties for failure to meet these obligations as well as reminders of the benefits of conforming to them. Intrinsic to the "spiritual penalties" of not conforming were warnings about angry ghosts that would return to haunt the living who fail to honor the spirits of the dead.[57] The other side of such warnings is that angry spirits can be appeased. The goal of funerary rites was "to help the dead spirit settle down and become purified" and to be transformed "into the body of the Buddha," even if the deceased currently dwells in a hungry ghost.[58] The results of bad karma were believed to issue in recurring illnesses, disabilities, and poverty that stem from not fulfilling one's religious responsibilities. Beyond the panoply of spiritual consequences there were adverse social effects of failing to fulfill their obligation to a temple.[59]

This system of economic support for temples reveals how the *danka* system defined the role of temples in relationship to the dead through "funerary rituals oriented toward the afterlife (*raise kuyō*)" and to the living through "practices that provided practical benefits in the present world (*genze riyaku*)."[60] The efficacy of rituals and other practices was underscored in the quest for protection in times of hardship and disaster as well as for benefits such as family harmony, wealth, good weather for crops, and safe travel. Of singular importance, as in Buddhism through the centuries, were concerns for healing and the alleviation of suffering. These rituals and their related beliefs were viewed as both accompanying the dead into the afterlife and protecting the living, curing illnesses, providing easy childbirth, and a host of other benefits. There is no doubt that this complementary approach to the living as well as to the dead had economic benefits for the temple in its interactions with the community.

By the late eighteenth century, however, the center of gravity in Japanese society was beginning to shift from village life, with all that this represented, to an urban existence in which the basic multigenerational nature of the family evolved into one that eventually became more nuclear in structure, with emphasis less upon the household at large and more upon the individuals in it. The move of families from village-situated family temples, to which households had been connected for generations, to the city amounted to a radical separation from a living past. Because of these extended associations over decades the funeral and the ongoing memorializing of their ancestors had been a central ingredient of a larger, more embracing, more intimate connection between the temple and its *danka*. Urbanization was to change much of this. Gradually disappearing in rural Japan were the earlier associations through which temples served their parishioners over the lifetimes of their members.

As large numbers of people moved into the cities, away from their family temples, these temples naturally experienced diminishing numbers of *danka* and therefore sources of financial support, a dilemma that only grew with time. The single most important variable was the correlation between how closely the *danka* felt to their local temple in generations past and how much these temples could therefore rely upon local support. While rituals were not the only variable, it is evident that these temples and their rituals were central to the life of their parishioners. It was clear that the extensive period of financial dependency under the *danka* system had left the average temple with an insufficient economic base. In Mark Rowe's words, Japanese Buddhist temples that are "entirely dependent on the traditional *danka* system are in serious trouble."[61] In his book *Japanese Temple Buddhism,* Stephen Covell analyzes the reasons for the final collapsing of the *danka* membership system, the resulting impact on the economics of temples, and the challenge to temples to reestablish their sense of purpose in a fundamentally different Japanese society than had existed in the Edo period.[62]

Compared with life in a small village, the likelihood of finding a spiritual home for those who relocated to a large metropolitan area proved far from easy. For one thing, the more open-ended social and cultural environment of city life promoted a diversity of secularized lifestyles. On the other hand, large numbers of people, cut adrift from familiar circumstances, were drawn to newer, lay-oriented forms of religion that place strong emphasis on one's daily life and that provide more dynamic experiences of community. In contrast, the temple-based, historic forms of Buddhism that had dominated the scene during the Edo period have suffered significant diminishment. Having been identified for so long with the rituals of death, these kinds of temples were less successful in becoming a vital force in the urban-based lives of their membership and thus remained in financial difficulty.[63] There are, of course, exceptions: temples possessing significant art treasures ("cultural assets") that are exhibited periodically or temples that are part of historic pilgrimages or are associated with major Buddhist figures. Also, there are temples around the country that, because of the natural beauty of their location, are able to capitalize on their appeal to large numbers of people, especially at certain seasons of the year

From these attractions there can be considerable income. The average temple has no such drawing power and thus derives little revenue from the general public. However successful a temple may be in attracting visitors, the main point is otherwise. It is to ask the question: For what fundamental purpose does a temple exist? There is perhaps no factor about Buddhist temples in the contemporary scene that is more revealing than the apparent confusion about their identity and their role in a society whose needs and values have changed fundamentally. What remains is the image of a "temple as a place only for postmortem practices."[64] While temples may serve a vital function of relating the living to the long line of their precursors, it is ironic that in contemporary Japan temple priests are less successfully relating the meaning of death (that is, one's mortality) to the meaning of life, particularly in a secularized and deracinated culture.

Only if temples are able to discover newly conceived roles, a deeper sense of purpose, will they attract followers who would value and thus support their services. The obstacles to this metamorphosis are considerable. "The sects of Temple Buddhism today are trapped between financial necessities, traditional postmortem rituals roles, and their desire to be seen as sincere Buddhist practitioners. Breaking free from this dilemma represents one of their greatest hurdles as they enter the next century."[65] According to Covell, the average source of temple income derived from funerals and memorial services, compared with other sources, was 72 percent in 2003. For many temples and other religious communities the plight of reduced income has contributed to the search for alternative sources of revenue, of which *mizuko kuyō* is one prominent example. A specific instance of this in a Jōdoshū temple in Kyoto is described in the appendices.

For these several reasons, one comes to understand the economic role that *mizuko kuyō* plays in the survival of many temples. At the same time, one can see the logic of linking *mizuko* to the ancestral tradition, even if that link has no historic connection. It may be even more the case that the transformation of a temple's role in the contemporary world will depend on an unprecedented reassessment of its basic purpose. On the other hand, if the role of *mizuko kuyō* can be other than having an economic value, it may be free to serve part of a larger purpose in helping men and women to experience whatever grief they may feel in losing a child or a fetus through stillbirth, miscarriage, or induced abortion. The issue involved is essentially one of grieving loss in some fundamental way, in a manner that cannot be reduced to some economic value.

One comes, therefore, to see the practice of providing *mizuko kuyō* along a wide continuum from commercialization and the promotion of guilt feelings (these are not necessarily combined) to a reluctance, if not a refusal, on the part of priests to offer these services at all. In other words, it is part of a larger, evolving religious and cultural context. In between lies a varied middle ground in which temples offer this service but do not accentuate or even advertise the fact. In numerous remunerative ways religious institutions combine the tension or paradox between "folk religion" and "established belief." Quoting Shinno Toshikazu again on this dialectic: Here we see the double-layered structure of these religious organizations. They have some sort of affiliation with "established" religious organizations, but they also have a side to them that deviates from the boundaries of traditional teachings and doctrines of the established organizations. In fact, it is precisely this aspect that tends to attract followers.[66]

Care of Ancestors and the Tension between Two Belief Systems

This *dialectic* raises questions about how religious traditions, let alone individual priests, reconcile the seemingly contradictory forms this confluence may take. Among the more provocative statements is one by the Jōdo Shinshū scholar Sasaki Shōten who has challenged his own tradition's stance that folk beliefs should be rejected and that these beliefs do not even merit discussion.[67] Sasaki refers to Satoru Kaneko's research over a ten-year period that reveals the wide gap in "faith structure" between temple priests and the laity they serve.[68] Kaneko identifies the beliefs of lay Shinshū people as a form of "this-worldly-benefit-oriented folk religiosity" combined with social "conservatism, blind faith in authority, and social (especially political) indifferentism."[69] Those interviewed by this research team were middle-aged and older women who had come to the Ishikiri Shrine in the Ikoma region east of Osaka in search of help with one problem or another. As a shrine located within a larger area of shrines and temples, Ishikiri is dedicated to the healing of bodily illnesses through intercession to kami, buddhas, bodhisattvas, and other supernatural beings.

This study sought to clarify the differences between two belief systems—"folk" or "popular" religion and mainstream Shinshū doctrine and practice. The findings indicate, however, that the same person may in different circumstances and for different reasons be embracing contradictory values and worldviews. While Jōdo Shinshū accents the grace of Amida Buddha, with the appropriate human response being one of gratitude for salvation already assured, folk religion seeks to remedy specific existing problems and to safeguard against future ones. Theoretically, Shinshū is free of utilitarian designs, while folk religion stimulates the seeking of such benefits.

> Jodo Shinshu believers engage in self-disciplined religious behaviors such as sutra-chanting, reading sacred texts and sutras, worship and missionary work, rather than in utilitarian practices such as consulting an oracle, visiting a fortune teller, wearing charms, praying for success in business (or for success on an examination or for the easy birth of a child. By contrast, the Ishikiri Shrine worshippers are very earnest in benefit-oriented prayer behaviors...[They] are decidedly oriented toward this-worldly benefits.[70]

Specifically, folk religion responds to and may even kindle anxiety about the curse of departed spirits who have not been properly memorialized. These studies of lay believers indicate that they have "a [strong] sense of gratitude and yearning toward their ancestors...[that they] may have been influenced by the folk religion of ancestor worship and that they have a consciousness of living together with the dead or a belief that communication with the dead is possible."[71] In these ways the two types of religious belief and practice overlap, but in terms of official Shinshū doctrine they are in radical contradiction.

Disturbed that these findings were being ignored by the leaders within Shinshū Buddhism, Sasaki Shōten called for a "grassroots theology" that would close the gap between priests in the field and theologians in their discourses, since there is little or no theological reflection on "what actually happens in the field."[72] Believing that such a field-oriented approach is not alien to the spirit of Shinran, founder of the Shinshū sect, Sasaki proposes a form of theological reflection that takes seriously folk practices, ritual, and religious community in contrast to the individualistic theology presently dominant in Shinshū. Intrinsic to this more community-centered theological approach would be an effort to understand what lies behind beliefs and practices that are dismissed as part of an "animist-shamanist complex," with its deep consciousness of "living together with the dead" and its fear of angry spirits (of ancestors and *mizuko*). To study such phenomena is not to endorse what they promote; it is to discover what they signify. Understanding of this kind, he asserts, is essential if one is to minister effectively to lay members.

Sasaki argues for the necessity of relating religious doctrine to folk practices and beliefs. Why do laypeople resort to these practices? And how does this situation become a proper topic for Shinshū theology to study? Theological discourse lacking contact with those in the field has little influence if it merely proclaims that curses do not exist. One needs to inquire as to why spirit belief flourishes in a modern urban society such as Japan. In the absence of a theology of folk belief that takes into account the deep connection Shinshū believers often feel with their ancestors, a vacuum is created. It is no surprise that these same believers seek solace and help from one of the new religions, for example, Mahikari or Reiyūkai. Sasaki argues that because Shinshū lacks a "doctrine for emergencies" it has no convincing theodicy, no way of helping people interpret tragic events in their lives. Nor does it have a theology of ancestor veneration that promotes respect for one's predecessors without believing that they have the power to curse the living. Nor does it exercise a theology of *genze riyaku* that both recognizes the importance of worldly concerns and at the same time helps people to encounter these concerns with less attachment.

Central among the implications of Sasaki's position is the importance of providing a broader education for priests, including the need to take into account research that is available through the social sciences. Otherwise, he argues, the sect cannot take seriously the actual circumstances in which people exist. While social concerns, especially in the new religions, are expressed in a variety of ways (for peace, environmental issues, and harmony in family life), there is little analysis by Buddhists that contributes to a deeper understanding of social problems. As Sasaki puts it, Buddhist priests are not trained to relate Buddhist teachings to complex social and political contexts. As long as this remains the case, there is little perceived relationship between Buddhist teachings and the life that most people live.

Who Is the Mizuko? Seeds of Disharmony Discovered and Healed

As we have indicated, another approach to understanding angry spirits is through awareness of how often society casts off those who live outside its norms. Those existing in conditions of nonrelationship (*muen*) threaten because they signify what has been excluded. They are the surds who are a challenge, who make no sense to the dominant culture, who are voiceless until they threaten the frameworks of the ordinary. In viewing the world of Ōe Kenzaburō, who writes frequently of the condition he calls *shūen* or margin, one is presented with persons or groups on the fringes of society, whose presence are haunting reminders of what refuses to go away. While it would be facile to equate *muenbotoke* with *mizuko*, there is in each the potential experiencing of brokenness. As it is ironic for a child to die before its parents, becoming thus their ancestor, their *senzo*, the same is true when whole categories of people who have been rejected refuse to go away and remain to disturb one's equanimity. In both there is the disordering of what had been expected. While Ōe's novel *A Personal Matter* is a classic expression of this reality, we present here adumbrations of the same by discussing Gedatsu-kai, a religious movement whose sense of ancestral connection has been stretched to include the full spectrum of the human world.

Gedatsu-kai: Returning to the Center

Gedatsu-kai is of interest to this study because of its concern for the spirits of dead children, including those of aborted fetuses, together with its strong focus on ancestors. Of even greater interest is the universality of its ancestral world. Founded in 1929, Gedatsu-kai, with roots in both the Shinto and Buddhist traditions, began as a movement strongly supportive of Japan's nationalistic efforts, but in recent decades it has moved toward the political center. As with most new religions in Japan today, its fundamental concerns are with the causes of disharmony within human society, the consequences of this disequilibrium, and the means by which this condition can be transformed into a potential for greater harmony. This particular movement's ritualistic enactment of harmonic power existing alongside the worlds of struggle, illness, and hatred affords one an extended view of ancestral lineage.[73]

In its version of *kuyō* Gedatsu-kai includes the spirits of aborted fetuses as belonging to the full network of human relationships.[74] This inclusion of a fetus as part of the family unit would seem to support Herman Ooms's theory that the contemporary process of greater social inclusiveness serves to redefine what it means to be human and, ironically, an ancestor these days. Gedatsu-kai's expanded sense of inclusiveness, ritualistically speaking, may be seen in its extraordinary range of those for whom memorial masses are conducted. The cosmology or religious universe evolving in Gedatsu-kai specifies two worlds interacting in continuously changing conditions of balance and imbalance, harmony and disharmony. Half of this universe is empowered by the beneficence of *kami*, buddhas, ancestors, and the movement's founder Okano Eizō (Seiken).[75] These evidences of spiritual power make them the central objects of worship. The universe's other half is the human world, with dilemmas and problems that require continual resolving. A key sign of cleavage in all the new religions is illness, whether physical or psychological. Healing is fundamentally a healing of the heart. Because an ungrateful, hate-filled heart has social consequences, restored harmony in a person's life is a combination of gratitude and the repayment of kindness. From a psychological and spiritual perspective the rituals of Gedatsu-kai manifest the community's efforts to combine approaches to personal healing with a larger vision of social health.

The principal rituals in this dialectic are the meditation rite (*gohō shugyō*), as a means of identifying and unlocking the reasons for one's turmoil, and the memorial rite (*amacha*) that pacifies the spirits of the ancestors and purifies the hearts of participants. Together with performing apologies and taking part in services to purify the inner spirit Gedatsu-kai observes monthly meetings for voicing gratitude for blessings received. This service of purification (*okiyome*) can be carried out anywhere. Its purpose is to express penitence for wrongdoings, to remove ill feelings, to conduct self-reflection, and to attain deep cleansing.[76] These acts of reflection identify the seeds of disharmony that exist in all persons and communities, including ancestors who also must be freed from their inner turmoil.

The transformative ritual in Gedatsu-kai is the memorial mass (*amacha kuyō*). Members are urged to perform this twice daily at home, in the morning and evening.[77] In performing this mass, members meditate on the names of the particular spirits they are memorializing. Theoretically, no one is excluded. The memorial mass is for all spirits and all souls. Interdependence with spirits of the dead is seen as a reality. In one form or another these spirits compose the body of our ancestral lineage. The challenge in identifying those for whom one should pray lies in discovering one's karmic tie with specific spirits, particularly those with whom the relationship has been injurious, unsatisfactory, or neglectful. In other words, while the memorial mass covers a vast sweep of existence it is at the same time pinpointed.

The guidelines for this dual focus are not intended to be exhaustive or prescriptive; they vary with need and circumstance. Different groups of memorial mass tablets are identified, each with its own subgroups. The *basic* tablets are subdivided into several categories: a general tablet for one's own family ancestors; family members who have become wandering spirits (*muenbotoke*) separated from the regular familial line; children lost in stillbirth or miscarriage as well as through abortion; family ancestors who have become disconnected for particular reasons (financial greed, sexual desire, sustained animosity); and those who have died unnatural deaths. The final categories are the "seeds" of plants, animals, and human beings (including eggs and sperm) that did not result in life, together with animals that were sacrificed for human existence, including laboratory experiments. The fact that all of these would be incorporated as "family ancestors," in various degrees of closeness, would seem to be unique in any ancestral lineage in Japan or elsewhere.[78]

While some of these categories may strike one as bizarre or at least speculative, their overall purpose is to extend the vista of one's universe.[79] Through personal counseling the list is tailored to each person's specific relationships, past and present. The act of reciting the mass is intended to be reflective and meditative, not magical or mechanical. This act is best done in the community of one's family, though it may be done alone. Part of Gedatsu-kai's success lies in combining formal and informal ways of communicating and strengthening its values. At the year's end all tablets for the memorialized dead are burned in a ceremony for all souls (*manbū kuyō*). This annual ceremony is to liberate (*gedatsu*) those spirits known and unknown from suffering and to transform them into protective spirits (*shugorei*) who can then benefit the living. The intent of the entire process is to enable its members to return to the center of their tradition and to its own potential for genuine harmony.

Because of extensive problems within contemporary Japanese family life, Gedatsu-kai's sense of a wider family has had its appeal; it ties individuals to a larger sense of interconnection. Its cosmology and complementary forms of ritual enact a vision that stretches the imagination and becomes an exuberant cataloguing of multifarious spirits, all of which require commemorating. Evolving from earlier emphases upon a narrow national loyalty, Gedatsu-kai encourages each family to link its own ancestral line to a more inclusive vision of human identity and at the same time tries to locate the sources of personal and social disharmony upon an infinitely broad canvas.

Within the phenomenon of *mizuko kuyō* there exists a similar tension. While representing a lost child, a stillborn child, an unborn fetus, each of these has been included within the ancestral connection. This process is at once a signal of unmet personal needs and evidence of unaddressed social problems. If it stimulates feelings of guilt in the lives of some, in others it widens their concern for all forms of existence. Its ritualistic expressions generate forms by which women can discover the authenticity of their feelings and enable them to see more clearly the social and cultural dimensions of personal suffering. In other words, it provides them with insight into what has been excluded and with a voice that articulates a more vibrant form of both compassion and interdependence.

Memorializing the Dead Intensifies Caring for the Living

However narrowly or broadly *mizuko* may be construed, they are challenges to settled values. Not being conventional ancestors whose destiny is more easily settled and who thereby enhance our welfare, *mizuko* have no living heirs. Unless they are seen as part of human experience, as inevitable ingredients of life and death, society is inclined to reject them as intrusions, as "anomalies," outside its *nomos* or recognized order. Yet, paradoxically, these anomalies are what challenge society's notions of what is "normative." When a society allows itself to be challenged, its *nomoi* or accepted norms are stretched. As this occurs, a community's capacity to imagine new realities is enlarged. Whenever marginalized by society, these anomalies threaten a society's definition of its own identity and embody a challenge to its worldview.

In how they point toward an expanded universe, there would seem to be parallels between Gedatsu-kai's ritualistic enactment of equilibrium between the worlds of humans, ancestors, and spiritual beings and Stephen Teiser's depiction of the *yü-lan-p'en* rite as a means of sustaining structures of meaning that keep individual, society, and nature in harmony. There is also a potential sense of interconnection between the worlds of the living and the worlds of the dead in the phenomenon of *mizuko kuyō*. In discussing Gedatsu-kai, Byron Earhart makes the point that members of this group are specific in claiming "that the aborted fetus had entered the human realm, and in fact the neglect of such fetuses caused misfortune or illness for the very reason that the family had neglected part of its unit."[80] The larger point is how *mizuko*, living persons, and ancestors exist in an interdependent psychic, social, and historic relationship. Without this sense of a more inclusive universe the meaning of *mizuko* is misunderstood. In Earhart's words:

> It seems to me that a crucial clue to illness and healing in Japan is the maintaining of a proper balance between the living family and dead ancestors (and local spirits). Illness may occur when there is disharmony between the living and dead (for example, the mistake of thinking that miscarried or aborted fetuses, and stillborn infants, are *not* part of the ongoing family unit); healing takes place when the rift between the living and the dead is repaired (through repentance which corrects the person's mistake, and through rituals such as the amacha rite which simultaneously purify the living and the dead).[81]

Having discussed contemporary examples of inclusive rites for spirits of the dead, it is appropriate to return to Teiser's interpretation of the *yü-lan-p'en* festival in China, since this was the precedent for what became the *urabon* festival for the dead in Japan, beginning in 657, now known as Obon. The question arises of whether or not *mizuko* should be seen as anomalies within the present Japanese understanding of memorial services for the dead. In other words, are memorial services appropriate for those who have been born into this world and lived for a time, however short, but not appropriate for miscarried or aborted fetuses?

In his discussion about the function and scope of the Chinese festival for the dead, Teiser raises an analogous question. After citing objections made by both Buddhist and Confucian apologists as to whether

FIGURE 6.1 Different wishes or prayers for safe childbirth, written on *ema* (wooden plaques).

FIGURE 6.2 *Omamori* or protective amulets for unborn mizuko's health and happiness.

ancestors or wandering ghosts receive the offerings in the *yü-lan-p'en* ritual, Teiser terms this an unfruitful question, saying that in fact "the historical record clearly shows that [these] offerings were made to both ancestors and ghosts."[82] His thesis is that ritual "provides a context that encompasses several polarities, a broader scheme in which these polarities make sense...As *recipients* of offerings, ghosts and ancestors represent two sides of the same process, the process whereby society ritualizes the passage of its members from one group (the living) to another (the reborn). This process comprises an intermediary period during which the dead exist as ghosts and a postliminal period in which the dead have been incorporated into a social group as ancestors."[83]

This parallels what we have said before, namely, that ancestral rites deal with those whose condition is unsettled for many reasons, whose disconnected (*muen*) nature makes them threatening to the living, and with those who are among the as-yet-unsettled dead but whose destiny is to become protective ancestors. For the living, the question is always whether there has been an orderly transition of the deceased through the liminal condition to their new state, in which one's relationship with them again becomes reciprocal. In a religion such as Gedatsu-kai the encompassing process can be all-inclusive, although there is recognition that some spirits are more deeply connected, for good or ill, to our lives and thus call for special attention. Are there no limits to the interdependency (reciprocity) that exists in the universe?

Theoretically, this position is analogous to what the *yü-lan-p'en* festival and rite were all about. By placing emphasis upon the ritual context, where reciprocity between the living and the dead can be imagined and reimagined, Teiser asserts that we "gain a greater appreciation of the plural functions of the festival and the multivocality of the symbols upon which it draws. *Yü-lan-p'en* celebrations are carried out in the home, in the village, in the temple, and in the cosmos, serving to invigorate these overlapping structures and the cultural values that permeate them. In this view, ritual...is viewed as a dynamic way of creating and sustaining structures of meaning that keep individual, society, and nature in harmony."[84] In the process, ritual both unites and differentiates between the innumerable categories of spirits for whom memorial masses can be performed. This cultivated ability to connect and to differentiate has implications for how we treat the living as well as the dead. Again, keeping alive the memory of the dead serves to intensify one's care for the living (Figures 6.1 and 6.2).

7

Mothers, Society, and Pregnancy Loss

RETHINKING THE MEANING OF NURTURE

THIS CHAPTER APPROACHES the social and cultural constructions of motherhood in a different way, in particular how these constructions have impacted the experiences of women in pregnancy loss and the ways varieties of feminist critique over the past thirty years have addressed the interconnections among power, identity, and human sexuality. This perspective reexamines the residual fears of *tatari*, looks at how the discourse about and practice of *mizuko kuyō* have been debated by a group of pro-choice Japanese women, and comparatively discusses the relationship between abortion and the politics of motherhood in Japan and the United States. The chapter includes fresh insights about the socially driven forms of women's agency in a patriarchal society by Meredith Underwood; together with rethinking women's grieving by Hashimoto Yayoi, a clinical psychologist; and reflections about deeper forms of nurturing and bonding among women by Ueno Chizuko, a prominent feminist and sociologist.

Confronting the Threat of Tatari*: "A Process of Ongoing Negotiation"*

As mentioned in Chapter 1, it is Meredith Underwood's conviction that unless one confronts the threat of *tatari* directly it will remain a barrier to seeing the practice of *mizuko kuyō* as something more than manipulation. It is thus important to ask how the issue of *tatari* may paradoxically be a means of understanding the contemporary sexual culture of Japan. Underwood raises a number of questions that have not been addressed before.

> We must seriously consider the possibility that women have instituted by popular demand a ritual that meets their religious needs in

a context where their sexual and reproductive freedom is seriously constrained and, more generally, where their status and role have been not only traditionally circumscribed by patriarchy but recently undergoing tremendous challenge and change.[1]

For instance, what if *tatari* were to be viewed as *society's threat* of punishment against women who subvert their traditional roles as "good wife, wise mother" rather than as a threat by spirits from another world? In other words, how might fears of reprisal from the spiritual world be construed as parallel to or homologous with whatever retribution women may experience when they exercise forms of agency in the social world? In addition, can the need for "appeasement" of angry spirits be a masquerading of individuals and institutions that are angry whenever women subvert the customary forms of subordination? On the other hand, if *tatari* seems exploitive, how might it be viewed not just as reflecting female subservience in a society that remains highly patriarchal but also as a means of negotiating with the elements of patriarchal power? This latter point is similar to what was discussed in the case of Nakaya Yasuko whose defense of her own rights, in her brief against Yasukuni Jinja, evoked "a barrage of threats and vituperation" from others, including large numbers of women. Typically, those who counter society's norms pay a huge price.

The other side of discussions about angry spirits is the awareness of how often society casts off those who fail to fit its norms, what Ōe Kenzaburō has called *shūen*, those who are marginal.[2] When what has been invisible, however, begins to be seen and heard, it appears everywhere. One becomes aware of persons or groups on the fringes of society, whose presence are haunting reminders of what refuses to go away. Marginal existence is deliberately on center stage in Ōe's works. It is ironic when that which has been rejected remains fixed in the depths of societal consciousness. Freud's term "the return of the repressed" is apt.

It is Underwood's belief that while women may manifest their traditional gender roles through *mizuko kuyō*, they do so in a manner that extends rather than limits their expression of *agency*. Underwood's approach "suggests that women, intuitively perhaps, have deeply understood their social and religious vulnerability and moreover have created strategies to manage it...[It enables] one to accept *tatari* as a legitimate aspect of *mizuko kuyō* not only worthy of investigating but also one of the keys to understanding the *instrumental effectiveness* of this ritual."[3] Though vengeful spirits would seem to target a woman's life at points where she is most vulnerable, having just lost a child, it is through ritual engagement that she becomes more able to counter the forces in society that ignore or minimize the pain she may experience.[4]

For Underwood, the key to unlocking the power of this ritual is an act of repentance (*zange*), through apologizing to the spirit of the dead child, in which she asks for forgiveness. Underwood utilizes Helen Hardacre's view of the *instrumental effectiveness* of repentance and apology as among the "multiple paradoxes" in the role of women in her book on Reiyūkai Kyōdan:

> They devote considerable energy to building up the egos of people with normally higher status even as they manipulate and control them from behind the scenes. While seeming to be (and telling other women they should be) weak and passive, they become active and strong...[At] the same time they strengthen their positions in the family, they entrench themselves ever more deeply in the ethic of economic dependence upon men and in the ideology of female subordination and inferiority.[5]

While Hardacre views *mizuko kuyō* as a denial of women's agency, thereby regarding women as passive recipients, Underwood sees this ritual as allowing women "to negotiate with the patriarchal powers that be and therefore survive the transgression of their accepted roles of wife and mother. This, then, is the instrumental effectiveness of *mizuko kuyō*."[6] In this sense, women can be both "negotiators of culture" and "active participants in the ongoing struggle over cultural meaning and power."[7] Underwood would locate this kind of paradox among the "strategies of weakness," including rituals, that exist worldwide in situations of systemic unequal power.[8] In this manner, a "tactic," as Michel de Certeau uses the term, becomes more than a tactic. It is a tactic that becomes a strategy.

Underwood's interpretation of the paradox entailed in "women as acting subjects under patriarchal conditions" underscores the tension between women's agency and women's circumscription within a society that is male dominated.[9] To Underwood, women in such circumstances exist in the *midst* of this tension, not apart from it. "In such a situation, words like 'resistance' and 'accommodation'...seem inadequate, for apparent resistance is constantly mitigated by collusion and compromise...just as accommodation may have unexpectedly subversive effects."[10] The problem of *agency* has been a central one that feminist theorists have struggled with in recent decades, though at times there has been the tendency to distinguish between forms of agency that seem *real* and *authentic,* and forms that seem inauthentic or are, at best, "anticipations of agency." Behind this lies an assumption that only *full* or *real* agency changes society. As a challenge to this value judgment, Underwood derives some of her insight from Dorinne Kondo, namely, that all forms of agency are *active,* whether they result in what we have called compliance, resistance, or subversion. They are all choices leading to certain actions, and they accomplish their result within an amalgam of *constraints and possibilities.*

The important distinction is not between *active* and *passive* subjects. Nor is it between the exercise of agency based on "appropriate" motivations that bring about normative consequences and forms of agency that do not meet these criteria. "In the early days of feminist notions about agency there was the tendency to discount forms of agency if they complied with, conformed to, or supported the status quo. Attitudes of that sort were expressed regarding third world women who fought for nationalist causes alongside men and were therefore seen as co-opted or anti-feminist, rather than as women who had made a particular strategic choice given their situation."[11]

In seeking to understand the ways Japanese women have acted as agents in the context of *mizuko kuyō,* it became more clear that the forms of their agency were as diverse as the women and situations one observes. It was necessary in this study first to identify and understand the coexistence of constraints and possibilities within which these women were acting. Chapter 6 approached the subject of angry spirits and the threat that they represent from the standpoint of cultural studies. This enables one to reexamine the meaning of *tatari* "as a legitimate aspect of *mizuko kuyō*" rather than as "the most troubling stumbling block to most interpreters of the phenomenon."[12]

Consistent with her understanding of agency, Underwood believes that Japanese women, in seeking to calm the spirits of angry *mizuko,* are engaged in the ancient rite of settling the spirits of the dead, who may be angry for any number of reasons. In a complex sense, *kuyō* as a memorial service underscores the continuing link between the living and the dead. The ritual's intent is to maintain and often to reestablish the reciprocity between ancestors and their descendants. The same rationale is at play in the relationship between a woman and her lost child or *mizuko.* Because the living often bears scars from their relationships with the dead, commemorating the dead is intended to acknowledge, understand, and heal the causes of unrest that may exist between the living and the dead and thereby to lay to rest *tatari* and whatever it may signify. On a larger scale, this care and respect serves to establish and maintain the interplay between the human world and the world of spirits. Underwood's position may be summarized in this statement:

> *Mizuko kuyō*, then, is a process of ongoing negotiation between Japanese women and the social/sacred order in which they live, one through which they seek to transform the demonic forces of patri-archy into forces that are protective and benevolent towards them and their children. Through its practice Japanese women enact a strategy that allows them to exercise what limited freedom of choice they do have by ritually managing the dangers incurred in that very exercise of their sexual and reproductive power.[13]

Confronting the Discourse and Practice *of* Mizuko Kuyō

Igeta Midori is among a small number of Japanese feminists who have addressed in writing the subject of *mizuko kuyō* directly.[14] In an article published in 1995 she cites issues in postwar Japan that have surrounded reproductive rights, namely, "a high rate of abortion, an expectation for women to bear children no matter what, an inadequate health policy and societal environment for mothers and children, lack of family planning, the trend toward increased sexual activity and abortion among teens, and the low status of women and [the] dominance of men in sexual relations."[15] In her view, the discourse about *mizuko kuyō* has not taken seriously these issues, and, in an approach shared by most feminists in Japan, she argues that this discourse has neglected to emphasize "how culture and history shape women's experiences of and emotions concerning sexuality."[16]

While more reliable procreative choice and better medical information about sex are essential, of comparable importance is the need for forms of education that help to "construct human relationships within which women and men [can be] on an equal footing."[17] In her mind, this applies especially to *mizuko kuyō*, in which Japanese women have been expected to have a sense of guilt in cases of miscarriage and abortion. She views the rit-ual itself as reinforcing religious and traditional structures that are created by men and in which women are "dependent subjects" within a culture that maintains conventional gender roles and mythologizes motherhood.

Igeta also notes the confusion caused by using the term *mizuko* to refer not only to aborted fetuses but to embryos that were miscarried involuntarily, stillborn infants, and children who died an early death. While recognizing the pain that a woman and her partner may suffer in any of the last three circumstances, she sees a serious problem whenever the same term is used for each, believing that this contributes to a fetocentric focus that accompanies many negative stances toward abortion. By this, she is not "denying that women need a way of expressing and a space for ritualizing the anguish and guilt they feel in their experiences of abortion... [rather she is stressing] that the problems and suffering faced by women who have lost their children are determined by their culture and society more than by anything else."[18]

One may see similar but more diverse comments made by a dozen women and two men who attended a meeting of the Kyoto Women's Group (*Fujinkai*) in October 1988.[19] The median age of this group was thirty-five (ranging from twenty-six to forty-six); their marital status included single, married, divorced, and others who were cohabiting but were not registered. Religious backgrounds or preferences were equally divided between those having "no religion" and those who were affiliated either with Jōdoshū or some form of the Zen tradition. While they agreed that *mizuko kuyō* practice tends to be commercialized, trades on guilt feelings, and fosters superstition about angry spirits, they also agreed that considerable misinformation about this practice existed among Japanese feminists. The following statements provide a rich variety of responses and are grouped here in three ways: one cluster discusses the inadequacy of birth control and the lack of significant education about sexuality in Japan; a second deals with the painful feelings a woman may experience in pregnancy loss and in going through many of these experiences by herself; and the third deals with the necessity of honest, healthy, and caring relations with her partner. These statements are not simply personal; they also raise questions about social values; and they are presented here in each of these categories without comment.

Inadequacy of Birth Control and the Importance of Sexual Responsibility

1. If the fetus had been hoped for and yet was lost, one might feel the same as losing a child after birth. The loss of a "child" is different from the case of a *mizuko* that is not yet a child in the same sense.

At present, *kuyō* seems to play a role in consoling the failure of contraception; as such, it discourages serious efforts toward more effective contraception.

2. Ordinarily, one becomes attached to one's child in the process of bringing it up. If one feels a sense of guilt for having an aborted fetus, it is because one has been led to feel this way by the world. After my abortion, I was happy to be liberated from the suffering of morning sickness and then felt truly relieved to be able to continue my study. Now that the burden of delivery and child raising are mostly on the woman's side, I suppose there is no other recourse than abortion. I myself don't use pills, a vaginal pessary, or an IUD [intrauterine device], which are more hazardous to a woman's body than the condom. In any case, we should have the kind of human relationship with our partner so that we can ask him to wear a condom when the risk of getting pregnant is high. In Japan, however, such a fundamental agreement has not been fully accepted.

3. The significant rate of failure in the use of condoms is the main reason for a high incidence of abortion. Besides, women often become pregnant because men are either reluctant to wear a condom or they engage in sex when they are intoxicated...In our case, the result was two abortions. My husband never acknowledged his fault, saying, "This is not something I should beg pardon for." To the contrary, I think men should beg pardon for this neglect, for it is the woman who suffers, even if it results from the lack of knowledge on the part of both parties. Japanese women remain in the weaker position and often do not make demands (in the use of contraception) upon her husband. This may be a principal reason for the high rate of abortion in the case of married women.

The Solitary and Painful Feelings a Woman May Experience in Pregnancy Loss

1. It is clear that the death of a child after having raised him or her would be heart-rending. But the loss of a child through abortion, miscarriage, or stillbirth should also be discussed from the side of the woman. It is the health and life of women that must be taken into account. *Mizuko kuyō* may help to relieve some women's sense of guilt, though this seems to be found especially in conservative views of motherhood and the sexual dynamics between a man and a woman.

2. As the experience of loss varies with the person, one may feel more depressed when one has actually seen the body of one's child—whether in early infant death, stillbirth, or miscarriage. Such a feeling probably remains with one throughout life. Though I don't know anyone who has experienced that kind of loss, I do know of cases of grown-up children who have committed suicide and have died in an accident. In these cases, the parents may live the rest of their lives spiritually unrelieved. While some may write down their recollections of the lost child or edit the writings of the deceased, I can only guess that their sorrows may never be fully assuaged, even if they have been profoundly moved by a memorial service. [Written by a male]

3. When a sick child dies after a long period of careful nursing, parents may be prepared, more or less, for the child's death, while in cases of accidental death it can be truly heart-rending, as with the death of my friend's six-year[-old] child in a traffic accident. With such a loss parents may be moved to do something for their child, including something like a *kuyō*.

4. When I was [a child], my mother expressed to me the grudge (*urami*) and anger (*ikari*) she felt toward my father. I think she was expressing her dissatisfaction about her sexual life or her life in general that had gone against what she had hoped for. Since *kuyō* means nothing to me, I can only guess that it may relieve someone of her sorrow or sense of guilt. Because I became incapable of pregnancy due to oviduct occlusion (*rankan heisoku*), I suffered after abortion. My own experience has influenced me to study how the medical system might be of help in cases of women who are sterile.

The Importance of Mutuality and Respect in a Relationship

1. Because Japanese women are less closely united with their husbands than in the West, they are probably more deeply attached to their children. If *kuyō* is sought by both mother and father it will deepen their relationship, but if it is only the woman and she does it in secret she could well become more estranged from her husband or partner.

2. Having no religious faith, I cannot believe that *tatari* or curse befalls anyone who has failed to perform a *kuyō* for *mizuko*. Recalling my own experience of abortion, I may sometimes regret what I did, but this has not prompted me to do *mizuko kuyō*. As for a woman's relationship with

her partner, it depends on whether they made the decision together and on how he behaves after such an experience. In any case, a woman may retain a deep-rooted [sense of] solitude since the ache and sorrow that her own body experienced cannot be understood fully by others.

3. How parents overcome whatever shock they may experience from losing a child is most important; if the couple does not support each other sincerely, serious problems may occur. In cases of abortion, genuine attention to a wife's opinion is needed. In any case, a couple should have confidence in each other. We are all possessed with the sense of helplessness (*muryokukan*) and the transitoriness (*mujōkan*) of existence. We feel remorse in having lost a life and will pray to have this feeling assuaged. *Mizuko kuyō* may, to a certain extent, provide a means of closure.

4. To begin with, pregnancy and abortion are thoroughly private matters whose responsibility should be shared by both partners. When the conclusion leads to an abortion, the couple should discuss fully the importance of the life and the hazard for a woman's health. I cried when my wife miscarried. It is true that there are many who can lessen their burden in life through a ritual, but we should also have courage to face the torment and try to probe the way for our future life. Sharing one's sorrow with one's partner or one's friends can help one to grow as a human being. *Mizuko kuyō* is not necessary, at least for me. [Written by a male]

Abortion and the Politics of Motherhood: Parallels and Contrasts—Japan and the United States

The dynamics of the abortion debate are distinctly different in Japan than in the United States, yet in both countries there are two clearly drawn opposing sides. While public attitudes toward abortion within these countries vary considerably, there is value in seeing the parallels that exist between them. Kristin Luker's evenhanded analysis of "pro-life–pro-choice" activists in America, in *Abortion and the Politics of Motherhood* (1984) provides a way of looking at conflicts over abortion that helps one to interpret the Japanese scene as well. In her view, abortion is but "the tip of the iceberg"; the real problems deal with larger issues. The same is true in Japan. Luker's book deals with "different beliefs about the roles of the sexes, about the meaning of parenthood, and about human nature... each side of the abortion debate has an internally coherent and mutually shared view of the world that is tacit, never fully articulated, and, most importantly, completely at odds with the world view held by their opponents."[20]

By employing a wider approach to the conflicts at stake, it is fair to suggest that the hidden agenda in both countries is principally about the evolving meaning of womanhood and motherhood. From this comparative perspective one discovers some unique ingredients within Japan that shed further light upon the significance of *mizuko kuyō*. While these ingredients were initially explored in Chapter 5, they need to be expanded here. Though the central focus in this book is not on abortion, one cannot avoid discussing the relationship between *mizuko kuyō* and issues of sexuality, including the pervasive recourse to abortion in Japan. It is clear that different worldviews come into play as one examines how social attitudes toward abortion have their counterpart in beliefs about what a woman's role should be and therefore the meaning of motherhood.

To begin with, the characteristics of a so-called pro-life worldview in America have their parallels in Japan. In both societies this position represents a strong affirmation of the divided responsibilities between husband and wife: "Men are best suited to the public world of work, and women are best suited to rear children, manage homes, and love and care for husbands."[21] Motherhood is a woman's "most fulfilling role." While working women should receive "equal pay for equal work," women "should be wives and mothers *first*."[22] Furthermore, conservatives in America who oppose abortion on religious grounds have their equivalents among conservative religious communities in Japan (e.g., Seichō no Ie), though the numbers of Japanese who voice opposition are small by comparison to the numbers in the United States. In both cases, abortion is viewed as the taking of human life. Conservatives in each society are opposed to extending access to effective birth control devices, which they see as encouraging extramarital sex on the part of married men and teenagers. In the United States the basic issue is abortion more than procreative choice, but activist pro-life women generally oppose the distribution of condoms to teenagers. In both countries those who espouse conservative positions about motherhood have often been opposed to sex education in schools beyond the minimal sort. Finally, there is a low tolerance for ambiguity and a fear of uncertainty among conservatives in both societies. Their ideal would be a return to earlier, "less ambiguous" times.

The opposite stance is equally comparable, represented by pro-choice women in America and the feminist critique of the century-old "good wife, wise mother" (*ryōsai kenbo*) ideology in Japan. While there is basic

agreement about the equality of men and women, meaning that opportunities in education and in career choice should essentially be available
to male and female alike, there is recognition that equal opportunities do
not, in fact, exist. The concept of a public domain for men and a private
domain for women is rejected as a social policy or goal. Though being a
mother can be a deeply satisfying experience, one's entire life should not
be defined in these terms. One's sense of self-respect is nurtured by many
roles and forms of relationship. While motherhood may often have central
meaning, parenting can be balanced over against other important roles
played by both men and women. This happens when extended forms of
child care by husbands and the community become available. This extension is valuable for the child as well, for preoccupation with children has
its downside for both parents and children. While this point meets greater
resistance among many Japanese women, it is now central to the discourse
among Japanese feminists.[23]

Feminist women in both cultures believe strongly that women should
have control over their own bodies and that men should share in the
responsibility of using reliable means of procreative choice. "Pro-choice"
to these women in Japan and America does not mean pro-abortion. It
is not the existence of legalized abortion per se that is the main problem. Instead, it is the fact that abortion remains in many instances the
principal recourse for those who wish not to be pregnant. While various
forms of birth control exist, the fact that procreative choice has largely
been restricted to the rhythm method and the condom means that abortion has been the most effective birth control method in Japan for the past
half century. Abortion represents either the clear choice in cases of rape
or incest or when a woman's life is in danger or when birth control measures have failed. On the other hand, while there is general opposition to
abortion as a routine form of birth control, feminists in Japan have until
recently settled for abortion rights but have failed to pursue vigorously
important social problems that surround the abortion issue.

Some of these problems are as follows: (1) the cultural denial of issues
concerning pregnancy loss and its impact upon women, including the
lack of feminist involvement in serious discourse about pregnancy loss;
(2) the lack of adequate procreative choice, resulting in a high incidence
of abortion; (3) the need for adequate sexual education, including effective
counseling for adults as well as youth; (4) the absence of a systematic program in family planning and the increased incidence of pregnancy among
unmarried women and young girls; (5) the fact that little communication,

even among young married couples, occurs about sexual matters and that counseling and support groups about these matters are rare; (6) the degree to which the medical profession, ob-gyn physicians especially, fail to take a responsible role in any of these areas; and (7) that little cooperation exists among parents, teachers, doctors, counselors, and religious leaders in the whole area of sex education for young people from junior high age and beyond. Almost thirty years ago Samuel Coleman pinpointed the inadequacies of family planning methods and sex education in Japan: "Modern contraceptive services are not readily available; the family planning movement is geared to providing condoms, and physicians are less committed to pregnancy prevention than to pregnancy termination."[24] In these circumstances, which still remain common, women find themselves confronted with abortion as the primary way out of an undesired pregnancy.

Of central importance is the fact that sex education beyond that of biological or anatomical information exists only minimally in Japan. From an extensive study, published in 1997 and updated in 2004, of the various sources of sexual knowledge in Japan today, one becomes aware of the principal issues.[25]

The current national *Course of Study* of the Ministry of Education does not include education for either value systems or for establishment of self- and sexual identity...This is causing some serious social problems, particularly when parents expect the public schools to assume complete responsibility for teaching all the codes of ethics, including sexual behaviors. (P. 10)

In order for sex education in Japanese schools to become the comprehensive sexuality education it needs to be, more consideration must be given [not just to the physiological but even more] to the psychological and sociological aspects of sexuality. (P. 19)

Since true sexuality education is absent from Japanese education, and parents and the community no longer communicate this essential information to youths, these [teen sex] magazines do perform an important function, providing limited but basic information about sexual anatomy. Unfortunately, their popularity depends on adolescent titillation that ignores the need to provide information on sexually transmitted diseases (STD) prevention and contraception. (P. 20)

Exposure to this information is not sufficient when they have to use it on their own, cognitively and affectively. They need to perceive this information in the context of actual human relations and experiences. In actuality, most contemporary Japanese children build their knowledge pertaining to sex in a passive manner that results in distortion and inflexibility. (P. 24)

This is a situation in which young males and females receive little help in coming to terms with their sexuality or what it means to be responsible in sexual relations. The notebooks at Jikishian, discussed in Chapter 3, reveal many facets of the sexual culture in contemporary Japan in which abortion may be seen as a consequence of inadequate procreative choice and the absence of a supportive social climate but is also the outgrowth of specific social attitudes and policies.

Again, in the collection of essays *Japanese Women: New Feminist Perspectives on the Past, Present, and Future,* one finds serious attention being given by its Japanese contributors, all of whom are women, to the issues of marriage, family, human sexuality, pornography, exploitation of women, and sexist portrayals in the media.[26] As those essays make clear, considerable attention is being addressed to these topics in many feminist circles. While abortion itself is not cast as the problem, the extent of its use helps to dramatize other issues that go unattended within the society at large.

Stereotyping of *mizuko kuyō*, however, fails to distinguish between those women who react passively and those who become agents of their own destiny. Restricting the discourse to abortion as a "right" paradoxically increases the recourse to abortion, for it fails to confront other social issues that make this recourse so common. Ironically, this results in undermining a woman's control over her own body. Out of these unattended issues emerges a breeding ground for women who develop serious emotional problems after miscarriage, stillbirth, and induced abortion. One consequence is that large numbers of women fall prey to those who hold out compensatory blessings, offer promises of healing and protection, but in effect reaffirm the passive role of Japanese women.

It is becoming clear to many feminists that a wide range of issues relating to sexuality as well as gender roles exist beyond that of procreative choice. While the following paragraph was written by Sandra Bartky about women in American society, the views she expresses here are strikingly similar to what has been said from feminist perspectives about Japanese women:

All sorts of women have known in their daily lives the low self-esteem that is attendant upon cultural depreciation, the humiliation of sexual objectification, the troubled relationship to a socially inferiorized body, the confusions and even the anguish that comes in the wake of incompatible social definitions of womanhood; women of all kinds and colors have endured not only the overt, but also the disguised and covert attacks of a misogynist society.[27]

On the other hand, I have stressed the diversity that exists in Japanese women's life experiences for at least three reasons: (1) to challenge the stereotyping tendency that remains by providing alternative images of women in different life situations; (2) to begin showing that resourceful women have been able to articulate their own forms of protest, even if these do not often precipitate social change; and (3) to see *mizuko kuyō* as another way in which some women have found their sense of agency within a social culture that fails to provide alternative procreative choices to abortion and effective education about human sexuality.

At the same time, these stereotypes have been highlighted, for they continue to define the nature and role of women and the manner in which these portrayals and the strong social values behind them have been constructed and remain culturally influential. In light of persisting constructs about mothering, it is no surprise that the ideology of passive Japanese women is at the center of the Japanese deconstructionist concern. It is also not surprising that there is disagreement about what the roles of women should be, let alone how motherhood might be redefined. As another way of looking at the issue of motherhood, this time with an emphasis upon the sometimes virulent ambiguity with which a mother may feel about her child and the anger with the role that society has imposed upon her, we look next upon this kind of life situation through the experience of a Japanese social and clinical psychologist, who was involved for several years in the Kyoto University research project on *mizuko kuyō*.

"Mizuko Kuyō *and Healing the Heart of the Mother*"

Hashimoto Yayoi's essay "*Mizuko Kuyō* and Healing the Heart of the Mother" may be the single most dramatic way of examining a mother's loss of her *mizuko*.[28] Though a critique of the overall *mizuko kuyō* phenomenon with its tendencies toward commercialism and its social conservatism, her essay explores in fresh ways what the loss of a child, in whatever form, may mean to a particular woman. While addressing the concept of a lost child (*mizuko*), Hashimoto sees the real loss to be the *subject* who is grieving more than the *object* (*mizuko*) she has lost. This rarely articulated source of a woman's grieving raises different questions about her sense of identity as a person who is a mother but is more than a mother and about her role within the family but also in other social contexts.

This study as a whole has sought to understand the powerful societal prescriptions, as the nation was moving into the modern era more than a century ago, that were designed to shape Japanese women into becoming "good wives and wise mothers" (*ryōsai kenbo*). The basic roles of women being redefined at that time were designed to be congruent with the characteristics and constraints of a changing social scene and its exposure to outside influences. While cognizant of this social history, Hashimoto proceeds to analyze the deep uneasiness (*fuan*) that characterizes the experience of so many Japanese women in a different way, asking why such discomfort has attached itself to the concept of a *mizuko* in recent decades.

With emphasis placed on the healing of a mother's heart, Hashimoto begins by describing the powerful amalgam of feelings that mothers often have toward their children, especially when children reject what their parents and society regard as accepted paths toward success. A primary case in point involves a child or young person who engages in school refusal, that is, who simply stops going to school. The effect is not simply upon the child; it is typically upon the mother since it indicates she has somehow failed in her capacity as a "wise mother" or resourceful parent. Because a father has normally not been expected to become involved in such situations, the mother's sense of having failed is heightened, along with her level of resentment at having to confront this issue alone.

At several points in this study the pitfalls of a mother whose entire being revolves around her child has been discussed. And because a child's success in school is a key source of the mother's inner well-being, she undergoes considerable confusion about what went wrong. As a result, she experiences strong ambivalence toward the child who fails to live up to her expectations as well as society's standards. Since the perceived measure of her worth as a person (her *ikigai*) is based upon her success as a mother, she may experience increasing self-doubt together with rage toward the child whose behavior reveals her failure.

In extreme cases, the mother carries an intense sense of emptiness, as though her life amounts to nothing. At the same time, Hashimoto writes, "there is strong criticism against mothers who have failed at childrearing," causing them to be profoundly wounded in spirit.[29] With this combination of self-blame and societal disparagement it is not uncommon for these women to express the desire to harm their children or to wish that these children had never been born. Because such negative emotions welling up inside her are the opposite of what she is supposed to feel, her sense of self-respect as a "good mother" is wounded, if not destroyed. These emotions are subconsciously "driven from the mother's awareness."[30] As a result, her guilt and the burdens of her "unease and pain are hidden in the shadows, and remain unhealed."

In cases where the mother seeks and finds a therapist who listens to, without judging these negative emotions she may be encouraged to speak at greater depths of her own "self-alienation." As Hashimoto emphasizes, this kind of focus by psychoanalysts on a mother's ambivalence toward her child is fairly recent in Japan. In her own work, employing several case studies of women who felt free to probe this painful dimension of their life, she came to realize that what is being mourned, beyond a mother's sense of failure and beyond her all-consuming anger, is the unborn nature of her own self, her own uniqueness (*kosei*) which had never been encouraged and which, in fact, had been chronically aborted. Because the socially scripted self, her *ikigai*, had remained her operative self-definition, what she brings to her various relationships is a continuing reminder of who she ought to be rather than the experience of one who might have grown into her own maturity. Hers is, therefore, a derivative self, lacking independence from what others think she should be. In a book that deals with the power of maternal ambivalence similar to what Hashimoto is saying, Rozsika Parker discusses the extensive literature on this subject in psychoanalytic circles and summarizes her own point of view:

> I am suggesting that it is the experience of maternal ambivalence that provides a woman with a sense of her independent identity. The pain of ambivalence, the distress in recognizing that the child hates her for frustrating its desires, and that she hates the child for frustrating her independent needs, can be a force for affirming her independent identity. Both mother and child need the mother's affirmation of her own needs, desires, opinions, rage,

love and hatred if separateness is to be established—and thus relationship.[31]

The upshot of such a process is what Hashimoto calls the mother's *killed self*, the self that was never permitted to exist. Lacking a sense of genuine individuality (*kosei*), what she brings to her relations with others is a truncated self that tends to be replicated in her children whom she bears and nurtures unwittingly in her own image. "A mother whose individuality [is] not respected cannot be expected to bring out her child's individuality."[32] Rather than viewing this as only a recent phenomenon, one may cite how the aspiration to be otherwise was strikingly expressed seventy years ago by the well-known Japanese writer Uno Chiyo: "Someday, when I am older, will I be able to get rid of this impulse, this wanting to be a 'good wife,' without feeling lost? Would I then be able to write my own story? I don't wish not to be a woman, but I'd certainly like to be a woman whose sense of purpose comes from within."[33]

Hashimoto's perspective on the concept of *mizuko* views it not only as a lost child or fetus but also as the unborn *mizuko* that is the mother's own, more fundamental, but unfulfilled potential. Her grasp of this larger truth unfolds as a basic paradigm shift. It makes real the unexpected question of "Who is the *mizuko*?" The pertinence of her analysis of *mizuko* is that while one may continue to regard a *mizuko* as a *killed child* there is a larger sense in which the mother's *own self* has failed even to be conceived. There are, in other words, two different but interconnected *mizuko* or eliminated selves. The second *child* is the root *mizuko*, without which the more conventional social concept of *mizuko* lacks adequate substance. "The mother's negative emotions towards [her own birth] child...have the same roots, psychologically, as the problem of the *mizuko*" that is the "eliminated child [that lies buried in] the darkness of the mother's heart."[34] Struggling to be born is the "individuality" of the Japanese woman that otherwise remains unborn:

> It is the *individual* that could not reflect on herself because of the system and the family; it is the *individual* that had unpleasant feelings and asserts herself; it is the *individual* that had different ideas than her husband and child; and it is the *individual* that has excited emotions. It is [also] the *individual* that can listen to the voice of the *spirit* inside [herself] and express it, rather than expressing her own intent about getting her child and husband to move.[35]

Essential to the healing process is for the mother to speak of her self-al-ienation (*mizukara no sogaisareta jōkyō*), to bring into the light that which has been consigned to darkness, personally as well as socially, namely, the "killed self," the unborn woman, the unconceived mother. "The *mizuko* [lying] in the darkness of the mother's heart must be brought out of dark-ness [in order to] be mourned."[36] It is this *mizuko*, representing symboli-cally a woman's unfulfilled self, that needs to be acknowledged and then to be mourned if she is to discover forms of individuality that enable her to engage in genuine interrelationship with others, including her ability to be a stronger woman and thus a more effective mother. This is a con-cept of individuality that is born out of its discovered connection with the larger world of human experience and that can in turn contribute to this fabric. It is not the same as "individualism"; it is rather a deeper sense of uniqueness that flourishes within both larger and smaller forms of interdependence.

To Hashimoto, it is the larger world of mother and nature that is "the source of life and death."[37] Into this expanded world a transformed sense of one's uniqueness may emerge. As to how "the discovered *individual* should live [this, she writes] is the problem about which the women in transition must now think."[38] This raises the central question about the relationship between self-determination and empowerment. Earlier, we discussed how achieving self-determination can be a catalyst in a woman's life toward becoming an empowered agent in other areas of her life, believ-ing that agency and empowerment are indivisible, that growth in one area helps to nurture growth in other areas. This concept is congruous with Hashimoto's assertion that a woman's discovery of her uniqueness, her subjectivity, is not self-preoccupation. Rather, it enables her to be a bet-ter mother, a better person in every context of her life. Coming to terms with her hostility, which is at the same time self-hatred, enables her capac-ity for love and affirmation to be discovered, expressed, and profoundly affirmed.

If one examines *mizuko kuyō* as a performative ritual, as occurs in the following chapter, realizing that the forms in which it can be found are multiple, one asks how Hashimoto's analysis may provide yet another understanding of what constitutes a ritual. Referring at the conclusion of her essay to the rite of a symbolic healing that has just been discussed, she contrasts it with her view of what ordinarily occurs in the popular forms of the *mizuko* ritual, that she regards as "a hollow thing, a formal rite carried out for money."[39] If one refrains from comparisons at this point, one sees that the healing of this kind is, in fact, a "rite." Paradoxically, the one who performs this ritual is the counselor to whom the woman goes in search of help. In a manner that permits and encourages the woman to speak freely out of her "resentment and anger that had been kept inside," one can imagine how that form of therapy has profound ritualistic implications.

As this happens, she eventually articulates her own sense of self-alienation. Without this ritualized permission to voice her true feelings, there can be no awareness of a "killed child" within her, no healing, no discovery of her own potential for "individuality." Obviously, the office of a counselor is not the typical location of a *mizuko* ritual, for there are no "typical locations." There are no references to sacred figures in the usual sense; sacred figures exist within the ordinary. Sacred texts and chanting play no role in this transformative process, for these are only some forms of articulation. Instead, one pays attention not to expected forms and institutional traditions for their own sake but only as ingredients of a process that can assist in continuing transformation from conditions of sickness and pain to those that can be agents of healing and new life.

Two Images of Japanese Woman—*as Scripted by Society/as Listening to Herself*

As Hashimoto makes clear, the task of affirming one's unique self seems remote given society's expectation that women be the ones who nurture not only their child but also their husband and elderly dependents for whom there are few caregivers. The embedded irony in Hashimoto's social-psychological analysis is that the woman-mother, woman-wife, woman-daughter is drained by the tasks she is given and experiences insufficient nurturing herself. As Suzanne Vogel asked years ago, where is the nurture for the one who is expected to nurture others? The person Hashimoto describes comes to the therapist in a state of anger, depression, loneliness, and profound resentment. Absent a sense of intrinsic self-worth, she brings in its wake an inability to be genuinely nurturing.

Among perceptive discussions of this complex issue are two chapters by Ueno Chizuko in her book *The Modern Japanese Family: Its Rise and Fall.*[40] The first of these is an extended discussion of Jun Etō's *Seijuku to sōshitsu* (Maturity and Loss: The Disintegration of Motherhood). As Ueno points out, this is "not about independence from mother." Instead, it is severance from socially defined canons of what motherhood is supposed to mean:

> Instead of lyrically describing a person's maturation as a story of the "loss of Mother," Etō described the required maturation as a story of the irreversible process of "disintegration of motherhood." By this attempt, [his] work, which discusses postwar literary texts, success-fully becomes a critique of civilization.[41]

Motherhood as a status of being is a product of modernity. It did not exist in agrarian Japan, in which there was no concept of good wife, wise mother but which arose in middle-class circles in the Meiji period and which became within the twentieth century the primary insignia of a woman's identity. Prior to that, caring for children was shared by others in the larger family, and children were not as emotionally dependent as they became in the nuclear families of modernity. Motherhood "occurred only after and only where mothers were expelled from production and became 'full-time mothers' whose identities relied solely on being moth-ers."[42] With the rapid unfolding of modernization, with its isolating of a woman from her extended family and the absence of her husband, the child became her obsessive concern.

While this scenario is a familiar one, what is more demeaning is a woman's *experience* of not being viewed as "an other" to whom her hus-band relates but instead being "a part of the husband." While such a relationship calls for responsibilities, it generates little responsiveness. Husband and wife are united through the "relationship between 'mother and child' rather than through an ethical relationship" between two people whose identities are prized because each is unique and each has needs that require reciprocity.[43] To be regarded as "an other" in a relationship is to have an identity that is not conditioned by role or social expectation. "Modernity, which attempted to confine women to neurosis, was naturally greeted by feminism with curses."[44]

A second chapter in Ueno's book provides images in the work by Shigeo Saitō titled *Tsumatachi no shisūki* (Housewives' Midlife Autumnal Period) that portray changes in Japanese family life and in the status of woman during the 1980s. What makes Saitō's work "epoch-making" in Japanese journalism was, in Ueno's estimation, its shift from covering women who cause troubles and disturb the public to focusing on the lives of ordinary women, including the trials they experience through "their relationships with their husbands and their children".[45] The subject of sex in marital relationships, about which people rarely communicate, is a case in point. To Saitō this signals "a huge pathological phenomenon in Japanese society." To Ueno, this approach represents a basic shift, precisely because each woman whom Saitō interviews falls "within the boundaries of ordinary women, each has something that makes her slightly out of the ordinary...[each] faces her own reality."[46] It is the same quality of respect and active listening that Hashimoto Yayoi models as a therapist to a client.

In an extended interview with Sandra Buckley, Ueno makes some of the same points in a more direct fashion. Addressing the subject of nurturing, she stresses that "in Japan the mothering, nurturing function is a key concern of feminists and seen as something that must be protected. Our primary goal is not to be like men but to value what it means to be a woman. This aspect of Japanese feminism is deeply rooted in the history of the women's movement in Japan as well as the individual experience of women."[47] While the quality of "nurturing" has sometimes been seen as the opposite of "equality and sameness," it becomes problematic only when "the maternal function" is the sole "acceptable or worthwhile function for all women." Ueno underscores the point that the quality of nurturing needs to be gender inclusive and that "unless women can teach men how to move into these areas [that is, into domestic and nurturing roles], I don't think things will change." [48]

> I agree with the early radical feminist position that the condition of the "feminine" is nurtured and not natural. We learn what it is to be feminine, and [that] it must be possible for men to learn. I realize that there are some feminist theoreticians who still argue for a feminist nature or essence that we are born with as women, but I feel uncomfortable with this idea ...The gap between the theoreticians [e.g., French feminists] and the activists seems to be immense there.[49]

Of pertinence here is what Ueno labeled years ago as the *mazākon* bond, the attachment or emotional bond of "mutual dependence and obligation" between a mother and a son that can be oppressive to both, that can last a lifetime, and that stems from Japan's gender-segregated system. The point

Ueno makes is apposite to what Hashimoto views as a woman's plight when her individual identity is obscured by the roles she is expected to play as a woman, a wife, and a mother.[50] In general, when a woman is genuinely listened to, she listens to herself. Of even greater importance, when she is treated as *an other*, as one who has her own integrity, she appreciates herself "as her self," not "as scripted by society." As she experiences being respected, as well as cared for, she becomes more sensitive as a caregiver but is not depleted in the process.

More than twenty years ago (1987) Ueno observed that the isolation typically experienced then by the average urban housewife was paradoxically being countered by renewed forms of *women's bonding*: "The traditional sexual segregation itself helps women to live in *sisterhood* [and] as long as women stay in the *new women's* world, Japanese husbands do not interfere. This [newly emerging kind of] bond is strong enough to provide mutual aid, and, importantly, is based neither on kinship nor on neighborhood relations but on shared tastes, feelings, activities, and orientations."[51] Twenty years later (2009) Ueno published a considerably revised version that accented the expanding possibilities for these different sorts of female bonds, ones that are based more upon a "free and pluralistic interpersonal relationship in which people can choose one another" in distinction from those into which one is born or enters through marriage. While differentiated from so-called associational bonds that are characterized by *nonselectivity* (that is, "one cannot get out of them or avoid them"), the option of these more selective bonds have the effect today of influencing associational bonds to become "somewhat more selective."[52] Ueno's depiction of the varieties that exist and the overlapping between them and associational bonds is nuanced, informative, and corroborated by the writings of others. Her overall assessment of this phenomenon is expressed in these words:

> Selective bond society becomes a place of self-realization for women through acceptance by others, together with [society's] sanction. They become "individuals" for the first time in the company of "other people with faces" who meet and appreciate one another as individuals with their own names, not as mothers or wives of someone, and regardless of their husbands' jobs or income... Japanese society holds the potential to grow a new type of interpersonal relationship that does not follow the *ie* or *mura*

model. The female bond has a lot to offer to selective bonds...as an advanced model. In today's society, where the population is rapidly aging and the traditional blood, territorial and associational bonds are no longer functional, we have come to the stage where both men and women have no choice but to find their future in selective bonds.[53]

As a way of highlighting the discernment expressed by Meredith Underwood, Hashimoto Yayoi, and Ueno Chizuko, it is helpful to put them side by side with Michel de Certeau's notion of how one relates to the "other" especially but not only in cross-cultural studies. In discussing Certeau, William Barbieri stresses the "aspect of otherness that goes beyond difference: that remains outside our grasp, in that it resists the bonds of conceptualization and reason...in which there is not only genuine encounter but an openness to revising one's own categories and assessments in light of the perspectives of the other."[54] The "other" exists within our own societies, within our bodies, within alien cultures, within our own psyches, and in the otherness of God.[55]

There is nowhere in which "otherness" does not exist. Embracing one's own otherness enables one to see and embrace the otherness of all existence. In that awareness one also recognizes interdependence. As with Hashimoto (with respect to a mother's child) and with Ueno (in relation to a woman's husband), a woman's identity and plight are obscured by the roles she is expected to play as a woman, a wife, and a mother. It is consonant with the subtlety of Certeau's sense of the fundamental "alterity" that "eludes capture, but continues to haunt and even undermine" the categories that imprison.[56] "To liberate the other," Certeau's "heterological quest" is to listen to the other:

> Certeau presses us here to strain to hear the voice of the other...Beyond this, he urges us to visit and converse with the other, to seek, inasmuch as we can, a genuine give and take, in a manner that places our own categories and values at risk. In the end, he commends a stance of vulnerability rather than mastery: we should be open to being wounded, transformed, even converted by the other. From this encounter, the voyager then returns to bear witness. As Certeau...frequently remarked, "No one ever returns unchanged."[57]

At this point we move to a chapter that deals with some of the ways a woman may not only respond to but also create rituals or "ritual-like activities" that enable her to connect her own experiences of loss more strongly to the broken features of social existence, especially but not only those of other women. Again, as Hashimoto Yayoi stresses, it is the larger world of mother and nature that is "the source of life and death." Into this expanded world a transformed sense of one's uniqueness may emerge.

PART THREE

Relating Mizuko Rei *to the* Larger Worlds of Profound Loss

8

The Revival of Death, the Rebirth of Grieving, and Ways of Mourning

When the goal of grief is to get over it and back to normal, then grief has been changed from being regarded as a core part of the human condition, and has been reconceptualized as a psychological process that is painful, but which, when the work is done, restores the survivor to the status quo ante...This psychological view of grief, they say, reduces a bereaved person's "experiences and concerns to stages or temporary feelings. Thus anger, and to a lesser extent, guilt, are dealt with not in substantive ways but only as transient feeling states—to be experienced and then surpassed."...Because contemporary culture does not easily include the idea of irreparable loss, it is very difficult to fit death into the spiritual frameworks in which humans have cast their grief for most of human history.[1]

A CENTRAL FOCUS of this research has been on rituals for the dead. Chapter 6 discusses the relationship between the living and the dead with respect to one's ancestors, how rituals for them are not simply expressions of gratitude for their existence but serve to keep alive some sense of their continued presence. Contemporary scholarship tends to approach ritual as both reflecting and "challenging cultural values."[2] Among theoretical approaches to the study of *mizuko kuyō* as a ritual are those that analyze it under the conceptual framework of *performance theory*.

Viewing rituals in this fashion opens one to how text and context interrelate and how both recipients and performers of rituals may receive and enact them differently each time they are conducted. Without such freedom performances are lifeless. Because performances are rarely just "spontaneous or accidental," they rely upon a "preexisting script," as in a play, a score, a liturgy.[3] In innumerable ways, a creative tension can exist "between the script and its enactment." To associate ritual, whether *religious* or not, with performance is a more recent theoretical development. From this perspective, the varied forms of *mizuko kuyō* can be seen as clearly performative in nature. Embedded in the process are numerous contingencies. Spontaneity occurs within a form or script but enables that form to be shaped anew.

Expressions of Grief and the Process of Mourning

In *mizuko kuyō* one sees how, in the whole ethos of memorial services, statuary, special days and places, sutras, and devotional songs about bodhisattvas, there is a continuing presence of the past and an ingenious creating of new elements woven into fabrics from the past. When experiences of pregnancy loss are discussed from intercultural and cross-disciplinary points of view, especially perspectives arising out of gender studies, anthropology, and ritual studies, one comes to understand the Japanese situation more fully. As a means of employing perspectives stemming from ritual studies and its grasp of the relationship between grief and mourning, it is appropriate to locate the Japanese discourse and practice of *mizuko kuyō* upon a wider screen, including examples from other cultures.

In Chapter 1 we referenced the perspectives of Susan Sered and the 1987 article by Hoshino Eiki and Takeda Dōshō in discussing the importance of communal support and rituals that assist a person in moving from a deep sense of personal loss to the ability to mourn that loss and to discover a greater awareness of wholeness. To locate Japanese experience upon a wider stage is not to engage in comparative judgments. To ignore, however, what has been unfolding in ritual studies on grief and mourning from the vantage point of many disciplines, beginning with anthropology and continuing with the history of mourning practices, deprives one of extensive resources. In a volume edited by Peter Homans titled *Symbolic Loss: The Ambiguity of Mourning and Memory at Century's End,* he makes important distinctions between grief and mourning.

> On the one hand, grief refers to 'the feelings of sorrow, anger, guilt, and confusion which occur when one experiences the loss of an attachment figure.' On the other hand, mourning refers to 'the culturally constructed social response to the loss of an individual.' Grief is a painful emotion that is, so to speak, looking for a 'cure.' Mourning is a ritual that, so to speak, 'heals' the pain of grief...

Mourning, it seems, enhances the capacity to 'let go' of the lost object and to be alone. Rituals of mourning heal human grief... In a nutshell, grief is an emotion, mourning is a grief-infused symbolic action. Both are a response to the loss of an attachment.[4]

The complexity of this subject makes it clear that the process of moving from grief to mourning may be among the most difficult of any journey, for *attachment* does not subside without a struggle, and the presence of the one lost may be enduring. To understand the larger process of mourning one needs to take seriously specific forms of grief and to highlight some of the possibilities that may constitute mourning. Mourning is not simply the cessation of grief; it is the transformation of a person who learns how to mourn, a process that can be lifelong. As one experiences the arduous, often mysterious process of mourning, one discovers that among its many expressive forms are not only through "ritual" in some restricted sense but through *ritual-like* activities or ways of thinking and acting that can effect powerful transformation as well. There may, for instance, be multiple expressions of sorrow and grief that take radically different forms, even in the same person. While the story of one woman's journey is not easily transferable to another, whether in Japan or elsewhere, some aspects of such an experience are, if not universal, still recognizable from another cultural perspective. In this sense, the experience is transcultural but still unique.

One such "crisis of soul" is reconstructed by Sue Nathanson, a clinical psychologist, out of her own experience as a mother who, having three children already, found herself pregnant and, even though wanting to have another child, reluctantly agreed to terminate that pregnancy.[5] While her level of grief was unusually profound and thus may seem atypical, her account serves to illuminate the range of what any woman may experience when she allows herself to entertain deeper dimensions of loss. One would not expect every person who chooses to terminate a pregnancy or even those losing a child through stillbirth or multiple miscarriage to go through a crisis of soul, though many do. Nathanson herself is shocked that this *wordless grief* "erupts and breaks through [her] normally strong controls."[6]

The enduring impact of her decision sharpens her need "to feel my grief in some way that will enable me to heal, to find a way to live with what I have done, with my loss. But I do not know where to turn for this source of healing."[7] Because she has always regarded her fertility as a sacred gift, not a commodity, she yearns for a ceremony that will help "to acknowledge the loss of this child within the circle of my family... For now this is not a shared loss, and I must carry its weight by myself."[8] Society too, she emphasizes, needs to acknowledge the depths of grief that mainly individuals can know in their aloneness. To endure this condition with dignity one needs to find forms of mourning that can channel one's grief in ways that extend one's sense of connection with others who also grieve. As she undergoes this aloneness in the midst of her family and in the presence of her therapist, she asks herself "where, in this culture, can I possibly find a mirror of my subjective experience... [a way of reaching] a sense of myself that is not influenced by the standards and assumptions of our culture?"[9]

That is precisely the core of this study of *mizuko kuyō*, that is, to mark ways in which women in Japan today are seeking not only to find their own voice but also to define themselves in relationship to others in a manner that prizes their own sense of self. In a Japanese context, it is the dilemma of how a woman can be a mother yet may not have a filiocentric relationship to her children. As mother and as therapist, living on an inescapable border, Nathanson testifies to "the special vulnerability and deep anguish that arise from attachment and inevitable loss, expectation and certain disappointment."[10] It is for these reasons that ceremonies for major transitions of life are vital; the importance of these rituals seems to be a growing realization.

Central to Nathanson's account is her awareness that there are many *triggers* for a crisis of the soul, "many issues that arise from being female—miscarriage, having a child with [serious] birth defects, infertility, menopause, hysterectomy, ovarian cancer, mastectomy. Any one of these might precipitate a profound crisis for a woman (and for men who are involved with women grappling with such crises)."[11] The very writing of her book was ritual-like, enabling her to become an agent in her own behalf and to help others break through the isolation caused by society's silence about matters of this importance. In the process of discussing the pertinence of these issues with Japanese women and men in their observance of *mizuko kuyō*, one is repeatedly brought back to the realization that, although this phenomenon is widespread, individuals experience it in differentiated ways. It is also clear that there are people for whom the experience of loss, of whatever kind, may be nowhere as traumatic as the one just described. May Sarton's well-known poem, however, speaks to both kinds of grief:

> *There are some griefs so loud*
> *They could bring down the sky,*
> *And there are griefs so still*
> *None knows how deep they lie,*
> *Endured. Never expended.*[12]

Among the central themes of Sue Nathanson's experience is the discovery that few rituals exist to help adults and young people to go through genuine crises of spirit and, just as important, that there is a vast silence about the subject of pregnancy loss. To find this silence among feminists as well as in the medical profession in her own society was, to her, deeply troubling. Among other women, Linda Layne has written extensively about the theme of silence in a series of articles, beginning about the same time as Nathanson's book (1989) and culminating in her own book *Motherhood Lost: A Feminist Account of Pregnancy Lost* (2003).[13] Having experienced multiple miscarriages, Layne regards this silence as both a "cultural denial of pregnancy loss" and as an area in which feminists need to be challenged.

By retaining a studied silence on the subject, feminists have simply given:

> the field to the antichoice activists while adding to the silence [that] members of pregnancy-support groups find so painful...to speak of pregnancy loss is automatically to make oneself suspect among feminists...The fear in the context of pregnancy loss is that if one were to acknowledge that there was something of value lost, something worth grieving in a miscarriage, one would thereby automatically accede the inherent personhood of embryos/fetuses. This is not the case, however, unless one accepts the anti-abortion view of personhood in the first place.[14]

Layne offers a number of suggestions by which her fellow feminists could deal constructively with the problems women may have in experiences of stillbirth, miscarriage, and other forms of pregnancy loss. As of 2003 when her book appeared, there were no or few "culturally sanctioned rituals by which to mark a pregnancy loss" in the United States.[15] Feminists could help to create both religious and nonreligious kinds of rituals. They could also urge the medical profession, especially, to take more seriously the impact that miscarriage can have on a woman. Feminists could become proactive in the creation of more adequate sexual education, dealing with the social, biological, psychological, and even the spiritual aspects of this issue. They could promote a more liberal discourse of pregnancy loss. In these ways, the involvement of feminists has not been prominent. In that sense, they contribute to furthering the silence. In Foucault's famous words, "There is not one but many silences, and they are an integral part of the strategies that underlie and permeate discourses."[16]

It is significant that all of these issues pertain in Japan: the cultural denial of pregnancy loss and its impact upon women; the lack of feminist involvement in serious discourse about pregnancy loss; the degree to which the medical profession is not engaged in these matters; the lack of adequate sexual education for adults as well as youth; the absence of responsible counseling; and, clearly, the lack of effective procreative choice. It is interesting that the most obvious area in which there is a ritual in Japan that is responsive to pregnancy loss is that of *mizuko kuyō*. While not every situation in which *mizuko kuyō* is conducted entails all of these matters, it is at least one response to some features of Japan's sexual culture.

Mizuko Kuyō, *Dharma Talk, and Two Discussions at Jikishian*

The core of this chapter discusses how the pain of pregnancy loss is experienced and a number of ways by which healing is sought. The discussion includes both Japanese and other cultural settings, forms of ritual that are religious and those that are not in any regular sense, those that are contemporary and others with a long history, and circumstances in which shared healing includes but a few people and some in which the community of shared pain and shared transformation is wide-ranging. The first two examples may be found together in a small Buddhist temple in Kyoto in 1990. After describing each of these, they will be looked at from the perspective of a recently published book (2009), *Mourning the Unborn Dead*, on *mizuko kuyō* practice mainly in the United States and also some of its antecedents in Japan.

The following portion of a dharma talk (*hōwa*) was given by Oda Hōryū, head priest at Jikishian, on October 23, 1990, to a gathering principally of Japanese visitors to the temple. This group also included Bardwell Smith, Shinji Kazue, Yvonne Rand, and three students of the Associated Kyoto Program. Following the service, Oda-san met with this small group to discuss the meaning of the service and how Buddhist teachings relate to daily life.

Oda-san starts by quoting a Buddhist saying, "When you see beauty in the flower, look to the roots for the source. Look how the chrysanthemums are now blooming. It is by viewing the flowers that our hearts become filled with peace. The roots of each family are parents, grandparents, and ancestors. At the very root is the life of the Buddha." Then he continues:

Muryōjin, muryōhō. Even though one may not understand the Buddha's ways, every object, plant and animal has *busshō*, or life given by the Buddha. That is why small children are called *hotoke no ko*. Nevertheless, we fail to notice our Buddha nature. The meaning of the temple's name "Jikishian" is to point one's finger back at one-self, at one's own *kokoro*, for each person has its own *busshō*. The reason we fail to notice the spirit/life of the Buddha within us is that we were born with three lusts (*kitanai kokoro*): (1) desire (*ton'yoku*); (2) anger (*ikari*); and (3) complaints (*guchi*). [He provides examples of each.] These sins become so large that they overshadow our awareness of original *busshō* and hamper our ability to practice it.

Because it is important not to be driven by our base desires, we must practice overcoming them. One fundamental practice is not to commit *sesshō* (the taking of life). Not performing criminal acts is not enough; we have to make the most of the life that we are given (*ikasu*). Not using our life to the fullest benefit is another form of *sesshō*. Is there anyone among us who can say with confidence that he has always done this? [No one speaks.]

In portrayals of the Buddha's death scene there are fifty-two animals. These pictures are called *nehan-zu*. But there is no cat in this picture. This is because cats perform *sesshō*; unlike other animals they take life when it is not necessary (that is, even when they are not hungry). There is also no swallow (the bird), because the swallow is overly concerned with fashion. When it was announced that the Buddha would die, most animals rushed there to witness it, but the swallows were too busy deciding what to wear to look fashionable.

This allegory has a practical meaning. We should not take more than we need. We must treat our life as a special gift (*ikasu*) and use it to its fullest. We are enjoined to pray before the *butsudan* (Buddhist shrine) in the morning, as a way of making our heart and the Buddha's one. Our body and the Buddha's body are not separate. While we cannot fully know another person's heart, the Buddha is able to discern our heart completely. We cannot lie to the Buddha.

Oda-san thanks the Japanese visitors for listening and ends with a brief chant.

Then Bardwell Smith (hereafter BLS) introduces the American visitors and requests that Oda-san talk about the purpose and structure of the service that was just performed.

ODA HŌRYŪ: We begin the service by a number of offerings. Initially, incense, candles, and flowers are offered to the Buddha, with chants accompanying the offerings. Incense (senkō) is offered so that all those who are present will be calmed by its fragrance. The way in which incense is burned is a symbol of transformation, as it slowly turns into ashes. Candles are offered in the hope that the hearts of everyone present will be lightened. Flowers of many colors, shapes, sizes and fragrances are offered, symbolizing the diverse elements of society, with the hope that the minds of everyone taking part may become as pure as the flowers.

Today's service was structured according to Pure Land Buddhist tradition. Following these offerings, the adoration of the Three Treasures of Buddhism (sanborai) is chanted, welcoming the buddhas (sanbujō) into the main hall of the temple. The head priest intones the nenbutsu (calling and honoring the name of the Buddha), and then reads the names of the mizuko written on the wooden memorial slats (tōba) that have been offered. The service concludes with ekō or transfer of merit, in this case, to the mizuko to help it reach Buddhahood. At the end of the service, a talk (hōwa) is usually given, which offers words of encouragement and advice on incorporating Buddhist teachings into one's own life.

1. *Waga mi kiyoki koto kōrō no gotoku* (My body is as pure as an incense burner). In other words, fire burns away impurities, leaving only ash. We want our mind to become pure; we want to follow the rules and disciplines (kai) of the Buddha and to keep a calm mind.
2. The next chant was the Three Treasures Chant: respect for the Buddha, respect for his teaching, and respect for each other.
3. The third chant was to welcome the Buddha into this *dōjō* (worship hall). This was followed by a chant to indicate that they would now begin.

4. This was followed by chanting to the rhythm of the *mokugyō* (wooden fish drum) as a way of revering Amida Nyorai (Buddha of the Pure Land). We admire Amida Nyorai because he saves every creature.
5. Oda-san continued by chanting the *Nenbutsu*, followed by chants for *mizuko*, including the *Jizō wasan* (dating from the Tokugawa Period.) This includes the tale of *sai no kawara*, where aborted fetuses pile stones to pray for their parents, but demons come and scatter the stones, saying it will do their parents no good, because they are so sad about their lost children that they cannot grow spiritually. At this point Jizō comes and saves the children.

The liturgy of the *kuyō* differs from temple to temple, and a variety of chants may be added to the ritual. The two most common chants are the *Hannya Shingyō* (Heart Sutra) and the *Jizō wasan* (song in praise of Jizō). Oda-san was then asked whether the meaning of this ancient tale, the tale of *sai-no-kawara* should be taken literally and, if not, what is its symbolical meaning?

ODA HŌRYŪ: Young people may not understand narratives about hell and paradise. However, because every human has *busshin* (Buddha-mind), this term can refer either to the Buddha's compassionate and enlightened mind or to the originally clear and pure mind inherent in all beings to which we must awake. We know we should strive to follow it, but we become distracted. So even if young people may laugh as they hear such stories, they can attain greater consciousness of their own deep shortcomings (*tsumi*). Genshin (Eshin Sōzū, 942–1017) said that these stories are for those who take life (*sesshō*) or give way to anger or become addicted to a life of pleasure. These habits of the heart make life itself unpleasant and difficult for ourselves and for others. The intent of *Jizō wasan* legends is to ask parents of a *mizuko* to reflect deeply about the decisions they have made.

The concept of *ekō* means to change directions, to take one's own good deeds and turn them to the benefit of others. In Pure Land Buddhism, we chant *Namu amida butsu*. By engaging in this, one dedicates one's honest heart and sincere feelings to the Buddha. The chant recalls the Buddha's promise to save all life. It is also *ekō* to pray that the departed *mizuko* can draw close to Buddha in heaven. Another kind is *gensō-ekō*. This means to pray that the departed person after attaining enlightenment will return [in some fashion] and help to guide us.

This can also be a prayer that our human teachers in this life will lead us on the right path.

STUDENT: What do you say to help these parents achieve a calm mind?

ODA HŌRYŪ: Those who attended the wake (*tsūya*) today received only the sermon, but for those who come for advice we talk more about Buddhist teaching. Fundamental to this teaching is that all human life is suffering. For instance, at some point we have to part from those we love. We cannot avoid or flee from suffering; rather, we must confront it and learn from it. In this manner it will no longer be suffering (*ku o norikoeru*). It will be overcome. While it is difficult to work up such courage, we must concentrate on our current way of being (*ikizama*) and come to understand its oneness with *busshin*.

We turn our suffering into enlightenment through changing our way of looking at existence. *Tenjukyōju* means that by taking the heavy burden off our backs (through Amida), we can accept our sufferings with greater dignity and insight. By offering all things to the Buddha (*tōmyō*), our heart becomes radiant and pure (like flowers). In any one vase there may be different colors and shapes of flowers, just as in families and communities there are many different forms of people. But like the flowers in a vase, we must coexist. In nature at large there is a vast interdependence.

The incense (*senkō*) burns away the old ash and refreshes the pure flame. In other words, rather than being too assertive, we should learn to compromise with other people. In that way, different substances give way to each other. As the incense gives away before the fire, people can learn how to give way to others. Incense is also fragrant; its fragrance quiets our hearts. *Kuyō* nurtures a calm state of mind. *Sonaeru* (offering sacrifices) also helps to calm our hearts and minds. *Kuyō* is not so much for the departed, as for one's own peace of mind. As one song says, "The services for the dead are really for the hearts of the living." The wake (*tsūya* or all-night vigil beside the corpse) is for the living and the dead, but it is more important for our own growth.

STUDENT: What are some topics you might address at this type of service?

ODA HŌRYŪ: A central topic is making the most of one's life (*inochi o ikasu*) and that every sentient thing has life. Because each person, each animal, each tree, each blade of grass has life, we should not use these things lightly. We must treat all living things as if they had their own importance (*mono o taisetsu ni suru*).

STUDENT: Do you tell parents of *mizuko* they have committed a sin (*tsumi*)?

ODA HŌRYŪ: Buddha's teaching is not to judge. While the realization of *tsumi* does not disappear, Buddha's teaching is to save people from their *tsumi*. [In other words, their *tsumi* is transformed.] This happens through repentance from the heart (*kokoro kara no sange*), in which one's promise is not to keep repeating the same mistake. We pray that the soul of the *mizuko* may go safely to paradise. Through *ekō* (saying the *Nenbutsu*) our prayer is for the *mizuko* to come back to us [in some fashion] and that we be made whole again.[7]

STUDENT: Are abortion, stillbirth, and miscarriage all treated the same?

ODA HŌRYŪ: One of the dangers of *mizuko kuyō* is to assume that if you just perform the memorial service your *tsumi* will be erased. So priests should give those who have aborted fetuses strong counseling so that they not do it again. In cases where there are unavoidable circumstances (such as miscarriage or rape), one instructs them to pray from their heart for the fetus, and in the process they too will be healed. One woman who was raped didn't know what to do; my counsel for her was to have an abortion but then to have *kuyō* performed for herself and for the *mizuko*.

Regardless of the causes of an abortion or miscarriage, there is no changing the fact that the child has a life, a soul. Buddhists treat the soul (*tamashii*) of each *mizuko* the same, regardless of the cause. In the case of miscarriage, even though the woman could not have avoided it (let's say, due to ill health). On the other hand, because it may stem from something related to one's way of life (one's *ikizama*), the person may engage mindfully in self-reflection (*hansei suru*) about the cause.

STUDENT: Does Oda-san counsel women about family planning?

ODA HŌRYŪ: Sometimes, depending on the person, we talk about contraception. Everyone has sexual desire, but it needs to be used "wisely" (*jōzu ni*) so that it does not have a bad result. One needs to be aware of the possible consequences of improper desire. This is part of what is discussed when we meet with men and women.

Yvonne Rand's Experience with Rituals for Pregnancy Loss in America

Attending the same *kuyō* service at Jikishian on October 23, 1990, was the well-known American Buddhist priest Yvonne Rand, who had been conducting *mizuko kuyō* services for women for nearly two decades in the San Francisco area who had experienced some form of pregnancy loss.

I asked her previously if she would be willing to discuss some of her experiences with Oda-san and others who attended his service and dharma
talk. This was the first time that Oda-san had known directly about this
American practice. Shinji Kazue interpreted Rand's description of how
she conducted *mizuko kuyō* in the United States. A fuller statement about
her practice is included in the Appendices.

> This past June [1990] I conducted a *mizuko kuyō* ceremony for thirty-
> two women. Before we began, I talked about Jizō Bodhisattva and
> his qualities. We then sat in a circle in silence, and everyone made a
> small bib from red cloth—for as many beings as they wished. Some
> made more than one.
>
> As we sat quietly, anyone who wanted to speak could say some-
> thing. But no one gave them advice or comfort [*nagusameru*]. We
> were just listening. One of the first to speak was a woman who said
> that forty-seven years ago she had an abortion to end a pregnancy
> from an incestuous relationship with her father. She said, "I've
> never been able to speak of that experience until today."

[She later wrote to Yvonne and expressed some sense of resolution (*kaiketsu/
kokoro no seiru*), a profound quieting of her disturbed mind.]

> Two other women had abortions when they were very young, and
> who, subsequently, were never able to have children. There was one
> woman who had an abortion because of a rape, and there were sev-
> eral who had experienced miscarriages.
>
> As we listened to each other, I emphasized that in the United
> States the issue of abortion is very heated, with people becoming
> almost violent, at both ends of the spectrum [*ryōkyokutan*]. In this
> circle, all points of view were represented: Some were against abor-
> tion, others approved of it, with every political position one could
> imagine. The common element was an experience of some deep
> suffering around a miscarriage or an abortion, whatever their polit-
> ical or philosophical position may have been.
>
> Listening to each other in that circle, we acknowledged [*sonchō
> shite ageru/mitomeru*] whatever had happened in the life of each one
> of us. After doing this for maybe an hour, we went out to a ter-
> race next to a room that was sheltered by trees. Here there was a
> kind of shrine with seven or eight figures of Jizō and one *Mizuko*

Jizō, and we stood in a circle around this altar. We had offerings of incense and flowers, and I performed a ceremony somewhat like the one that was just done by Oda-san, and we stated our intention in doing this ceremony for the sake of the spirit of the unborn children to whom we were dedicating these practices. Following this, we chanted the Heart Sutra [*Hannya Shingyō*] and a chant to Kannon Bosatsu.

One by one each person came forward, offering incense and putting a child's bib they had made on the figure they had chosen. Many of these women remained at the altar for a few minutes and would say something silently, just for themselves. Afterward, as each person bowed before the altar, we would all bow with them. As this occurred, the circle of women became a kind of safe chamber, holding each woman in their hearts as she went to the altar. This created for each a sense of being held by the others who were present. After about half an hour, I offered [*sasaeru*] a kind of dedication [*ekō no yō na mono*].

Since that occasion, many of these women have written to me about the sense of healing [*iyashi no kimochi*], or settling [*kokoro ga ochitsuku/ shizumaru*], or deep feeling of quietness that they had not experienced before. One woman had participated vicariously for her daughter's miscarriages.

At another time I did this particular ceremony at a conference on Women in Buddhism, attended by approximately 250 women. Within an hour everyone at the conference knew about the ceremony; the word spread throughout the group like a kind of grass fire. It was very powerful.

I had been doing ceremonies like this for quite a while [since the early 1970s]. What always surprises me is how a power for healing comes from acknowledging that a genuine form of dying has occurred. A ceremony that includes this quality of repentance [*sange/zange*] and that speaks to a place within ourselves [*fukai kimochi o shiru* (to know) or *fukai kimochi ni fureru* (to touch)] and to this other being whose life was ended contributes to something deeply effective in the healing process. It seems to arise from doing this combination of activities.

Shinji Kazue, the interpreter, mentioned how impressed she was by the universality (*fuhensei*) of such experiences, particularly when cultural differences are so "extremely big" and how something that is understood (*tsūjiru*) in one culture may be completely foreign or not understood (*tsūjinai*) in another. Yvonne mentioned that both she and Robert Aitkin, a Zen teacher in Hawaii at the time, started conducting their ceremonies before they ever knew about *mizuko kuyō* in Japan. Nevertheless, experiencing Japan's practice of *mizuko kuyō* provided her with a kind of affirmation (*kakushin o motsu*) and encouragement that gave her a sense of how to go even deeper.

Other Forms of Memorial Services for the Unborn in America

In his book *Mourning the Unborn Dead: A Buddhist Ritual Comes to America* (2009), Jeff Wilson discusses many forms of similar memorial rituals within various cultural settings.[18] Of special interest in these comparisons is how they provide a richer sense of what pregnancy loss means to a woman, whether Japanese or American, and how this experience is shaped by the mores of her time.

In the American context there are normally no fees for the performance of this ritual and therefore no form of economic exploitation. This does not mean there are no restrictions. The expectation in most American settings is that the person for whom this is done should participate actively in the service, while in Japan it is more common for those attending *mizuko kuyō* to be essentially "passive recipients" in settings that are conducted by priests, though in the newer forms of religion in Japan lay participation can be much more active. As an example, Wilson cites how differently the Heart Sutra is chanted. While the chanting may be vigorous in Japanese temples, the premium in these settings is not on understanding its meaning but in producing "spiritual merit (*kudoku*) for subsequent ritual offering and dedication to a variety of beings and purposes."[19] Because these purposes are not mutually exclusive, both may be sought in many Buddhist communities in each society.

A second feature differentiating American from Japanese forms of practice is that in Japan there is rarely encouragement for participants "to express to strangers their feelings or reasons for their presence at the ceremony," in contrast to what one finds in Rand's descriptions.[20] In American Zen communities, opportunities are regularly created for men as well so that they too may share their feelings about pregnancy loss, including loss by induced abortion. As one Zen abbess wrote: "I facilitated a healing circle on abortion [in 2000], an intimate gathering of five women and four men. The circle was open to women who have had an abortion, whether therapeutic or by choice, and to men who were partners to an abortion."[21] One would seldom find such gatherings in Japan. She continues, "No one who has ever had an abortion, or been partner to one, escapes its pain. This is not a loss we grieve openly, if we allow ourselves to grieve at all. Our grief and guilt live... *as a shadow in the heart.* The cultural, legal, and religious postures around abortion offer little support for women and men who have lived through it... I've rarely experienced such profound grief and better understand how this emotion is necessary to letting go."[22] It would seem clear that feminists who are supportive of a woman's choice have increasingly expressed similar feelings, in America and even in Japan, in recent years.

Another major difference between what occurs in America and what still exists in Japan is a belief that spirits of the dead may haunt the living unless they have been properly memorialized. Wilson makes a distinction in saying that "what in Japan [tends to be] a strongly shame-based practice becomes a relatively nonjudgmental one in America—the only judgments are ones the woman brings to the ceremony herself, which are neither encouraged nor discouraged by the clergy."[23] On the other hand, as we discussed earlier about the meaning of *tsumi*, it is often the case that the origins of these feelings may be several, not simply *inner* or *outer*.

In general, the memorial service in American Buddhist communities is intended to promote "the mental and spiritual health of the grieving mother (and/or father)."[24] It is "to remember an abortion, miscarriage, stillbirth, or the death of a young infant," yet a service of this kind may also "honor runaway children, children given up for adoption, children lost through post-divorce custody disputes, or adult children alienated from their parents...[or] on behalf of their own 'lost childhood.'"[25] In other words, "it is the parent who is the main object of concern in the ritual [not the *mizuko*]. The point is to produce healing for these mourners."[26] Therapeutic in nature, it allows "hidden emotions to come into the conscious mind, where they [can] be acknowledged, expressed, and realized."[27]

As a way of summarizing the larger picture of ceremonies for the unborn dead found in the American scene, Wilson identifies three fundamental needs.[28] The first is for an increasing number of women to voice their experience of pregnancy loss, since women often have difficulty doing so due to a culture or *code* of silence toward experiences of this kind, as illustrated by Sue Nathanson and Linda Layne. Wilson's first point is therefore the importance of "finding a voice," enabling individuals to find their own voice and to express this within a community that recognizes the necessity for this. The second need is for a community of listeners, who having faced similar grief can listen actively to and share this plight with others. The third feature is the creation of ways by which this loss can be mourned. "Pregnancy loss precipitates a tremendous feeling of power-lessness...along with a frustration that there seems to be little or nothing available. It is here that rituals like *mizuko kuyō* appear to offer a society with little history of ritualization of pregnancy loss a way to actively deal with grief."[29]

While similar needs exist in Japan, it is rare to find contexts in which they are discussed openly among people with comparable experiences. On the other hand, an interesting comment by the head priest at Hasedera, mentioned in Chapter 2, stressed that the practice of *mizuko kuyō* became a factor in drawing younger women into temple life, normally participated in by older women.[30] However important a common experience of miscar-riage or abortion may be, a deeper sense of bonding may emerge, based on sharing their fuller experiences as a wife and particularly as a mother in contemporary Japan. The sharing of a greater commonness lessens their sense of isolation, provides a range of models for what being a woman can mean, and enlarges a woman's horizon at the same time that it closes the door on an anguishing chapter in her life.[31] Pain shared creates the possi-bility of community beyond the common experiences of loneliness.[32]

In her book *Grief Unseen: Healing Pregnancy Loss through the Arts* (2006), Laura Seftel raises the problematic of what she calls a "grief without a shape." Having experienced pregnancy, abortion, miscarriage, and giving birth herself, she discovered how these are "multilayered and interwoven" with each other. Whether stillbirth, neonatal loss, ectopic pregnancy, or infertility, each was located under the rubric of "losing a dream." And each may become "an invisible loss...[in which] open and in-depth discussion of pregnancy loss is still culturally forbidden."[33] Cultural silence about these forms of loss furthers the sense of isolation a woman may endure.

We move now from how the work of grieving pregnancy loss may be expressed through innumerable forms of the arts. The intent of *Grief Unseen* is to illustrate how both artists and ritual leaders, who may not find sustenance in conventional responses to pregnancy loss, may experience "the power that visual imagery, song, movement, and storytelling...draw upon both personal and universal symbols in order to give form to their formless grief, to purge their lingering guilt and anger, and to make meaning and reconnect with the world around them."[34] This giving of form provides the invisible with texture, shape, and significance, enabling the formlessness of grief to be woven into a larger body of meaning. Toward this end, the next portion of the chapter explores how the relationship of the living to the dead has been enacted through Japanese drama, devotional songs (*wasan*), and invocations to the deceased. Each art form may exist either within or outside religious jurisdiction; it may challenge but also enhance the power of conventional Buddhist praxis. The following three sections exemplify how Japanese culture through drama, visualization, and the invocations (*kuchiyose*) of blind mediums portray other means by which the living seek communication with the dead.

It is the specificity of what is performed or portrayed that enlivens the imagination and employs one's senses in new ways. Art gives shape to experiences that cry for other images of the significant. In this regard, Michel de Certeau's perspective helps by telling us to look in the "gaps and lacunae in texts, in form instead of content, in those things that are present in their very absence."[35] By using stories or narratives as "modes of writing that aim to open themselves up to the workings of what has been hidden, silenced, smothered," one comes upon the energy of otherness.[36] It is this energy that enlivens and brings about rebirth and transformation, including the sense of otherness that is hidden or repressed within oneself.

Relating the Living to the Dead in Post-Medieval Japan: Confluence of Noh Drama, Buddhist Cosmology, Ritual, and Social Issues

The first two examples of how ancient drama still speaks to the living may be seen in the Noh play *Sumidagawa* and the tradition of devotional songs (*wasan*) in praise of Jizō connected with legends about *sai-no-kawara*. The effectiveness of these expressions lies to a significant degree in their dramatic and poetic forms.[37] A third example is illustrated throughout Japan wherever sizable numbers of people seek connection with the recently deceased. Among prominent sites of this kind is Osorezan where one finds the meeting of ancestors, ghosts and, in recent decades, *mizuko*. In this sense it is a newly sensed presence of the deceased (Figure 8.1).

FIGURE 8.1 Sai-no-kawara scene at Chōshō-ji Rinzai Zen temple in Shiga-ken.

Of special interest for the study of *mizuko kuyō* is how these earlier, premodern forms of communicating with the dead retain their power to open up an invisible reality that continues to haunt contemporary existence. It is Gavin Brown's insight that rituals can be dynamic and transformative precisely when they "manifest indeterminacy," that is, when they engage in "privileging the moment."[38] Because "ritual is a declaration of form against indeterminacy…indeterminacy is [ironically] present in the background of any analysis of ritual."[39] The voices of the past emerge from the background. They become open to some sense of indeterminacy when they are congruent with similar life experiences in the present. Because life itself is indeterminate, performances that lack a sense of indeterminacy are lifeless. In other words, rituals or ritual-like performances can be transformative not despite their inherent structure or morphology but *because* of it.[40] It is through performances, therefore, in theater, music, and liturgies of healing that new life can often be discovered and expressed (Figure 8.2).

Sumidagawa: *"In This Grief-Laden World…"*

While *Sumidagawa* deals with themes that address spiritual realities, including a memorial service, and while the context of its setting occurs

FIGURE 8.2 Elizabeth Harrison, Charlotte Smith, Kanai Gudō, Nishimura Eshin at Chōshō-ji temple.

outside a temple, it incorporates forms of ritualistic practice that lie below the surface of ordinary consciousness. In many ways, the action of Noh plays moves within and speaks to the boundary between this world and the realm of the dead. The tales found in Noh drama are typically of the spirits of warriors, of deranged women, and of demons who make audible for a moment the unvoiced language of tormented spirits. In an agonizingly real manner, these figures exist at the margins (*shūen*) of everyday life. In this case, it is a deranged mother looking for her lost child.

Within the category of plays about deranged women there is no more highly revered story about child loss in Japanese literature than *Sumidagawa*.[41] In graphic form it depicts the sorrow of losing one's child and of a *kuyō* held on the banks of a river in the child's behalf, memorializing his death that occurred one year before. It situates the placement of this loss within a specific social and metaphysical cosmology. In this context the contrasting notions of transitoriness and the enduring grace of Amida intertwine. Written by Motomasa Jūrō (1395–1459), son of Zeami (Kanze Motokiyo), this play belongs to the genre *kyōjo mono* or "mad woman piece." In the Muromachi period (1334–1573), when this play was written, "the unit of mother and child signifies total world perfection, and when this perfection is shattered, the mother becomes deranged."[42] With her world now devoid of meaning, she wanders in her aloneness in quest of this lost child.

The scene is set on the banks of the Sumida River in what is now Tokyo. A ferryman (*waki*) is about to take an unnamed traveler to the other shore (a metaphor for Amida's Pure Land) when an obviously distraught woman (*shite*) appears, seeking passage. Unknown to others at this stage, she is the widow of Lord Yoshida of Kita-Shirakawa in Kyoto and the mother of a twelve-year-old boy who was abducted the previous year by a slave trader. Ever since, she has searched with "frenzied longing" for her lost son, Umewaka-maru (*kokata*). As the boat makes its way across the river, the woman divulges the reason for her search. The ferryman belatedly realizes that she is the mother of the boy whose death anniversary is just then being memorialized on the opposite shore by villagers who remember his valor in the face of sudden illness and death. To see this play is to appreciate the emotion portrayed by the mother as she takes part in the *kuyō* for her son. In her grief she seeks, as it were, to exist in two worlds at once:

> *Before the mother's eyes the son appears*
> *And fades away*
> *As does the phantom broomtree.*
> *In this grief-laden world*
> *Such is the course of human life . . .*
> *Now eyes see how fleeting is this life.*[43]

On stage, the ghost of Umewaka-maru emerges from the burial mound, disappears, and reappears again. Each time the mother tries to touch him, but she cannot cross the boundary of life and death. The child speaks to her and echoes the villagers who are chanting the Buddha's name (*nenbutsu*). She reaches for his hand once more.

> *The vision fades and reappears*
> *And stronger grows her yearning.*
> *Day breaks in the eastern sky.*
> *The ghost has vanished;*
> *What seemed her boy is but a grassy mound*
> *Lost on the wide, desolate moor.*
> *Sadness and tender pity fill all hearts . . .*[44]

In a dramatic sense *Sumidagawa* not only incorporates a *kuyō* service, it becomes one. By its very length on stage it draws out the feelings of grief in extended catharsis. While the tragedy of the child's death remains, greater prominence is given, by means of this long enactment, to the facing of this reality. Grief not encountered is a grief denied, and one thereby retains the "frenzied longing" in one guise or another. Only upon realizing that what she "sees" is a ghost can she accept his death, mourn her loss, and begin to regain her wholeness of mind.

A vital part of the drama is the manner in which her loneliness is transformed into the beginnings of human community. For a year she has walked a solitary path in search of her lost son, estranged by her loss and her madness from normal social bonds. As she approaches the ferry it is clear to the viewer that she is beside herself, for reasons that none can know. In medieval Japan there was a tradition for onlookers, out of amusement, to ask mad women to display their "amusing" (*omoshiroi*) mad behavior, which frequently takes the form of dance. This curious spectacle serves only to isolate the woman further from her viewers. In *Sumidagawa*, however, as the ferryman tells those on the boat what is happening on the far shore he becomes aware by the mother's reactions to this tale that she is, in fact, the boy's mother.

Suddenly, his manner toward her changes from what had been one of distance and condescension to one of tenderness. Others in the boat, as represented by the Traveler from Miyako (*waki-zure*), catch this shift in mood and are also deeply affected. This subtle change is the first sign of an inclusive community. As the boat docks on the far shore, one form of separation has been breached: the mad woman-mother is now seen in human terms. The party moves to where the villagers are conducting the memorial service. Other than the recognition that she has located her son but that he is dead, the most powerful elements of this scene are twofold. First, the villagers gather the grieving mother into the fullness of human community, and, second, this community and the audience itself are confronted with the most liminal of situations, namely, the cleavage between life and death. This combined cleavage and connection create for the viewer the sense of a complex cosmology. Though the play ends on a note of "sadness and tender pity," it reaffirms the mystical connection between transient existence and some larger reality represented here by the chants of "Namu Amida Butsu" (homage to the name of Amida Buddha).

While retaining a tragic ending, *Sumidagawa* lends deeper meaning to the many worlds of suffering and in the process ritualizes the promise of a transformed existence. It is by memorializing the dead and through embracing those who suffer loss that compassion is expressed. It is particularly in Noh drama that one is in the presence of tormented spirits that must be laid to rest. In *Sumidagawa* it is ironically the case that the principal tormented spirit is not the child but the "crazed woman" (*kyōjo*), the child's mother, whose frenzied spirit is in need of being healed of grief, symbolized by the *fukai* mask worn by those whose anguish is boundless. It is her spirit that cannot be put to rest because of the tragic manner in which the child's life was lost, but it is through the muted voice of her child from the dead that her sanity is restored, and the connection made between the mother and her child (Figure 8.3).

FIGURE 8.3 The Mother in Sumidagawa, afflicted by the loss of her son, experiences healing through dramatized ritual.

The specific purpose in focusing on this Noh play is to depict it as an artistic example of how grieving the loss of a child can be powerfully portrayed and experienced in modern Japan. Having seen it performed in different productions in Tokyo in the 1980s as well as in the United States, I have been impressed by how well it comes across as a *kuyō* in a different guise. Earlier, this chapter discussed how performative ritual and ritual-like activity can be seen in a variety of art forms. In this sense, *Sumidagawa* is a performative enactment of how the living relate to the deepest forms of human loss and how skillfully it portrays the indeterminacy of the human condition, regardless of how long ago this Noh play was written.

In another respect, in an article dealing with the genre of Noh plays about child loss, Erika Ohara Bainbridge underscores the link between the social backgrounds of women in the Muromachi period (1334–1573) and the role of crazed mothers in these plays.[45] Central to her thesis is how the issue of child loss may be set within this larger historical, social, and cultural series of connections, namely, (1) between that society's view of women as mothers, (2) the stake that women had in being mothers because of their diminished social roles, and (3) the derangement that women experienced when they had lost a child.

In this manner, one may see similar connections between these same three features and the experience of women and child loss in contemporary Japan. The dramatic power of this Noh play lends deeper meaning to contemporary forms of devastating loss, its ritualized significance, its expanded cosmology and the difficulty with which many women respond to "child loss." To ignore these features would be to trivialize a woman's experience of loss. And to emphasize only the experience of loss, ignoring social and cultural circumstances of Japanese women today, is to view women in general as an abstraction, as another form of "the other."

Jizō Wasan *and* Sai-No-Kawara *Legends: Tokugawa and Contemporary Versions*

The popularity of hymns of praise to the bodhisattva Jizō (*Jizō bosatsu wasan*) for his wondrous acts began to arise in the Tokugawa period (1603–1868). Each of the legends about the dry river bed (*sai-no-kawara*) upon which dead children pile up stones as prayers for their grieving parents presents an ongoing struggle between the forces of destruction and those of healing. In such stories one is presented with a world that appears as devoid of hope. It is a drama with no apparent resolution, providing only ongoing forms of ritualized contention and release. Its meaning in premodern times, at least in Pure Land Buddhism, is primarily focused on Jizō as the compassionate guide from the *shaba* world of birth, suffering, and death along the path of darkness and obscurity (known as *meido*), through the world of hell ruled over by King Yama, where each person is judged according to his karma and finally attains to the Pure Land through the grace of Amida.

In contemporary Buddhism, on the other hand, Jizō is beloved primarily for his help to people who are at the crossroads of human experience. And in *mizuko kuyō* this figure is regarded as the central bodhisattva to whom people turn in anguish when they have experienced child loss, including loss through abortion. What the *sai-no-kawara wasan* does in the contemporary context of *mizuko kuyō* is to establish the link between the bodhisattva Jizō and the care of dead children. Although the children in the hymn worry about their parents, and while parents of *mizuko* today worry about their children as they chant, the central image of the hymn is of a bond of concern between parents and children and of Jizō stepping in to help: Jizō takes care of the children in the same way that parents would.[46]

The *wasan* and the *kuyō* service in general establish a strong link among parents, *mizuko*, and the religious place where the memorial service occurs, for it is through the formal service at its particular place that the parent–absent child bond is continually celebrated and, perhaps, made real. In many places where the *sai-no-kawara* story is told there are vivid portrayals in art form that show the children on the dry riverbed, the menacing *oni* or demons who treat the children cruelly, and the salvific figure of Jizō who rescues these children from their suffering. In the oft-repeated text, its art forms, and in ritualized staging the scene is portrayed in complementary forms.

In a similar respect, reverence for Jizō is expressed in modern *wasan* or hymns. One begins by identifying the ingredients of a *Jizō wasan* that came out of Tokugawa times, underscoring the forlorn cosmology that it portrays. A well-known text of this story is located in the Appendices.[47] It is clear that the narrator of this story seeks to touch the heartstrings of the desolate parent whose child has been snatched away but at the same time provides assurance that the child is being cared for by the compassionate Jizō. While the story is familiar to most who hear it being told, it rarely ceases to affect the listener. It is akin to the Noh play where the lineaments of the tale are well-known but where the enactment of the scene, like a much-practiced ritual, elicits fresh reactions.

FIGURE 8.4 Sanmyōji sai-no-kawara scene, Toyokawa, Aichi-ken. Jizō responds to the pain of desolate parents and rescues their forlorn children.

While different in many respects, similar motifs are present in the Noh play *Sumidagawa* and in this *wasan* about *sai-no-kawara*. In both, there is an extended experience of unrelieved desolation. For a full year the mother of the lost child wanders grief-stricken, on her own, with no sense of where her missing child might be. In like fashion, small children in the *wasan* have been plucked from their comfortable homes and now exist in the timeless and barren condition of death. In both, the surviving parents look prayerfully but in vain for their children, with little hope of seeing them again. Though driven by their grief, they yearn to reestablish this connection. In each story, we are presented with an impenetrable divide between the worlds of life and death, yet at the same time we are shown the means of establishing a ritualistic interplay between them. In each, we are confronted with the obvious but powerful theme of the inseparable bond existing between a parent, especially a mother, and a child. In the Noh play the name of this child is known, as is the identity of its mother; in the *wasan* no names are provided, but the sense of agony is no less vivid. In both, we have a portrayal of the human condition in which there can be no dissociating of life and death. Both are central to a universal cosmology in which they are inseparably linked. In both stories, the note of tragedy remains (in that the dead are not brought back to life), but it is combined with a note of resolution (as one comes to terms with the fact of death as part of the larger cosmology of existence). And in one, the child is party to the bringing of Amida's larger message; in the other, the messenger is the bodhisattva Jizō.

Ancestors, Ghosts, and Mizuko: Osorezan—Where the Living Meet the Dead

We deal thirdly with the nature of the occult in Japanese religion and society and how this has influenced some forms of *mizuko kuyō*. Central to any form of "occult practice" is the belief that communication occurs between the living and the dead. In her analysis of Osorezan (Mt. Osore), located on the furthermost peninsula of northeast Honshu, Marilyn Ivy examines different modes of encountering death at this site.[48] It is a place of considerable renown and is cast as a site where ancient folk practices are still believed to exist. As one of many sites in Japan where spirits of the dead are said to reside, it is where large numbers of people come to seek connection with the recently deceased through the efforts of female mediums (*itako*). The drama of Osorezan serves to confront visitors with the inexplicable, suggesting that we have no choice but to live with the liminal ambiguities that constitute life as much as death. We are destined to seek bridges between what we know and what we do not know, indeed, between what we think we know and what we can never fully understand—including our finite worlds.

The purpose of discussing Osorezan in this chapter is not to portray the many functions of this site as these evolved ever since the mid-seventeenth century but to note that, as recently as the past forty years, "new rites such as prayers for aborted or miscarried fetus, known as *mizuko*" have been added.[49] Instead, the focus here is much more limited. It is upon the belief that through the medium of a traditionally blind female shaman in northern Japan, there can be communication with the dead, of which a mother's desire to commune with her *mizuko* is but one example.

In the midst of Osorezan's rugged site is located a Sōtō Zen temple, Entsūji, which represents the more conventional approach of consoling, pacifying, and settling the spirits of the dead in order that the living may be blessed by their ancestors. The world of Osorezan (the "mountain of terror") disconcerts—that is, indeed, its power. An interesting modus vivendi has evolved between the relative orthodoxy of Buddhist rituals of the dead within the temple with "their narratives of redemption" and the counterpoint to this as found in ghost narratives that represent unpredictability. In between lie further tensions. On one hand is the virtually unpredictable manner whereby ghosts of the dead are encountered and summoned by the medium who calls down (*kuchi-yose*) these spirits. In contrast, there is the more standard approach used by Buddhist priests in their efforts to memorialize the recently dead in their unsettled condition. The intent in both is to entice these spirits to protect and bestow blessings on their descendants. The role of the medium is to facilitate communication between the living and the dead and to divine the client's future through advice coming from the deceased.

The official Buddhist practices are represented by a person's purchasing, inscribing, offering, and receiving back the priestly blessed wooden marker (*tōba*) that substitutes for the dead person's body. This "act of buying a memorial tōba brings the dead person more securely within the domain of controlled, orderly ancestorhood."[50] This is analogous to reinforcing the social and cosmic order. It helps the deceased to make the dangerous transition from one realm to another and to assist the mourner through the process of dealing with the "weight of words left unsaid," as one of Ivy's informants put it.

Another ingredient of Buddhist encounters with the dead is for each person to make her pilgrimage through the liminal terrain of the recently dead—nature's simulation of *sai-no-kawara*. It is here that the bodhisattva Jizō comforts the children as they engage in a "meaningless accumulation and disaccumulation" of stones as prayers for their disconsolate parents. In making this brief pilgrimage visitors participate in the piling up of stones and pebbles, thereby delineating the boundary between this world and the next. As Ivy indicates, this process is doomed to fail—our offerings are never adequate. It is meant not to evoke resignation but to highlight the need for the living to join in what Jizō symbolizes, namely, remembering and caring for the dead. Severing such connections deflates what it means to be human; measured against the needs of the living and the dead these are lessons in humility. Even the presence of grace, personified by Jizō, reveals the enormous odds that Buddhist metanarratives of salvation take on.

The other principal forms of encountering death at Osorezan are represented by ghost narratives and are reported by those who have seen these unsettled spirits of the recently dead and by the blind mediums in bridging the divide between the living and the dead. As to what ghosts and mediums signify about our normal canons of expectation, one is confronted with the fact that we live in a world that cannot be measured by human standards or controlled by human wills. Ivy's discussion of ghosts conveys how to the Japanese imagination "there are gaps in the edifice of memorialization, [and that] through these gaps the dangerous, unsettled dead appear."[51] It is ghosts who "reveal an irruption of the other world that is beyond the...reach of memory or the predictability of the senses. They indicate a point where the control of the dead is called into question."[52]

This revelation is an embarrassment to the Buddhist skills of ordering reality. While Buddhist orthodoxy does not promote these kinds of ghost narratives, it maintains at least an ambivalent stance with respect to the telling of them. These stories represent the ongoing surds in human experience; they are the irrational at the heart of our systematizing. This is why it is both difficult and necessary for a woman who has lost a child to *find her own means of representing* that child, her own need to give that child a specific name and form. By this, she comes to terms with what does not make sense. In *mizuko* research, one keeps finding instances in which women have created their own rituals and talismans, becoming agents in their own behalf.

On the other hand, what is highly personalized needs to be set into a larger ritualistic context. The interchange between medium and client occurs not in charismatic trance but in conventionalized formats. In the hands of a skilled practitioner it resembles more ritual language than shamanic convulsion or dance. In its archaic style, the ritual sets the stage for an encounter to occur across the divide separating the worlds of the living and the dead. This contextualization is akin to hearing the words of the Mass from the depths of a cathedral in a language one does not understand. Its deepest meaning exceeds comprehension. It is more mood and expectation than intelligibility, or it is like experiencing a Noh play before reading the libretto or even afterward. It employs all of one's senses if one is desperate for communication with a beloved dead one. Of greater importance than the words and their meaning is the sensed presence of the deceased. It is here that one realizes "the irretrievability of what is lost, signaled by the irresolvable gap between the voice of the medium and the dead person's remembered voice."[53]

What can occur is a brief experience of simultaneity; it generates belief in a multivalent dimension of time. Without denying that the past is past, it signifies that the past becomes genuinely present. By experiencing time afresh, the past is brought up into the present and provides different images of the future. The present is renewed when its doors are open to the past, without being controlled by it. This is what Osorezan seems to be saying.

For Ivy, the great temptation is for people "to situate themselves against loss."[54] As was implied in Chapter 6, this temptation is what Yasukuni Jinja represents: it is restiveness in the face of uncertainty. It finds meaning primarily in past values. This temptation, Ivy suggests, may now be happening to the *itako* tradition itself. The process that signifies mortality is ironically slated to be lost. As present practitioners pass from the scene, the temptation is to replicate that past. Lacking the courage to face what is irretrievably lost (parts of one's culture or persons of immense importance to one) is a mark of tragedy. "The realization of loss is forestalled, denied...by an idealization, a memorialization of place, a bracketing of practices, an assertion of continuity."[55] Holding on to fixed images of the past consigns life to what is already familiar and at the same time hinders one from coping with the unknown.

The authentic medium, on the other hand, holds up for momentary recognition the past one wishes to reclaim but that is irrecoverably gone. In the process, false hopes are exorcised. With such recognition, the past can be incorporated in a manner that helps to transform. Becoming an agent in one's own life is to do for oneself what others cannot do for you. The central meaning of Osorezan goes beyond even the question of agency; it sets the human condition within a more complex cosmos that cannot be defined by transient social values, political ideology, or religious teachings without minimizing the impact of these.

If there are common factors existing within the Noh play *Sumidagawa*, the art forms and legends of *sai-no-kawara*, and in places such as Osorezan where the living meet the dead they may be along the following lines: (1) In each there is a search for contact with the dead, the one who is irretrievably lost; (2) each search confronts the inexorable line separating life from death; (3) coming to terms with the finality of death, one discovers forms of gaining communication; (4) it is the nature of these discoveries that another kind of *presence* of the deceased emerges, as we saw before in the elderly couple on pilgrimage in Shikoku; and (5) in the process, one may find a path out of devastating aloneness into some form of community, however small, however transient and thereby experience a connection with a larger whole, a genuine sense of interdependence. This is the subject of the final chapter.

9

Rituals of Affliction

AN INVITATION TO SOBRIETY

AT THIS POINT in the narrative the objective is to view the phenomena of *mizuko kuyō* and a variety of perspectives on Japanese women in larger social and cultural frameworks. Beliefs in expanded forms of existence contain structures by which to comprehend social and psychological realms that define human worlds. Cosmologies are religious and artistic ways of portraying human experiences, providing means by which people perceive "order" or "continuity" within a universe of continuous change. They are ways of imagining universes that escape everyday recognition. At the same time, cosmologies themselves require and invite reinterpretation.

Even a single visit to a temple confronts one with images and symbols that represent universes of meaning. While many ingredients in earlier cosmologies and rituals have been retained in the beliefs and practices associated with *mizuko kuyō*, they have been modified and supplemented by newer constructions in belief and practice. *Mizuko kuyō* may, therefore, be viewed as a case study in a conglomerating process that has existed throughout the history of Japanese religions.[1]

Yet the very concept of a worldview seems out of place in modern times. "For a couple centuries now we have been living in a world in which these points of reference no longer hold for us ... The very idea that one such order should be embraced to the exclusion of all the others ... ceases to have any force."[2] What has become more typical in the modern era is that men and women discover alternative forms of meaning.[3] Employing the perspective of Michel de Certeau, there are various "ways of speaking," various "rhetorics of practice" that allow for "a certain play within a system of defined places" by which these places are made "habitable" or even imaginable.[4] Entry into subjunctive worlds takes one by surprise; it opens up unimagined possibilities. Alternately, one finds possibilities within what may seem to be traditionally scripted cosmologies. While all worldviews are of human construction, the question is about the significance of worldviews that seem outmoded.

We are reminded once more of the comment made by the head priest of the Hasedera temple in Kamakura, who, when asked if he believed literally in the ancient teachings about Amida's Paradise or the miracles of Jizō, replied that they are "too important to be taken literally." In ways that are similar, Certeau suggests that it is by means of stories, narratives, and drama that one enters worlds that have hidden meanings. Hidden meanings are the true sense of "skillful means."[5] In the previous chapter we encountered these as "wondrous tales," ghost narratives, devotional songs (wasan), performative rituals, and artistic portrayals. These are worlds in which infinite dimensions can be encountered only if not taken literally. To be literal is to shut the door on fresh experience. As Akira Sadataka writes, the "Buddhist conception of the universe [has undergone] numerous changes over time."[6] To use terms such as "cosmology" or "worldview" can be exercises in imagination, but what do they construe?

In the words of the Japanese Buddhist philosopher Junjirō Takakusu: "The universe, according to the Buddhist idea, is not homocentric. It is instead a co-creation of all beings...everything inevitably comes out of more than one cause; in other words, all is mutually relative, a product of interdependence."[7] This is a powerful corrective to any form of human certitude and, indeed, welcomes the play of imagination, alternative views of existence, and all social perspectives without endorsing a stance of relativism.

Within the concept of interdependence exists a cosmology that while vast in scope and implication includes all forms of being. As was stressed earlier, this-worldly needs are congruent with the path of becoming a buddha. Rather than discarding earlier cosmologies one looks at them anew and at the same time beyond them. This is clearly the case as one tries to understand the phenomenon of mizuko kuyō and, indeed, what being a women means either in contemporary Japan or in earlier periods of history. While homocentric perspectives can easily become a default tendency, this is not inevitable. The intent of this final chapter is to highlight as well as to challenge that propensity.

Ritual and Cosmology in a World of Suffering and Conflict

"In this generation one is influenced by experiences within one's own tiny world, but one's true emotion comes from outside this material existence."[8]

From such perspectives one understands the continuing emotional tie to figures such as Jizō and Kannon in contemporary Japan, as in the past. In their metaphoric connotation they are seen as purveyors of succor and worldly benefits but also as embodying qualities that are life authenticating. The coincidence of worldly benefits with life-giving spiritual sustenance, as reflected in the architectural plan of Hasedera in Kamakura, mirrors the balance one also finds in the *Lotus Sūtra*, the *Jizō bosatsu reigenki*, and the *Jizō hongankyō*, as was discussed in Chapter 2. The point is that there is a balance between these two forms of human need. By examining parallels between Jizō and *mizuko*, one sees a juxtaposition of older and newer cosmologies and the possibility for *mizuko kuyō* to serve as a ritual that responds to suffering but does not promise a world in which there is no suffering. Based upon what one finds throughout Buddhist history in Japan, the emphasis in *mizuko kuyō* upon worldly benefits and protection should be no surprise. It suggests a fuller dimension of what the concept *mizuko* signifies.

Because Jizō identifies with those in any form of suffering, this figure symbolizes an apt counterforce in worlds where strife, violence, and discouragement are rife. In such a world Jizō represents the prospect of hope where this appears to be absent. In this sense, he assists in the confrontation of death and death equivalents (that is, situations of broken connection). If Jizō is considered a salvific boundary figure between forms of life and death, one symbolic meaning of *mizuko* lies in its representation of radical isolation, as one having no connection to anything living or dead, one whose "spirit" remains in limbo (another sense of *sai-no-kawara*) unless freed ritualistically to reenter the world in which one already exists. Potentially a symbol pointing toward redressive action, Jizō identifies with situations of brokenness. It is within fragmented cosmological contexts especially that *mizuko kuyō* can be understood.

As we know, a standard term in Japanese Buddhism for someone who has died without relatives is *muenbotoke*, one who has lived but who dies without descendants to make offerings for their spirits. *Muenbotoke* are symbols of those outside any cosmological or ancestral designation. While it would be overly simple to equate *mizuko* with *muenbotoke*, each is a spirit that has not been put to rest. The function of ritual is to assist in transforming unsettled spirits (psychologically, socially, and culturally restive spirits) into ones capable of being protective, restorative to the living. In the Buddhist sense, all mortuary ritual has transformation as a central purpose. If the symbols of both *mizuko* and *muenbotoke* represent human experience in some universal sense, the question arises of how rituals can assist persons and communities to confront obstacles to genuine community. For this purpose, it is useful to explore the notion of redressive ritual as a means of comprehending the "potential" of *mizuko kuyō* to illuminate the problems that women, as well as other people, face. The value of such rituals lies in inviting plural, often contending interpretations. At this point, theodicy, ritual, and cosmology intertwine. It is in diagnosing where the sources of disorder lie that one foresees a potential for more inclusive forms of community.

In cases of spirit possession it is not always clear why someone has become possessed or who the possessing spirit may be.[9] "Diagnosis" of what causes this affliction is intrinsic to the "cure." It becomes a means of perceiving who among family members, neighbors, or society on a larger scale might be generating situations that are conflictive. So-called demonic spirits are viewed not as foreign to the natural or human realms but as continuing ingredients within a more overarching frame of reference. Clearly, demonic spirits play a prominent role in Japanese mythology, but they also have a psychic presence in the contemporary world. As such, they are spirits within a dramatized cosmology. Demons are allowed their place. Symbolically, they personify the possibility of disorder, confusion, injustice. In other words, they are seen *within* a deeper framework of social and cosmic order, not as independent of this order.

A perspective of this kind is not foreign to Japanese culture, in which mythology, literature, drama, and film have paid considerable attention to the shadow side of life. Long before the appearance of *mizuko* malevolent ancestors have occasioned "misfortune for their living kin as a consequence of their own suffering."[10] Avenging ghosts bear grudges from wrongs "suffered at the hands of those expected to be trusted," seeking redress against perceived injustice.[11] Raging deities (*araburu kami*) represent unchecked nature or unrestrained passions, for which ritual becomes an appropriate transforming vehicle.[12] Demonic beings are expressions of "confusion and chaos [and] therefore manifest themselves in those areas where the power of order which drives things *to* the outside and the power of chaos which invades *from* that outside overlap."[13]

The place where this overlap occurs constitutes the boundary of two worlds, or two worldviews. These exist at the interstices between the seemingly familiar and the inevitably unknown or the time intervals between past and present, present and future. In other words, the present recrudescence of *tatari*, as seen in some ingredients of *mizuko kuyō*, may seem surprising in a secular age, but it may in fact be another face of the violent dimensions within human experience (whether in literal, metaphoric, or psychological guise). It has its own extended history throughout Japanese culture. However manifested, the demonic is the disordering potential in all times and places. It is a warning sign that what we call "order" may, in actuality, be the locus of what is unstable, incomplete, unjust.

A prominent proponent of a conflictive *worldview* is Michel Foucault, who portrays the domain of the political at least as "a heterogeneous ensemble of power relations operating at the microlevel of society. The practical implication of [this] model is that resistance must be carried out in local struggles against the many forms of power exercised at the everyday level of social relations."[14] It is a contest that is ongoing. The social and historical field that he describes is "a battleground, a field of struggle."[15] It is "a network of intersecting practices and discourses, an interplay of non-egalitarian, shifting power relations. Individuals and groups do not possess power but rather occupy various and shifting positions in this network of relations—positions of power and resistance."[16] These forms of interplay in Japanese society have been discussed in previous chapters, whether in relationships between the genders or in different expressions of social and political philosophy or in various types of religious belief and practice.

From the perspective of Jana Sawicki, whose interpretation of Foucault's social and political philosophy seems particularly apposite to understanding the conflictive feature of human existence in any society, "a Foucauldian feminist would describe the present situation as the outcome of a myriad of micro-practices, tactics and counter-tactics among such agencies."[17] She depicts his approach as a "bottoms-up analysis." While the language is different, its point of view is akin to what Certeau is saying in *The Practice of Everyday Life*. It serves also to reinforce Meredith Underwood's thesis, discussed in Chapter 7, of how female subservience in a society that remains highly patriarchal can be a means of negotiating with the elements of patriarchal power. This is an apt point of departure for the next section, which, while bearing some resemblance to Foucault's philosophy of enduring struggle, provides an additional perspective.

Hārītī, the "Demon-Mother": She Who Staves Off Demonic Forces

For a personification of unstable "order" and the conflictive nature of human existence, we turn to the figure of Hārītī whose roots in India and China are as long-term as those of Kannon and Jizō. She makes her appearance in Mahayana Buddhism in the Lotus Sutra but has been less influential throughout East Asia except in the Nichiren sect in Japan. Of particular interest here is her role as a prominent personage in contemporary expressions of *mizuko kuyō*. Hārītī, known as Kishibojin in Japan, represents an important influence in the relationship of cosmology to ritual, art, and personal devotion in modern religious life in Japan.

The legend of Hārītī (Ch. *Kuei-tzu-mu*, J. *Kishibojin*) is the epitome in Buddhist tradition of one who, having lost her youngest, most precious child, is consumed by grief and who, when given this child back, becomes a consummate protector of children. The story of Hārītī is complex. Sometimes regarded as a smallpox goddess, especially inimical to children, there are many versions of the legend about her in India, Central Asia, China, and Japan.[18]

According to an important textual account of this figure, the *Mūlasarvāstivāda Vinaya*, as the mother of 500 sons she was known at the time of the Buddha as one who stole and ate the children of others.[19] After trying to placate this demonic figure (*yakṣa*), the people of Rājagṛha in northern India implored the Buddha to stop her evildoings. Using skillful means, the Buddha proceeds to steal and hide her youngest child, Priyaṅkara. Upon returning and finding the child missing, she searches in vain and in her grief becomes panic-stricken. Beseeching the god Vaiśravaṇa (overlord of demons), she is told to confer with the Buddha. The Bhagavat listens to her lament and then asks about the grief of those whose children she has consumed. Getting the point, she replies, "Their grief is as great as mine." When convinced she is repentant, he tells her to stop these practices and gives back the child.

The conditions laid down for her are that she protect all Buddhist monasteries of Jambudvīpa (narrowly construed as India) and that she assist each childless couple that turns to her for help in conceiving children. As bestower and protectress of children in Japan especially, she often presents two visages to the world—one fierce and frightening to those who would harm the Buddha dharma, the other benign and tender to those who come to her in need. Her conversion to the Buddhist faith and practice is a classic instance of how non-Buddhist deities and practices are absorbed into the Buddhist worldview.

This ambiguous feature of Hārītī may have been the face she assumed in tantric forms of Buddhism, perhaps in China during the seventh century and soon thereafter in Japan. However transformed, her perceived nature retains seeds of the demonic.[20] The great Chinese pilgrims Hsüan-Tsang (Xuanzang) and I-jing (Yijing) in the seventh century comment on the existence of altars to Hārītī at every monastery they visited in northern India. This presence was a Buddhist reminder to keep the demonic in check. The presence of Hārītī is admonition that ordinary human existence is conflictive, not irenic. She presents a graphic image of this inner tension, with its outer consequences, and signals the task of heeding her or other forms of ambivalent power. This figure should not be seen as a model for women alone but also as a prototype of transformed karma for both genders.

In the guise of a transformed demon-mother Hārītī becomes a protectress not only in Indian legend but even more so in Japanese religious devotion. The force she represents prompted Nichiren in the thirteenth century to order "an image of Kishimojin to be placed in every temple and monastery of his sect" in her capacity as defender of the Lotus Sutra.[21] In the figure of Kishibojin (alternatively, Kishimojin), one sees destructive power being transmuted into life-affirming power, thus retaining its capacity to offset evil forces. In other words, she is not just a protective figure in the abstract; she also symbolizes the possibility of transformative power in the practice of everyday affairs. The concept of transformation is of great significance, for in essence the chapter of the Lotus Sutra known as Dhāranī (esoteric spell) comes near the end of the text and is designed to ensure that this sutra will be guarded and protected. The particular intent of this protection is to ward off demonic figures, hungry ghosts, and others that commit crimes against teachers of the dharma. That this protection is thought to proceed from the hands of demons that have become protective deities of the Buddhist law signals belief in the great power of the dharma to transform.

Over the centuries the cult of Kishibojin has contributed to a strong emphasis upon healing within Nichiren Buddhism. "In a work called the *Kitōkyō*, Nichiren culled from the Lotus Sutra numerous passages endorsing healing ritual and promising that...the sick would be cured by belief in the sutra's healing power."[22] Throughout the nineteenth century, especially in the Kanto area, there were many religious associations (*kō*) based upon faith in Kishibojin, particularly for her powers in effecting safe delivery (*koyasu*) of children. *Koyasukō*, groups based upon this conviction, were common, and events or festivals connected with such beliefs drew large crowds. This was especially the case on the night of the seventeenth of each month (*ennichi* or festival day for Kishibojin) at the Hokkekyōji, temple of the Nakayama sect of Nichiren in Ichikawa City of Chiba Prefecture.[23]

Since World War Two Kishibojin has been petitioned for help in conceiving a child, childrearing, child protection and safety in the home, and dealing with child loss (including from abortion); for exorcism of harmful or neurosis-producing spirits; and for protection against mental and bodily diseases.[24] In the past generation, increasing attention has been given to problems connected with *mizuko kuyō*. While Kannon and Jizō have been regarded as responsive to women's needs in the areas of safe childbirth, the rearing of children, and the tragedy of child loss, the cases of Jizō and Kishibojin add another element, namely, forms of exorcistic ritual that confront the negative causes behind one's suffering. In today's terminology this would be called *redressive ritual*, or rituals of affliction.

In the personage of Kishibojin is a figure that exemplifies both the agonistic nature of existence and the possibility for conflict to be transformed. What is labeled as *demonic* may be the recognition of the chaotic or conflictive within what we believe to be *order*. It signals the Buddhist belief that while negative forces cannot be eliminated from human experience they can be harnessed for new life potential. To put it another way, the demonic can be exorcised out of individuals, even for a time out of communities, but not out of existence itself. It is possible, therefore, to see Kannon, Jizō and Kishibojin as three different symbolic means by which Buddhism responds to the human condition and, for our purposes, as figures whose significance for women and child loss in Japan remains of special importance. This would not be to take them literally but to recognize how they challenge and expand our frames of reference, our imagination.

Rituals of Affliction and the Process of Healing

Throughout this study of Japanese women and pregnancy loss we have been drawn to evidences within Japanese mythology and society of discordant forces in everyday life. When a woman loses a child, by what-ever means, she may be consumed by grief, longing, anger, and confusion and may express these feelings in ways that cry for attention. Her per-sonal world seems to be broken. Of equal importance, she may experience a community's denial of social factors that contribute to her condition. That agonistic elements are present in the experience of women who may remain stuck in the grieving process in modern Japan should occasion no astonishment. If one recognizes her plight not primarily as conceived by priests who prey upon her vulnerable condition but as part of a woman's subordination to what Hardacre calls misogynist patterns, the phenom-enon of *mizuko kuyō* may also be seen as an indicator with both deeper social and personal significance.

The heart of Hashimoto Yayoi's analysis, as discussed in Chapter 7, is not on a woman's anguish in losing a child but on her sense of diminish-ment as a person, her loneliness in not being listened to, and in failing to develop her own voice. The substance of that analysis is what may happen to a wife or mother when she is not encouraged to express her own selfhood. Along with Hashimoto's perspective, other chapters in this book provide examples of women whose selfhood seems more derived than nurtured through their own uniqueness. On the other hand, there are striking examples of women who have rejected one-dimensional forms of what it means to be a woman, as, for instance, Ueno Chizuko's discussion of sexual relationships in contemporary Japan. "By discuss-ing sex, women's studies revealed a tremendous gap between man and woman in what sex—the most intimate of all activities—means to them in reality…When sex between husband and wife is close to rape, the two live different realities in the same bed. It is not a matter of which is right."[25] Ueno highlights the existence of different worlds experienced by men and women, and therefore the absence of significant communica-tion between them:

> This unclosable gap between husband and wife in the way they live a reality—in fact, they do not even share 'one reality'—speaks to us, more eloquently than anything else, of the horror of the realities. Can't we adopt a method that…shows multiple realities just as they are—those pluralistic realities that remain inconsistent with each other, never to become consistent or reconciled…What we need is a method to describe multiple realities.[26]

This expression of the need for "a method to describe multiple realities" is what is at stake in concepts of cosmology or worldview. Traditionally, a so-called cosmos represents a common search for an inclusive system of order and harmony, a concept of oneness within which manifold, "pluralistic realities" exist, even though in infinite and shifting relationship to each other, and despite the fact that each condition of *harmony* is evanescent. Furthermore, in Ueno's judgment, these "realities" are frequently "inconsistent with each other." It is also the perspective of this study of *mizuko* that social existence is inevitably conflictive and is more realistically addressed when harmony is viewed as a fragile, uneven process, not as a goal to be finally or fully achieved.

Attempts to impose concepts of reality, including concepts of social order, on any segment of society fail to honor the inherent diversity of human existence and therefore become forms of violence. In that sense, it has what we earlier called a demonic impact and can be found anywhere within the social and political worlds. *Demonic* is a term for what may emerge in everyday contexts of family and neighborhood and is present *within* a world of pain, not as some foreign intrusion. Its existence is part of contingent reality, *not* as extrinsic to it.

As an instance of redressive ritual, exorcism of the demonic (of which *tatari* can be seen as one example) serves as a common means of reestablishing *equilibria*, however temporary, but occurs only when the social and cultural roots of disharmony have been identified, confronted, and, in a liturgical sense, harnessed. The relationship of order to disorder is ritualistically similar as that of life to death, in that they coexist, inherently. And unless the threats of fundamental disorder and death equivalents are confronted (personally and communally) in symbolic, cognitive, and liturgical ways, one avoids, even denies, the dark side of existence and hence remains paralyzed by it.

To perceive this discussion within a more theoretical framework it is useful to refer to Robert J. Lifton's research, which has focused on the importance and the difficulty of grieving, on the process by which one confronts death, and on imagery and therapy relating death to the continuity of life.[27] Studies of this kind reveal that persons who are overcome by grief are typically unable to move from this condition until they confront their death-like experience. A grief not confronted *is* a death denied. Central to his approach is the importance of images of continuity or of life equivalents such as connection, integrity, and movement. Lifton's point is that life-promoting connections are possible only as one learns to handle factors within oneself and the human community that resist the facing of death or of death equivalents such as the collapse of earlier forms of communal order and the loss of personal or social meaning.

This twofold approach—of realism in the face of death equivalents and of hope when these are seriously faced—speaks also to the problem of how one responds to the experience of child loss. So far, little attention has been paid to the implications these sorts of studies have for the social and religious phenomenon known as *mizuko kuyō*. This seems ironic, since at the heart of this phenomenon lie both the experience of death and the difficulty of encountering it. Lifton's analysis confirms one's suspicion that the issues underlying the experience of child loss, even that of abortion in Japan are not only more serious than is often acknowledged but also involve a number of rarely discussed complex factors. In the process of this research one becomes convinced of the interplay between the experiences of child loss by women at the very time that so many women are undergoing confusion about their role and identity in modern Japan.

Among the more helpful ways of understanding and addressing this process is through the theory of "rituals of affliction" or "redressive rituals," as advanced by Victor Turner. Intrinsic to rituals of this kind is "divination into the hidden causes of misfortune, conflict, and illness," along with curative rituals that seek to move the afflicted person through and ultimately beyond the particular causes of this affliction.[28] There is a similarity between Turner's thesis of ritual's potential within conflictive or agonistic situations and Lifton's psychoanalytically based research into how one copes with life's broken connections. Both recognize the pervasiveness of conflict, and in both there is emphasis on encountering these situations directly and discovering how to experience their ever-changing forms anew.

It is precisely in the genre of rituals of affliction that one might be tempted to locate *mizuko kuyō*, for the sources of anguish are within not only each person's experience but also within a larger cultural and social environment.[29] The anguish felt is not simply idiosyncratic, even though it is deeply personal. It is societally stimulated but not just by groups that have sought to make women feel guilty for having had an abortion. Ironically, it is because of society's neglect of women's experiences that the practice of *mizuko kuyō* has become so pervasive. While this practice rarely serves as a ritual of affliction, assisting men and women to face their own inner conflicts, frustration, and anger, it—or a more deeply probing successor to it—has the potential to create life equivalents in personal and communal experience.

Here again the figure of Kishibojin and the role she plays in ritualized therapy make it clear that healing does not occur without the willingness to engage the conflictive in its many forms. At any rate, a cosmology, however this-worldly, that does not include *the conflictive* will be of no earthly use. This again corresponds with what is "perhaps the most distinctive feature of Foucault's view of history [namely] that as a type of knowledge, it must allow for reversal, discontinuity, and conflict because, as a real world process, it is intensely political."[30] Within the arenas of conflict the central issue is how one engages this reality.

Encounters with Otherness, within and beyond Oneself

Since addressing the nature of the conflictive in its ever-evolving forms is, to a significant degree, an epistemological matter, this narrative concludes with a reference to Rachel Carson's "worldview" as scientist and as human being who faced the impact of the human species upon the natural order with seriousness but without conceit or illusion. Hers is a story about the "interconnectedness" of all life, the consequences of "human interference in nature," and the false assumption that the otherness of nature and of the human condition can be fully understood, defined, and therefore controlled. Central to her reflections is a lack of arrogance and a nonprescriptive approach. At the same time, hers is an invitation to sobriety.

This approach represents an axial shift of perspectives. It is even more fundamental to social theories than to scientific exploration. Implicit in her assessment is a note of tragedy about the damage done to the environment by man's failure to perceive the limits of his ability to comprehend. The tragedy arises not simply from ethical insensitivity but also from a distorted epistemology. Chapter 1 of *The Edge of the Sea* recounts her oft-quoted experience of nature's "otherness." At night, with her flashlight, she walks by the water's edge, "at the edge of where we couldn't see," and spots a small ghost crab.[31] Vera Norwood's article is a sensitive depiction of this encounter:

> The night, the individual crab, the alien seascape all conspire to deny her a comfortable sense of identification with the world she sees ...This grasp of the "elusive," "tantalizing," "obscure," "inscrutable" meaning of nature, coupled with her understanding of the very human need to make patterns, is the basic source of the trespasser images. For Carson, one of the most important aspects of

human interaction with nature is the realization that the protean quality of the natural world cannot be caught by our pattern-hungry minds but that it is our "nature" continually to seek the pattern.[32]

At the moment of realizing that she lacked even the slightest idea of what the *world* of a ghost crab was all about, she saw herself within a fabric whose strength depends upon a healthy relationship between the natural world and its human members. This combination of being professionally informed about but not truly understanding that she and this small mysterious entity had a shared existence was a profound realization. In effect, this realization of a shared existence is a kind of cosmology. Human beings are part of a larger universe that they cannot control but with which they are inseparably interdependent. Paradoxically, this "changed vision" is not a new shift; it is a return to a nonadversarial relationship to the earth and its infinite creatures. Throughout, she "emphasizes the need to move away from comfortable, assumed visions of the environment and to see it as new, astounding, unusual."[33]

For the contemporary world this amounts to a break from all forms of anthropocentrism and the willingness to see ourselves "as part of a larger order that can make [its own] claims on us."[34] This sense of nature's "otherness" deepened Carson's respect for its intrinsic worth, totally apart from whatever utilitarian value it may have for humans. Aware of nature's exploitation by human beings, she recognized how the "interconnectedness of all life becomes sinister as we come to understand [how] the webs of death [are inevitably] interwoven with the webs of life [and envision] the consequences of human interference in nature for all life."[35] The implications of her transformed vision are enormous. In Vera Norwood's words:

> Carson's place as a liminal individual, able to deconstruct traditional frames of reference and offer new visions, is the result of her lifelong fascination with what [Thomas] Kuhn calls "progress toward no goal"...Rather than espousing a vision of nature's otherness as nasty and uncontrollable, she is 'tantalized' by the alien, the mysterious. Rather than seeing in the 'wild' an obligation to control and tame, she delights in the unharnessable quality of nature.[36]

Her delight in this quality of nature is more than reverence for the *otherness* of all existence; it is a realization that the inherent wildness of nature invites the human species to a higher order of respect. The cruelest form of irony would be to suppose that disrespect for the natural world—the closest part of the universe to us—would eventuate in anything but disregard for ourselves. In contrast, to see and act upon an inherent bond between the worlds of nature and of humankind has the potential to fashion a more intimate kind of cosmology.

This is to say that all forms of cosmology or worldviews challenge the imagination to find dimensions of reality *within* ordinary experience that we cannot understand but that call us into being beyond what we can ever understand. It is never a matter of saying that here is what we know and there is what we do not know. Instead, right in the heart of what we think we know lies the infinity of what we do not know and will never fully understand. Imagination of this sort is the opposite of arrogance. It is to recognize the relativity of our vision and at the same time to thirst for new vision. Carson's "nature of knowing" is based on respect for seeing our own world with transformed meaning. From a similar perspective, it is the willingness to "face life within the context of our own utter smallness . . . [and] to go where we are small and where we need to respect the power and objectivity of nature."[37]

In a genuine sense, the perspective of Carson is akin to the discovery of the two elderly Japanese pilgrims with whom we began this narrative. Out of that couple's sense of loss there evolved an awareness of deep paradox—namely, that through the experience of mourning their son his renewed presence became more vivid in their memory. And from that experience their lives acquired a richer sensitivity to the pain of others.

How does sensitivity of this quality, especially when the pain is incapacitating, square with viewing life as fundamentally conflictive? While conflict is *inevitable* and while the resolution of conflict is often problematic, arduous, sometimes seemingly futile, there is exceptional power in the kind of sensitivity that stems from a revolution in how we regard the human scene, how we engage in self-examination, and how we pay "attention [to] the risks involved in becoming too comfortable with oneself, one's community, one's sense of reality . . . [and with] the ground on which one's . . . consciousness emerges."[38] The price one pays for openness of this kind is "making oneself vulnerable in acts of engagement with others."[39] It is generosity with no thought of recompense, a by-product that may arise from the genuine practicing of interdependent relationships.

In Chapter 7 we quoted the Buddhist priest Yvonne Rand in her discussions with Oda Hōryū, the head priest at Jikishian in Kyoto, about how each has conducted *mizuko kuyō* services for those who seek help with their experiences of pregnancy loss. It is appropriate at this stage to hear what she has learned in listening to others who have undergone not only personal anguish but also painful forms of social denial about the importance of this kind of loss:

> Attitudes about abortion have given birth to heartbreaking polarization and violence. The need for a safe and respectful meeting ground for everyone concerned now overrides the issues themselves... Each of those who attend our ceremonies has suffered the death of one or more small beings. Strangers assemble with their grief and unresolved dismay. Over time I have been struck by how successfully the ceremony has provided a container for the process of acknowledging what is so, for encompassing what is difficult, and for bringing about resolution and healing... What, then, is the solution? My experiences as a Buddhist priest continue to teach me that looking into a situation in detail, without glossing over what is unpleasant or difficult, is what helps us to stay present and clear and break through ignorance. This is certainly true in the potent realms of sexuality, fertility, and gestation... I have seen that there is no easy or "right" answer. I think that each woman must stay with her experience and be with what is so in as simple and clear a way as she can.[40]

Perhaps the most apt way to conclude this attempt to understand the diverse experiences of Japanese women, and women elsewhere, who have endured the pain of pregnancy loss, which is a form of death, is to cite again the prescience of Hashimoto Yayoi, who observes that it is the larger world of mother and nature that is "the source of life and death."[41] Into this expanded world a transformed sense of one's uniqueness may emerge. As to how "the discovered *individual* should live, this [Hashimoto writes] is the problem about which the women in transition must now think."[42]

It remains my own experience that while I have learned a good deal over the past twenty-five years about child death and the many other forms of pregnancy loss, I remain profoundly impressed by these ongoing narratives of sorrow and dignity. And, as I look back upon what I have written, I am impressed only by how much I have learned and how much more there is to discover.

Acknowledgments

I AM GRATEFUL to the Fulbright Commission for a research fellowship enabling me to spend eighteen months in 1986–88 affiliated with the Institute for Research in Humanities at Kyoto University and to Professor Toshio Yokoyama for being my sponsor and guide in many senses of those words; to Carleton College for a Faculty Development research grant in 1986–87; and to the National Endowment for the Humanities (NEH) for providing Elizabeth Harrison and me with a Three-Year Collaborative Research Grant (1991–94) for our continuing research on women and child loss in Japan.

My appreciation to a large number of persons is considerable, especially those with whom I have been in correspondence and had extended conversation about the topic of this research over many years. This includes those who have read earlier versions of this manuscript and whose suggestions have been taken seriously. The primary focus in this research began and has remained the experience of death and the process by which one mourns a loss that has proved to be overwhelming. The longer one is intellectually engaged in such a study, the more one sees the multidisciplinary and cross-cultural implications of this topic. Because of this and because this research has spanned two decades, it was important to consult with colleagues not only in religion and psychology but also in anthropology, feminist and ritual studies, as well as Japanese history, literature, and cultural studies. Beyond the value of these disciplines, it was the sensitivity that so many have brought to this subject that enriched my own perspective beyond what I could have imagined by myself.

Among those who provided research assistance to me in Japan, in some cases over a period of twenty years, the following have been of special help: Hara Satoshi, Kato Kazusei, Kitamura Takao, Kurokawa Machiko,

Nishimura Eshin, Oda Hōryū, Sakakibara Yasuo, Shinji Kazue, Takahashi Saburō, Takahashi Yoshinori, and Yokoyama Toshio.

A second group consists of friends and colleagues whose perception and encouragement have expanded my understanding of complex issues in fresh ways. These include Janet Eimon Abraham, Akiyama Taeko, Barbara Ambrose, Paula K. R. Arai, John Barbour, Doris Bargen, Karen Beall, Judith Berling, Carly Born, Scott Carpenter, Liz Coville, Patricia Crosby, Winston Davis, James Dobbins, Van Dusenbery, H. Byron Earhart, Gary Ebersole, Dale Haworth, Jamie Hubbard, Chang-tai Hung, Jerri Hurlbutt, Anne Godfrey, Roger Jackson, Yukio Kachi, Mariko Kaga, Kato Masae, Robert Kent, Hiroshi Kitamura, William LaFleur, Beth McKinsey, Eileen Mikals-Adachi, Hollis Otsuka, Charles Priore, Yvonne Rand, Asuka Sango, Noriko Tamura Sasaki, Robert J. Smith, Kathryn Sparling, Oliver Statler, Andrew Tsubaki, Meredith Underwood, Mark Unno, Gudrun Willett, Jeff Wilson, William Woehrlin, Patricia Yamada, and Richard Young.

My appreciation as well to Paul Swanson, Michael Williams, Ronald Grimes, and José Cabezón who, by including one of my essays on *mizuko kuyō* in their own collections of essays, provided further incentive and stimulus, direct and indirect, to completing this extended research project.

I am grateful to Marnie Jorenby for her nuanced help in translating and discussing with me the rich variety of materials, especially those written by Japanese women, among the eight published volumes of the *Omoidegusa* notebooks collected at Jikishian in Kyoto. And in understanding taped interviews with Hara Satoshi from 1986 to 2002 and with Oda Hōryū from 1986 to 2010. I am appreciative also for the genuine insight of Diane Burry who assisted me in translating portions of the volume edited by Takahashi Saburō, director of the Sociological Research Group on Contemporary Religion at Kyoto University (*Gendai shūkyō shakaigaku kenkyūkai*). This group's published volume, *Mizuko kuyō: gendai shakai no fuan to iyashi (Mizuko Kuyō: Healing the Unrest of Modern Society)* appeared in 1999. Chapters 3 and 5 of that volume supplied part of the primary material that is analyzed in Chapter 4 of this book.

Once more, my gratitude to Elizabeth Harrison for the extent and quality of our collaboration over many years, to the large number of persons in Japan who were interviewed over this same period of time, and to Carleton College and the Associated Kyoto Program (AKP) for their support of faculty in ways by which scholarly research and field study approaches to teaching may be effectively combined.

Finally, I would like to express genuine appreciation to the external reviewers for their comments on my manuscript as well as to Ronald Grimes, Cynthia Read, Charlotte Steinhardt, and Cammy Richelli for their competence, professional guidance, and encouragement throughout the process of readying this book for publication by Oxford University Press.

Appendices

Commentary on the Mizuko Kuyō *Service at Adashino Nenbutsuji, Kyoto*

Namu Mizuko Jizō

Mizuko (Unseen Mizuko)
Without ever seeing the light of this world,
nor having seen your mother's or father's face,
your tiny life vanished like a dew drop.

Mizuko Jizō is the Buddha (*hotokesama*) who helps (*sukuu*) the souls of children.

Welcome to our service. Please offer incense to *Mizuko Jizō*. Please light a candle and present it. Then, please join your hands in prayer, and let us worship with a peaceful (*shizuka ni*) heart.

With our whole hearts, let us worship. Buddha (*hotokesama*) always listens to your prayers (*negai*). With our whole hearts, let us perform this memorial service (*kuyō*). The teachings of the Buddha will surely save your soul. Let us pray with our whole hearts. *Mizuko Jizō* watches over (*mamoru*) many, many babies.

There are many different Buddhas (*hotokesama*), including Sakyamuni (*Shaka Nyorai*) who explained the teachings, and Amitabha Buddha (*Amida Nyorai*) who leads the way to the Pure Land (*Jōdo*). Amongst these figures, it is *Mizuko Jizō* who is the savior (*sukui*) of babies.

Mizuko Jizō helps the spirits of babies who have become *mizuko*, no matter what the circumstances. Let us open our hearts and worship him. He will surely respond to your feelings (*kimochi ni kotaeru*).

If that tiny budding life that you plucked for the sake of convenience had been born into this world, what sort of life would it have led? The snatching away (*ubau*) of this tiny life is a great offense (*tsumi*).

What must that child be thinking [of you]? Put yourself in your baby's place.

Let us mourn (*kuyamu*) for your all-too-brief life, and let us reflect (*hansei suru*) upon your deep sin (*tsumi*), vowing in your hearts never to repeat the same act again. From deep within yourselves and facing *Mizuko Jizō*, let us frankly and openly (*sunao ni*) repent (*zange*).

The following are the sutras explaining the teachings of the Buddha (*hotokesama*).

Please add your wholehearted prayers to the priest's chanting of the sutra.

The spirit of your *mizuko* must surely be crying all alone.

Let us pray to *Mizuko Jizō* to guide your *mizuko*.

Let us pray that your *mizuko* be enveloped (*tsutsumareru*) in the peace of *Mizuko Jizō*.

Let us pray to *Mizuko Jizō* to help (*sukuu*) your *mizuko*.

Doubtless you are now looking upon the figure (*sugata*) of *Mizuko Jizō*. [In the temple sanctuary there is a large painting of Jizō holding in his palm the figure of a *mizuko* within a sphere.] Do you see how the *mizuko* is held in the palm of *Mizuko Jizō*? This figure symbolizes the spirit of a *mizuko* whose life vanished like a dewdrop; without ever having walked down life's many-decades-long path; without ever having experienced joy, anger, sorrow, and pleasure as a human being; and had never known the preciousness that is life. The lives of such *mizuko* are lost due to a variety of causes: illness, accident, stillbirth, miscarriage, and abortion. Each situation surely has its own set of circumstances.

Surely, you too had your own set of circumstances. Even if your action was condoned by society, do you think your baby has forgiven you? A life was consigned to oblivion, for the sake of a mother's and a father's convenience. We cannot allow this child, who never had the chance to become a light of this world (*kono yo no hikari to narieru*), to wander in a world of darkness. A child left alone is so piteous (*kawaiisō*). In its loneliness, it forever calls out to its mother. We must reach out a helping hand (*sukui no te*) to these children.

Please ask *Mizuko Jizō* to help the spirits of the *mizuko*.

As the baby's father or mother, this is your responsibility. You too may be sad, and your sadness is also your baby's sadness. Let us [make it so] that the child grieves no more, and that it is no longer lonely. Call out to your baby with your own voice. With all your might (*seiippai*), call out to your baby, and ask [your baby] how it is doing. And then pray to *Mizuko Jizō*. The priest here is only passing on [communicating] your feelings (*kimochi*).

If you do not perform *kuyō*, then who will? Let us always preserve an attitude of *kuyō*. Let us pray that your *mizuko* as well will be cradled in the palm of *Mizuko Jizō*.

Please chant wholeheartedly for your baby. *Mizuko Jizō*, please shower (*okage kudasai*) your benevolent love on this baby. Please watch over this baby [child]. We ask that this baby [it] may live peacefully in the midst of *Mizuko Jizō*'s loving-kindness (*jion*).

Namu amida butsu. Homage to Amida Butsu (10 times).

In a brilliant world overflowing with light, your baby is surrounded by the kind ness (*yasashisa*) of *Mizuko Jizō*. Your baby is well on its way to being saved. Your heartfelt prayers and your sincere *kuyō* have found their way to *Mizuko Jizō*. Your baby is being watched over, so that it will no longer be wandering alone.

Namu amida butsu. Homage to Amida Butsu (Keep repeating, countless times).

Your baby is not alone. Other babies, like yours, who through no fault of their own were unable to become the treasures of this world, are all playing together in the brilliant, shining world of *Mizuko Jizō*. Your baby is there, too, playing with its many friends. They are all playing together at the knees (*hizamoto ni*) of *Mizuko Jizō*.

Please worship with all of your heart, for the sake of your baby.

Mizuko Jizō has heard your prayers. Please continue to pray for your baby, that it may never wander alone again, but be embraced (*tsutsumareta*) by *Mizuko Kuyō* in benevolent love, and thus live in peace and comfort for a long time.

Mizuko Jizō, we ask this of you. (Repeat 3 times.)

Thank you for worshiping here today. *Mizuko Jizō* will always help you, you who have come to this *kuyō*, to connect with your baby. Even surrounded by the compassion and love of *Mizuko Jizō*, there is nothing greater than a parent's love.

If you do not look after your child, it will surely be lonely. From time to time, come and talk to your baby, and ask it whether it is lonely. And later, should you give birth to little brothers and sisters of your *mizuko*, pray to *Mizuko Jizō* that they grow up safely. Your baby, along with *Mizuko Jizō*, will gaze warmly on those brothers and sisters, praying for their happiness. Please do not forget to perform *kuyō* for them.

Repeating the kuyō many times, building up the number of *kuyō*, the baby, too, will be reborn and become happy. And now, make a vow to *Mizuko Jizō* that you will never again repeat these things.

Namu amida butsu. Homage to Amida Butsu.

Notes

This Japanese commentary is not an interpretation of the sutras. It is something unique to Adashino Nenbutsuji. It was written for those who come to worship *Mizuko Jizō*, with the thought of having them worship with whatever feelings they bring to this service. On the other hand, we do not say that they must come with these particular feelings.

Prepared and Written by: Nenbutsuji Temple Office. Reproduction, duplication, or reprinting without permission is strictly prohibited.

Comment by the author: Tentative permission to reprint this commentary for the purpose of this book was given to me by Hara Satoshi when we last met in 2002, but official permission was granted in 2011 by the Temple Office. It was translated from the Japanese by Marnie Jorenby, Diane Burry, and Bardwell Smith. In a number of instances the original Japanese words have been put in parentheses to provide those with a reading knowledge of Japanese a sense of why certain English equivalents have been selected. This was done particularly in cases where the meaning of the words was regarded as having particular significance or when the connotation was ambiguous.

Jizō: Protector of Travelers into and out of Life

YVONNE RAND

Attitudes about abortion have given birth to heartbreaking polarization and violence. The need for a safe and respectful meeting ground for everyone concerned now overrides the issues themselves. My own view on the issues may appear inconsistent on the surface, for I am antiabortion and prochoice, but what concerns me these days is the intolerance and intemperance that prevent any harmony between the contending camps. I see remarkable grief in people as an aftermath to abortions and miscarriages and no container in which to heal that grief.

The perspective on abortion I present here has developed through my experiences as a practicing Buddhist and as a Zen priest. In conducting memorial ceremonies under the benevolent auspices of Jizō bodhisattva, I have come to appreciate the capacity the Buddha Dharma gives us to accept what is painful and difficult. In Japan, Jizō is the much loved form of the bodhisattva of the underworld; he is the emanation of compassion, which guides and protects travelers into and out of life.

My first encounter with Jizō happened in 1969 after a dear friend of mine died in a train accident in Japan. Several years earlier, my friend had gone on a search for himself, which ended at a Zen monastery. His sudden death was a blow, and I grieved his passing deeply. Later that year I found myself driving Suzuki Roshi to Tassajara Zen Mountain Centre from San Francisco. When I told him that I had been taking care of a footlocker holding my friend's precious belongings (music, a flute, essays, books, drawings), Suzuki Roshi suggested that we burn the belongings in the stone garden near his cabin at Tassajara. After a proper funeral and fire ceremony, we buried the ashes in the rock garden and marked the spot with a small stone figure of Jizō.

This, my first meeting with Jizō, affected me deeply. For some years afterward, I could not explain my pull to the figure of this sweet-faced monk with hands in the mudra of prayer and greeting.

Subsequently, I began spending time in Japan and became reacquainted with Jizō. Figures of Jizō are everywhere there. I saw firsthand that Jizō ritual and ceremony involved not just graveyards and death in general but particularly the deaths of infants and fetuses through abortion, miscarriage, or stillbirth. Back home, during the 1970s and 1980s, women had begun coming to me and asking if I could help them with their difficulties in the aftermath of an abortion or a miscarriage. Consequently, I began doing a simple memorial service for groups of people who had experienced the deaths of fetuses and babies. After many years of counseling both men and women I decided in 1991 to spend several months in Japan doing a focused study of practices around Jizō.

Initially, I did the ceremony only with women. But now I include men and children as well. The participants are neither all pro-choice nor all pro-life in their politics; a full spectrum of opinion and belief is represented in the circle we make. Many of the people who come are not Buddhists. Yet somehow this old Buddhist way seems to absorb whoever does come.

Each of those who attend our ceremonies has suffered the death of one or more small beings. Strangers assemble with their grief and unresolved dismay. Over time I have been struck by how successfully the ceremony has provided a container for the process of acknowledging what is so, for encompassing what is difficult, and for bringing about resolution and healing. When I initially performed the Buddhist Memorial Ceremony, I followed a quite traditional form. Slowly I have modified and added to it in a way that seems to work better for Americans.

The ceremony is as follows. We sit in silence, sewing a bib or hat for one of the compassion figures on the altar. The figures are from different cultures: Jizō, Mary with Jesus, "Spirit entering and leaving" from the Eskimo people, or a mother and child. Our commitment is to listen to those who wish to talk without attempting to give advice or comfort. Some of us know from twelve-step meetings the important practice of simply listening.

The principle of "no cross-talk" provides safety from uninvited comforting and solicitude, and many find it to be the most healing of possible attentions. After this, we form a circle and go through a simple ceremony of acknowledging a particular life and death. One by one, each person says whatever is in his or her heart while offering incense, placing the sewn garments on one of the altar figures and bowing. We then chant the Heart Sutra, give the unborn beings names, and say good-bye to them. Prayer sticks are made and inscribed with prayers for forgiveness and for the well-being of those who have died. No names are signed. The prayers are hung from the bushes and trees in the meditation garden, thus committing our messages to the wind and the rains. Afterward we have a cup of tea, walk in the garden, and go home with a quieter heart.

Over the years, I continue to learn from the people who participate. About seven or eight years ago, at a conference for Women in Buddhism, I led the Jizō ceremony for a large group of conference participants. At the end of the ceremony a woman spoke about her own experience. She described herself as a nurse midwife who did a lot of abortion counseling. After undergoing an abortion herself, she had begun to ask women who came to her for help to first go home and talk to the fetus they were carrying. She encouraged each woman to tell the baby all the reasons for her inner conflict about the pregnancy. She reported that the number of spontaneous miscarriages that occurred was remarkable.

After hearing this woman's story, I began to hear about a similar practice of speaking to the fetus in other cultures: People in Cambodia, the Netherlands, and Native Americans, to name a few, find great sense in this practice. Speaking to the fetus is a way to recognize and acknowledge that the being in utero also is a presence. I continue to be struck by the deep rightness of such an attitude in the midst of the suffering that comes with conflict over a pregnancy.

I have added modern touches to the ceremony. Yet the wisdom it embraces comes from traditional Buddhist teachings, which, although steeped in history, nevertheless offer profound guidance for the current conflict over abortion. For me, the Buddha's first grave precept—not to kill intentionally—cannot be denied, much less minimized. Since I am convinced that the teaching embodied in the precept is correct, both conventionally and ultimately, and, since adherence to it is a necessary step on the path that leads away from suffering, I feel compelled to encourage each of us to consider whatever range of options we can see.

At the same time, I can readily and willingly keep someone company when abortion is the choice she has arrived at. I am strongly in favor of the freedom of each individual to choose what to do for herself regarding a conflicted pregnancy. I could not and would not advocate a return to the years when the government controlled the woman's decision. In 1955 when abortion was illegal, almost one of four American women had an abortion by the age of forty-five, and some perished in the process.

What, then, is the solution? My experiences as a Buddhist priest continues to teach me that looking into a situation in detail, without glossing over what is unpleasant or difficult, is what helps us to stay present and clear and break through ignorance. This is certainly true in the potent realms of sexuality, fertility, and gestation. The premise of restraint, which underlies all the Buddha's precepts and is fundamental in the practice of compassion, is also of critical importance in how we lead our sexual lives. Through the precepts and through the practice of awareness of what is so, we can understand our previous actions and make wise decisions about future actions. By contrast, action based on unexamined and habitual thought patterns—implanted in childhood and reinforced by the generalities, platitudes, and superficialities of the common culture—perpetuate ignorance and sentence us to ever-renewing suffering.

The solution I propose is neither tidy nor quick. I have seen that there is no easy or "right" answer. I think that each woman must stay with her experience and be with what is so in as simple and clear a way as she can. I feel that it is important, whatever one's starting point on the abortion issue, to study its history in this nation. By doing so, we will benefit from a wider framework and a more open point of view.

3

The Tale of Sai-no-Kawara[1]

In the words of the narrator:

This story of a dry riverbed situated at the foot of a mountain across which goes a rocky path on which people travel after death is a tale remote from the world in which we presently live. It is a pitiable account of small children, mostly two to five years of age, who are doomed to endless suffering. It is a place that bears no resemblance to the *shaba* world [the corrupt world] into which these children were born but never lived for long. In the other world they had known so briefly they slept next to their mothers, who bestowed parental smiles upon them and clothed them in beautifully decorated dresses, protecting them from the harsh elements.

Now in utter contrast they lack even a single layer of clothing. On this dimly visible riverbed, each child has in its hands small stones to erect towers of prayers with which to transfer merit (*ekō*) to their parents and to pray for their solace. Yearning for their fathers and mothers, their crying voices penetrate one's very bones. Despite the many *kuyō* said for their children, these parents weep over the tiny remnants of clothing that have been left behind. And, seeing other children play with their toys, they keep wondering why their own child had to die. Grief-stricken, the parents are as pitiable as the children. The divide that separates them from their children is unalterable, yet suffused with memories. On the riverbed on which they sit or stand, placing one layer of stones for their fathers and another for their mothers, these children put their infant hands together in prayer. And they pile high other layers for the siblings they have left behind. However endearing their action, it only reinforces the unbridgeable distance between themselves and home.

Throughout each day they play by themselves, in a community of iso-lated selves, but at the gathering of dusk demons (*oni*) from hell appear before the little children, shouting at them, "Hey, what are you doing? Are you indulging yourselves, imagining that you are still in the *shaba* world? You have embarked on a trip into the land of perpetual darkness. Your parents, who remain in *shaba* observing *kuyō*, grieve for you from dawn to dusk. But their mourning only sows the seeds of your further suffering." So saying, these demons brandish cast-iron bars, smash the towers the children have built, and snatch away flowers from their hands. Taunting the children, these demons tell them to rebuild their towers. Overwhelmed with grief the children put their hands together, like tiny autumn leaves in color, and prostrate themselves in prayer, begging to be forgiven. Instead, the ruthless *oni* merely jeer at them: "How dare you suppose that you are innocent? As you cry on, half-asleep, for your mother's breast that can no longer give you milk, your cry resounds through 80,000 hells. Your weep-ing voice, as you hold on to your mother while your father wants to pick you up, reverberates throughout heaven and earth." With these words, the demons disappear.

As the storms blow against the mountain tops the children wake up imagining that their father has called. When they hear stream waters rus-tling by, they run down believing their mother now summons them. They look around and find her nowhere. Pounding the sand to make a sleep-ing hollow, using rocks as their pillows, crying on and on, they finally fall asleep. Endlessly, each day brings the same pitiable pattern. This is the world that lies waiting for us all along the mountain path into the land of death. Though they stumble and fall, they do not cease to yearn for succor.

In the midst of this bleak condition a halo of light appears from a valley in the distance. A figure stands in front of the children and speaks: "What are you wailing for? Great is the distance between this place and the world you have left. In this place of desolation you may trust me as your father and mother; day and night you may depend upon me." So saying, this fig-ure, who is none other than Jizō, picks some of them up, tucking others within the skirt of his robe, and lets still others walk clinging to his staff. Holding them close to his breast, he caresses and comforts them.

Addressing those who read or listen to his words, the narrator concludes with these words: "If you are grieving for your children who have departed this world before you, turn to the west and do *gasshō* the remainder of your lives, for in a little while longer you too must meet Jizō-son, the one who guides us with the palm of his lotus flower. It is therefore mete to chant Amida's name each morning and evening, kneeling in front of the family *butsudan*."

4

Economic Development and Temple Economics in Japan

Yasuo Sakakibara, Professor Emeritus of
Economics, Doshisha University, Kyoto

For twenty-five years the author was the priest-in-residence (*jūshoku*) of a small temple of the Jōdo Sect in Kyoto until 2001. His father was the priest of the same temple before him for forty-six years. His father was the twenty-seventh and the author was the twenty-eighth *jūshoku* of the temple established in the early seventeenth century (exact date of the temple's establishment is unknown). The temple has at present about 150 *danka* (supporting families)and about eighty of these families have graves in the cemetery behind the temple.

Born as the eldest and only son in his family, the author was trained as a priest since he was very small. His father read sutras in the morning and evening, holding the author on his knee. The father taught the boy how to properly dust the statutes, clean the scripture tables, and cook rice and vegetables to give as offerings to the buddhas and bodhisattvas of the temple. By the time the author entered senior high school he had learned by heart almost all the sutras necessary to conduct the temple rituals.

Toward the end of World War II, the author was a naval cadet in Hiroshima when the atomic bomb exploded over that city. After the war the author was enrolled at Doshisha University, an institution affiliated with the Congregational Church. He studied economics and pursued the career of a university professor, doing part of his graduate work in the United States, thanks to the Fulbright Program. He has taught economics in both countries.

When his father died in 1977, the author had no choice but to succeed him at the temple. At the same time, he did not want to quit research and teaching and therefore maintained both professions until 2001. Since the temple was always in financial difficulties, the author used his stipend from Doshisha to help support the temple. He has referred to this situation as a "cross-subsidization between religions."

The Danka *System and Its Achievements*

As is well-known, the Tokugawa Shogunate initiated the *danka* system in the seventeenth century as a means to ferret out hidden Christians. According to the system, every Japanese was forced to belong to a Buddhist temple that became the place of registration for all the births, marriages, and deaths in the person's family.

In the Genroku Period (1788–1804) the average citizens started having individual family graves made of sandstone that were usually kept on the temple grounds where the family was affiliated. The *danka* system that included the family graves successfully protected Buddhism from intrusion by other religions. Even today, most Japanese families belong to Buddhist temples, while the number of Christians is only about 1 percent of the total population.

The *danka* system made it possible for temples to plan for the ultra long-term. In their decision making, temple priests thought in terms of generations rather than decades. The temple compound, buildings, and gardens were all designed with future generations in mind. European churches enjoyed a similar situation in the Middle Ages. This gave remarkable stability to the society in which the average adult life span was only twenty to twenty-five years. Reciprocal in nature, the *danka* system also provided a secure economic base for the temple; not all temples were rich, and some small temples in both urban and rural areas were neglected and abandoned. But as compared with the period preceding the *danka* system, the temple economy became more stable after the seventeenth century. This system has continued to exist into the twenty-first century chiefly because of the merits of the temples and the sense of continuity with the past that they provide for the public. However, for the first time in history the *danka* system is facing serious challenges for reasons that will be explained shortly.

Ofuse *(Contributions) within a Market Economy*

What a priest and a temple can offer to the public is a service—not material goods— that gives people some sort of spiritual comfort. Services are difficult to measure in terms of value and are diverse in quality. For this reason, temples invented *ofuse* or "contributions" in which the receiver of the service could pay according to his means and level of satisfaction. This can be thought of as "price discrimination" or "Ramsay price." But this method of payment was a rational price system that functioned within a premodern economy and has existed in some form almost everywhere in the world.

Before World War II contributions to family temples in Japan were often in-kind donations rather than an exchange of money. Here the *ofuse* usually assumed the currency of rice. Rice contributed by the parishioners was enough to provide for a priest and his family's needs as well as the requisite offerings to the buddhas. What remained was used for meals for visitors (including hungry beggars) and for *danka* at the time of festivals. But during World War II, rice was severely rationed, and no family had enough to eat. Thus, contributions had to be converted into money. Since that time, temples have never reverted to in-kind donations.

In addition, temples started to set prices for various services—memorial services marking death anniversaries, monthly visits to the *danka*'s shrines, funerals, and other services during the mourning period. The *danka* now have to buy stupas, candles, and incense to offer to the buddhas at the temple. Temples also charge the *danka* monthly or yearly fees for keeping the graveyard clean. From the *danka*'s perspective, they often find it easier to just pay those set prices since they do not need to fret over the appropriate amount of contribution for the services performed.

Thus, the market economy has gradually taken a firm hold in temple economics. The problem then becomes the inflationary trend in these set prices and fees. When one looks at major items of expenditure at the temple, they are mostly human costs: (1) salary for the priest; (2) schooling for the eldest son who will inherit the temple; (3) skilled gardeners; (4) helpers to clean the temple and weed; (5) repairs and maintenance; and (6) water, gas, and electricity.

As the cost of service labor rises, prices have also risen. Temples with large buildings and spacious gardens have been hit especially hard. The cost of maintaining them has risen much faster than the revenue of the temples themselves. The entrance fees to well-known temple gardens in Kyoto has also risen to such an extent that tourists now complain. No way to ameliorate the situation seems to exist except through subsidies from the local government. But neither the government nor the temples were ready to accept such a drastic measure.

The Religious Corporation Law

In 1951 the Diet passed the Religious Corporation Law. Under this law temples became Religious Corporations. Besides being a religious leader, the *jūshoku* or "head priest" was now also the chief executive of a corporation, and the *sodai* or "elders" became executives in the enterprise. By law, religious corporations and their revenues from religious activities are exempt from real estate tax. But any nonreligious activity they may conduct is taxed, and the land used for such activities is excluded from the tax-exempt status applicable to real estate. This includes the parking lots they often have on their premises. The corporation also pays the priest a salary that is taxable.

After the enforcement of this law many priests could not adjust to the new regulations. The temple revenue and the priest's income were the same in the minds of most priests, but the executive board did not really function since the *danka* were not interested in the management of the temple. Whether good or bad, these regulations gradually led to an increasing dependence on a market system within the temple.[1] To report the revenue of the temple to the executive board composed of laypeople, a priest has to specify the amount of *ofuse* for a funeral and other services he conducts. Extreme differences in the amount of *ofuse* will certainly be questioned. Therefore, a certain degree of transparency becomes a necessity. The long-run thinking that was once fundamental to temple operation has now become a luxury for most temples.

Urbanization, Increased Mobility, and the Danka *System*

The *danka* system was initiated at the time when there was little mobility in Japanese society. During the Edo period, 80 percent of the population consisted of farmers tied to the land. Artisans in urban areas were organized into guilds. But after the Meiji Restoration in 1868, social mobility increased gradually with the introduction of Western-style education. Geographical mobility also increased with the construction of a railroad system.

Such increased mobility accelerated after World War II. Higher education was shifted from a European to an American model in which education formerly restricted to elites had become one of mass education. College-educated youth were able to find solid jobs in Tokyo, Osaka, or even further afield in New York, Frankfurt, or Paris. Very few would succeed their fathers in the family business or similar professions. Improvements in transportation also facilitated this process. After 1970 the *shinkansen* and an expanded highway system further increased geographical mobility. Prior to this it took seven hours by a special express train to get from Tokyo to Osaka. Now it takes only two and a half. No matter how remote their domicile, 95 percent of all Japanese today can travel round-trip anywhere in Japan in a single day.

Increased mobility, social change, and changes in job structure are all factors that have contributed to making the Japanese household much smaller. In 1950 the average household size was 4.52 persons, in 1970 it shrunk to 3.69, and at present it is only 2.66. These changes have had negative effects on the *danka* system as a whole. The number of *danka* who regularly visit family graves has decreased. Those who formerly accepted monthly visits by priests now simply say, "No thanks." Grandmothers who used to come to the temple with grandchildren now come alone. For the most part, grandchildren do not even know the location of their family graves or the temples to which their families are affiliated. In the case of the author's temple, of a total of 150 *danka*, about 50 live in the Tokyo area and abroad, 20 live in Osaka, and only 80 now live in Kyoto.

In 2006, 66 percent of the Japanese population lives in cities where the population is more than 100,000. Urbanization has made it difficult for temples in the countryside to survive. For this reason, one priest may now be managing two or three separate temples. Suburbanization creates another kind of problem. Temples located in the urban centers are losing *danka*, and the priest who happens to have his temple in the suburbs cannot provide for all the needs of new inhabitants in the area. A temple with a graveyard cannot readily migrate to a new location. Furthermore, developers have no plan whatsoever to build religious facilities. Poor allocation of religious resources exists, yet no one seems to be paying much attention to it.[2]

There are some who think Buddhism is now in a state of revival. They are thinking mostly of the Buddhist faith of individuals. However, the *danka* system itself is in sad decline. Some would argue for the need to revive the system since the number of elderly people is increasing, and they tend to be more serious Buddhists. According to estimates of the Bureau of Statistics, by 2130 30 percent of all Japanese will be over sixty-five. Thus, in order for Buddhism to revive it must begin to attract younger people. Otherwise, Buddhist temples will not be able to avoid the fate of a progressive decline.

Consider the average lifestyle of young people who work in business corporations in Tokyo. They live in small apartments where they have no room for family shrines. If the couple is without children, then the wife too may have a job. Or if they have children, the wife may take a job after the child has reached school age. During the day, nobody is at home, and the only occasional visitors are salespeople, not priests. The spare time of these working couples becomes a precious commodity that cannot be squandered in religious activities. The only exception is when their parents might ask them to return to the family home in order to attend the thirty-third anniversary memorial service for a late grandfather.

Competition from Other Religions and Secularization

The Jōdo sect of Buddhism has largely depended on the *danka* system for much too long. Its solution to competition from other religions has been to make the distinction between individual faith and family religion. In this view, one may be a Christian while his or her family religion belongs to the Jōdo sect of Buddhism. Such a person will attend Buddhist memorial services for his grandfather but then go to church on Sunday. Yet the acceptance of this kind of accommodation accepted by Buddhist sects is no real solution to the problem.

Secularism also plays a role in the decline of the *danka*. It has gained momentum in Japan with economic development. More Japanese are interested in yen rather than in zen. The dual standard in Japanese Buddhism may free dogmatic thinking, but it also fosters secular thinking. More and more intellectuals choose nonreligious funerals or prefer a private farewell within the family to big and lavish ceremonies. Increasingly, more people tend to omit the role of priests as an ornamental component of a funeral service rather than the necessary presence of a spiritual leader capable of leading the dead to *gokuraku* or "paradise." The priest wears a *kesa* or "surplice" made of beautifully colored and high-quality silk. In a solemn voice he reads sutras that nobody understands. He may also give a sermon to which nobody listens. The problem is that these people think that what the priest represents belongs to the past, and few are enchanted by the mysticism it represents. In addition, some competition to temples comes from business corporations that specialize in ceremony services. They own many large funeral halls and in this way take a large share of funerals away from temples, although they may still think cooperation with temples is vital and necessary for their business. In the future they may well hire priests of their own to reduce the cost of funeral ceremonies.

Conclusion

It is clear from the previous analysis that the *danka* system is in crisis. Unfortunately, however, there is little sense of crisis among Jōdo sect temples. The maintenance of family graves has reached crisis levels. These graves are still based predominately on the primogeniture system that functions as a central structural principle of Japanese Buddhism. The eldest son in a family is responsible for the care and maintenance of the family grave. When the author was teaching at universities, he was surprised to find that 80 percent of the students were either eldest sons or the eldest daughters. If eldest sons and elder daughters should marry each other, the new couple would have to take care of two family graves. If the couple had just one son and he happened to marry another eldest daughter, the young couple would have to take care of four graves. It is impossible to do this if one considers the cost of keeping graves at four different temples, each of which will charge him maintenance fees. Another issue is that many families do not permit the ashes of a person with a different surname to be buried in the family grave. Yet more Japanese women are choosing to keep their maiden name after marriage.[3]

Religious faith is basically a matter of individual conscience. In Japan where individualism has grown to full-scale in the last hundred years, the *danka* system with its family graves will naturally be eroded. The emphasis in Buddhism has shifted from the family unit to the individual who is more concerned with enlightenment and salvation. It is here that esoteric Buddhism can make the greatest contribution. Its significance will increasingly come to be recognized. Buddhism should continue to play its proper function in society since the spiritual needs of the Japanese will continue to exist even if the *danka* system should fail.

Notes

CHAPTER 1
Mizuko Kuyō: *Memorial Services for Child Loss in Japan*

1. For twenty years (1983–2002) the Pilgrimage to the 88 Sacred Places of Shikoku has been an important part of our personal life. The first time was in 1983 with Oliver Statler. Twice, it has been with sizable groups of students, all of whom were spending their college year as juniors in Japan on the Associated Kyoto Program (AKP). Four other occasions have been in smaller groups of both Japanese and America academics.

2. Along the way this couple had heard the early Buddhist story of Kisa Gotami, who had lost her only child and was so aggrieved she was unable to bury the child. She was advised by friends and neighbors to go see Gotama the Buddha, who suggested that she collect mustard seeds from every house in the village where death had never occurred. Having collected no seeds by the time she returned to Gotama, she realized that death is intrinsic to the human condition. As part of her mourning, she buried her son and in time became a prominent disciple of the Buddha.

3. Peter Homans, *The Ability to Mourn: Disillusionment and the Social Origins of Psychoanalysis* (Chicago: University of Chicago Press, 1989). A similar observation is found in Walter Brueggemann, *First and Second Samuel, Interpretation* (Louisville, KY: John Knox Press, 1990), 1: "Although we may have lost our capacity for public grief, we still know from interpersonal relationships that where loss is not grieved there are barriers to newness."

4. Michel de Certeau, *The Practice of Everyday Life*. Trans. Steven F. Rendell (Berkeley: University of California Press, 1984).

5. Elizabeth G. Harrison, "'I Can Only Move My Feet towards *mizuko kuyō*': Memorial Services for Dead Children in Japan," in *Buddhism and Abortion*, ed. by Damien Keown (Honolulu: University of Hawaii Press, 1999), 104.

6. Takahashi Yoshinori was part of the research team of social scientists at Kyoto University who, in the 1980s and early 1990s, produced an extensive study of *mizuko kuyō* in Japan. This is discussed at length in Chapter 4.

7. Children who died at a young age were traditionally not acknowledged in Buddhist memorial services in Japan, in part because these children were not

seen as individuals distinct from their mothers. As with other religious practices in Japan, however, one finds wide variations in funeral practice: Funerals were performed and graves and memorial tablets were created for some children. See Robert Smith, *Ancestor Worship in Contemporary Japan* (Stanford: Stanford University Press, 1974).

8. Harrison, "'I Can Only Move My Feet towards *mizuko kuyō*'," 108.

9. See Helen Hardacre, *Marketing the Menacing Fetus in Japan* (Berkeley: University of California Press, 1997), 12. As she writes, "The complexity of *mizuko kuyō* requires that multiple perspectives must be brought to bear upon the problem, but this provides no guarantee of a final solution. Interpretations of so complex and contentious an issue as *mizuko kuyō* will inevitably be partial and contingent."

10. Ann Braude, *Radical Spirits: Spiritualism and Women's Rights in Nineteenth-Century America* (Boston: Beacon Press, 1989), 49. For instance, "in the nineteenth century [America], more frequently than today, death entered every life, and each individual had to find a way to continue in its face."

11. Robert E. Goss and Dennis Klass, *Dead but Not Lost: Grief Narratives in Religious Traditions* (Walnut Creek, CA: AltaMira Press, 2005), 258–262.

12. There is considerable clinical evidence in the United States that a woman may experience similar feelings after placing a child for adoption, despite the fact that she had relinquished her child willingly. Leverett Millen and Samuel Roll, "Solomon's Mothers: A Special Case of Pathological Bereavement," *American Journal of Orthopsychiatry* 55(3) (1985): 416. See also Anne B. Brodzinsky, "Surrendering an Infant for Adoption: The Birthmother Experience," in *The Psychology of Adoption*, ed. by David M Brodzinsky and Marshall D Schechter (New York: Oxford University Press, 1990), 295–315.

13. Ueno Chizuko in Sandra Buckley, ed., *Broken Silence: Voices of Japanese Feminism* (Berkeley: University of California Press, 1997), 291.

14. This statement was among a dozen comments made by those who attended a meeting in October 1988 of the Kyoto Women's Group (*Fujinkai*) at which Elizabeth Harrison gave a talk on our *mizuko kuyō* research.

15. Goss and Klass, *Dead but Not Lost*, 269.

16. This is #55086 of the questionnaires made available to individuals in the mid-1980s who came to Adashino Nenbutsuji in Kyoto for *mizuko kuyō*. This particular survey was conducted by Tokyo Polytechnic University Collaborative Research Group (Tokyo Kōgei Daigaku Kyōdō Kenkyū Han) in cooperation with the Kyoto University research group. This project is hereafter referred to as the Kōgei survey. The results of the 1,127 completed responses that were given to us appear in tabulated form in the appendices to Takahashi Saburō, ed., *Mizuko kuyō: gendai shakai no fuan to iyashi* [Mizuko Kuyō: Anxiety and Healing in Contemporary Society] (Kyoto: Kōrosha, 1999).

17. Kōgei survey, #55197.

18. Kōgei survey, #55089.

19. Kōgei survey, #25160.

20. Kōgei survey, #55089.

21. Sono Ayako, *Watcher from the Shore*, Trans. Edward Putzar (Tokyo: Kodansha International Ltd., 1990). Because Sono is a Catholic writer and because the novel focuses on an abortion clinic, a non-Catholic reader may be predisposed to see this work as an antiabortion tale and thereby dismiss it on ideological grounds. To do so would be to miss the complex issues that are raised by the author. Sono provides a series of vignettes that are meant to prompt questions, not suggest remedies. See Hardacre, *Marketing the Menacing Fetus in Japan*, 97, in which she characterizes Sono's novel as "a didactic Catholic critique of abortion." The fact that Sono is a Catholic may incline one to this conclusion, but the novel would be less interesting if that were its basic thrust.

22. Sono, *Watcher from the Shore*, 1990, 319–320.

23. Ibid., 320.

24. Ibid., 320–321.

25. Hoshino Eiki and Takeda Dōshō, "Indebtedness and Comfort: The Undercurrents of *Mizuko Kuyō* in Contemporary Japan," Trans. Paul L. Swanson, *Japanese Journal of Religious Studies* 14(4) (1987): 4.

26. Shinno Toshikazu, "From Minkan-shinkō to Minzoku-shūkyō: Reflections on the Study of Folk Buddhism," *Japanese Journal of Religious Studies* 20(2–3) (1993): 196.

27. Susan Starr Sered, *Priestess, Mother, Sacred Sister: Religions Dominated by Women* (New York: Oxford University Press, 1994), 90. While mentioning abortion only in passing, she identifies *mizuko kuyō* as a form of religious ritual that women have performed for dead children.

28. Sered, *Priestess, Mother, Sacred Sister*, 99; Sered, "The Domestication of Religion: The Spiritual Guardianship of Elderly Jewish Women," *Man* (N.S.) 23 (1988): 516.

29. Sered, *Priestess, Mother, Sacred Sister*, 111.

30. Sered, "Domestication of Religion," 512.

31. Ibid., 516.

32. Pierre Bourdieu and Loïc Wacquant, *An Invitation to Reflexive Sociology* (Chicago: University of Chicago Press, 1992), 30, italics added. See also Pierre Bourdieu, *Outline of a Theory of Practice*, Trans. Richard Nice (Cambridge: Cambridge University Press, 1977).

33. Bourdieu and Wacquant, *Invitation to Reflexive Sociology*, 34–35.

34. Michel de Certeau, *The Practice of Everyday Life*, Trans. Steven Rendall (Berkeley: University of California Press, 1988).

35. Faye Ginsburg and Rayna Rapp, eds., *Conceiving the New World Order: The Global Politics of Reproduction* (Berkeley: University of California Press, 1995), 1.

36. Certeau, *Practice of Everyday Life*, 24.

37. Michèle Lamont, "Review of Michel de Certeau, *The Practice of Everyday Life,*" *American Journal of Sociology* 93(3), (1987): 270.
38. Ibid.
39. Ibid.
40. Certeau, *Practice of Everyday Life,* 37.
41. Ibid., 123.
42. Ibid., 125.
43. Ibid., 41.
44. Ibid., 127.
45. Ibid., 105–106.
46. Ibid., 203.
47. Ibid.
48. Ibid. 31.
49. Bourdieu and Wacquant, *Invitation to Reflexive Sociology,* 167–168.
50. Ibid., 168, n.122.
51. Ibid., 170.
52. Ibid., 173.
53. Ginsburg and Rapp, *Conceiving the New World Order,* 1.
54. Ibid., 2.
55. Ibid., 4.
56. Ibid., 3–4.
57. Masae Kato and Margaret Sleeboom-Faulkner, "Meanings of the Embryo in Japan: Narratives of IVF Experience and Embryo Ownership," *Sociology of Health & Illness* 33(3) (2011): 434–447. Each interview was from one to four hours.
58. Ibid., 435–436.
59. Ibid., 434.
60. Ibid., 435.
61. Ibid., 443, italics added.

CHAPTER 2
Architectural, Iconographic, Doctrinal Features of Mizuko kuyō

1. For fuller discussions of Indian origins and the significance of this deity, known as Mahākāla in Hindu and Indian Buddhist traditions, and for other features of Daikoku-ten in Japan, see Dwijendra Nath Bakshi, *Hindu Divinities in Japanese Buddhist Pantheon* (Calcutta: Benten Publishers, 1979), 77–82.
2. After World War II a new religious sect, Benten-shū, was founded, with its headquarters and main shrine dedicated to Benzai-ten located near Osaka, now functioning largely for the purpose of *mizuko kuyō.* See Bakshi, *Hindu Divinities,* 107–127, for various Shinto and Buddhist holy places for Benzai-ten in Japan, for the forms in which she is worshipped at shrines and temples and for her role in shops and homes. This grouping of seven deities exemplifies

the interrelationship of different religious traditions (in this case, Hinduism, Buddhism, Taoism, and Shinto), whose favors and blessings are sought for one kind of need or another. For discussion of how "Buddhist cosmology and doctrine were combined with indigenous notions and practices," see Allan G. Grapard's analysis of the Kasuga-Kōfukuji multiplex in his book *The Protocol of the Gods* (Berkeley: University of California Press, 1992), especially 186–236.

3. Permission to use this abbreviated version of a 1988 brochure of "The Hase Kannon Temple" in Kamakura, Kanagawa Prefecture was granted by the temple's office.

4. Stephen F. Teiser, *Reinventing the Wheel: Paintings of Rebirth in Medieval Buddhist Temples* (Seattle: University of Washington Press, 2006), 257.

5. The *Konjaku monogatari-shū* was assembled by an unknown compiler about 1100 C.E. Its extant version contains 1,039 stories, 32 of which relate principally to Jizō. In any case, it has twenty-five stories portraying the wondrous actions of Jizō. This text and the *Konjaku* provide evidence of Heian belief concerning Jizō.

6. W. Michael Kelsey, *Konjaku monogatari-shū* (Boston: Twayne Publishers, 1982), 4, 9–10. See William R. LaFleur, *The Karma of Words: Buddhism and the Literary Arts in Medieval Japan* (Berkeley: University of California Press, 1983), 49–59, for a discussion of the many theories of salvation in "medieval" Japan.

7. More recently, this has been documented at length in Teiser, *Reinventing the Wheel*; and Zhiru Ng, *The Making of a Savior Bodhisattva: Dizang in Medieval China* (Honolulu: University of Hawaii Press, 2007). Because of its focus on Dizang (J. Jizō), Zhiru's work is especially pertinent to our study. Using "indigenous and accretionary scriptures," art and epigraphy, and narrative literature with an emphasis on "miracle tales," she presents a view of Dizang and of medieval Chinese Buddhism that exceeds what has been available previously. There was no comparably rich study of Jizō in Japan that utilizes this threefold approach until Hank Glassman, *The Face of Jizo: Image and Cult in Medieval Japanese Buddhism* (Honolulu: University of Hawaii Press, 2012).

8. Marian Ury, *Tales of Times Now Past: Sixty-Two Stories from a Medieval Japanese Collection* (Berkeley: University of California Press, 1979), 18. For an outline of the chapters of the *Konjaku* see Ury, *Tales of Times Now Past*, 1–13; and Kelsey, *Konjaku monogatari-shū*, 60–83.

9. Yoshiko Kurata Dykstra, "Jizō, the Most Merciful: Tales from *Jizō bosatsu reigenki*," *Monumenta Nipponica* 33(2) (1978): 185. The *Reigenki*'s Chinese counterpart is *Ti-ts'ang p'u-sa hsiang ling-yen chi*. See also Hayakawa Seiko, "Heian makki ni okeru Jizō shinkō" [*Belief in Jizō in the Late Heian Period*], *Shichō* 96 (1966): 31–52. Iconographically, one begins to see Buddhist altars in Heian Japan with statues of Jizō and Kannon as part of Amida triads. The Chinese version *Ti-ts'ang p'u-sa pen-yüan ching* describes the compassionate deeds of Ti-ts'ang (Jizō) in previous lifetimes.

10. Zhiru Ng, *The Making of a Savior Bodhisattva: Dizang in Medieval China* (Honolulu: University of Hawaii Press, 2007), 49. In her chapter on narrative literature, she notes that these locally transmitted miracle tales serve "as fairly reliable mirrors of religious attitudes and practices observed by the larger population across the diverse social strata of medieval Chinese society... [and thus] offer a de facto vehicle for accessing otherwise elusive dimensions of daily medieval life" (168).

11. Zhiru, *Making of a Savior Bodhisattva*, 117.

12. Besides the *Hongankyō*, two other Chinese sutras should be mentioned: *The Sūtra on the Ten Wheels* (Ch. *Ta-ch'eng-ta-chi-ti ts'ang-shih-lun-ching*; Jpn. *Jūringyō*₁ and *The Sūtra on the Ten Kings* (Ch. Yu-hsiu-shih wang-sheng-ch'i-ching; Jpn. *Bussetsu Jizō bosatsu hosshin innen jūōkyō*). In short form, these are known as *Jūringyō* and *Jūōkyō*, respectively.

13. *Sūtra of the Past Vows of Earth Store Bodhisattva*, Trans. Bhiksu Heng Ching (New York: Institute for Advanced Studies of World Religions, 1974), 82. This is the first English translation from Chinese of the *Ti-ts'ang p'u-sa pen-yüan ching* (Jpn. *Jizō bosatsu hongankyō*). It is accompanied by lectures on the text by the Tripitaka Master Hsuan Hua. The translation from Sanskrit to Chinese was rendered by Śikṣānanda (652–710) in the seventh century C.E.

14. Dykstra, "Jizō, the Most Merciful," 180.

15. Ibid., 188. This evidence was recorded in the *Kammon gyoki* of the Kamakura period. Dykstra indicates that these kinds of meetings, whether in honor of Jizō or Kannon or Amida, became especially popular "among the commoners, merchants, and townsfolk throughout the Muromachi and Edo periods ... [and] functioned as community gatherings until quite recent times."

16. M. W. DeVisser, *The Bodhisattva Ti-tsang (Jizō) in China and Japan* (Berlin: Oesterheld & Co., 1914), 68. The connection between Jizō and his devotees is spelled out in a spurious sutra, attributed to the famed Tantric master Amoghavajra (704–774 C.E.) and was translated from Sanskrit by a Japanese priest in the seventeenth century. With this text, the *Sūtra Spoken by Buddha on the Bodhisattva Ksitigarbha, the Lengthener of Life* (*Bussetsu emmyō bosatsu kyō*), one has an updated compendium from the early Tokugawa period of what had been believed for centuries about the many blessings accruing from devotion to Jizō (DeVisser, 162–168). It is claimed that this text was written in Japan in the thirteenth century. In it, an intrinsic relationship (*en*) was felt to exist between Jizō and women. "It is quite logical that the 'Womb of the Earth' [Jizō] was believed to be one of the most appropriate deities for giving easy birth and general protection to women" (DeVisser, 108). In this manner Jizō, the earth-womb figure—in touch with the souls of the dead—became the prototype of restorative hope in medieval cosmology.

17. Edward Kamens recognizes the role of "expedient devices" as a means of cultivating greater spiritual effort and awareness, not simply to secure benefits

of a worldly nature. This twofold use of skillful means is central to the message of the *Lotus Sutra*. See Kamens, "Dragon-Girl, Maidenflower, Buddha: The Transformation of a Waka Topos, 'The Five Obstructions,'" *Harvard Journal of Asiatic Studies* 53(2) (1993): 389–442; and Kamens, *The Buddhist Poetry of the Great Kamo Priestess: Daisaiin Senshi and 'Hosshin Wakashū'* (Ann Arbor: Center for Japanese Studies, University of Michigan, 1990).

18. Zhiru Ng, *Making of a Savior Bodhisattva*, 223–224.

19. Diana Y. Paul, *Women in Buddhism: Images of the Feminine in Mahāyāna Tradition* (Berkeley, CA: Asian Humanities Press, 1979), 220–221, 318. All quotes carry the pagination of the 1979 edition. The second edition, *Images of the Feminine in Mahāyāna Tradition*, was published by the University of California Press in 1985.

20. Duncan Ryūken Williams, *The Other Side of Zen: A Social History of Sōtō Zen Buddhism in Tokugawa Japan* (Princeton, NJ: Princeton University Press, 2005), 4–5.

21. Ibid., 4.

22. Ibid., 12.

23. Hur, Nam-lin, *Death and Social Order in Tokugawa Japan: Buddhism, Anti-Christianity, and the Danka System* (Cambridge, MA: Harvard University Press, 2007), 195.

24. Ibid.,162 n. 74. Duncan Williams, "Funerary Zen: Sōtō Zen Death Management in Tokugawa Japan," in *Death and the Afterlife in Japanese Buddhism*, ed. by Jacqueline I. Stone and Mariko Namba Walter (Honolulu: University of Hawaii Press, 2008), 243 n. 59, writes that "the age at which children might receive funerals is a complex issue, differing by region."

25. Williams, *Other Side of Zen*, 38, 54.

26. Ibid., 47.

27. Ibid., 56. This belief in the spirits of children began to play a role that changed over centuries with the practice of infanticide.

28. Fabian F. Drixler, "Infanticide and Fertility in Eastern Japan: Discourse and Demography, 1660–1880" (Ph.D. diss., Department of History, Harvard University, Cambridge, MA, 2008), 129, n. 50.

29. Ibid.

30. Williams, "Funerary Zen," 223.

31. Bryan J. Cuevas and Jacqueline I. Stone, eds., *The Buddhist Dead: Practices, Discourses, Representations* (Honolulu: University of Hawaii Press. 2007), 9.

32. Ibid., 8–9.

33. John Bolitho, *Bereavement and Consolation: Testimonies from Tokugawa Japan* (New Haven, CT: Yale University Press, 2003), 9.

34. Ibid., 27.

35. Ibid., 28–29.

36. Ibid., 29–30.

37. Ibid., 171.
38. Ibid., 186–187.
39. Ibid., 187.
40. This conversation took place on October 17, 1988, between Elizabeth Harrison, Bardwell Smith, and the head priest of Hasedera. The return to Japan in 1945–46 of thousands of Japanese soldiers, their wives, children, and grandchildren from Manchuria and North China was a process in which Bardwell Smith was involved. At that time, he was in the First Marine Division in Tientsin (Tianjin), North China. His battalion's responsibility was to repatriate the Japanese troops and their families to Japan in an orderly process over a six-month time period.
41. This interview with the head priest at Hasedera Temple occurred on July 29, 1988. The priest's description of the involvement of younger women in the temple's life sounded similar to what occurs in many newer, nonclerical forms of Buddhism in Japan.
42. Of these, all but five were women. The age range was from nineteen to sixty-seven, with the median at thirty. Most were from Kanagawa-ken and the Tokyo area. The religious affiliations included "none" (3); Shingon-shū (3); Nichiren-shū (1); Jōdoshin-shū (3); Shinto (1); "Buddhist" (3); and "no answer" (6).
43. Copies of the Harrison–Smith questionnaire were distributed in 1986–88 to a large variety of religious sites in Honshu and Kyushu. In each case, permission was granted by the head priest, and self-addressed stamped envelopes were provided for the responses to be mailed to us.

CHAPTER 3
Situating the Rites of Mourning: Two Temples and a Variety of Visitors

1. Doris G. Bargen, "Ancestral to None: *Mizuko* in Kawabata," *Japanese Journal of Religious Studies* 19(4) (1992): 337–377. In a footnote Bargen writes that Kawabata's novel was "originally serialized in *Fujin kōron* (1961–1963), a woman's magazine, [indicating that] the author wished to address a largely gender-specific problem." In her article Bargen writes how "the geographically ambiguous concept of *sai no kawara* represents a children's limbo (*meido*), which precisely reflects the liminal position of *mizuko*" (341).
2. In the Edo period this area was probably a wide field with tall grasses, into which people were cautious to enter, afraid of ghosts or apparitions, which is why the area was called Adashino, literally the field of ghosts. Fabian Drixler states that in the Heian period "non-elites commonly disposed of their dead without burial, a practice sanctioned by Buddhism as 'wind funeral' and motivated by a long-standing abhorrence of the pollution emanating from death." And, he adds, that in the Tokugawa period there was "a changing balance between the fear of dead souls and a concern for their wellbeing." See Drixler, "Infanticide and Fertility in Eastern Japan," 126–127. Donald Keene, *Essays in Idleness: The Tsurezuregusa*

of Kenkō (New York: Columbia University Press, 1967), 8, translates *adashi* as "impermanence," adding that this "accounted for the frequent use of Adashino in poetry as a symbol of impermanence."

3. This interview of Hara Satoshi was conducted by Elizabeth Harrison and Bardwell Smith at Adashino Nenbutsuji on November 4, 1988.

4. The original series was a big hit; it not only caused a *"furin* drama" boom but also was a social phenomenon in its own right. The nickname for this series, *kintsuma*, became synonymous with the word *furin*. In response, the following year a second series was released (also as a "Friday drama"), and the year after that a third. Each of these series received a big reaction from the public. All three screenplays are by Kamata Tetsuo and comprise one of his representative works. In the online dictionary (*Eijiro*) there is the following use of *furin*: *Furin o suru tsuma yori, onna asobi o suru otto no hō ga dōjō o erarenai* [husbands who philander with women gain less sympathy than wives who commit adultery]. This seemingly makes a distinction between *furin* and the more traditional type of "playing around."

5. The class as a whole, which I taught in fall 1990, numbered about twenty students and was subdivided into six smaller groups, each of which had three or four members. The AKP consortium is based at Doshisha University in Kyoto and is currently composed of fifteen American liberal arts colleges, each of which offers four years of Japanese language. The AKP junior year program, which includes a ten-month home stay with Japanese families, is the heart of this offering.

6. Interview conducted by Bardwell Smith and Shinji Kazue at Adashino Nenbutsuji on October 3, 1992.

7. Prior to this time Hara-san provided us with copies of these questionnaires. While planning to use them in some way himself, he died before doing anything with them.

8. In retrospect, Hara-san was unaware of the detailed results of the Kyoto University research into the practice of Japanese sectarian headquarters and of temple priests, a volume that was published in 1999.

9. Another Jōdoshū priest refers to this trait as *ippōtsūkō* (one-way traffic), by which he means the importance of listening to a woman talking freely about her concerns.

10. Originally, Jikishian was a Rinzai Zen hut and later was the residence of the Chinese Obaku Zen priest Ingen Ryūki (1592–1673). Since the end of the Tokugawa period it has been a temple affiliated with the Jōdo-shū (Pure Land sect), with Amida Buddha as its main image. It is also part of the Fudō Myōō pilgrimage.

11. Hirose Zenjun Ni, ed., *Jikishian omoidegusa yori: Ichirin no ai o kudasai*, Vol. 2 [Please Give Me One Flower of Love] (Tokyo: Chōbunsha, 1997), 10.

12. This interview of Oda Hōryū, priest in charge of Jikishian in the Sagano area of Kyoto, was conducted by Elizabeth Harrison on November 27, 1986. Bardwell Smith was also present.

13. Hirose Zenjun Ni, ed., *Jikishian omoidegusa yori: Ichirin no ai o kudasai* [Please Give me One Flower of Love], vol. 2, 8, 10.

14. Ibid., 157.

15. Ibid., Vol. 4, 216–218. (Tokyo: Chōbunsha, 1979).

16. Ibid., Vol. 1, 1977, 30.(Tokyo: Chōbunsha, 1977).

17. Ibid.,180–181. The caption for this quote is translated as "Beautiful Flowers," but the literal meaning is "[I will keep loving] only Beautiful Flowers." *Flowers* here stand for *women*.

18. Ibid., Vol. 2, 8–9.

19. Ibid., 86–88.

20. Oda Hōryū, *Ai no kiroku* [Documents (Records) of Love], Vol. 6 (Tokyo: Tokuma Shoten, 1980), 13–17, 44.

21. Ibid., 37–38, 44.

22. Ibid., 18–19.

23. The concept *folie à deux* conveys the folly or madness of two people who lean upon each other as a way of creating their own identity. Ironically, they become enablers of their own narcissism. See Eric Fromm, *The Art of Loving* (New York: Harper & Bros., 1974).

24. Hirose Zenjun Ni, ed., *Jikishian omoidegusa yori*, Vol. 2, 96–97.

25. Ibid., Vol. 2, 68.

26. Oda Hōryū, *Ai o komete* [Devote One's Whole Heart], Vol. 8, 1982, 284–285.

27. Oda Hōryū, Ai no kiroku, Vol. 6, 16.

28. Ibid., Vol. 6, 29. Oda-san adds this comment: "As the nineteenth-century French writer Stendhal, author of *Black and Red* and *On Love*, said: 'Love is like having a fever. It comes and goes without having much control.'"

29. Ibid.,, 16–17.

30. Ibid., 19–20.

31. Ibid., 20–21.

32. Ibid., 21–22.

33. Ibid., Vol. 8., 85–86.

34. Ibid., Vol. 6., 26–28.

35. Ibid., 28.

36. Ibid., 32–33.

37. Ibid., 33.

38. Ibid., 39.

39. Ibid., 37, 44–45.

40. Ibid., 47.

41. Ibid., 47–48.

42. Ibid., Vol. 8, 155–156.

43. Ibid., Vol. 6., 48–49.

44. Questionnaire 3 was sent to local religious organizations. Among the questions asked was No. 28: "What does your group think about abortion (*jinko chūzetsu*)?"

This questionnaire was one of five conducted by the Sociology of Contemporary Religion Research Group, based at Kyoto University.

CHAPTER 4

The Phenomena of Mizuko kuyō: *Responses to Pregnancy Loss*

1. While these words are not drawn from any one service, they are typical of what one might hear and observe at a Buddhist *mizuko kuyō* (memorial service).

2. The results of these surveys are included as appendices in the book *Mizuko kuyō: gendai shakai no fuan to iyashi* (Mizuko Kuyō: Anxiety and Healing in Contemporary Society), edited by Takahashi Saburō and published in Kyoto by Kōrosha in 1999. Two of these surveys, carried out in 1986, were of various religions sects, denominations, and other religious organizations (209 responses with a response rate of 41.0%) and of religious organizations and spiritualists that publicly indicated they performed *mizuko kuyō* (152 replies and a response rate of 40.4%). Three other surveys were conducted in 1991. Of these, one was a survey of Buddhist temples that advertised they performed *mizuko kuyō* (284 responses at a rate of 81.4%) and of spiritualists (*reinosha*) performing *mizuko kuyō* (59 responses at a rate of 35.5%). The third is a shorter survey of all Buddhist temples in the city of Kyoto, with 681 responses at a response rate of 40.9%. The results of these five questionnaires appear on pages 259–299 of this book.

3. Of the questionnaires made available to individuals in the mid-1980s who came to Adashino Nenbutsuji in Kyoto for *mizuko kuyō*, the 1,127 completed responses also appear in tabulated form in the appendices to the same book edited by Takahashi Saburō (1999). This particular survey, conducted by *Tokyo Kōgei Daigaku Kyōdō Kenkyū Han* [Tokyo Polytechnic University Collaborative Research Group], was in cooperation with the Kyoto University research group. Of considerable importance are the personal responses added by people at the end of this questionnaire. This particular survey and its tabulations appear on pages 243–258 in the appendices of the Takahashi book. Because some of the questions and responses of this survey were of less pertinence to the subject matter of this chapter, they have not been included here, though more of this material is discussed in later chapters.

4. Page numbers for the responses and tabulations appearing in the appendices in the book edited by Takahashi Saburō are indicated in brackets. Percentage numbers are rounded off to the nearest percent, with the exception of numbers within accompanying tables, as these are part of the Kyoto University volume (referred to again as the Kyōdai project).

5. This is response #55028 in the survey conducted at Adashino Nenbutsuji by the Tokyo Kōgei University survey. These numbers represent statements by respondents to the questionnaire administered in the mid-1980s. For the most part, this questionnaire was a "closed survey" in that the options were already

provided, but in various places the respondents were invited to expand on their reactions.

6. Kōgei University survey, #25257, #55087, #55197, respectively.

7. Kōgei University survey, #55010.

8. Kōgei University survey, #55041.

9. Kōgei University survey, #55166.

10. Kōgei University survey, #55148.

11. Suzuki Kentarō, "Divination in Contemporary Japan: A General Overview and an Analysis of Survey Results," *Japanese Journal of Religious Studies* 22(3–4) (1995): 249–266. This article focuses primarily on astrology, tarot cards, palmistry, physiognomy, and Chinese augury.

12. Figures on what temples charge women and their families for *kuyō* and for statues of one sort or another are included in the appendices.

13. Shinno Toshikazu, "From Minkan-shinkō to Minzoku-shūkyō: Reflections on the Study of Folk Buddhism," *Japanese Journal of Religious Studies* 20(2–3) (1993): 202.

14. This questionnaire is one of five surveys done by the Kyoto University Sociological Research Group on Contemporary Religion. This particular survey was sent to Buddhist temples in the Kyoto area that advertise the fact that they provide *mizuko kuyō*. See question 20 on page 283.

15. This questionnaire was sent to various religious groups and spiritualists (*reinosha*) that identify the fact that they perform *mizuko kuyō*. See question 22 on page 270.

16. Kōgei University survey, #25280.

17. Kōgei University survey, #55197.

18. Kōgei University survey, #25250.

19. Kōgei University survey. #55046.

20. Kōgei University survey, #55038.

21. Kōgei University survey, #55002.

22. Kōgei University survey, #55183.

23. Kōgei University survey, #55198.

24. Richard W. Anderson and Elaine Martin, "Rethinking the Practice of *Mizuko Kuyō* in Contemporary Japan: Interviews with Practitioners at a Buddhist Temple in Tokyo," *Japanese Journal of Religious Studies* 24(1–2) (1997): 121–143.

25. Kōgei University survey, #55027.

26. This question is from the survey sent to Buddhist temples in the Kyoto area. See question 25 on page 285.

27. Kōgei University survey, #25280.

28. This survey was sent to the headquarters of a large number of religious organizations in Japan. See question 10 on page 262.

29. Kōgei University survey, #55107.

30. Again, as we have seen, Oda Hōryū (Jikishian) is clearly an exception to this.

31. Kōgei University survey, #25254.

32. This question was also addressed to Buddhist temples in the Kyoto area that performed *mizuko kuyō*. See question 3 on pages 276–277.

33. Takahashi Yoshinori, "*Futatsu no mizuko kuyō*," in *Mizuko kuyō: gendai shakai no fuan to iyashi* (*Mizuko Kuyō: Anxiety and Healing in Contemporary Society*), ed. by Takahashi Saburō, Kyoto: Kōrosha, 1999, Chapter 3.

34. Ibid., 120.

35. Kōgei University survey, #25199.

36. Takahashi, "*Futatsu no mizuko kuyō*," 132–133.

37. Ibid., 130.

38. Ibid., 134.

39. Ibid., 139–142.

40. These statements are summaries derived from a large number of responses to questionnaires sent by the Kyoto group of social scientists to the headquarters of religious groups in Japan and to clergy or officials at temples, shrines, churches, or newer forms of religions. The statements as they appear here are my own generalizations; they do not represent the formal position of any group. Rather, they provide a sketch of important differences as well as common features among these various groups.

CHAPTER 5
Japanese Woman as Housewife, Mother, and Worker (1868–2010)

1. Kathleen S. Uno, "Women and Changes in the Household Division of Labor," in *Recreating Japanese Women, 1600–1945*, ed. by Gail Lee Bernstein (Berkeley: University of California Press, 1991), 18.

2. Ibid., 25.

3. Niwa Akiko, "The Formation of the Myth of Motherhood in Japan," Trans. Tomiko Yoda, *U.S.-Japan Women's Journal* (English Supplement) 4 (1993): 76. A useful bibliographical essay may be found in Kuzume Yoshi, "Images of Japanese Women in U.S. Writings and Scholarly Works, 1860–1990: Formation and Transformation of Stereotypes," *U.S.-Japan Women's Journal* (English Supplement) 1 (1991): 6–50.

4. Niwa, "Formation of the Myth of Motherhood in Japan," 72.

5. Ibid., 73–75. For a view of motherhood among the aristocracy in Japan that provides a different perspective from what is found in the middle or lower classes, Takie Sugiyama Lebra's research is of great interest: Lebra, "Fractionated Motherhood: Status and Gender among the Japanese Elite," *U.S.-Japan Women's Journal* (English Supplement) 6 (1994): 3–25.

6. Niwa, "Formation of the Myth of Motherhood in Japan," 75.

7. Uno, *Recreating Japanese Women*, 40–41.

8. See William Reynolds Braisted, ed., *Meiroku Zasshi: Journal of the Japanese Enlightenment* (Cambridge, MA: Harvard University Press, 1976), xvii–xlvii.

9. While *Onna daigaku*, a book on women's education published in 1729, is ascribed to Kaibara Ekken, it may have been written by a later scholar making use of Kaibara's views.

10. Carmen Blacker, *The Japanese Enlightenment: A Study of the Writings of Fukuzawa Yukichi* (Cambridge: Cambridge University Press, 1964), 84–85.

11. Fukuzawa Yukichi, *Fukuzawa Yukichi on Japanese Women: Selected Works*, Trans. and ed. by Eiichi Kiyooka (Tokyo: University of Tokyo Press, 1988), 20–21.

12. Yoshiko Miyake, "Doubling Expectation: Motherhood and Women's Factory Work under State Management in Japan in the 1930s and 1940s," in Bernstein, *Recreating Japanese Women*, 276, n. 19. See Sharon L. Sievers, "Feminist Criticism in Japanese Politics in the 1880s: The Experience of Kishida Toshiko," *Signs: Journal of Women in Culture and Society* 6(4) (1981). Sievers writes that "*ryōsai kembo* was not a term rescued from some Tokugawa Confucian text for women but the creation of Nakamura in the Meiji period" (604, n. 4). See Sievers, *Flowers in Salt: The Beginnings of Feminist Consciousness in Modern Japan* (Stanford, CA: Stanford University Press, 1983); and Sharon H. Nolte and Sally Ann Hastings, "The Meiji State's Policy Toward Women, 1890–1910," in Bernstein, *Recreating Japanese Women*.

13. Robert J. Smith, "Gender Inequality in Contemporary Japan," *Journal of Japanese Studies* 13(1) (1987): 7. A useful depiction of the American scene is Barbara Welter, "The Cult of True Womanhood: 1820–1860," *American Quarterly* 18 (1966): 151–174. This account shows how the ideals presented to American women in the early to mid-nineteenth century are parallel to yet different from those presented to Japanese women during the Meiji period. This emphasis gives rise to the importance of a woman's piety, purity, submissiveness, and domesticity. The similarities between these qualities and those singled out by the Tokugawa scholar Kaibara Ekken (i.e., gentle obedience, chastity, mercy, and quietness) and those eventually underscored by the Meiji Civil Code of 1898 are evident.

14. See Doi Kōka, *A Theory of Civilization and the Greater Learning for Women (Bunmeiron onna daigaku)*, 1876, for an influential work that was strongly critical of Kaibara Ekken's *Onna daigaku*, especially on the issues of child care and the mother's role in educating her children.

15. Barbara Rose, *Tsuda Umeko and Women's Education in Japan* (New Haven, CT: Yale University Press, 1992), 52. As Mori Arinori put it, "The foundations of national prosperity rests upon education; the foundations of education upon women's education"; quoted in Sharon H. Nolte, "Women, the State, and Repression in Imperial Japan," Working Paper 33 (Office of Women in International Development, Michigan State University, 1983), 5.

16. E. Patricia Tsurumi, *Factory Girls: Women in the Thread Mills in Meiji Japan* (Princeton, NJ: Princeton University Press, 1990), 3.

17. Tsurumi, *Factory Girls*, 10.

18. Marjorie Wall Bingham and Susan Hill Gross, *Women in Japan from Ancient Times to the Present* (St. Louis Park, MN: Glenhurst Publications, Inc., 1987), 198.

19. Rose, *Tsuda Umeko and Women's Education in Japan*, 113.

20. R. P. Dore, *City Life in Japan: A Study of a Tokyo Ward* (Berkeley: University of California Press, 1958), 92. See also Carol Gluck, *Japan's Modern Myths: Ideology in the Late Meiji Period* (Princeton, NJ: Princeton University Press, 1985).

21. Margit Maria Nagy, "'How Shall We Live?': Social Change, the Family Institution and Feminism in Prewar Japan" (Ph.D. diss., University of Washington, 1981), 38. The evolving nature of Japanese family law from the Meiji Civil Code of 1898 to the present may be traced in Toshitani Nobuyoshi, "The Reform of Japanese Family Law and Changes in the Family System," *U.S.-Japan Women's Journal* (English Supplement) 6 (1994): 66–82. For another discussion of *ie* structure, see Dorinne Kondo, *Crafting Selves* (Chicago: University of Chicago Press, 1990), 121–131.

22. Rose, *Tsuda Umeko and Women's Education in Japan*, 115–117. Other features of this code were more specific: "In this new Civil Code only men were legally recognized as persons; a married woman (placed in the same classification as the 'deformed and the mentally incompetent') could neither enter into a legal contract nor bring legal action without her husband's consent. The husband had the right to dispose of his wife's property as he saw fit and the right to any of its profits ... Adultery was a crime only for married women; only the wife's adultery was legal grounds for divorce. The husband was not obligated to support the wife after a divorce, and any children were considered to be solely the father's" (116).

23. Dore, *City Life in Japan*, 92–93. See also Susan J. Pharr, *Losing Face: Status Politics in Japan* (Berkeley: University of California Press, 1990), 18–28.

24. Nolte and Hastings, "The Meiji State's Policy Toward Women, 1890–1910," in Bernstein, 1991, 171.

25. For a similar separation of public and private spheres in an earlier period of New England life and society, see Nancy F. Cott, *The Bonds of Womanhood: "Women's Sphere" in New England, 1780–1835* (New Haven, CT: Yale University Press, 1977).

26. Margit Nagy, "Middle-Class Working Women During the Interwar Years," in Bernstein, *Recreating Japanese Women*, 200. See also Barbara Molony, "Activism among Women in the Taishō Cotton Textile Industry," in Bernstein, *Recreating Japanese Women*, 217–238, which carries the discussion of Japanese textile workers up through the 1920s.

27. Sheldon Garon, *Molding Japanese Minds: The State in Everyday Life* (Princeton, NJ: Princeton University Press, 1997), 132.

28. Garon, *Molding Japanese Minds*, 144.

29. Uno, Kathleen, S., "The Death of 'Good Wife, Wise Mother'?" in *Postwar Japan as History*, ed. by Andrew Gordon (Berkeley: University of California Press, 1993), 303.

30. Ibid., 304–305.
31. Richard K. Beardsley, John W. Hall, and Robert E. Ward, *Village Japan* (Chicago: University of Chicago Press, 1959), 228.
32. Ibid., 232.
33. Ibid., 330.
34. Fukutake, Tadashi, *Japanese Rural Society* (Ithaca, NY: Cornell University Press, 1972), 59.
35. Ochiai Emiko, *Nijūisseiki no kazoku e* [Toward the Twenty-First Century Family] (Tokyo: Yūhikaku, 1996), 78–83. In Chapter 6 we discuss further the opposition by feminists of the remnants of the *ie* system, including in a practice such as *mizuko kuyō*.
36. Robert J. Smith and Ella Lury Wiswell, *The Women of Suye Mura* (Chicago: University of Chicago Press, 1982).
37. See Judith Modell's review article of *Haruko's World* and *The Women of Suye Mura* in *Journal of Japanese Studies* 12(1) (1986): 141–150. This quotation is from page 148.
38. Kyoko Yoshimizu, "Marriage and Family: Past and Present," in *Japanese Women: New Feminist Perspectives on the Past, Present, and Future*, ed. by Kumiko Fujimura-Fanselow and Atsuko Kameda (New York: Feminist Press, 1995), 183–197.
39. Ochiai presents an interesting analysis of the emergence of the role of professional housewives in Japan as linked to the postwar shift from rural agricultural to urban industrial economy. See Ochiai, *Nijūisseiki no kazoku e* [*Toward the Twenty-first Century Family*], 12–30.
40. Robert J. Smith, *Kurusu: The Price of Progress in a Japanese Village* (Stanford: Stanford University Press, 1978), 10–11.
41. Susan Orpett Long, *Family Change and the Life Course in Japan*, in Cornell East Asia Papers (Ithaca, NY: Cornell University, 1987), 40, 54. In 1993 the average number of children for a Japanese woman was 1.3.
42. For an important study of this issue see Muriel Jolivet, *Japan: The Childless Society? The Crisis of Motherhood*, Trans. Anne-Marie Glasheen (London: Rutledge, 1997).
43. Long, *Family Change and the Life Course in Japan*, 50.
44. See Anne Allison, "Producing Mothers," 135–155, in *Re-Imaging Japanese Women*, ed. by Anne E. Imamura (Berkeley: University of California Press, 1996). See also Anne Allison, *Permitted and Prohibited Desires* (Boulder, CO: Westview Press, 1996), especially Chapters 4 and 5.
45. Long, *Family Change and the Life Course in Japan*, 49.
46. Ariyoshi Sawako, *The Twilight Years*, Trans. Mildred Tahara (Tokyo: Kodansha International, 1984), 167. The novel details the strongly mixed feelings of Akiko, the daughter-in-law whose fate was to take care of her husband Nobutoshi's rapidly aging parents. It captures Akiko's frustration and anger yet also her sense of duty. See page 88 especially.
47. Mariko Asano Tamanoi, "Women's Voices: Their Critique of the Anthropology of Japan," *Annual Review of Anthropology* 19 (1990): 17–37. See pages 19–25 for a

critique of approaches that tend to generalize about Japanese women's existence yet to ignore "what women have to say about their own experiences, emotions, and thoughts" (17).

48. For a depiction of part-time women workers in a small, family-owned confectionery factory in an industrial area of Tokyo, Dorinne Kondo differentiates the attitudes of these women as well as their work and family lives from the lifestyles and class backgrounds of the two types of women just mentioned. Kondo, *Crafting Selves: Power, Gender, and Discourses of Identity in a Japanese Workplace* (Chicago: University of Chicago Press, 1990).

49. Ueno Chizuko, "Genesis of the Urban Housewife," *Japan Quarterly* 34(2) (1987): 138.

50. Ochiai, *Nijūisseiki no kazoku e*, 94–99.

51. Muriel Jolivet, *Japan: The Childless Society?* (London and New York: Routledge, 1997). Jolivet's study is based on Japanese sources "as well as discussions held with a study group made up of some thirty Japanese women," which frequently included pediatricians and psychiatrists whose practice dealt principally with women's problems. She derived part of her information from the battered children's help line, whose callers are often women who are sick of being a mother and are afraid they will harm their children but have nowhere else to turn.

52. Ibid., 29.

53. Suzanne H. Vogel, "Professional Housewife: The Career of Urban Middle Class Japanese Women," *Japan Interpreter* 12(1) (1978): 32.

54. Ibid., 32.

55. Takie Sugiyama Lebra, *Japanese Women: Constraint and Fulfillment* (Honolulu: University of Hawaii Press, 1984), 163. Hers is an ethnographic study of Japanese women and their life histories, with life cycles as a primary point of focus.

56. Lebra, *Japanese Women*, 164.

57. Ibid., 216.

58. Gail Lee Bernstein, *Haruko's World: A Japanese Farm Woman and Her Community* (Stanford, CA: Stanford University Press, 1996). Originally published in 1983, it was reprinted in 1996, with an epilogue that updated the story from 1982 to 1995. Bernstein lived with this family from October 1974 to May 1975 and then revisited the Utsunomiya family briefly in 1982 and 1993, with another briefer time in Tokyo seeing Haruko's husband Shō-ichi in November 1995.

59. Ibid., 99.

60. Ibid., 55–56.

61. Ibid., 105.

62. Uno, "The Death of 'Good Wife, Wise Mother'?" 303–320. This essay is valuable also for its rich bibliographic references. Garon, *Molding Japanese Minds*, widens the perspective on the women's movement over the last fifty years. Other useful essays include Sandra Buckley, "Altered States: The Body Politics of 'Being Woman,'" in Gordon, *Postwar Japan as History*, 347–372; Sandra

Buckley and Vera Mackie, "Women in the New Japanese State," in *Democracy in Contemporary Japan*, ed. by Gavan McCormack and Yoshio Sugimoto (Armonk, NY: M.E. Sharpe, Inc., 1986), 173–185; and Ehara Yumiko, "Japanese Feminism in the 1970s and 1980s," *U.S.-Japan Women's Journal* (English Supplement) 4 (1993): 49–69.

63. Omori Maki, "Gender and the Labor Market," *Journal of Japanese Studies* 19(1) (1993): 100. For an article with a broader perspective, see Mary C. Brinton, "The Social-Institutional Bases of Gender Stratification: Japan as an Illustrative Case," *American Journal of Sociology* 94(2) (1988): 300–334.

64. Fujita Mariko, "'It's All Mother's Fault': Childcare and the Socialization of Working Mothers in Japan," *Journal of Japanese Studies* 15(/1) (1989): 67–91, describes this problem from her experience as a Japanese mother returning with her husband and child after ten years in the United States.

65. Sandra Buckley, "Altered States: The Body Politics of 'Being Woman'," in Andrew Gordon, 359.

66. Ibid., 362. Her two examples of this kind of literature are Hamao Minoru, *How to Bring Up Girls: A Guide to Raising a Nice Child* [Onna no ko no shit-sukekata—yasashii kodomo ni sodateru hon] (Tokyo: Kobunsha, 1972); and Kawakami Gentarō, *I'd Like to See Their Parents' Faces* [Oya no kao ga mitai] (Tokyo: Shobo, 1975). As Buckley says, "Unfortunately, Kawakami and Hamao cannot be ignored as extreme examples. Their books were quite representative of the tone and moral content of the genre of guide books to femininity" (363). One response to these books is Keiko Higuchi, *Bringing Up Girls: Start Aiming at Love and Independence (Status of Women in Japan)*, Trans. Akiko Tomii (Kyoto: Shoukado Booksellers Private Company, 1985). Higuchi's book challenges the ideas of Hamao and Kawakami and was translated into English through the Women's Bookstore in Kyoto.

67. Buckley, "Altered States," 365. See Fujimura-Fanselow and Kaneda, *Japanese Women*, 75–180. (1995). For an important discussion of these issues see Nancy Rosenberger, "Fragile Resistance, Signs of Status: Women between State and Media in Japan," in Imamura, *Re-Imagiing Japanese Women*, 12–45.

68. Susan J. Pharr, "The Japanese Woman: Evolving Views of Life and Role," in *Asian Women in Transition*, ed. by Sylvia A. Chipp and Justin J. Green (University Park: Pennsylvania State University Press, 1980), 36–61. For other works on the variety of women's roles and expectations and the importance of seeing women's roles from a life cycle perspective, see Sumiko Iwao, *The Japanese Woman: Traditional Image and Changing Reality* (New York: Free Press, 1993); Anne E. Imamura, *Urban Japanese Housewives: At Home and in the Community* (Honolulu: University of Hawaii Press, 1987); and Jane Condon, *A Half Step Behind: Japanese Women of the '80s* (New York: Dodd, Mead & Company, 1985).

69. Pharr, "Japanese Woman: Evolving Views of Life and Role," 51. For further discussion of Japanese feminist issues and activities see Vera Mackie, "Feminist

Politics in Japan," *New Left Review* 167 (1988): 53–76. Mackie contends that there are positions between the "New Women" and the "Radical Egalitarians." For another sense of the spectrum among Japanese feminists, see Ehara Yumiko, "Japanese Feminism in the 1970s and 1980s," *U.S.-Japan Women's Journal,* English Supplement No. 4 (1993): 49–69.

70. Chieko Ariga, "Dephallicizing Women in *Ryukyo shinshi*: A Critique of Gender Ideology in Japanese Literature," *The Journal of Asian Studies* 51(3) (1992): 576–577.

71. Noriko Mizuta, "Symposium on Women and the Family: Post-Family Alternatives," *Review of Japanese Culture and Society* 3(1) (1989): 82.

72. Nancy J. Chodorow, *Feminism and Psychoanalytical Theory* (New Haven, CT: Yale University Press, 1989), 80.

73. Dorinne K. Kondo, *Crafting Selves: Power, Gender, and Discourses of Identity in a Japanese Workplace* (Chicago: Chicago University Press, 1990), 50.

74. Kondo, *Crafting Selves,* 280–282.

75. Jamie Hubbard, *The Yamaguchi Story: Buddhism and the Family in Contemporary Japan* (60-minute film with English subtitles). London and Washington, DC: BBC/Educational Communications International, 1988.

76. Dore, *City Life in Japan,* 184–185. In these words Dore captures the power of social expectation.

77. A similar instance of how a husband's guilt over his infidelity is triggered by his wife's nonrecriminatory strategy is reported in Helen Hardacre, *Lay Buddhism in Contemporary Japan: Reiyūkai Kyōdan* (Princeton, NJ: Princeton University Press, 1984), 215.

78. Sandra Buckley, *Broken Silence: Voices of Japanese Feminism* (Berkeley: University of California Press, 1997), 362.

79. Masako Tanaka, "Maternal Authority in the Japanese Family," in *Religion and the Family in East Asia,* ed. by George A. DeVos and Takao Sofue (Berkeley: University of California Press, 1984), 233.

80. Ibid., 234. She continues: "The suppression of sexuality in the marital relationship, the continuous maternal interest in her son, and the conceptualization of the wifely care [for her husband] after the model of maternal care, all make the wife–husband relationship and the mother–son relationship dangerously similar."

81. Philip E. Slater, *The Glory of Hera: Greek Mythology and the Greek Family.* (Boston: Beacon Press, 1968), 33. Ronald V. Bell, "Lovers, Leavers, Sons and Mothers: Breaking the Spell of Japanese Romance," *Kyoto Journal* 17 (1991): 27, discusses the same phenomenon in Japanese society: "Emotionally abandoned by their husbands, many wives pour their passion on their sons ... It is not surprising, then, that sons of passionless marriages should unconsciously try to fill the emotional gaps left by father whose main bonds are with their workmates." Lengthier discussions of this theme are found in Nicholas Bornhoff, *Pink Samurai: An*

Erotic Exploration of Japanese Society (London: Grafton, 1992); and Ian Buruma, *A Japanese Mirror* (New York: Viking Penguin Inc., 1985), especially 18–112.

82. Funabashi, Kuniko. "Pornographic Culture and Sexual Violence," in Fujimura-Fanselow and Kameda, *Japanese Women,* (1995), 255.

83. See the extended interview of the feminist poet Kora Rumiko in Buckley, *Broken Silence,* 102–130, in which Kora stresses the importance of the erotic experience of a woman's own body and her belief that a woman is ineluctably body-centered in ways a man is not.

84. Ibid., 131.

85. Ibid., 141. See also Buckley's chapter on Matsui Yayori, 131–151.

86. Ariga, Chieko M., "Who's Afraid of Amino Kiku? Gender Conflict and the Literary Canon," in Fujimura-Fanselow and Kameda, *Japanese Women,* 43–60. For a discussion of the Japanese woman writer Miyamoro Yuriko (1899–1951), who created another kind of subversive fiction. For this, see Michiko Niikuni Wilson, "Misreading and Un-reading the Male Text, Finding the Female Text: Miyamoto Yuriko's Autobiographical Fiction," *U.S.-Japan Women's Journal* (English Supplement) 13 (1997): 26–55.

87. Ariga, "Who's Afraid of Amino Kiku?" 55.

88. Ibid.

89. Ibid.

90. Sandra Buckley and Vera Mackie, "Women in the New Japanese State," in *Democracy in Contemporary Japan,* ed. by Gavan McCormack and Yoshio Sugimoto (Armonk, NY and London, England: M.E. Sharpe, Inc.), 181.

91. Ibid., "Women in the New Japanese State," 181–182.

92. Ibid., 178–179.

93. Ehara Yumiko, "Japanese Feminism in the 1970s and 1980s," 55.

94. Buckley, *Broken Silence,* provides important evidence of this expanding diversity through interviews with ten Japanese feminists whose perspectives, while often diverging, present a complementary picture of current feminist views in Japan.

95. Lebra, "Fractionated Motherhood," 3.

96. Ibid., 4–5.

97. Kanai Yoshiko, "Issues for Japanese Feminism," in *Voices from the Japanese Women's Movement,* ed. by AMPO-Japan Asia Quarterly Review (Armonk, NY: M.E. Sharpe, Inc., 1996), 9.

98. Ibid., 16.

99. Ibid., 9.

100. Certeau, *Practice of Everyday Life,* 39.

101. Ibid., 37. For parallel strategies and tactics see James C. Scott, *Weapons of the Weak: Everyday Forms of Peasant Resistance* (New Haven, CT: Yale University Press, 1985); and Scott, *Domination and the Arts of Resistance: Hidden Transcripts* (New Haven, CT: Yale University Press, 1990).

102. Jolivet, *Japan: The Childless Society?* 191. Examples of resistance in Japan have addressed the following sorts of issues: the dominance of young wives and mothers

by mothers-in-law; the noninvolvement of husbands in childcare and tasks around the house; the refusal of society to make adequate daycare provisions; and the insensitivity of employers who expect full commitment by husbands and fathers at the cost of life within the family. For a discussion of new patterns of relationships within the Japanese home, see Deborah M. Aoki, "Gender, Class, and Age in the Microcosm of the Family: The Household Division of Labor in Hokkaido, Japan," *U.S.-Japan Women's Journal* (English Supplement) 13 (1997): 87–103.

103. Margaret Lock, "Protests of a Good Wife and Wise Mother: The Medicalization of Distress in Japan," in *Health, Illness, and Medical Care in Japan: Cultural and Social Dimensions,* ed. by Edward Norbeck and Margaret Lock (Honolulu: University of Hawaii Press, 1987), 131.

104. Ibid., 141.

105. Ibid., 152.

106. Susan R. Bordo, "The Body and the Reproduction of Femininity: A Feminist Appropriation of Foucault," in *Gender/Body/Knowledge: Feminist Reconstructions of Being and Knowing, ed.* by Alison M. Jaggar and Susan R. Bordo (New Brunswick, NJ: Rutgers University Press, 1989), 20.

107. Chieko Irie Mulhern, "Japanese Harlequin Romances as Transcultural Woman's Fiction," *Journal of Asian Studies* 48(1) (1989): 57–58. Janice Radway, *Reading the Romance: Women, Patriarchy, and Popular Literature* (Chapel Hill: University of North Carolina Press, 1991), deals with the American scene and has become a classic in cultural studies.

108. Mulhern, "Japanese Harlequin Romances," 60.

109. Ibid., 67.

110. Fumiko Enchi, *The Waiting Years,* Trans. John Bester (Tokyo: Kodansha International, 1984). Enchi worked on this novel for eight years; it was published in Japan [*Onna zaka*) in 1957. During that time she was working on other versions of the same story.

111. Ibid., 28.

112. Ibid..

113. Ibid., 78–79.

114. Ibid., 148.

115. Ibid., 188.

116. Ibid., 189–190.

117. Ibid., 199.

118. Ibid., 200.

119. Ibid., 201.

120. Ibid., 201–202.

121. Ibid., 203.

122. The impact of possessed power is the import of this novel. While Tomo's "request" can be seen as a "strategy of weakness," its strength lies in its devastating disclosure of the codes of human conduct that prevailed in Meiji Japan and that are still echoed in different forms a century later.

123. See Eileen B. Mikals-Adachi, "Reflections: Enchi Fumiko and the Sequel to *Onna zaka*," unpublished manuscript, given as a paper at the Association for Asian Studies meetings in Chicago, March 13–16, 1997. Here Mikals-Adachi discusses Enchi's short story "Hansēki" [Half a Century], *Enchi Fumiko Zenshū*, Vol. 5 (Tokyo: Shinchosha, 1978), in which Enchi reflects on her relationship to the model for the protagonist Tomo in *Onna zaka* [The Waiting Years], namely, her maternal grandmother. While Enchi's search for an "ideal" modern woman, one with "the strength to come to terms with [her own] self," was a lifelong literary quest, it is pertinent here that because she found that kind of strength in her own grandmother who lived, like Tomo, in the mid-Meiji period. Therefore, she could represent Tomo as a woman whose strength was to express "her own true self." Mikals-Adachi's essay is an important corroboration of seeing the fictionalized Tomo as a strong woman who, while caught in the midst of Meiji conventions, was able to defy them in a manner that undermined their posture of rectitude.

CHAPTER 6

Ancestors, Angry Spirits, and the Unborn: Caring for the Dead

1. Meyer Fortes, "An Introductory Comment," in *Ancestors*, ed. by William H. Newall. (The Hague: Mouton, 1974), 6. See also C. Takeda, "Family Religion in Japan: Ie and Its Religious Faith," in *ibid.*, 119–128. R. P. Dore, "The Japanese Family System," in *City Life in Japan*, 91–120, spells out both the ideal and the actual dimensions of the pre-World War II *ie* family system in Japan.
2. Kenneth Ch'en, "Filial Piety in Chinese Buddhism," *Harvard Journal of Asiatic Studies* 28 (1968): 97. See also Ch'en, *Buddhism in China: A Historical Survey* (Princeton, NJ: Princeton University Press, 1964); and Ch'en, *The Transformation of Buddhism* (Princeton, NJ: Princeton University Press, 1973).
3. For a critique of Ch'en's assumption that Buddhist monks as well as laypeople in South Asia were not prone to practice filial piety through acts of *pūjā* (religious ritual in reverence and honor) for their living or deceased parents, see Gregory Schopen, "Filial Piety and the Monk in the Practice of Indian Buddhism: A Question of 'Sinicization' Viewed from the Other Side," in Schopen, *Bones, Stones, and Buddhist Monks: Collected Papers on the Archaeology, Epigraphy, and Texts of Monastic Buddhism in India* (Honolulu: University of Hawaii Press, 1997), 56–71.
4. Richard Gombrich, "'Merit Transference' in Sinhalese Buddhism: A Case Study of the Interaction between Doctrine and Practice," *History of Religions* 11(2) (1971): 203–219. For a focus on the *Petavatthu* ("Stories of the Departed") literature, see John C. Holt, "Assisting the Dead by Venerating the Living: Merit Transfer in the Early Buddhist Tradition," *Numen* 28(1) (1981): 1–28; and Schopen, "Filial Piety and the Monk in the Practice of Indian Buddhism." *T'oung Pao* 70(1–3) (1984): 110–126.

5. P.D. Premasiri, "Significance of the Ritual Concerning Offerings to Ancestors in Theravada Buddhism," in *Buddhist Thought and Ritual*, ed. by David Kalupahana (New York: Paragon House, 1991), 157–158.

6. The apocryphal Chinese sutra known as *Fo-shuo hsiao-tzu ching* (*Sutra on a Filial Son*) appeared in many versions, had immense popularity among laypeople, and served to assimilate Buddhism into the Chinese social structure. For a Japanese Buddhist sense of the parent–child bond that begins in life and continues after death, see the apocryphal *Sutra on the Heavy Indebtedness to One's Parents* [*Bumo onjūkyo*], Trans. John Doami and ed. by Hisao Inagaki (Kyoto: Ryukoku Translation Center, Ryukoku University, 1965), 16.

7. Stephen F. Teiser, "Ghosts and Ancestors in Medieval Chinese Religion: The Yü-lan-p'en Festival as Mortuary Ritual," *History of Religions* 26(1) (1986): 50–51. See also Teiser, *The Ghost Festival in Medieval China* (Princeton, NJ: Princeton University Press, 1988).

8. Teiser, *Ghost Festival in Medieval China*, 9–10; Robert J. Smith, *Ancestor Worship in Contemporary Japan* (Stanford, CA: Stanford University Press, 1974), 15–17.

9. Smith, *Ancestor Worship in Contemporary Japan*, 148–149. Many of the same reasons are given by those requesting memorial services for lost children or for an aborted fetus. See Dore, *City Life in Japan*, 317–325.

10. Herman Ooms, "The Religion of the Household: A Case Study of Ancestor Worship in Japan," *Contemporary Religion in Japan* 8(3–4) (1967): 274.

11. Matthews Masayuki Hamabata, *Crested Kimono: Power and Love in the Japanese Business Family* (Ithaca, NY: Cornell University Press, 1990), 59.

12. Fortes, "Introductory Comment," 7–15. Fortes analyzes these ingredients against the backdrop of his research in West African cultures.

13. Tu Wei-ming, *Humanity and Self-Cultivation: Essays in Confucian Thought* (Berkeley, CA: Asian Humanities Press. 1985), 68.

14. Herman Ooms, "A Structural Analysis of Japanese Ancestral Rites and Beliefs," in Newall, *Ancestors*, 85, 87.

15. Ooms, "Religion of the Household," 251.

16. Ōmusu, Heruman, *Senzo sūhai no simborizumu* [*Symbolism in Ancestor Worship*] (Tokyo: Kōbundō, 1987).

17. Ibid., 182. In the writings of Ōe Kenzaburō one also finds a larger vision of what constitutes the human community, one that includes previously marginalized persons (*shūen*).

18. Octavio Paz, *Conjunctions and Disjunctions*. Trans. Helen R. Lane (New York: Viking Press, 1974). Reflecting on the steady returning of death into the midst of the living, he writes: "As the wheel of time revolves, it allows the society to recover buried, or repressed, psychic structures so as to reincorporate them in a present that is also a past. It is not only the return of the ancients and antiquity; it is the possibility that each individual possesses of recovering his living portions of the past" (10).

19. Smith, *Ancestor Worship in Contemporary Japan*, 41. *Muen* means "having no connection or tie"; *hotoke (botoke)* stands for the deceased.

20. Ooms, "Structural Analysis," 68.

21. Smith, *Ancestor Worship in Contemporary Japan*, 19–20. There is a tradition that Kūkai brought this ritual back from China in the early ninth century.

22. Ooms, "Religion of the Household," 251–256, 282–284, 319.

23. Winston Davis, *Dojo: Magic and Exorcism in Modern Japan* (Stanford, CA: Stanford University Press, 1980). For other discussions of angry spirits in Japan, see Takie Sugiyama Lebra, "Ancestral Influence on the Suffering of Descendents in a Japanese Cult," 219–230, in Newell, *Ancestors*, 219–230; Karen Kerner, "The Malevolent Ancestor: Ancestral Influence in a Japanese Religious Sect," in ibid., 205–217; and Janet R. Goodwin, "Shooing the Dead to Paradise," *Japanese Journal of Religious Studies* 16(1) (1989): 63–80.

24. Davis, *Dojo*, 147.

25. Ibid., 156. As Davis notes, ancestors may also be seen to apologize, when scolded by exorcists, for disturbing the living. See Richard W. Anderson, "Social Drama and Iconicity: Personal Narratives in Japanese New Religions," *Journal of Folklore Research* 32(3) (1995): 177–205. Part of Davis's focus is on the role of ancestors in the experiences of suffering and healing.

26. Davis, *Dojo*, 197.

27. For an extended discussion of Winston Davis's book on Mahikari, see Kanako Shiokawa, "Children of the Bright Light: A Folkloric Inquiry into a 'True-Light' Religious Sect in Japanese Cosmological Contexts" (Ph.D. diss., University of Pennsylvania, 1994), especially "Spirits, Ancestors, and Experiences," 271–309.

28. Kiyomi Morioka, "The Appearance of 'Ancestor Religion' in Modern Japan: The Years of Transition from the Meiji to the Taisho Periods," *Japanese Journal of Religious Studies* 4(2–3) (1977): 199–203.

29. Franziska Seraphim, *War Memory and Social Politics in Japan, 1945–2005* (Cambridge, MA: Harvard University Asia Center, 2006), 13. See also John Nelson, "Social Memory as Ritual Practice: Commemorating Spirits of the Dead at Yasukuni Shinto Shrine," *Journal of Asian Studies* 62(2) (2003): 443–467; and John Breen, ed., *Yasukuni, the War Dead, and the Struggle for Japan's Past* (New York: Columbia University Press, 2008).

30. Seraphim, *War Memory and Social Politics in Japan*, 13.

31. Klaus Antoni, "Yasukuni-Jinja and Folk Religion: The Problem of Vengeful Spirits," *Asian Folklore Studies* 47(1) (1988): 128.

32. Helen Hardacre, *Shintō and the State, 1868–1988* (Princeton, NJ: Princeton University Press, 1989), 38. For a different version of Yasukuni's symbolism prior to the strong emergence of patriotism with the Russo-Japanese War, see Tsubouchi Yūzō and Yoshida Tsukasa, "Yasukuni Shrine as a Symbol of Japan's Modernization," *Japan Echo* 26(3) (1999): 48–51.

33. Hardacre, *Shintō and the State*, 146. This postwar fifty-year history includes attempts by the Supreme Court to expand the scope of state-supported

religious activity allowable by the Constitution. Allies in this effort included the "Association of Shinto Shrines, patriotic and rightwing groups, and right-leaning new religions such as Reiyūkai Kyōdan and Seichō no Ie." Those resisting state-promoted religious ideology and observance have, thus far, been successful. Principal resistance has come not only from left-wing political circles but also from Sōka Gakkai, the Union of New Religions (especially Risshō Kōseikai), and various Christian elements.

34. Norma Field, *In the Realm of a Dying Emperor: A Portrait of Japan at Century's End* (New York: Pantheon, 1991).

35. Ibid., 108. Article 20 of the Japanese Constitution reads as follows: "Freedom of religion is guaranteed to all. No religious organization shall receive any privileges from the State, nor exercise any political authority. No person shall be compelled to take part in any religious act, celebration, rite or practice. The State and its organs shall refrain from religious education or any other religious activity."

36. Ibid., 136. See Mark R. Mullins, "From 'Departures' to "Yasukuni Shrine:' Caring for the Dead and the Bereaved in Contemporary Japanese Society," *Japanese Religions* 35(1–2) (2010): 101–112. His main interest is "the way in which the war dead have been unilaterally enshrined in the postwar period without regard for the wishes or feelings of many bereaved families" (106).

37. Field, *In the Realm of a Dying Emperor*, 136.

38. Ibid., 162.

39. Gail Lee Bernstein, ed., *Recreating Japanese Women, 1600–1945* (Berkeley: University of California Press, 1991). Until recently most materials in English on women in Tokugawa Japan are general in nature; the essays in this volume provide specificity and diversity. In particular, see Kathleen S. Uno, "Women and Changes in the Household Division of Labor," 17–41. See also Wakita Haruko, "Women and the Creation of the Ie in Japan: An Overview from the Medieval Period to the Present," *U.S.-Japan Women's Journal* (English Supplement) 4 (1993): 83–105. Uno's essay focuses on the social significance of the *ie* system and the several positions and functions of the housewife in the home, arguing that women's roles in the medieval period were not "confined to activities related to motherhood but included managerial responsibilities" (see 27–30). For a discussion of the economic and cultural evolution of the *ie* system, see Murakami Yasusuke, "Ie Society as a Pattern of Civilization," *Journal of Japanese Studies* 10(2) (1991): 281–363.

40. Morioka, "Appearance of 'Ancestor Religion' in Modern Japan," 194.

41. Sheldon Garon, *Molding Japanese Minds: The State in Everyday Life* (Princeton, NJ: Princeton University Press, 1997), reveals the manner in which large numbers of women's groups beginning in the 1920s pressured the government to deal with issues of central concern to women. While these groups have sometimes been portrayed as instances of the state co-opting women for its own purposes, Garon argues that these were women who involved themselves in causes

for the express purpose of advancing their own goals. This is another example of women becoming agents in their own behalf, of those whose agency was a form of resistance to cultural norms that they be compliant and obedient. Because the story of this collaboration between the state and activist women had not been sufficiently told prior to this book, Garon's work was groundbreaking.

42. Ibid., 98. For a "gender-based analysis of the symbiotic relationship between the Japanese imperial institution and the patriarchal *ie* (household) system," see the discussion of the Japanese social critic Aoki Yayoi in Sandra Buckley, *Broken Silence: Voices of Japanese Feminism* (Berkeley: University of California Press, 1997), 1–31.

43. Earlier we saw a twist on the old *ie* funereal practice in Enchi Fumiko, *The Waiting Years*, Trans. John Bester (Tokyo: Kodansha International, 1984), situated in mid-Meiji times. After decades of being misused by her philandering husband, Tomo Shirakawa, on her deathbed, informs him through a niece that she wants no funeral. Such a move is clearly more radical than not sharing the same grave. It is a declaration of independence not just from her husband but also from a culture in which such a declaration would be scandalous.

44. Kathleen Uno, "Questioning Patrilineality: On Western Studies of the Japanese Ie," *Positions* 4(3) (1996): 569–594. In this she examines the manner in which this system has been conceptualized in English-language scholarly materials from the 1950s to the present. She cites Anita Levy, *Other Women: The Writing of Class, Race, and Gender, 1832–1898* (Princeton, NJ: Princeton University Press, 1991), which discusses how late nineteenth-century anthropology has contributed to the misunderstanding of women from different backgrounds.

45. Uno, "Questioning Patrilineality," 583. To document her point, Uno provides extensive citations of studies, available in English and Japanese, during the past twenty years.

46. Ibid. 585.

47. Helen Hardacre, *Marketing the Menacing Fetus in Japan* (Berkeley: University of California Press, 1997), 257.

48. Hur, Nam-lin, *Death and the Social Order in Tokugawa Japan: Buddhism, Anti-Christianity, and the Danka System* (Cambridge, MA: Harvard University Press, 2007), 9.

49. Ibid. In his own words, Hur's study is an integrated approach to the *danka* system and funerary Buddhism that takes into account the "wider political, cultural, and socioeconomic contexts of early modern Japan." He writes: "The *danka* system was not an exclusive domain of any one party. *Danna* patrons, Buddhist temples, and public authorities all had vested interests in the *danka* system—interests that reflected, and were affected by, the mode of the *danna* relationship, family structure, the religious needs of *danna* households, competition between *danna* temples, state regulations, and local customs relating to funeral services and ancestral rites" (108). Italics in the original have been removed here.

50. "All in all, the entire country was subjugated to the absolute mandate of anti-Christian politics—all in the name of protecting the administrative apparatus of Buddhism, Buddhist institutions set themselves up as trusted anti-Christian agents, and, in return, they succeeded in turning the entire population into loyal Buddhist patrons who would remain within the *danka* system. Anti-Christianity, in alliance with Buddhism, was an institutional fixture of Tokugawa Japan." Ibid., 103.

51. Duncan Ryūken Williams, *The Other Side of Zen: A Social History of Sōtō Zen Buddhism in Tokugawa Japan* (Princeton, NJ: Princeton University Press, 2005), 13. As mentioned in Chapter 2, with access to newly uncovered historical archives, religious manuscripts, and temple records from the Tokugawa period, Williams documents the "ordinary life" of Sōtō Zen priests and laypeople.

52. Stephen G. Covell, *Japanese Temple Buddhism: Worldliness in a Religion of Renunciation* (Honolulu: University of Hawaii Press, 2005), 25.

53. Ibid., 29.

54. Gail Lee Bernstein, *Isami's House: Three Centuries of a Japanese Family* (Berkeley: University of California Press, 2005), 24–25. In her book, which deals with three centuries of a particular Japanese family, Bernstein provides a clear sense of how important ancestral ties were to the living and, by implication, the dead. As we regard members of an extended family in rural Japan relating to each other and the dynamics of the times, we also see a family expressing its loyalty to the ongoing generations through memorial rituals and the many annual observances that highlight their sense of interconnection year after year.

55. Hur, *Death and the Social Order in Tokugawa Japan.* "The *danka* system, leveraged by the shogunal policy of anti-Christianity, had far-reaching ramifications. For Buddhist temples, it provided a major source of income and socio-religious influence; for *danna* households, it provided assurance of religious welfare and continued prosperity; and for the state, it provided an institutional apparatus for socio-religious control and political maneuvering. Within this triangular structure, no one party could fully control the whole system—not even the *bakufu*" (219). Italics in the original have been removed here.

56. See ibid., 232–243, 255–261, for an extended discussion of the various sources of income available to temples as well as a depiction of the increasing expenditures on funerals and burial practices. Hur underscores how in the Edo period "Buddhist monks and *danna* temples were all involved in mortuary rituals, memorial services, and ancestral rites. Their multifaceted involvement in the household institution through the *danka* system ranged from officiating rituals to chanting Buddhist sutras, to taking care of graves, to responding to the special needs of *danna* patrons" (195). For a thorough treatment of the phenomenon of *kanjin* campaigns in Kamakura (1185–1333) Japan, see Janet R. Goodwin, *Alms and Vagabonds: Buddhist Temples and Popular Patronage in Medieval Japan* (Honolulu: University of Hawaii Press, 1994).

57. Hur, *Death and the Social Order in Tokugawa Japan.* "In Tokugawa society, people believed that if a new spirit was denied access to Buddhist death rituals and postmortem services, then it was doomed to be a wandering ghost, unable to attach itself to its descendants and forever flitting about in the wilderness of the other world. Furthermore, when deprived of the divine protection of ancestral deities, a household was believed to run the risk of losing its divine wall of protection and eventually ceasing to exist" (219). Italics removed from this quote.

58. Williams, *Other Side of Zen*, 47.

59. Ibid., 25.

60. Ibid., 9. Williams continues: "Laypeople looked to priests to perform special rites for the dead women and their stillborn because of a popular belief that women who died in childbirth wandered as a ghost in the 'intermediary stage' after death ... People thought that because such female ghosts were unable to achieve salvation, they would haunt the living and wreak havoc on local communities out of resentment. Most manuals of this genre therefore detailed rituals to separate the mother and child so that both would receive proper funerary attention" (55). And he writes: "During the Tokugawa period ... Sōtō Zen priests were part of the small but growing trend to provide children who died with special funerary rites and separate graves" (56).

61. Mark Rowe, "Grave Changes: Scattering Ashes in Contemporary Japan," in *The Buddhist Dead: Practices, Discourses, Representations*, ed. by Bryan J. Cuevas and Jacqueline I. Stone (Honolulu: University of Hawaii Press, 2007), 431.

62. Covell, *Japanese Temple Buddhism*, 31. He adds: "Funerals, graveyards, and memorial services color the image of Japanese Buddhism to such an extent that the vast majority of Japanese claim only to associate with temples at death and, moreover to associate temples and priests themselves with death" (167).

63. As a supplement to the larger picture we include in the Appendix an essay by Yasuo Sakakibara on "Economic Development and Temple Economics in Japan" arising out of his experience as a professional economist and as the head priest for twenty-five years of a Kyoto-based Jōdoshū temple in the second half of the twentieth century.

64. Covell, *Japanese Temple Buddhism*, 183. See also Kenneth A. Marcure, "The Danka System," *Monumenta Nipponica* 40(1) (1985): 39–67, in which he focuses on his and his wife's five-year experience of being tenants of Konrenji, a Jōdo temple in Shiga-ken that was without a resident priest since 1953. While this is a special situation, it provides another view of how the *danka* system affects a small rural temple in contemporary Japan.

65. Covell, *Japanese Temple Buddhism*, 190. Covell, 140–190, provides an extensive and current financial analysis, based on Japanese sources, of Japanese Buddhist temples. He writes: "The pressure to raise the funds needed to maintain the temple and to meet the demands of *danka* members for ritual services (primarily funerals and memorial services) often forces priests away from striking out

into new realms of proselytizing or social welfare. When attempts are made at creating new, or improving old, methods of proselytizing (such as re-creating pilgrimage routes), so strong is the bias against the intermixing of money and religion that such efforts, no matter how sincerely engaged in, are often seen as little more than thinly veiled attempts at fund-raising" (148).

66. Shinno Toshikazu, "From Minkan-shinkō to Minzoku-shūkyō: Reflections on the Study of Folk Buddhism," *Japanese Journal of Religious Studies* 20(2–3) (1993): 202. Also quoted in Chapter 4.

67. Sasaki Shōten, "Shinshū and Folk Religion: Toward a Post-Modern Shinshū 'Theology,'" *Nanzan Bulletin* 12 (1988): 13–35. Translated by Jan Van Bragt in an abridged translation of the original text (1986), which appeared in the *Chūgai Nippō*, a religious newspaper. While Sasaki's critique of his own sect's position on these matters aroused strong reactions among his fellow scholars in Jōdo Shinshū, there is clear evidence that large numbers of Shinshū adherents use *mizuko kuyō*.

68. Satoru Kaneko, "Dimensions of Religiosity among Believers in Japanese Folk Religion," *Journal for the Scientific Study of Religion* 29(1) (1990): 1–18. See also Satoru Kaneko, "Religious Consciousness and Behaviors of Believers in Jōdo Shinshū Buddhism" [in Japanese], in *A Research Paper on the Current Status of the Jōdo Shinshū Sect*, ed. by the Research Center of the Current Status of the Jōdo Shinshū Sect (Kyoto: The Planning Department of Jōdo Shinshū Hongwanji-ha, 1986), 65–86.

69. Sasaki, "Shinshū and Folk Religion," 17.

70. Satoru Kaneko, "Dimensions of Religiosity among Believers in Japanese Folk Religion," 13. Roughly 77% of those interviewed in this study of visitors to Ishikiri Shrine were between fifty and seventy-nine years old, and over two-thirds were women. In 1986 this study also surveyed the religious beliefs and practices of Jōdo Shinshū adherents, of whom the average age was sixty-six, similar to those interviewed at Ishikiri Shrine. Emiko Ohnuki-Tierney discusses the Ishikiri Shrine and the Nakayama Temple in the Ikoma area in Ohnuki-Tierney, *Illness and Culture in Contemporary Japan: An Anthropological View* (Cambridge: Cambridge University Press, 1984), 123–144; and discusses health care in contemporary Japanese religions in *Healing and Restoring: Health and Medicine in the World's Religious Traditions*, ed. by Lawrence E. Sullivan (New York: Macmillan, 1989), 59–87.

71. Satoru Kaneko, "Dimensions of Religiosity among Believers in Japanese Folk Religion," 13.

72. Sasaki, "Shinshū and Folk Religion," 18. See also Yasuaki Nara, "May the Deceased Get Enlightenment! An Aspect of the Enculturation of Buddhism in Japan," *Buddhist–Christian Studies* 15 (1995): 19–42. Nara's article compares the approaches of Jōdoshin-shū and Sōtō-shū to the "two religious levels of Buddhism," namely, the so-called doctrinal and cultural levels, and argues not only that they coexist but also that "interaction between the two is necessary, which, if established satisfactorily, helps the faith to take root and flourish" (36).

73. H. Byron Earhart, *Gedatsu-kai and Religion in Contemporary Japan: Returning to the Center* (Bloomington: Indiana University Press, 1989). Earhart's study of this movement, with approximately 250,000 members, is enriched by his use of nine case studies among its members.

74. Ibid., 252–253. The fact that Gedatsukai lumps together all categories of "child" loss does not mean there are no important differences between how one loses a child or fetus.

75. Posthumously known as Gedatsu Kongō Sonja.

76. The Japanese terms for these, respectively, are *zange, urami, hansei,* and *jōka.*

77. Based upon a questionnaire handed out to 5,686 members in the late 1980s, with 79% responding, Earhart underscores how seriously this discipline was taken at that time. Of those responding, nearly 36% perform the memorial service sixteen to forty-five times monthly; another 52% do it forty-five times or more each month.

78. Earhart, *Gedatsu-kai and Religion,* 175. This is perhaps the only instance that embraces sperm and eggs, independent of conception, as being *mizuko.*

79. Ibid., 174–176. The group of *standard* tablets include *muen* spirits with ties to one's family land or buildings; customers or employees of family business; and spirits of fish, birds, trees, or shrubs related to one's business. Beyond these are tablets reserved for individual *muen* spirits without connection to Gedatsu-kai members but whose identity was revealed through the meditation rite or in counseling sessions. Subcategories of disconnection (*muen*) may arise out of bad sexual relations or shady financial dealings. Other subcategories may include the following: those outside the family lineage dying in infancy; aborted fetuses; unnatural death victims; living spirits consumed with hatred; enemies related to the land one owns or rents, spirits of animals one has raised; and a blank tablet for the spirits of other deceased persons in need of a memorial service. Finally, there are *public* memorial tablets to pacify the *muen* spirits of those who die in traffic accidents, in natural disasters, at the hands of enemies in warfare, and as a sacrifice in war damage as well as for all deceased members of Gedatsu-kai.

80. Ibid., 252.

81. Ibid., 253.

82. Stephen F. Teiser, "Ghosts and Ancestors in Medieval Chinese Religion: The Yü-lan-p'en Festival as Mortuary Ritual," *History of Religions* 26(1) (1986): 61.

83. Ibid., 63.

84. Ibid., 65–66.

CHAPTER 7

Mothers, Society, and Pregnancy Loss: Rethinking the Meaning of Nurture

1. Meredith Underwood, "Strategies of Survival: Women, Abortion, and Popular Religion in Contemporary Japan," *Journal of the American Academy of Religion* 67(4) (1999): 740–741.

2. Michiko N. Wilson, *The Marginal World of Ōe Kenzaburo: A Study in Themes and Techniques* (Armonk, NY: M.E. Sharpe, Inc., 1986), 105. Ōe Kenzaburō, writing of similar situations, calls these persons *shūen*. Within his fictional world the reader's imagination is stretched to perceive dimensions of human experience that are positioned at the periphery. His commitment to face the "condition of being marginal and peripheral [is what] enables one to look at the *official* culture from the margins." For years, Ōe has questioned these standards of respectability by confronting society with its own victims and creating literary images that contrast sharply with conventionally perceived reality.

3. Underwood, "Strategies of Survival," 741.

4. Ibid., 762.

5. Helen Hardacre, *Lay Buddhism in Contemporary Japan: Reiyūkai Kyōdan* (Princeton, NJ: Princeton University Press, 1984), 223.

6. Underwood, "Strategies of Survival." 761. See her extended discussion of this on pp. 761–766. Underwood's critique is based on Hardacre, *Marketing the Menacing Fetus in Japan* (Berkeley: University of California Press, 1997).

7. Underwood, "Strategies of Survival," 740.

8. There is a rich discussion of how rituals of affliction in other cultures combine lamenting for the dead with social grievance. For examples of this, see Anna Caraveli, "The Bitter Wounding: The Lament as Social Protest in Rural Greece," in *Gender and Power in Rural Greece,* ed. by Jill Dubisch (Princeton, NJ: Princeton University Press, 1986), 169–194; Anna Caraveli-Chaves, "Bridge between Worlds: The Greek Women's Lament as Communicative Event," *Journal of American Folklore* 93(368) (1980): 128–157; Elizabeth L. Johnson, "Grieving for the Dead, Grieving for the Living: Funeral Laments of Hakka Women," in *Death Ritual in Late Imperial and Modern China,* ed. by James L. Watson and Evelyn S. Rawski (Berkeley: University of California Press, 1987), 135–163; Seong Nae Kim, "Lamentations of the Dead: The Historical Imagery of Violence on Cheju Island, South Korea," *Journal of Ritual Studies* 3(2) (1989): 251–285; Seong Nae Kim, "Chronicle of Violence, Ritual of Mourning: Cheju Shamanism in Korea" (Ph.D. diss., University of Michigan, Ann Arbor, University Microfilms International, 1989); and Kilsong Ch'oe, "The Symbolic Meaning of Shamanic Ritual in Korean Folk Life," *Journal of Ritual Studies* 3(2) (1989): 217–233.

9. Underwood, "Strategies of Survival," 753.

10. Ibid. Underwood quotes here Dorinne K. Kondo, *Crafting Selves: Power, Gender, and Discourses of Identity in a Japanese Workplace* (Chicago: University of Chicago Press. 1990), 299.

11. Part of my correspondence with Meredith Underwood, March 1998.

12. Underwood, "Strategies of Survival," 741.

13. Ibid., 766. I am indebted to Underwood, through extensive conversation and correspondence over several years, for her insight regarding the whole issue of agency and especially how this applies to the current situation among both women and men in Japan.

14. Igeta Midori, "A Response," *Journal of Feminist Studies in Religion* 11(2) (1995): 95–100. This is a response to Elizabeth G. Harrison, "Women's Responses to Child Loss in Japan: The Case of *Mizuko Kuyō*," *Journal of Feminist Studies in Religion* 11(2) (1995): 67–93.

15. Ibid., 95.

16. Ibid., 97. For an influential statement along these lines, see Ueno Chizuko, "Collapse of Japanese Mothers," *U.S.-Japan Women's Journal* (English Supplement) 10 (1996): 3–19. See also Niwa Akiko, "The Formation of the Myth of Motherhood in Japan," *U.S.-Japan Women's Journal* (English Supplement) 4 (1993): 70–82; Wakita Haruko, "Women and the Creation of the Ie in Japan: An Overview from the Medieval Period to the Present," *U.S.-Japan Women's Journal* (English Supplement) 4 (1993): 83–105; and Ehara Emiko, "Japanese Feminism in the 1970s and 1980s," *U.S.-Japan Women's Journal* (English Supplement) 4 (1993): 49–69.

17. Igeta, "Response," 96.

18. Ibid., 97–98. See also Yamaori Tetsuo, "*Hahagokoro no gen-fūkei: Umarekawari no reikon-kan*" [The Original Scene in Mother's Mind: Views on the Soul or Spirit in "Rebirth"], *Taiyō* (Special Issue) (Spring 1992): 136–142.

19. This was a session at which Elizabeth Harrison discussed our research on *mizuko kuyō*. Her talk was followed by conversation and written comments about *mizuko kuyō* as well as about their own personal experiences.

20. Kristin Luker, *Abortion and the Politics of Motherhood* (Berkeley: University of California Press, 1984), 158–159.

21. Ibid., 160.

22. Ibid., 161.

23. Examples of this discourse may be found in the following articles: Emiko Ochiai, "The Modern Family and Japanese Culture: Exploring the Japanese Mother–Child Relationship," *Review of Japanese Culture and Society* 3(1) (December 1989): 7–15; Iwamura Miki, Kunishige Atsuko, Tanaka Hiroshi, Tomiie Emiko, and Yamamoto Itsuki, "A Comparative Analysis of Gender Roles and the Status of Women in Japan and the U.S.," Trans. Sue Y. Yan, *U.S.-Japan Women's Journal* (English Supplement) 3 (1992): 36–53; Amy Beth Borovoy, "Sticky Relations, Interpersonal Addiction, and Unspoken Understandings: The Politics of 'Japanese Interdependence,'" *Proceedings of the Fifth Annual Ph.D. Kenkyukai Conference on Japanese Studies* (Tokyo: International House of Japan, 1994), 25–40; and "Symposium—Women and the Family: Post-Family Alternatives," *Review of Japanese Culture and Society* 3(1) (December 1989): 79–96. This symposium includes discussions by Taeko Tomioka, Chizuko Ueno, Noriko Mizuta, Miriam M. Johnson, Myra Strober, and Miho Ogino (facilitator).

24. Samuel Coleman, *Family Planning in Japanese Society: Traditional Birth Control in a Modern Urban Culture* (Princeton, NJ: Princeton University Press, 1983), 17.

For more recent studies of birth control in Japan, see Tiana Norgren, *Abortion before Birth Control: The Politics of Reproduction in Postwar Japan* (Princeton, NJ: Princeton University Press, 2001); and Special Issue, "Pregnancy and Childbirth in the Context of Modernity," *U.S.-Japan Women's Journal* 24 (2003). For discussion of the reasons for a comparably high rate of induced abortion in Russian society, see Larissa I. Remennick, "Patterns of Birth Control," in *Sex and Russian Society*, ed. by Igor Kon and James Riordan (Bloomington: Indiana University Press, 1993), 45–63.

25. Hatano, Yoshihiro and Tsuguo Shimazaki, *The International Encyclopedia of Sexuality* (New York: Continuum, 1997), Vol. 2, Japan, 1–86. Updated version of *Encyclopedia*, 2004, ed. by Robert T. Francoeur and Raymond J. Noonan. *The Continuum Complete International Encyclopedia of Sexuality (Japan)*, 2004, 636–646.

26. Kumiko Fujimura-Fanselow and Atsuko Kameda, eds., *Japanese Women: New Feminist Perspectives on the Past, Present, and Future* (New York: Feminist Press at the City University of New York, 1995). Another resource of great value on gender studies in Japan is the *U.S.-Japan Women's Journal*, a semiannual journal that began publication in August 1991. See also *AMPO-Japan Asia Quarterly Review*, ed., *Voices from the Japanese Women's Movement* (Armonk, NY: M.E. Sharpe, 1996). This is the third special issue on Japanese feminist perspectives published by this review. The first two were *Japanese Women Speak Out* (1975) and *The Challenges Facing Japanese Women* (1986).

27. Sandra Lee Bartky, *Femininity and Domination: Studies in the Phenomenology of Oppression* (New York: Routledge, 1990), 9.

28. This essay by Hashimoto Yayoi appears in Takahashi Saburō, ed., *Mizuko Kuyō: Gendai shakai no fuan to iyashi* [Mizuko Kuyō: Healing the Unrest of Present Day Society] (Kyoto: Kōrosha, 1999). This publication discusses the research by social scientists based at Kyoto University, to which we often refer in this volume.

29. Hashimoto Yayoi, "Haha oya no kokoro iyashi to mizuko kuyō" [Mizuko kuyō and Healing the Heart of the Mother], in *Mizuko kuyō: gendai shakkai no fuan to iyashi* [Mizuko kuyō: Healing the Unrest of Modern Society], ed. by Takahashi Saburō (Kyoto: Kōrosha, 1999), 214.

30. Ibid., 223. "Eliminated child" is *haijo sareta ko* in Japanese.

31. Rozsika Parker, *Mother Love/Mother Hate: The Power of Maternal Ambivalence* (New York: Basic Books, 1995), 137. Describing similar phenomena, Parker suggests that the emotional reality mothers experience is often ignored because the hostility a mother may feel toward her child is so threatening to social and cultural stability. At the same time, Parker emphasizes that along with facing her hostility toward her child it is equally important to understand the depth of her love. In other words, the focus is on the power of maternal *ambivalence*.

32. Hashimoto, "Haha oya no kokoro iyashi to mizuko kuyō," 231. Individuality is *kosei* in Japanese.

33. Uno Chiyo, *A Genius of Imitation* (*Mohō no tensai*), Trans. Yukiko Tanaka (1936). See reference in Barbara Rose, *Tsuda Umeko and Women's Education in Japan* (New Haven, CT: Yale University Press, 1992).

34. Hashimoto, "Haha oya no kokoro iyashi to mizuko kuyō," 223.

35. Ibid., 237.

36. Ibid., 225.

37. Ibid., 231.

38. Ibid., 238.

39. Ibid., 237.

40. Ueno Chizuko, *The Modern Family in Japan: Its Rise and Fall* (Melbourne: Trans Pacific Press, 2009). This was initially published as *Kindai kazoku no seiritsu to shūen* (Iwanami Shoten, 1994).

41. Ibid., 163.

42. Ibid., 165.

43. Ibid., 170.

44. Ibid., 180.

45. Ibid., 185.

46. Ibid., 188.

47. Ibid. Other articles germane to the issues in this chapter are Susan Orphett Long, "Nurturing and Femininity: The Ideal of Caregiving in Postwar Japan," in *Re-imaging Japanese Women*, ed. by Anne E. Imamura (Berkeley: University of California Press, 1996), 156–176; Margaret Lock, *Encounters with Aging: Mythologies of Menopause in Japan and North America* (Berkeley: University of California Press, 1993), especially 233–255; Masami Ohinata, "The Mystique of Motherhood: A Key to Understanding Social Change and Family Problems in Japan," in Fujimura-Fanselow and Kameda, *Japanese Women*, 199–211; Ueno Chizuko, interview by Sandra Buckley, *Broken Silence: Voices of Japanese Feminism* (Berkeley: University of California Press, 1997), 272–301; Mioko Fujieda, "Japan's First Phase of Feminism," in Fujimura-Fanselow and Kameda, *Japanese Women*, 323–341; Kazuko Tanaka, "The New Feminist Movement in Japan, 1970–1990," in Fujimura-Fanselow and Kameda, *Japanese Women*, 343–352; Mioko Fujieda and Kumiko Fujimura-Fanselow, "Women's Studies: An Overview," in Fujimura-Fanselow and Kameda, *Japanese Women*, 155–182; and Evelyn Nakano Glenn, "Social Constructions of Mothering: A Thematic Overview," in *Mothering: Ideology, Experience, and Agency*, ed, by Evelyn Nakano Glenn, Grace Chang, and Linda Rennie Forcey (New York: Routledge, 1994), 1–29.

48. Buckley, *Broken Silence*, 280–281. Her entire interview of Ueno Chizuko is pertinent to the subject of this chapter.

49. Ibid., 283. Ueno states this point in a manner that is different from the one developed by Sandra Lee Bartky in *Femininity and Oppression* (New York: Routledge, 1990). On the other hand, Bartky's analysis in her final chapter "Feeding Egos

and Tending Wounds" (99–119) is a major contribution to the understanding both of the double-edged meaning of nurturing and of *instrumental effectiveness* of repentance and apology, as advanced in different ways by Helen Hardacre and Meredith Underwood. See the earlier part of this chapter.

50. Buckley, *Broken Silence*, 285–288.

51. Ueno Chizuko, "Genesis of the Urban Housewife," *Japan Quarterly* 34(2) (1987): 130–142.

52. Ueno, *Modern Family in Japan*, 225, 227.

53. Ibid., 235. For a lively and informative discussion of this phenomenon, see Veronica Chambers, *Kickboxing Geishas: How Modern Japanese Women Are Changing Their Nation* (New York: Free Press, 2007).

54. William A. Barbieri Jr., "The Heterological Quest: Michel de Certeau's Travel Narratives and the 'Other' of Comparative Religious Ethics," *Journal of Religious Ethics* 30(1) (2002): 23.

55. Ibid., 26.

56. Ibid., 34.

57. Ibid., 39–40.

CHAPTER 8

The Revival of Death, the Rebirth of Grieving, and Ways of Mourning

1. Robert E. Goss and Dennis Klass, *Dead but Not Lost: Grief Narratives in Religious Traditions* (Walnut Creek, CA: AltaMira Press, 2005), 106–107.

2. Gavin Brown, "Theorizing Ritual as Performance: Explorations of Ritual Indeterminacy," *Journal of Ritual Studies* 17(1) 2003: 3.

3. Ibid., 5.

4. Peter Homans, ed., *Symbolic Loss: The Ambiguity of Mourning and Memory at Century's End* (Charlottesville: University Press of Virginia, 2000), 2–3.

5. Sue Nathanson, *Soul Crisis: One Woman's Journey through Abortion to Renewal* (New York: New American Library, 1989).

6. Ibid., 43.

7. Ibid., 62.

8. Ibid., 68.

9. Ibid., 121.

10. Ibid., 190.

11. Ibid., 228–229.

12. May Sarton, "Of Grief," in *Selected Poems of May Sarton* (New York: W.W. Norton, 1978), 77. Quoted with permission from W.W. Norton.

13. Linda L. Layne, *Motherhood Lost: A Feminist Account of Pregnancy Lost* (New York: Routledge, 2003).

14. Layne, "Breaking the Silence: An Agenda for a Feminist Discourse of Pregnancy Loss," *Feminist Studies* 23(2) (1997): 304–305.

15. Ibid., 309. An exception to this may be found in Rosemary Reuther, *Women-Church: Theology and Practice of Feminist Liturgical Communities* (San Francisco: Harper & Row, 1985), in which she discusses briefly several rites of healing under the general rubric "Healing Our Wounds: Overcoming the Violence of Patriarchy" (149–152, 161–164). These situations include incest, violence (physical and psychological), abortion, miscarriage or stillbirth, and divorce. These are significant examples of sensitivity in the Roman Catholic tradition among women, especially in the past thirty years.

16. Michel Foucault, *The History of Sexuality*, Vol. 1, An Introduction (New York: Random House, 1980), 27.

17. The notion that the soul of a *mizuko* will "come back" or "return" is one that can be interpreted in many ways. Again, many priests and laypeople may read this literally; others may not. My own sense of what Oda Hōryū is saying is that the presence of the *mizuko rei* (spirit of the *mizuko*) may literally be present psychologically and that this may remain a reality to a woman and her partner, a reality that can be an important part of the healing process.

18. Jeff Wilson, *Mourning the Unborn Dead: A Buddhist Ritual Comes to America* (Oxford: Oxford University Press, 2009).

19. Ibid., 96.

20. Ibid., 94.

21. Ibid., 63.

22. Ibid., italics added.

23. Ibid., 98.

24. Ibid., 101.

25. Ibid., 102.

26. Ibid., 102

27. Ibid., 103.

28. Ibid., 177–189.

29. Ibid., 183.

30. Bardwell Smith interviewed the head priest at Hasedera in Kamakura on July 29, 1988.

31. Bardwell Smith (1988). My description here is adapted from Smith, "The Social Contexts of Healing: Research on Abortion and Grieving in Japan," in *Innovation in Religious Traditions: Essays in the Interpretation of Religious Change*, ed. by Michael A. Williams, Collett Cox, and Martin S. Jaffee (Berlin: Mouton de Gruyter, 1992), 297–298.

32. A seventeenth-century English classic, the *Religio Medici*, expresses this well: "It is not the teares of our owne eyes onely, but of our friends also, that doe exhaust the current of our sorrows ..." David A. Garrick, "The Work of the Witness in Psychotherapeutic Rituals of Grief," *Journal of Ritual Studies* 8(2) (Summer 1994): 91. The reference here is to Sir Thomas Browne (1643, 74). "Religio Medici." *The Prose of Sir Thomas Browne*, 3–89. Ed. Norman J. Endicott. (New York: W.W. Norton).

33. Laura Seftel, *Grief Unseen: Healing Pregnancy Loss through the Arts* (London: Jessica Kingsley Publishers, 2006). Seftel is an art therapist and mental health counselor, whose book contributes to understanding the role that art can play in the grieving process.

34. Ibid., 137. Stephen F. Teiser makes a similar point that is central in Teiser, *Reinventing the Wheel: Paintings of Rebirth in Medieval Buddhist Temples* (Seattle: University of Washington Press, 2006, 41): "[Ordinary] people were likely to encounter visual images and oral teaching at the same time ... In almost all these situations, then, painting is conjoined to preaching, and the canonical text, around which the discipline of Buddhist studies continues to circumambulate is at the margins ... [In this context] the category of ritual plays a prominent role ... each piece of visual and textual documentation [is placed] in its original performative setting."

35. Barbieri, 'Heterological Quest," 42.

36. Ibid., 44.

37. An interesting parallel to these two examples may be found in Barbara Ruch, "Medieval Jongleurs and the Making of a National Literature," in *Japan in the Muromachi Age*, ed. by John Whitney Hall and Toyoda Takeshi (Berkeley: University of California Press, 1977), 279–309. In depicting vocal literature during the Muromachi period, Ruch discusses the *Kumano bikuni* (nuns) whose proselytizing put in the hands of common people books or tracts that served as talismans and protective devices (*omamori*) for oneself and one's home. This form of vocal literature "calmed destructive demons, cured the sick, protected the home, asserted one's ties to clan and land, confirmed the compassion of the deities, saved one's soul, and affected one's karma" (306).

38. Brown, "Theorizing Ritual as Performance," 11.

39. Ibid., 12. Quoted from Sally F. Moore in Moore and Barbara G. Myerhoff, *Secular Ritual* (Amsterdam: Van Gorcum, 1977), 17.

40. Richard Schechner, *Between Theater and Anthropology* (Philadelphia: Pennsylvania University Press, 1985, 35). Schechner's insight was that the very *morphology* of ritual, its essential structure, is what enables transformation to occur in each ritual performance.

41. *Sumidagawa* [The Sumida River], published in *The Noh Drama: Ten Plays from the Japanese* (Tokyo: Charles E. Tuttle Company, 1960), 141–159, by the special Noh Committee, Japanese Classics Translation Committee, Nippon Gakujutsu Shinkōkai (Japanese Society for the Promotion of Scientific Research). Other Noh plays in this same genre (madwoman piece) are: *Miidera, Sakuragawa, Asukagawa, Kashiwazaki,* and *Hyakuman. Miidera* is also published in *The Noh Drama,* 51–75; and *Sakuragawa* (Cherry River), attributed to Zeami, was translated into English by Robert N. Huey in *Monumenta Nipponica* 38(3) (1983): 195–312. *Sumidagawa* is the only play in this genre in which there is not a reunion of a mother with her living son. For an unusually creative way in which *Sumidagawa* has been transformed from a Noh play to a British opera (*Curlew*

River by Benjamin Britten) to a poem for television, see Bardwell Smith, commentator with Andrew Tsubaki, James Brandon, Reiko Brandon, and Philip Brett for the televised film "The Mad Woman and the Mask: A Transformation from a Japanese Noh Play into a British Opera into a Poem for Television." Written and read by Freya Manfred and produced by Patty Hegman for KTCA-TV, St. Paul, MN, 1993.

42. Erika Ohara Bainbridge, "The Madness of Mothers in Japanese Noh Drama," *U.S.-Japan Women's Journal* (English Supplement) 3 (1992): 84–104, see 84.

43. *Sumidagawa*, 156.

44. Ibid., 159.

45. Bainbridge's thesis is that as the patriarchal family system became established in Japanese society there was a steady decline in women's political power at court, as had existed in Heian Japan, along with a narrowing of women's domestic sphere first among the warrior class, then in society at large. Because of poverty and social unrest during feudal times it was not uncommon for mothers to end up being separated from their children due to abandonment (a form of birth control), kidnapping, or selling them to make ends meet. The frequency with which children were lost during this period contributed to circumstances where being a mother put one in a vulnerable position emotionally. "Many women could project their personal situation onto the deranged mother's characterization, find vicarious atonement in her derangement, and gain catharsis through witnessing the final reunion [actual or symbolic] with the lost child" (93–94).

46. This three-way relationship can be seen in the statues of Jizō used to give form to *mizuko*. The boyish, round-headed Jizō resembles and, indeed, *becomes* the child, whom the parents then take care of in this world with offerings of food, clothing, toys, and other children's paraphrenalia..

47. The account retold and paraphrased here is of a poetic version found in Manabe Kōsai, *Jizō-bosatsu no kenkyū* [Research on Jizō Bodhisattva] (Kyoto: Sanmitsudō shoten, 1960), 198–202. This is a Pure Land (Jōdoshū) derived *sai-no-kawara Jizō wasan* song or hymn and is translated here by Yukio Kachi and Bardwell Smith.

48. Marilyn Ivy, *Discourses of the Vanishing: Modernity, Phantasm, Japan* (Chicago: University of Chicago Press, 1995). Her chapter on Osorezan (141–191) is an important addition to this conversation. This is an excellent study of discourses in modern Japan that seek "to preserve the vanishing by valorizing it as the traditional" (see Ivy, 1988, 7). One of these discourses concerns itself with the "language of loss" related specifically to spirits of the dead and the role of blind female mediums in facilitating communication between the living and the dead.

49. Miyazaki Fumiko and Duncan Williams, "The Intersections of the Local and the Translocal at a Sacred Site: The Case of Osorezan in Tokugawa Japan," *Japanese Journal of Religious Studies* 28(3–4) (2001): 432. This is an important discussion

of the historical development of Osorezan, based on "evidence from local archives, travel records, temple collections, and inscription from stone monuments" (399).

50. Ivy, *Discourses of the Vanishing*, 154–155.

51. Ibid., 164.

52. Ibid., 167.

53. Ibid., 180.

54. Marilyn Jeanette Ivy, "Discourses of the Vanishing in Contemporary Japan (Ph.D. diss., Cornell University, Ann Arbor, MI: University Microfilms International, 1988), 265.

55. Ibid., 191.

CHAPTER 9
Rituals of Affliction: An Invitation to Sobriety

1. Scholarship on these composite and changing formations is crucial to an understanding of Japanese religious history and practice. Among many examples of this, see Allan G. Grapard, "Japan's Ignored Cultural Revolution: The Separation of Shintō and Buddhist Divinities in Meiji (shinbutsu bunri) and a Case Study: Tōnomine," *History of Religions* 23(3) (1984): 240–265; and "Institution, Ritual and Ideology: The Twenty-Two Shrine-Temple Multiplexes of Heian Japan," *History of Religions* 27(3) (1988): 246–269; Neil McMullin, "Historical and Historiographical Issues in the Study of Pre-Modern Japanese Religion," *Japanese Journal of Religious Studies* 16(1) (1989): 3–40.

2. Charles Taylor, *The Ethics of Authenticity* (Cambridge, MA: Harvard University Press, 1992), 83–87.

3. Victor Turner, "Acting in Everyday Life and Everyday Life in Acting," in Turner, *From Ritual to Theatre: The Human Seriousness of Play* (New York: PAJ Publications, 1982), 122. As he indicates, alternative forms of meaning may be found in "the subjunctive world of monsters, demons, and clowns, of cruelty and poetry, in order to make sense of [their] daily lives."

4. Michel de Certeau, *The Practice of Everyday Life*, Trans. Steven F. Rendell (Berkeley: University of California Press, 1984), 106.

5. This is akin to John Keats's theory of *negative capability*, namely, when a person becomes "capable of [residing] in uncertainties, mysteries, doubts, without any irritable reaching after fact and reason." See Keats's letter to his brother, December 21, 1817, in Duncan Wu, *Romanticism: An Anthology*, 3d ed. (Malden, MA: Blackwell, 2006), 1351.

6. Akira Sadataka, "The Buddhist View of the Universe Today," *Dharma World* (1994): 49.

7. Junjirō Takakusu, *The Essentials of Buddhist Philosophy*, 3d ed. by Wing-tsit Chan and Charles A. Moore (Honolulu: University of Hawaii Press, 1956), 192–193.

8. Lan T'ing-su [Lan Ting Xu], "Prelude to the Orchid Pavilion Collection," composed in 353 A.D. by Wang His-chi (Wang Xizhi, 321–379) at a gathering of about forty calligraphers in Shaoxing, China.

9. An example of plural diagnosis and redressive rituals may be found in Bruce Kapferer, *A Celebration of Demons: Exorcism and the Aesthetics of Healing in Sri Lanka* (Bloomington: Indiana University Press, 1983). See also David Scott, *Formations of Ritual: Colonial and Anthropological Discourses on the Sinhala 'Yaktovil'* (Minneapolis: University of Minnesota Press, 1994) for a critique of various anthropological interpretations of exorcism and demonic experience.

10. Karen Kerner, "The Malevolent Ancestor: Ancestral Influence in a Japanese Religious Sect," in *Ancestors*, ed. by William H. Newall. (The Hague: Mouton, 1974), 211.

11. Anthony C. Yu, "'Rest, Rest, Perturbed Spirit!' Ghosts in Traditional Chinese Prose Fiction," *Harvard Journal of Asiatic Studies* 47 (1987): 416.

12. W. Michael Kelsey, "The Raging Deity in Japanese Mythology," *Asian Folklore Studies* 40(2) (1981): 228.

13. Mori Masato, "Konjaku Monogatari-shū: Supernatural Creatures and Order," *Japanese Journal of Religious Studies* 9(2–3) (1982): 155.

14. Sawicki, Jana, *Disciplining Foucault: Feminism, Power, and the Body* (New York: Routledge, Chapman and Hall, Inc. 1991), 23.

15. Ibid., 25.

16. Ibid., 80.

17. Ibid., 81.

18. Étienne Lamotte, *History of Indian Buddhism*, Trans. (from French) Sara Webb-Boin (under the supervision of Jean Dantinne) (Louvain-La-Neuve: Institut Orientaliste, 1988); Julia K. Murray, "Representations of Hariti, the Mother of Demons, and the Theme of 'Raising the Alms-Bowl' in Chinese Painting," *Artibus Asiae* 43 (1981–82): 253–268. For further iconographical discussion of this cult see Alexander C. Soper, "Aspects of Light Symbolism in Gandharan Sculpture," Parts 1–3, *Artibus Asiae* 12: 252–283, 314–330; 13: 63–85; Alice Getty, *The Gods of Northern Buddhism: Their History, Iconography and Progressive Evolution through the Northern Buddhist Countries* (Rutland, VT: Charles E. Tuttle, 1962), 84–87, 97–99; and Dietrich Seckel, *Kariteimo: Die "Buddhistische Madonna" in der Japanischen Kunst* (Tokyo: Deutsche Gesellschaft fur Natur- und Volkerkunde Ostasiens, 1943), 1–53 and Plates 1–20. See also David Kinsley, *Hindu Goddesses: Visions of the Divine Feminine in the Hindu Religious Tradition* (Berkeley: University of California Press, 1986), 153–160, in which he places Hārītī in the category of *mātrkā(s)* or divine mothers who are customarily portrayed with inauspicious, dangerous, and child-afflicting traits, though when appeased become protective deities.

19. A detailed examination of the Hārītī legend is found in Noël Peri, "Hārītī la mère-de-démons," *Bulletin de l'École Française d'Extrême-Orient* 17 (1917): 1–102,

in which he translates into French the important texts about this figure. Key texts on Hārītī are reprinted in the Tokyo edition (1962–79) of the Buddhist Tipitaka (*Taishō shinshū daizōkyō,* abbreviated as T): T.XXI, 1260, 1261, 1262 and T. XXIV, 1451. The *Sutra on the Mother of Demons* (Hārītī sūtra) was translated into Chinese in the third century with the title *Kuei-tzu-mu ching.* A cult to this figure was known in China, it is said, by at least the sixth century.

20. See John S. Strong, *The Legend and Cult of Upagupta: Sanskrit Buddhism in North India and Southeast Asia* (Princeton, NJ: Princeton University Press, 1992), especially 36–37, 303, n. 66, 67 for bibliographical references to the Hārītī cult in South and Southeast Asia.

21. Getty, *Gods of Northern Buddhism,* 98.

22. Helen Hardacre, "The Transformation of Healing in the Japanese New Religions," *History of Religions* 21(4) (1982): 308.

23. Miyazaki, Eishū, ed., *Kishimojin Shinkō* [Religious Belief in Kishimojin] (Tokyo: Yūzankaku shuppan, 1992), 186–187.

24. Ibid., 187–188.

25. Ueno Chizuko, *The Modern Family in Japan: Its Rise and Fall* (Melbourne: Trans Pacific Press, 2009), 189.

26. Ibid.

27. Robert Jay Lifton, *The Broken Connection: On Death and the Continuity of Life.* (New York: Basic Books, Inc. Publishers, 1983), 53. See also Willis Stoesz, "Death and the Affirmation of Life: Robert Lifton's 'Sense of Immortality,'" *Soundings: An Interdisciplinary Journal* 62 (1979): 199.

28. Victor W. Turner, "Dewey, Dilthey, and Drama: An Essay in the Anthropology of Experience," in *The Anthropology of Experience,* ed. by Victor W. Turner and Edward M. Bruner (Urbana: University of Illinois Press, 1986), 41.

29. *Mizuko kuyō,* as normally practiced, is not a ritual of affliction or a redressive ritual; it is a ritual that helps women to address painful aspects of their own condition. At such times, a variety of social issues may rise to the surface.

30. Charles C. Lemert and Garth Gillan, *Michel Foucault: Social Theory as Transgression* (New York: Columbia University Press, 1982), 132.

31. Vera L. Norwood, "The Nature of Knowing: Rachel Carson and the American Environment," *Signs: Journal of Women in Culture and Society* 12 (1987): 757. Some of the phrases in this depiction of Rachel Carson were part of a talk I gave at the Poynter Center for the Study of Ethics and American Institutions, Indiana University, that was published by the center in July 1992.

32. Ibid., 751.

33. Ibid., 757.

34. Taylor, *Ethics of Authenticity,* 89. Taylor adds, "It would greatly help to stave off ecological disaster if we could recover a sense of the demand that our natural surroundings and wilderness make on us" (90).

35. Norwood, "Nature of Knowing," 755.

36. Ibid., 759.
37. Ann Bancroft, Forward to Eric Sevareid, *Canoeing with the Cree* (Wadena, MN: Borealis Books, 2005), xiv. With a friend, Sevareid canoed 2,200 miles from Minneapolis to Hudson Bay, Canada, over a four-month period in 1930. His book records that journey in great detail. To Sevaried, as well as to Carson, it is the juxtaposition of the human scale with the vastness of nature that provides a fundamentally different perspective.
38. Sawicki, *Disciplining Foucault*, 107.
39. Thomas A. Tweed, "Toward an Ethic of Civic Engagement: Reflections on a Kinetic and Relational Theory of Religion," unpublished manuscript.
40. Yvonne Rand, *Jizo: Protector of Travelers into and out of Life* (revised title 2012). The full version of her statement is included in the Appendices.
41. Hashimoto Yayoi, "Haha oya no kokoro iyashi to mizuko kuyō" [Mizuko kuyō and Healing the Heart of the Mother], in *Mizuko kuyō: gendai shakkai no fuan to iyashi* [Mizuko kuyō: Healing the Unrest of Modern Society], ed. by Takahashi Saburō (Kyoto: Kōrosha, 1999), 238.
42. Ibid., 237.

APPENDIX 3
The Tale of Sai-no-Kawara

1. The account retold and paraphrased here is of the poetic version found in Manabe Kōsai. *Jizō-bosatsu no kenkyū* [Research on Jizō Bodhisattva]. Kyoto: Sanmitsudō shoten, 1960, 198–202. This is a Pure Land (Jōdoshū) derived *Sai-no-kawara Jizo wasan* song or hymn. Upon hearing this tale, one bows down in devotion to the Honorable Jizō, the central figure in this legend and its complex cosmology. Translated by Yukio Kachi and Bardwell Smith.

APPENDIX 4
Economic Development and Temple Economics in Japan

1. One extreme case the author encountered revealed a loophole in the new tax laws. Since the cost of funerals is deductible from the inheritance tax, one *danka* reported to the tax office the huge amount of money he paid as *ofuse* to the temple: for example, charges for a posthumous name, many visits by the priest, payment to accompanying monks. His report to the tax office was deceptive since the temple received only a fraction of that amount. Because the temple usually did not issue receipts, the tax office had no way of identifying the swindle. After this incident, the author decided to issue receipts for *ofuse*.
2. The temple where the author was *jūshoku* was located in an urban area. The previous *jūshoku* (the author's father) was able to visit some eighty homes to pay tribute to the family shrines in a period of three days during the Bon festival

season. That was possible because the *danka*'s houses were closer to each other! It took five days for the author to visit the same number of houses even on a motorcycle.

3. At the time when the average life span was short, the second and third marriage was common among wealthy people. In the case when they had the son in the first marriage, the second wife kept the premarriage name and was buried in a different grave usually built nearby in the same graveyard to avoid friction in the family.

Note on Transliteration

For Romanization of Japanese words, the Modified Hepburn System is used, with macrons over long vowels o and u. Commonly used Japanese and Sanskrit terms and place names that are found in English dictionaries, such as Mahayana, Theravada, nirvana, samsara, and the like, are presented without diacritics. Sanskrit terms are used principally to cite Indian and Chinese prototypes of a Japanese text, a bodhisattva figure, or a Buddhist school. For Sanskrit terms the traditional diacritical marks are used throughout the book.

Glossary of Terms

Heian Period	794–1185
Kamakura Period	1185–1333
Muromachi Period	1334–1573
Momoyama Period	1573–1603
Tokugawa (Edo) Period	1615–1868
Meiji Period	1868–1912
Meiji Civil Code	1898
Taishō Period	1912–1926
Shōwa Period	1926–1989
Revised Civil Code	1948
Heisei Period	1989–

Proper names, historical places, including names of Japanese religions and temples, are not italicized in this glossary.

Adashino Nenbutsuji	あだしの念仏寺	Jōdoshū temple in Arashiyama area of Kyoto
akachan	赤ちゃん	baby
aku	悪	evil, malice badness
amacha	甘茶	rite to pacify ancestral spirits, purify hearts of participants (Gedatsu-kai)
Amida butsu	阿弥陀仏	Amida Buddha of the Western Pure Land
Amida Nyorai	阿弥陀如来	Japanese equivalent to Skt. Tathāgata
ano yo	あの世	the "other world"
anzan	安産	safe childbirth
Arashiyama	嵐山	"Storm Mountain," western outskirts of Kyoto

atotsugi	跡(後)継ぎ	heirs in the same lineage (Japanese)
bakufu	幕府	Tokugawa central government
Bentenshū	弁天宗	Benten temple in Ibaragi City, Osaka Prefecture
Benzaiten	弁財天	Skt. Sarasvatī, goddess sought for wisdom, learning, progeny
bosatsu	菩薩	bodhisattva
o-bon	お盆	festival for returning spirits of the dead in July or August
bonnō	煩悩	illusion, afflictions, evil passions (Skt. *klesa*)
bosei	母性	motherhood
būmu	ブーム	"boom," fad, fashion, often used for *mizuko kuyō*
busshō	仏性	Buddha nature; one's original nature
butsu	仏	Buddha
butsudan	仏壇	Buddhist home altar, for keeping in touch with deceased family
Chōshōji	長勝寺	Rinzai Zen temple in Shiga Prefecture
chūkun aikoku	忠君愛国	loyalty and patriotism (key to Meiji education in morals)
chūzetsu	中絶	interrupted or aborted pregnancy (妊娠中絶 *ninshin-chūzetsu*)
Daikokuten	大黒天	one of the Seven Gods of Good Fortune (*shichifukujin* 七福神)
Daishidō	大師堂	Hall honoring Kōbō Daishi 弘法大師 (Kūkai, 空海, 774–835), founder of Shingon-shū
danka	檀家	temple parishioners
dankaseido	檀家制度	Tokugawa period family Buddhist temple registration system
danson johi	男尊女卑	ideology of male superiority and female inferiority
darani	陀羅尼	mystical invocations or phrases (Skt. *dhārani*)
datai	堕胎	abortion
de Certeau, Michel		French scholar (1925–1986) whose work combined history, psychoanalysis, philosophy, and the social sciences.

dharma (Skt., Jap. 法 *hō*)		central notion of Buddhism, used in various meanings
eitai (*eidai*) *kuyō*	永代冑供養	"Extended Rites," literally "perpetual services"
ekō	回向	saying mass for the dead; transfer of merit
ema	絵馬	wooden votive tablets
en	縁	intimate, karma-like connection, relation, bond
Enmei Jizō	延命地蔵	Jizō of long life
ennichi	縁日	a day of religious festival
Foucault, Michel (1925–84)		French philosopher, social theorist, and historian of ideas
fuan sangyō	不安産業	"fear industry"
fukai	深い	a particular mask worn in Noh plays representing "profound emotion"
fukō	不幸	ill fortune
Fukuzawa Yukichi	福澤 諭吉	author, translator, political theorist, Meiji intellectual (1835–1901)
fushiawase	不幸せ	misfortune, unhappiness, heartache, suffering
fuyūrei	浮幽霊	wandering, floating, unsettled spirits of the dead
ga	我	ego, self-importance
gaki	餓鬼	hungry ghost (Skt. preta; Pali peta)
gakidō	餓鬼道	realm of hungry ghosts (*gaki*)
gakugyō jōju	学業成就	achievement in schoolwork
gakureki shakai	学歴社会	academic achievement society
gakureki shinkō	学歴信仰	school career worship
Gedatsukai	解脱会	one of the new religions (*gedatsu* = liberation)
Genshin	源信	Tendai monk (942–1017) responsible for the *Ōjōyōshū* (985 CE)
gense riyaku	現世利益	this-worldly blessings (health and wealth)
gō	業	(Skt. *karma*) a deed or a result caused by mind, body, or words
gohō shugyō	誤報修行	rite to identify and unlock the reasons for one's turmoil
gōka	豪華	the effect of karma

goryō-e	御霊會	ceremony to appease dead spirits from doing harm
gōshō	業障	karmic hindrances
hanashi	話	a Buddhist priest's sermon or talk at a service
Hannya shingyō	般若心経	a short, popular sutra representing the gist of *Mahayana* wisdom
hansei suru	反省する	self-reflection, retrospection, reflection, soul searching
Hara Satoshi	原慧	the late priest at Adashino Nenbutsuji who conducted *mizuko kuyō*
Hārītī		Skt. for *Kishibojin/Kishimojin*/Ch. *Kuei-tzu-mu*
Hasedera Kannon	長谷寺観音	Jōdo-affiliated temple in Kamakura
Hashimoto Yayoi	橋本やよい	Kyoto University social and clinical psychologist
higan	彼岸	festival of the dead in fall equinox, literally "the other shore"
hinin-yaku	避妊薬	birth control medicine
Hirose Zenjun ni	広瀬善順尼	Jōdoshū nun, in charge of Jikishian before Oda Hōryū
hōben	方便	skillful means (Skt. *upāya*; Ch. *fang-pien*)
hōkachō	奉加帳	a register for donations to temple
Hokekyō	法華経	Lotus Sutra (a central Mahayana scripture)
Hokkegenki	法華験記	*Miraculous Tales of the Lotus Sutra* (ca. 1040–1044)
hōmotsu-kan	宝物館	Treasure Hall at a temple
hōmyō	法名	Dharma name, given at initiation or posthumously
hondō	本堂	main hall of a temple
Hōnen Shōnin	法然上人	Founder (1133–1212) of the Japanese Pure Land sect
hongan	本願	"original vow" (to save others) of Amida, Jizō, et al.
honzon	本尊	main image of a temple
hōon	報恩	debt of gratitude for another's kindness
hōon kansha	報恩感謝	combination of gratitude and repayment of kindness

hotoke	仏	buddha(s), ancestors, deceased person
hotoke-sama	仏様	deceased person
hōwa	法話	Buddhist sermon
Ichirin no ai o kudasai		*Please Give Me One Cycle of Love* (part of *Omoidegusa* notebooks)
ie	家	Japanese family system based on feudal samurai codes
ihai	位牌	Buddhist memorial tablet, representing spirit of *mizuko* (same as *tōba*)
ikigai	生き甲斐	one's sense of self-worth, that which is worth living for
ikizama	生き様	one's life, one's current way of being
inga (kankei)	因果関係	cause and effect (connection, karmic relation)
ikasu	生かす	to give life, to bestow life
innen	因縁	direct and indirect causes, karma, fate, negative or harmful relations
innushi	院主	temple or shrine priest
itako	いたこ	blind female mediums, whom people consult to speak to the dead
jigoku	地獄	Buddhist hell
Jikishian	直指庵	Jōdoshū temple in Sagano area of Kyoto
jikkai	十界	the ten different realms of Buddhist cosmology
jinkō ninshin chūzetsu	人工妊娠中絶	artificial abortion
Jizō	地蔵	C. Dizang, Ti-Tsang; Skt. Kshitagarbha
Jizō bosatsu	地蔵菩薩	the bodhisattva Jizō
Jizō bosatsu reigenki	地蔵菩薩霊験記	*Miraculous Stories about Bodhisattva Jizō* (mid-11th c.)
Jizō bosatsu hongankyō	地蔵菩薩本眼鏡	*Sutra on Original Vow of Bodhisattva Kshitigarbha*
Jizō-dō	地蔵堂	Jizō Hall
Jizō-kō	地蔵講	association of Jizō devotees
Jizō shinkō	地蔵信仰	faith in, belief in Jizō

Glossary

jōbutsu	成仏	enter nirvana; go to heaven
Jōdo	浄土	Pure Land of Amida Buddha
Jōdoshū	浄土宗	Pure Land Sect, founded in Japan by Honen Shōnin
Jōdo Shinshū	浄土真宗	True Pure Land Sect, founded in Japan by Shinran Shōnin
jōka	浄化	purification
josei wa katei ni	女性は家庭に	"women's place is in the home"
joseiteki fuan	女性的不安	"feminine anxiety or troubles"
Jūichimen Kannon	十一面観音	famous 11-faced Kannon statue, Hasedera temple (Kamakura)
juken sensō	受験戦争	entrance exam warfare
juku	塾	extra schooling to prepare students for the next level
jūshoku	住職	head priest of a Buddhist temple
juzu	数珠	rosary or string of beads
Kaibara Ekken	貝原 益軒	Japanese neo-Confucian scholar (1630–1714), to whom the *Onna daigaku* (The Great Learning for Women) was attributed
kai	戒	precept, discipline, rule; Skt. *śīla*
kaimyō	戒名	posthumous Buddhist name, given to newly deceased
kaiun	開運	good fortune in general
kakochō	過去帳	death registries
kami	神	gods, divine beings
kanai anzen	家内安全	safety in the home
kanashimi	悲しみ	grieving
Kannon bosatsu	観音菩薩	bodhisattva attending Amida; (Ch. *kuan-yin*; Skt. *Avalokitesvara*)
Kannon-dō	観音堂	Kannon Hall
kansha	感謝	gratitude
katsuai	割愛	Buddhist concept of thirst or craving
Kisa Gotami		early female disciple of Gotama Buddha
Kishibojin	鬼子母神	demon turned protector (Skt. *Hārītī*; Ch. *Kuei-tzu-mu*)
kitanai	汚い	impure qualities: *tonyoku* (desire), *ikari* (anger), *guchi* (complaints)
kitō	祈祷	prayers and incantations (Ch. *hsiao*)

kiyomeru	清める	to purify, cleanse; *okiyome*, purification
kō	孝	filial piety (*pietas*), veneration of parents and ancestors
kō	講	religious associations of followers
kokoro	心	heart, mind; feeling; will
kokoro no sasae	心の支え	heartfelt support
kokoro no yasuragi	心の安らぎ	peace of mind (*kimochi ga yasuraida* 気持ちが安らいだ)
komori	子守り	lower class providers of child care in small towns
Konjaku monogatari-shū	今昔物語集	A *Collection of Tales of Long Ago* (ca. 1100)
koseki	戸籍	family register
kosodate	子育て	for good upbringing of children
Kosodate Jizō	子育て地蔵	good upbringing of children, helped by Jizō (or Kannon)
kōtoku	公徳	virtuous behavior
kōtsū anzen	交通安全	traffic safety
koyasu	子安	easy childbirth (*Koyasu Jizō*)
Kshitigarbha		Sanskrit term for *Jizō* and *Chinese Ti-tsang (Dizang)*
ku	苦	Buddhist concept of suffering (*dukkha*), pain
kuchiyose	口寄せ	invocations of blind mediums (see *itako*)
kudoku	功徳	virtuous activity, spiritual merit
Kūkai	空海	founded Jpn. Shingon; posthumously known as Kōbō daishi (774–835)
kuyami	悔み	regret, mourn, condolences
kuyō	供養	memorial ritual offering of food and services, to venerate and soothe
kyō	経	sutras, scriptures that convey the teachings of the Buddha
kyōhaku sangyō	脅迫産業	"threat or intimidation industry"
kyōiku mama	教育マ	a mother whose raison d'être is her child's schooling
Kyōkai (ca. 757-822)		compiler of the *Nihon ryōiki* (日本霊異記)

Mabiki Jizō	間引き地蔵	an 18th-century form of *mabiki Jizō* resorted to in times of famine
Mabiku	間引く	"to weed out" unwanted children by infanticide, abortion
Mahikari	真光	Sukyō Mahikari, meaning True Light, was "officially" founded in 1959
mappō	末法	last age and decay of the Buddhist dharma
mayoke	魔よけ	good luck talismans, charms, amulets
mazākon	マザーコン	mother complex
meido	冥途	path to or region of darkness and obscurity; Hades; underworld
meinichi	命日	anniversary of a person's death
Migawari Jizō	身替わり地蔵	bodhisattva who sacrifices self for others (e.g., Jizō)
mikkyō	密教	esoteric or secret teachings
Minamoto Yoritomo	源 頼朝	founder and first shogun of the Kamakura Shogunate (1147–1199)
minzokugakusha	民俗学者	Japanese folklorists
Miroku bosatsu	弥勒菩薩	the Buddha to come (Skt. *Maitreya Buddha*)
mitomeru	認める	to acknowledge, recognize
mizuko	水子	stillborn, miscarried, or aborted fetuses
mizuko kuyō	水子供養	memorial services for miscarried or aborted children
Mizukokuyōdera	水子供養寺	*Jōdoshū* temple in Kyoto
mizuko rei	水子霊	spirits of *mizuko*
mokugyō	木魚	a wooden drum used in temple services
Mokuren	目連	(Skt. Maudgalyāyana), great disciple of the Buddha
Monju Bosatsu	文殊菩薩	(Skt. Manjusrī) bodhisattva of wisdom
Myōenji	妙円寺	Nichiren temple in Matsugasaki area of Kyoto
muen	無縁	quality or state of fundamental brokenness
muenbotoke	無縁仏	the "unconnected dead," with no one to pray for them

mujō	無常	Buddhist concept of impermanence (Skt. *anitya*)
mumyō	無明	(Skt. *avidyā*) ignorance, darkness of mind
myōtai furi	妙対不利	we and the Buddha are one
nagusame	慰め	consolation, comfort
"*Namu Amida Butsu*"	南無阿弥陀仏	*Nembutsu*; homage to, invocation of Amida's name
nayami	悩み	afflictions, suffering, anguish
nenbutsu	念仏	invocation of the Buddha's name
Nichiren-shū	日蓮宗	Nichiren Buddhist sect
nigai	苦い	bitterness
nikumi	憎み	hate, loathing
ninshin chūzetsu	妊娠中絶	artificial abortion (see *datai*)
nyoirin	如意輪	Skt. *cintāmani*, wish-fulfilling jewel, attribute of Jizō and Kannon
nōkotsudō	納骨堂	ossuary or a place where ashes of the dead are stored
nōkyōchō	納経帳	pilgrim's album to record and authenticate one's pilgrimage
Ōe Kenzaburō	大江 健三郎	major figure in contemporary Japanese literature (born 1935)
Oda Hōryū	小田芳 隆	current head priest of Jikishian, a Jōdoshū temple in Kyoto
ofuda	お札	amulets, tablets, or tags on which prayers are written
ogamu	拝む	to pray, worship, bow to
okonai	行い	rituals, practices
okyō	お経	Buddhist sutras or scriptures
omairi	お参り	visit, worship at a temple or shrine
omamori	お守り	protection amulet, "to guard or protect"
Omatsuri	お祭り	a festival
omikuji	お神籤	a written oracle or prediction
Omoidegusa	思い出草	recollections, often recorded in temple notebooks
omoiyari no kokoro	思いやりの心	heart or mind of being considerate or empathic
oni	鬼	demon, fiend, devil, ogre
Onna daigaku	女大学	*Greater Learning for Women*
onryō	怨霊	angry, vengeful spirits of the dead
onryōgami	怨霊神	vengeful gods

Oshakasama	お釈迦様	the historical Gotama Buddha; Shakyamuni Buddha
osonae	お供え	offering
Osorezan (NE Honshu)	恐山	"Mountain of Dread" to which spirits of the dead return in mid-July
otsuya	お通夜	wake
owabi	お詫び	apology, repentance
paritta		ancient Buddhist rituals for protection
raise kuyō	来世供養	rituals oriented toward the afterlife
raise riyaku	来世利益	benefits for the next life
Rand, Yvonne		well-known American Sōtōshū priest, who conducts *mizuko* services
reijō	霊場	sacred place
reikai	霊界	spirit world
reikan shōhō	霊感商法	schemes of making money by capitalizing on people's fears
reikon	霊魂	a person's spirit or soul, including spirits of the aborted
reinōsha	霊能者	spiritualists
Reiyūkai Kyōdan	霊友会教団	lay-based new religion, derived from Nichiren Buddhism
Risshō Kōseikai	立正佼成会	lay-based new religion, originally derived from Reiyūkai
rokudō	六道	six realms or worlds of desire (lower states of existence)
ryōsai kenbo	良妻賢母	"good wife, wise mother" ideology adopted in Meiji era
ryūkō	流行	fashion, fad
ryūzan	流産	miscarriage (*ryūzanji*, miscarried children)
Sai no kawara	賽の河原	Legends about a place where spirits of dead children exist
Sakakibara Yasuo	榊原康夫	Retired temple priest, economics professor at Doshisha University
sanborai	三簿来	Bowing to the Three Buddhist Treasures: teachings, precepts, philosophy
Sanmyōzenji	三明禅寺	an eclectic temple in Toyokawa, with Buddhist and Shinto features

sanpai	参拝	worship
Sawicki, Jana		Author of *Disciplining Foucault: Feminism, Power, and the Body*. Her special fields are women's, gender, and sexuality studies
segaki-e	施餓鬼会	ritualized ceremony, festival of feeding the hungry ghosts (*gaki*)
senkō	線香	incense stick
senzo kuyō	先祖供養	memorial services for ancestors
seirei	精霊	spirit
sekibutsu	石仏	stone (Buddhist) image
sentō kuyō	千頭供養	1000 lantern memorial service at Adashino Nenbutsuji and Osorezan
senzo	先祖	ancestor
sesshō suru	殺生する	to kill (against the Buddhist principle of killing)
sesshō-kai	殺生戒	Buddhist precept not to kill
setsuwa bungaku	説話文学	legendary tales of merit-producing virtuous deeds
shaba	娑婆	our mundane world (Skt. *sahā*), the world of "endurance"
shiawase	幸せ	good fortune
shichifukujin	七福神	the seven gods of good fortune and happiness
shindai	身代	prosperity and wealth
Shingonshū	真言宗	*Shingon* (mantra) sect, founded by Kūkai (774–835)
shinkō	信仰	religious belief, faith
Shinnyōen	真如苑	a Buddhist school for lay practitioners, with variety of religious beliefs
Shinran Shōnin	親鸞上人	founder (1173–1262) of *Jōdoshin* sect
shirei	死霊	spirit of the newly dead
shizan	死産	stillbirth
shōbai hanjō	商売繁盛	success in business
shōgan jōju	賞玩成就	success in completing all requests
shōkonsha	招魂社	shrines dedicated to spirits of those who died in war
shōrō	鐘楼	a bell tower
shōryō	精霊	spirits of the dead

shūen	周縁	people deemed on the outskirts or fringes (of society)
Shugendō	修験道	the way of practicing mystical rites in the mountains
shugorei	守護霊	protective spirits
shugyō	修行	ascetic practice or training
shūkyō	宗教	religion, or religious belief
shūshin	就寝	morals course in schools from late 19th century to 1945
sōdan	相談	counseling, discussion, instruction, consultation
sonaeru	備える	to offer, provide, dedicate (as on an altar)
sorei	祖霊	ancestral spirits
sosen-kuyō	祖先供養	consolation of the spirits of the dead
sosen-sūhai	祖先崇拝	reverence for the ancestors
sōshiki bukkyō	葬式仏教	"funerary Buddhism," when memorial rites are its primary function
sugaru	縋る	rely on, depend on (e.g., Jizō), cling to
taiji	胎児	aborted fetuses
Takahashi Saburō	高橋三郎	Kyoto University professor, director of the Kyōdai Project (see chapter 3)
Takahashi Yoshinori	高橋由典	Kyoto University, School of Human and Environmental Studies
tamashii	魂	a soul, a spirit
tatari (*tataru*, to curse)	祟り	curses inflicted on the living by the unrequited dead
te o awaseru	手を合せる	to pray
teikyō suru	提供する	to make offerings
Tripitaka (Skt.)		"Three Baskets" of Buddhist scriptures: sutras, precepts, commentaries
Ti-Tsang (Dizang)		Chinese name for *Jizō* (Skt. *Kshitagarbha*)
tōba (sotoba)	塔婆	wooden marker or tower for deceased persons (Skt. *stupa*)
Togenuki Jizō	とげ抜き地蔵	*Jizō* of pulling thorns

tōmyō	灯明	votive light
tomurau	弔う	console, mourn
tsuizen kuyō	追善供養	doing good deeds (e.g., *kuyō*) to increase one's merits
tsumi (munen)	罪 (無念)	feelings of having committed a deep offense (regret)
tsumi no ishiki	罪の意識	awareness of having committed such an offense
tsumi o okasu	罪を犯す	to commit an offense
tsutome	勤め	religious service
tsuya	夜	a wake, a vigil, a death watch
tsūzoku dōtoku	通俗道徳	popular or common morality
Underwood, Marilyn		examines *mizuko kuyō* from a cultural studies approach
Ueno Chizuko	上野千鶴子	a leading postmodernist feminist critic
Urabonkyō	盂蘭盆業	Skt. *Ullambana Sutra* relating to feeding the spirits of the dead
urami	恨み	ill will, resentment, grudge
uranaishi	占い師	fortuneteller
wasan	和讃	a hymn or song eulogizing the merits of Jizō, Amida, et al.
Yakushi Nyorai	薬師如来	the healing Buddha
yakudoshi	厄年	the unlucky years for men and women
yakuyoke	厄除	good luck and protection from various dangers
yami	闇	world of darkness (*yami no ko*, children of the darkness)
yashinau	養う	to feed, nourish, nurture (as with a child or dead spirit)
Yasukuni Jinja	靖国神社	national shrine in Tokyo, especially for the war dead
Yü-lan-p'en	盂蘭盆	Chinese festival for departed spirits, forerunner of *Obon*
Yūseihogohō	優生保護法	Eugenic Protection Law (1948), legalizing abortion
zaiaku kan	罪悪感	awareness of sin
zaishō	罪障	karmic hindrances
zange (sange)	懺悔	repentance for one's bad deeds; deep regret

Bibliography

JAPAN LANGUAGE REFERENCES

Committee on Non-Christian Religions, ed. *Sosen to shisha nitsuiteno katorikku shinja no tebiki* [The Church's Teaching on Reverence for Ancestors and All the Dead]. Tokyo: Catholic Bishops' Conference of Japan, rev. ed., 1986, 1–32.

Fujii Harue. *Gendai hahaoya-ron* [On Contemporary Motherhood]. Tokyo: Meiji Tosho Shuppan, 1975.

Fujita Shōichi. "Mumyō no tenshō gendai ni mizuko kuyō" [Transmigration of the Soul in Darkness: Mizuko Kuyō in the Present Day]. *Taiyō*, Spring (1992): 125–136.

Hashimoto Mitsuru. "*Mizuko kuyō to josei no iyashi*" [Mizuko Kuyō and Healing for Women]. In *Sei no polyphony: Sono jitsuzō to rekishi o tazunete* [Polyphony of the Sexes: Seeking Its True Face and History], ed. by Harada Heisaku and Mizoguchi Kohei. Kyoto: Sekaishisōsha, 1990, 284–295.

Hashimoto Mitsuru. "*Gendai nihon no fuan to iyashi*" [Healing the Unrest of Modern Japan]. In *Mizuko Kuyō: Gendai shakai fuan to iyashi* [Mizuko Kuyō: Healing the Unrest of Modern Society], ed. by Takahashi Saburō. Kyoto: Kōrosha, 1999, 13–79.

Hashimoto Yayoi. "*Haha oya no kokoro no iyashi to mizuko kuyō*" [Mizuko Kuyō and Healing the Heart of the Mother]. In *Mizuko kuyō: Gendai shakai no fuan to iyashi* [Mizuko Kuyo: Healing the Unrest of Modern Society], ed. by Takahashi Saburō. Kyoto: Kōrosha, 1999, 207–239.

Hashimoto Yayoi. *Hahaoya no shinri ryōhō: Haha to mizuko no monogatari* [Psychotherapy for Mothers: The Story of Mothers and *Mizuko*]. Tokyo: Nihon Hyōronsha, 2000.

Hatano Yoshihiro and Tsuguo Shimazaki. "Japan (Nippon)." In *The International Encyclopedia of Sexuality*, ed. by Robert T. Francoeur. New York: Continuum, 2004, 1–86.

Hayakawa Seiko. "*Heian makki ni okeru jizōshinkō*" [Belief in Jizō in the Late Heian Peiod]. *Shichō* 96 (1966): 31–52.

Hayami Tasuku. "*Jizō shinkō no nagare*." [Trends in Jizō Worship]. In *Jizō-sama nyūmon* [Introduction to Jizō], ed. by Ishihara Kunitarō. Tokyo: Daihōrin Senshū, 1984.

Hibino Yuri. "*Chūzetsu no katari kara mita josei no jikohenyō to kea no kanōsei.*" [Care for Women Who Have Undergone Induced Abortion: Focusing on Psychological Changes of Women in Their Narratives]. *Japanese Society of Maternal Health* 48(2) (2007): 231–238.

Hirose Zenjun Ni, ed., Vol. 1. *Ichirin no ai o kudasai.* [Please Give Me One Flower of Love]. Jikishian Omoidegusa yori. Tokyo: Chōbunsha, 1977.

Hirose Zenjun Ni., ed., Vol. 2. *Ichirin no ai o kudasai.* [Please Give Me One Flower of Love]. Jikishian Omoidegusa yori. Tokyo: Chōbunsha, 1977.

Hirose Zenjun Ni, ed., Vol. 3. *Ichirin no ai o kudasai, zoku zoku.* [Please Give Me One Flower of Love]. Jikishian Omoidegusa yori. Tokyo: Chōbunsha, 1978.

Hirose Zenjun Ni, ed., Vol. 4. *Ichirin no ai o kudasai.* [Please Give Me One Flower of Love]. Jikishian Omoidegusa yori. Tokyo: Chōbunsha, 1979.

Ishihara Kunitarō, ed. *Jizō sama nyūmon* [An Introduction to Jizō]. Tokyo: Daihōrin Senshū, 1984.

Iwamoto Kazuo. "*Mizuko kuyō ni miru shūkyōsei no mondai*" [Religiosity in Mizuko Kuyō]. Faculty of Engineering, Tokyo Institute of Polytechnics: *Academic Reports* 10(2) (1987): 42–50.

Kamihara Kazuko. "*Mizuko kuyō ni miru reikon no mondai*" [How the Soul Is Regarded in Mizuko Kuyō]. Faculty of Engineering, Tokyo Institute of Polytechnics: *Academic Reports* 8(2) (1985): 24–32.

Katsumata Saori, Matsuoka Megumi, Misumi Junko, and Simizu Kiyomi. "*Jinkō ninshinchūzetsu o ukeru josei ni taisuru kangosha no kea taiken to kangokan no buseki*" [Nurses's Experiences in and Views about Caring for Women Undergoing Abortion]. *Nihon josei shinshin igakkai zasshi [Journal of the Japanese Society for Psychosomatic Obstetrics and Gynecology]* 10(2) (2005): 85–93.

Katsumata Saori, Matsuoka Megumi, and Sekine Kenji. "*Jinkō ninshinchūzetsu jutsu o uketa josei no naiteki sekai—Nijū dai zenhan mikon josei no dēta kara*" [The Inner world of Woman Who Received an Induced Abortion Procedure: Data Collected from Women in Their Early 20s]. *Nihon josei shinshin igakkai zasshi [Journal of the Japanese Society for Psychosomatic Obstetrics and Gynecology]* 12(1) (2007): 317–326.

Kinefuchi Emiko. "*Baransushīto to utsushakudo kara mita jinkō ninshinchūzetsu o ukeru*" [Women's Ambivalence in the Process of Decision-Making on Induced Abortion]. *Nihon jōsei shinshin igakkai zasshi [Journal of the Japanese Society of Psychosomatic Obstetrics and Gynecology]* 13(3) (2008): 115–126.

Komatsu Kazuhiko. "*Kogoroshi no keifu*" [The History of Child Murder]. *Taiyō* 30(375) (September 1992).

Manabe Kōsai. *Jizōson no sekai* [The World of Jizō]. Tokyo: Aoyama Shoin, 1959.

Manabe Kōsai. *Jizō-bosatsu no kenkyū* [Research on Jizō Bodhisattva]. Kyoto: Sanmitsudō Shoten, 1969.

Masaki Akira. "*Jizō shinkō to kodomo kyūsai*" [Faith in Jizō and the Rescue of Children]. *Taiyō* 77(Special Issue) (Spring 1992): 142–145.

Minoru Hamao. *Onna no ko no shitsukekata: Yasashii kodomo ni sodateru hon* [A Guide to Parenting Girls: Raising a Kind Child]. Tokyo: Kobunsha, 1972.

Miyazaki Eishū. *Nichirenshū no shugoshin: Kishimojin shinkō to Daitoku Tenjin shinkō* [The Protective Deities of Nichiren Sect: Kishimojin Faith and Daitokujin Faith], 10th ed. Kyoto: Heirakuji Shoten, 1980.

Miyazaki Eishū. *Kishimojin shinkō* [Religious Belief in Kishimojin]. Tokyo: Yūzankaku Shuppan, 1992.

Mizoguchi Akiyo. "*Mizuko kuyō to josei kaihō*" [Mizuko Kuyō and Women's Liberation]. In *Bosei o kaidoku suru: Tsukurareta shinwa o koete* [Interpreting Motherhood: Beyond the Constructed Myth], ed. by Gurūpu Bosei Kaidoku Kōza. Tokyo: Yūhikaku, 1991, 74–94.

Muraguchi Kiyo. "*Kikonsha no ninshinchūzetsu no genjō: Zōkasuru kongaikankei ni yoru ninshinchūzetsu*" [The Status of Early-Induced Abortions in Married Women: An Increase in Abortions in Extramarital Relationships]. *Nihon seika gakukai [Japanese Journal of Sexual Science]* 28(1) (2010): 35–46.

Ochiai Emiko. "*Taiji wa dare no mononanoka: Chūzetsu to datai no rekishi*" [To Whom Does the Fetus Belong?: The History of Contraception and Abortion]. *Gendai-Shisō* 18(6) (1990): 80–97.

Ochiai Emiko. *Nijūisseiki no kazoku e* [Toward the Twenty-First Century Family]. Tokyo: Yūhikaku, 1996, 78–83.

Oda Hōryū, ed. *Jikishian yori: Ashita ni saku kono ai* [Tomorrow This Love Will Blossom]. Tokyo: Gakushū Kenkyūsha, 1979.

Oda Hōryū, ed. *Jikishian yori: Ai no kiroku* [Documents (Records) of Love]. Tokyo: Tokuma Shoten, 1980.

Oda Hōryū, ed. *Jikishian yori: Ai o komete* [Devote One's Whole Heart]. Tokyo: Gakushū Kenkyūsha, 1982.

Onishi Noboru. "*Mizuko kuyō ni miru jujutsu no mondai*" [Mizuko Kuyō from the Standpoint of Sorcery]. Faculty of Engineering, Tokyo Institute of Polytechnics: *Academic Reports* 8(2) (1985): 33–38.

Ōmusu, Heruman (Herman Ooms). *Senzo sūhai no shinborizumu* [The Symbolism of Ancestor Worship]. Tokyo: Kobundō, 1987.

"*Shinshū no tachiba kara mita 'mizuko' mondai*" [The Mizuko Problem as Seen from the Shinshū Position]. In *Dendoin tokutei kadai kenkyūkai* [Rebirth by Women], ed. by Nyōnin ōjō. Kyoto: Honganji Shuppanbu, 1988, 67–93.

Sokabe Mieko, Ohi Keiko, Kishi Emiko, Hayakawa Yuko, and Takamura Hisako. "*Jinkō ninshinchūzetsu o ketteisuru made no keii to shinriteki henka*" [The Process and Psychological Change for Decision-Making on an Induced Abortion]. *Nihon jōsei shinshin igakkai zasshi [Journal of the Japanese Society of Psychosomatic Obstetrics and Gynecology* 5(2) (2000): 190–196.

Sumisu, Bādoweru (Bardwell Smith). "Buddhism and Abortion in Contemporary Japan: Mizuko Kuyō and the Confrontation with Death." [Japanese translation *Mizuko kuyo ni okeru shi to no chokumen.*" ("Facing Death in Mizuko Kuyō").] In *Ibunka kara mita nihon shukyo no sekai* [The World of Japanese Religions Looked at from Another Culture], ed. by Paul Swanson. Kyoto: Hōzōkan, 2000: 34–71.

Takahashi Bonsen. *Datai mabiki no kenkyū* [Abortion and Infanticide Research]. Tokyo: Daiichi Shobō, 1981.

Takahashi Saburō. *'Mizuko kuyō' ni kansuru tokei chōsa shiryō* [Statistical Data on Mizuko Kuyō]. Kyoto: Kyoto Daigaku Kyōyōbu Shakaigaku Kyōshitsu, 1992.

Takahashi Saburō, ed. *Mizuko kuyō: Gendai shakai no fuan to iyashi* [Mizuko Kuyō: Healing the Unrest of Modern Society]. Kyoto: Kōrosha, 1999.

Takahashi Yoshinori. *"Futatsu no mizuko kuyō"* [Two Types of Mizuko Kuyō]. In *Mizuko kuyō: Gendai no fuan to iyashi* [Mizuko Kuyō: Healing the Unrest of Modern Society], ed. by Takahashi Saburō. Kyoto: Kōrosha, 1999, 113–147.

Tokiwa Yōko, Doeda Narumi, and Watanabe Takashi. *"Jinkō ninshinchūzetsu zengo no shinriteki hannō to kokoro no kea ni kansuru kenkyū no genjō to kadai"* [Psychological Response and Mental Care concerning before and after Induced Abortion: An Integrative Review of the Literature]. *Annals of Gunma University of Health Sciences* 24 (2004): 53–64.

Uchino Kumiko. *"Kishimojin shinkō ni miru minshū no inori to sugata"* [Public Prayer and Form as Seen in the Cult of Kishimojin (goddess of childbirth and children)]. In *Nichirenshū no shomondai* [Various Problems in Nichirenshū], ed. by Nakao Takashi. Tokyo: Yūzankaku shuppan, 1975.

Yamaori Tetsuo. *"Hahagokoro no genfūkei: Umarekawari no eikon-kan"* [The Background to a Mother's Heart: Views on the Rebirth of a Departed Spirit]. *Taiyō* (Special Issue) (Spring 1992): 136–142.

WESTERN LANGUAGES REFERENCES

Ackroyd, Joyce. "Women in Feudal Japan." *Transactions of the Asiatic Society of Japan*, Third Series, 7 (1959): 31–68.

Aitken, Robert. *The Mind of Clover: Essays in Zen Buddhist Ethics*. San Francisco: North Point Press, 1984.

Akima, Toshio. "The Songs of the Dead: Poetry, Drama, and Ancient Death Rituals of Japan." *Journal of Asian Studies* 41(3) (1982): 485–509.

Albanese, Catherine L. "The Poetics of Healing: Root Metaphors and Rituals in Nineteenth-Century America." *Soundings* 63(4) (1980): 381–406.

Alexiou, Margaret. *The Ritual Lament in Greek Tradition*. Cambridge: Cambridge University Press, 1974.

Allison, Anne. *Nightwork: Sexuality, Pleasure, and Corporate Masculinity in a Tokyo Hostess Club*. Chicago: University of Chicago Press, 1994.

Allison, Anne. *Permitted and Prohibited Desires: Mothers, Comics, and Censorship in Japan*. Berkeley: University of California Press, 2000.

Allison, Anne. "Producing Mothers." In *Re-Imaging Japanese Women*, ed. by Anne E. Imamura. Berkeley: University of California Press, 1996, 135–155.

Ambros, Barbara R. *Bones of Contention: Animals and Religion in Contemporary Japan*. Honolulu: University of Hawaii Press, 2012.

AMPO: Japan-Asia Quarterly Review, ed. "Voices from the Japanese Women's Movement." Armonk, NY: M.E. Sharpe, 1996.

Amstutz, Galen. "Ambivalence Regarding Women and Female Gender in Premodern Shin Buddhism." *Japanese Religions* 35(1–2) (2010): 1–32.

Anderson, Richard W. "Social Drama and Iconicity: Personal Narratives in Japanese New Religions." *Journal of Folklore Research* 32(3) (1995): 177–205.

Anderson, Richard W. and Elaine Martin. "Rethinking the Practice of Mizuko Kuyō in Contemporary Japan: Interviews with Practitioners at a Buddhist Temple in Tokyo." *Japanese Journal of Religious Studies* 24(1–2) (1997): 121–143.

Antoni, Klaus. "Yasukuni-Jinja and Folk Religion: The Problem of Vengeful Spirits." *Asian Folklore Studies* 47(1) (1988): 123–136.

Aoki, Deborah McDowell. "Widow's Rites in Japan: An Interpretive Study of Women's Participation in Memorial Rituals and the Transformation of Family Practices." *U.S.-Japan Women's Journal, Center for Inter-Cultural Studies and Education, Josai University* 18 (English Supplement) (2000): 84–106.

Aoki, Michiko and Margaret B. Darness. "The Popularization of Samurai Values: A Sermon by Hosoi Heishu." *Monumenta Nipponica* 31(4) (1976): 393–413.

Arai, Paula Kane Robinson. *Bringing Zen Home: The Healing Heart of Japanese Women's Rituals*. Honolulu: University of Hawaii Press, 2011.

Arai, Paula Kane Robinson. "The Dead as "Personal Buddhas": Japanese Ancestral Rites as Healing Rites." *Pacific World: Journal of the Institute of Buddhist Studies*, Third Series, 5 (2003): 3–17.

Ariga, Chieko. "Dephallicizing Women in Ryūkyō Shinshi: A Critique of Gender Ideology in Japanese Literature." *Journal of Asian Studies* 51(3) (1992): 565–586.

Ariga, Chieko. "Literature and the Institution: Erasure of Women in Schools' Kokugo." *U.S.-Japan Women's Journal* (English Supplement) 9 (1995): 7–28.

Ariga, Chieko. "Who's Afraid of Amino Kiku? Gender Conflict and the Literary Canon." In *Japanese Women: New Feminist Perspectives on the Past, Present, and Future*, ed. by Kumiko Fujimura-Fanselow and Atsuko Kameda, 1995, 43–60.

Ariyoshi Sawako. *The Twilight Years*. Trans. Mildred Tahara. Tokyo: Kodansha International, 1984.

Asquith, Pamela J. "The Monkey Memorial Service of Japanese Primatologist." In *Japanese Culture and Behavior: Selected Readings*, ed. by Takie Sugiyama Lebra and William P. Lebra. Honolulu: University of Hawaii Press, 1986, 29–32.

Baba Sachiko, Tsujita Satoshi, and Morimoto. "The Analysis of Trends in Induced Abortion in Japan: An Increasing Consequence among Adolescents." Osaka University Graduate School of Medicine: *Environmental Health and Preventive Medicine* 10 (2005): 9–15.

Bainbridge, Erika Ohara. "The Madness of Mothers in Japanese Noh Drama." *U.S.-Japan Women's Journal* (English Supplement) 3 (1992): 84–104.

Bakshi, Dwijendra Nath. *Hindu Divinities in Japanese Buddhist Pantheon: A Comparative Study*. Calcutta: Gopal Ray and Gouri Bakshi, 1979.

Barbieri, William A., Jr. "The Heterological Quest: Michel de Certeau's Travel Narratives and the 'Other' of Comparative Religious Ethics." *Journal of Religious Ethics* 1 (2002): 23–48.

Bargen, Doris G. "Ancestral to None—Mizuko in Kawabata." *Japanese Journal of Religious Studies* 19(4) (1992): 337–77.

Bargen, Doris G. "Twin Blossoms on a Single Branch: The Cycle of Retribution in Enchi Fumiko's Onnamen." *Monumenta Nipponica* 46(2) (1991): 147–174.

Bartky, Sandra Lee. "Femininity and Domination: Studies in the Phenomenology of Oppression." In *Thinking Gender*, ed. by Linda J. Nicholson. New York: Routledge, 1990.

Bartky, Sandra Lee. *"Sympathy and Solidarity" and Other Essays*. Lanham, MD: Rowman & Littlefield Publishers, Inc., 2002.

Bays, Jan Chozen Roshi. *Jizo Bodhisattva: Modern Healing & Traditional Buddhist Practice*. Boston: Tuttle Publishing, 2002.

Beardsley, Richard K., John W. Hall, and Robert E. Ward. *Village Japan*. Chicago: University of Chicago Press, 1959.

Beichman, Janine. *Embracing the Firebird: Yosano Akiko and the Birth of the Female Voice in Modern Japanese Poetry*. Honolulu: University of Hawaii Press, 2002.

Bell, Catherine. *Ritual Theory, Ritual Practice*. New York: Oxford University Press, 1992.

Berentsen, Jan-Martin. "The Ancestral Rites in Missiological Perspective." *Japanese Religions* 13(1) (1983): 2–27.

Berger, Michael. "Japanese Women—Old Images and New Realities." *Japan Interpreter: A Journal of Social and Political Ideas* 11(1) (1976): 56–67.

Bernstein, Andrew. *Modern Passings: Death Rites, Politics, and Social Change in Imperial Japan*. Honolulu: University of Hawaii Press, 2006.

Bernstein, Gail Lee. *Haruko's World: A Japanese Farm Woman and Her Community*, reprinted with an Epilogue. Stanford, CA: Stanford University Press, 1996.

Bernstein Gail Lee, ed. *Recreating Japanese Women, 1600–1945*. Berkeley: University of California Press, 1991.

Bestor, Theodore C. "Gendered Domains: A Commentary on Research in Japanese Studies." *Journal of Japanese Studies* 11(1) (1985): 283–287.

Bingham, Marjorie Wall and Susan Hill Gross. *Women in Japan from Ancient Times to the Present*. St. Louis Park, MN: Glenhurst Publications, Inc., 1987.

Birnbaum, Raoul. "Chinese Buddhist Traditions of Healing and the Life Cycle." In *Healing and Restoring: Health and Medicine in the World's Religious Traditions*, ed. by Lawrence E. Sullivan. New York: MacMillan Publishing Company, 1989, 33–57.

Birnbaum, Raoul. *The Healing Buddha*. Boulder, CO: Shambhala Publications, Inc., 1979.

Blacker, Carmen. *The Japanese Enlightenment: A Study of the Writings of Fukuzawa Yukichi*. Cambridge: Cambridge University Press, 1964.

Bolitho, Harold. *Bereavement and Consolation: Testimonies from Tokugawa Japan*. New Haven, CT: Yale University Press, 2003.

Bordo, Susan R. "The Body and the Reproduction of Femininity: A Feminist Appropriation of Foucault." In *Gender/Body/Knowledge: Feminist Reconstructions of*

Being and Knowing, ed. by Alison M. Jaggar and Susan R. Bordo. New Brunswick, NJ: Rutgers University Press, 1989, 13–33.

Bourdieu, Pierre. *Outline of a Theory of Practice*, Vol. 16. Trans. Richard Nice, Cambridge Studies in Social Anthropology, ed. by Jack Goody. Cambridge: Cambridge University Press, 1977.

Bourdieu, Pierre and Loïc Wacquant. *An Invitation to Reflexive Sociology*. Chicago. University of Chicago Press, 1992.

Bozarth-Campbell, Alla. *Life Is Goodbye Life Is Hello: Grieving Well through All Kinds of Loss*, 2d ed. Minneapolis, MN: CompCare Publications, 1986.

Bradbury, R. D. "Fathers, Elders, and Ghosts in Edo Religion." In *Anthropological Approaches to the Study of Religion*, ed. by Michael Banton. London: Tavistock, 1966, 127–153.

Braisted, William Reynolds, ed. *Meiroku Zasshi: Journal of the Japanese Enlightenment*, 1976.

Braude, Ann. *Radical Spirits: Spiritualism and Women's Rights in Nineteenth-Century America*. Boston: Beacon Press, 1989.

Breen, John, ed. "Yasukuni and the Loss of Historical Memory." In *Yasukuni, the War Dead, and the Struggle for Japan's Past*, ed. by John Breen. New York: Columbia University Press, 2008, 143–162.

Breen, John, ed. *Yasukuni, the War Dead, and the Struggle for Japan's Past*. New York: Columbia University Press, 2008.

Bregman, Lucy. "Three Psycho-Mythologies of Death: Becker, Hillman, and Lifton." *Journal of the American Academy of Religion* 52(3) (1984): 461–479.

Brinton, Mary C. "The Social-Institutional Bases of Gender Stratification: Japan as an Illustrative Case." *American Journal of Sociology* 94(2) (1988): 300–334.

Brodzinsky, Anne B. "Surrendering an Infant for Adoption: The Birthmother Experience." In *The Psychology of Adoption*, ed. by David M. Brodzinsky and Marshall D. Schechter. New York: Oxford University Press, 1990, 295–315.

Brooks, Anne Page. "Mizuko Kuyō and Japanese Buddhism." *Japanese Journal of Religious Studies* 8(3–4) (1981): 119–147.

Brown, Gavin. "Theorizing Ritual as Performance: Explorations of Ritual Indeterminacy." *Journal of Ritual Studies* 17(1) (2003): 3–18.

Buckley, Sandra and Vera Mackie. "Women in the New Japanese State." In *Democracy in Contemporary Japan*, ed. by Gavan McCormack and Yoshio Sugimoto. Armonk, NY: M.E. Sharpe, Inc., 1986, 173–185.

Buckley, Sandra. "Body Politics: Abortion Law Reform." In *The Japanese Trajectory: Modernization and Beyond*, ed. by Gavan McCormack and Yoshio Sugimoto. Cambridge: Cambridge University Press, 1988, 205–217.

Buckley, Sandra. "Altered States: The Body Politics of 'Being Woman.'" In *Postwar Japan as History*, ed. by Andrew Gordon. Berkeley: University of California Press, 1993, 347–372.

Buckley, Sandra, ed. "Writing Japanese Women/Japanese Women Writing." *U.S.-Japan Women's Journal* (English Supplement) 9 (Special Issue) (1995): 3–126.

Buckley, Sandra. "Are the Japanese Feminine? Some Problems of Japanese Feminism in Its Cultural Context [Includes interview of Ueno Chizuko]." In *Broken Silence: Voices of Japanese Feminism*, ed. by Sandra Buckley. Berkeley: University of California Press, 1997, 272–301.

Buckley, Sandra. *Broken Silence: Voices of Japanese Feminism*. Berkeley: University of California Press, 1997.

Burns, Susan. "When Abortion Became a Crime: Abortion, Infanticide, and the Law in Early Meiji Japan." In *History and Folklore Studies in Japan*, ed. by David L. Howell and James C. Baxter. Kyoto: International Research Center for Japanese Studies, 2006, 37–55.

Cabezón, José Ignacio. "Buddhist Studies as a Discipline and the Role of Theory." *Journal of the International Association of Buddhist Studies* 18(2) (Winter 1995): 240.

Caraveli, Anna. "The Song beyond the Song: Aesthetics and Social Interaction in Greek Folksong." *Journal of American Folklore* 95(376) (1982): 129–158.

Caraveli, Anna. "The Bitter Wounding: The Lament as Social Protest in Rural Greece." In *Gender and Power in Rural Greece*, ed. by Jill Dubisch. Princeton, NJ: Princeton University Press, 1986, 169–194.

Caraveli-Chavez, Anna. "Bridge between Worlds: The Greek Women's Lament as Communicative Event." *Journal of American Folklore* 368 (1980): 129–157.

Carmichael, Elizabeth and Chloe Sayer. *The Skeleton at the Feast: The Day of the Dead in Mexico*. Austin: University of Texas Press, 1991.

Chambers, Veronica. *Kickboxing Geishas: How Modern Japanese Women Are Changing Their Nation*. New York: Free Press, 2007.

Charmaz, Kathy. "Grief and Loss of Self." In *The Unknown Country: Death in Australia, Britain and the USA*, ed. by Kathy Charmaz, Glennys Howarth, and Allan Kellehear. New York: St. Martin's Press, Inc., 1997, 229–241.

Ch'en, Kenneth. "Filial Piety in Chinese Buddhism." *Harvard Journal of Asiatic Studies* 28 (1968): 81–97.

Childs, Margaret Helen. *Rethinking Sorrow: Revelatory Tales of Late Medieval Japan*. Ann Arbor: Center for Japanese Studies, University of Michigan, 1991.

Chimoto, Akiko. "The Birth of the Full-Time Housewife in the Japanese Worker's Household as Seen through Family Budget Surveys." *U.S.-Japan Women's Journal* (English Supplement) 8: 37–63.

Chodorow, Nancy J. *Feminism and Psychoanalytical Theory*. New Haven, CT: Yale University Press, 1989.

Coleman, Emily. "Infanticide in the Early Middle Ages." In *Women in Medieval Society*, ed. by Susan Mosher Stuart. Philadelphia: University of Pennsylvania Press, 1976, 47–70.

Coleman, Samuel. *Family Planning in Japanese Society: Traditional Birth Control in a Modern Urban Culture*. Princeton, NJ: Princeton University Press, 1983.

Coleman, Samuel. "The Tempo of Family Formation." In *Work and Lifecourse in Japan*, ed. by David W. Plath. Albany: State University of New York Press, 1983, 185–214.

Condon, Jane. *A Half Step Behind: Japanese Women of the '80s*. New York: Dodd, Mead & Company, 1985.

Copeland, Rebecca. "Mother Obsession and Womb Imagery in Japanese Literature." *Transactions of the Asiatic Society of Japan*, Fourth Series, 3 (1988): 131–150.

Copeland, Rebecca. "Motherhood as Institution." *Japan Quarterly* 39(1) (1992): 101–110.

Cornell, L. L. "Hajnal and the Household in Asia: A Comparativist History of the Family in Preindustrial Japan, 1600–1870." *Journal of Family History* 12(1–3) (1987): 143–162.

Cornell, Laurel L. "Infanticide in Early Modern Japan? Demography, Culture, and Population Growth." *Journal of Asian Studies* 55(1) (1996): 22–50.

Cott, Nancy F. *The Bonds of Womanhood: "Woman's Sphere" in New England, 1780–1835*. New Haven, CT: Yale University Press, 1977.

Covell, Stephen G. *Japanese Temple Buddhism: Worldliness in a Religion of Renunciation*. Honolulu: University of Hawaii Press, 2005.

Covell, Stephen G. "The Price of Naming the Dead: Posthumous Precept Names and Critiques of Contemporary Japanese Buddhism." In *Death and the Afterlife in Japanese Buddhism*, ed. by Jacqueline I. Stone and Mariko Namba Walter. Honolulu: University of Hawaii Press, 2008, 293–324.

Crawford, Douglas R. and Michael T. Mannion. *Psycho-Spiritual Healing after Abortion*. Kansas City, MO: Sheed & Ward, 1989.

Cuevas, Bryan J. and Jacqueline I. Stone. "Introduction." In *The Buddhist Dead: Practices, Discourses, Representations*, ed. by Bryan J. Cuevas and Jacqueline I. Stone. Honolulu: University of Hawaii Press, 2007, 1–31.

Cuevas, Bryan J. and Jacqueline I. Stone, eds. *The Buddhist Dead: Practices, Discourses, Representations*. Studies in East Asian Buddhism 20. Honolulu: University of Hawaii Press, 2007.

Davis, Winston. *Dojo: Magic and Exorcism in Modern Japan*. Stanford, CA: Stanford University Press, 1980.

De Certeau, Michel. *The Practice of Everyday Life*. Trans. Steven F. Rendell. Berkeley: University of California Press, 1984.

De Silva, Lily. "Paritta: A Historical and Religious Study of the Buddhist Ceremony for Peace and Prosperity in Sri Lanka." *Spolia Zeylanica* 36, Part I (1981).

De Silva, Lily. "The Paritta Ceremony of Sri Lanka: Its Antiquity and Symbolism." In *Buddhist Thought and Ritual* ed. by David Kalupahana. New York: Paragon Press, 1991, 139.

Denes, Magda. *In Necessity and Sorrow: Life and Death in an Abortion Hospital*. Harmondsworth: Penguin Books, 1977.

DeVisser, M. W. *The Bodhisattva Ti-Tsang (Jizō) in China and Japan*. Berlin: Oesterheld & Co., 1914.

DeVos, George and Hiroshi Wagatsuma. "Value Attitudes toward Role Behavior of Women in Two Japanese Villages." *Anthropologist* 63(6) (1961): 1204–1230.

DeVos, George A. and Takao Sofue, eds. *Religion and Family in East Asia.* Berkeley: University of California Press, 1986.

Doi Kōka. A Theory of Civilization and the Greater Learning for Women. [*Bunmeiron onna daigaku*, 1876].

Doi Takeo. *The Anatomy of Dependence.* Trans. John Bester. Tokyo: Kodansha International, 1973.

Doi Takeo. *The Anatomy of Self: The Individual versus Society.* Trans. Mark A. Harbison. Tokyo: Kodansha International, 1986.

Dore, R. P. *City Life in Japan: A Study of a Tokyo Ward.* Berkeley: University of California Press, 1958.

Dore, R. P. "Education: Japan." In *Political Modernization in Japan and Turkey*, ed. by Robert E. Ward and Dankwart A. Rustow. Princeton, NJ: Princeton University Press, 1964.

Dore, R. P. *Education in Tokugawa Japan.* Berkeley: University of California Press, 1965.

Dore, R. P. "The Legacy of Tokugawa Education." In *Changing Japanese Attitudes toward Modernization*, ed. by Marius B. Jansen. Princeton, NJ: Princeton University Press, 1965, 99–131.

Dore, Ronald P. *Shinohata: A Portrait of a Japanese Village.* New York: Pantheon Books, 1978.

Downing, Christine. *The Goddess: Mythological Images of the Feminine.* New York: Crossroad Publishing Company, 1987.

Driver, Tom F. *The Magic of Ritual: Our Need for Liberating Rites that Transform Our Lives and Our Communities.* New York: HarperCollins, 1991.

Drixler, Fabian F. "Infanticide and Fertility in Eastern Japan: Discourse and Demography, 1660–1880." Ph.D. dissertation, Harvard University, 2008.

Du Boulay, Juliet. "Women—Images of Their Nature and Destiny in Rural Greece." In *Gender and Power in Rural Greece*, ed. by Jill Dubisch. Princeton, NJ: Princeton University Press, 1986, 139–168.

Dubisch, Jill. "Introduction." In *Gender and Power in Rural Greece*, ed. by Jill Dubisch. Princeton, NJ: Princeton University Press, 1986, 3–41.

Dubisch, Jill, ed. *Gender and Power in Rural Greece.* Princeton, NJ: Princeton University Press, 1986.

Dykstra, Yoshiko Kurata. "Jizō, the Most Merciful: Tales from Jizō Bosatsu Reigenki." *Monumenta Nipponica* 33(2) (1978): 179–200.

Dykstra, Yoshiko Kurata. *Miraculous Tales of the Lotus Sutra from Ancient Japan: The Dainihonkoku Hokekyōkenki of Priest Chingen*, trans. and annotated with introduction. Hirakata City, Osaka-fu: Intercultural Research Institute, Kansai University of Foreign Studies, 1983.

Earhart, H. Byron. *Gedatsu-Kai and Religion in Contemporary Japan: Returning to the Center.* Bloomington: Indiana University Press, 1989.

Earhart, H. Byron. "Amulets as Mechanism and Process: Capturing the Formless within Form." *Dharma World* 21 (September–October 1994): 47.

Ehara Yumiko. "Japanese Feminism in the 1970s and 1980s." *U.S.-Japan Women's Journal* (English Supplement) 4 (1993): 49–69.

Embree, John F. *Suye Mura: A Japanese Village*. Chicago: University of Chicago Press, 1939.

Enchi Fumiko. "Enchantress." In *Modern Japanese Short Stories*, ed. by John Bester, E. G. Seidensticker, and Ivan Morris. Tokyo: Japan Publications, Inc., 1970, 72–93.

Enchi Fumiko. *The Waiting Years [Onna zaka]*. Trans. John Bester. Tokyo: Kodansha International, 1980.

Enchi Fumiko. *Masks*. Trans. Juliet Winters Carpenter. Tokyo: Charles E. Tuttle Company, 1984.

Enchi Fumiko. "Skeletons of Men." *Japan Quarterly* 35(4) (1988): 417–426.

Eng, Robert Y. and Thomas C. Smith. "Peasant Families and Population Control in Eighteenth-Century Japan." *Journal of Interdisciplinary History* 6(3) (1976): 417–445.

Federman, Asaf. "Literal Means and Hidden Meanings: A New Analysis of Skillful Means." *Philosophy East and West* 59(2) (2009): 125–141.

Field, Norma. *The Splendor of Longing in the Tale of Genji*. Princeton, NJ: Princeton University Press, 1987.

Field, Norma. *In the Realm of a Dying Emperor: A Portrait of Japan at Century's End* (New York: Pantheon, 1991).

Fiorenza, Elizabeth Schussler. *In Memory of Her: A Feminist Theological Reconstruction of Christian Origins*. New York: Crossroad, 1994.

Florida, R. E. "Buddhist Approaches to Abortion." *Asian Philosophy* 1(1) (1991): 39–50.

Fortes, Meyer. "Pietas in Ancestor Worship." *Journal of the Royal Anthropological Institute of Great Britain and Ireland* 91(1–2) (1961): 166–191.

Fortes, Meyer. "An Introductory Commentary." In *Ancestors*, ed by William H. Newell. The Hague: Mouton Publishers, 1974, 1–16.

Foucault, Michel. *Power/Knowledge: Selected Interviews and Other Writings, 1972–1977*. Trans. Leo Marshall, Colin Gordon, John Mepham, Kate Soper, and edited by Colin Gordon. New York: Pantheon Books, 1980.

Freed, Anne O. *The Changing Worlds of Older Women in Japan*. Manchester, CT: Knowledge, Ideas & Trends, 1993.

Freud, Sigmund. "Mourning and Melancholia." In *The Standard Edition*. London: Hogarth Press, 1957, 247–268.

Fridell, Wilbur M. "Government Ethics Textbooks in Late Meiji Japan." *Journal of Asian Studies* 39(4) (August 1970): 823–833.

Friedl, Emestine. "The Position of Women: Appearance and Reality." In *Gender and Power in Rural Greece*, ed. by Jill Dubisch. Princeton, NJ: Princeton University Press, 1986, 45–52.

Friedman, Rochelle and Bonnie Gradstein. *Surviving Pregnancy Loss: A Complete Sourcebook for Women and Their Families*, rev. ed. New York: Carol Publishing Group, 1996.

Fujii Sadakazu. "The Relationship between the Romance and Religious Observances: Genji Monogatari as Myth." *Japanese Journal of Religious Studies* 9(2–3) (1982): 127–146.

Fujimura-Fanselow, Kumiko and Atsuko Kameda, eds. *Japanese Women: New Feminist Perspectives on the Past, Present, and Future.* New York: Feminist Press at the City University of New York, 1995.

Fujita Mariko. "'It's All Mother's Fault': Childcare and the Socialization of Working Mothers in Japan." *Journal of Japanese Studies* 15(1) (1989): 67–91.

Fujiwara Takanori. "Japanese Rites of Passage and the Mission of the Church, Part I." *Missionary Bulletin* 42(2) (1988): 59–71, 98–105.

Fukutake Tadashi. *Japanese Rural Society.* Trans. R.P. Dore. Ithaca, NY: Cornell University Press, 1972.

Fukuzawa Yukichi. *Fukuzawa Yukichi on Japanese Women: Selected Works.* Trans. and ed. Eiichi Kiyooka. Tokyo: University of Tokyo Press, 1988.

Funabashi Kuniko. "Pornographic Culture and Sexual Violence." In *Japanese Women: New Feminist Perspectives on the Past, Present, and Future,* ed. by Kumiko Fujimura-Fanselow and Atsuko Kameda. New York: Feminist Press at the City University of New York, 1995, 255–263.

Garon, Sheldon. "Women's Groups and the Japanese State: Contending Approaches to Political Integration, 1890–1945." *Journal of Japanese Studies* 19(1) (1993): 5–41.

Garon, Sheldon. *Molding Japanese Minds: The State in Everyday Life.* Princeton, NJ: Princeton University Press, 1997.

Garrick, David A. "The Work of the Witness in Psychotherapeutic Rituals of Grief." *Journal of Ritual Studies* 8(2) (Summer 1994): 85–113.

Gelb, Joyce. "Tradition and Change in Japan: The Case of Equal Employment Opportunity Law." *U.S.-Japan Women's Journal* (English Supplement) 1 (1991): 51–77.

Gessell, Van C. "Echoes of Feminine Sensibility in Literature." *Japan Quarterly* 35(4) (1988): 410–416.

Gessell, Van C. "The 'Medium' of Fiction: Fumiko Enchi as Narrator." *World Literature Today: Literary Quarterly of the University of Oklahoma* 32 (Special Issue "Contemporary Japanese Literature") (1988): 380–385.

Ginsburg, Faye. "Procreation Stories: Reproduction, Nurturance, and Procreation in Life Narratives of Abortion Activists." *Journal of the American Ethnological Society* 14(4) (1987): 623–636.

Ginsburg, Faye. *Contested Lives: The Abortion Debate in an American Community.* Berkeley: University of California Press, 1989.

Gjertson, Donald E. "Ghosts, Gods, and Retribution: Nine Buddhist Miracle Tales from Six Dynasties and Early T'ang China." In *Occasional Papers Series 2.* Amherst, MA: International Area Studies Programs, University of Massachusetts, 1978, 1–51.

Glassman, Hank. "A Cloak of Ambivalence: Mothers and Monks in Medieval Japan." *Japanese Religions Bulletin: New Faces in the Field* (February 1998 Supplement): 12–19.

Glassman, Hank. "The Tale of Mokuren: A Translation of Mokuren-no-Sōshi." *Buddhist Literature* 1(1) (1999): 120–161.

Glassman, Hank. "Chinese Buddhist Death Ritual and the Transformation of Japanese Kinship." In *The Buddhist Dead: Practices, Discourses, Representations*, ed. by Bryan J. Cuevas and Jacqueline I. Stone. Honolulu: University of Hawaii Press, 2007, 405–437.

Glassman, Hank. "At the Crossroads of Birth and Death: The Blood Pool Hell and Postmortem Fetal Extraction." In *Death and the Afterlife in Japanese Buddhism*, ed. by Jacqueline I. Stone and Mariko Namba Walter. Honolulu: University of Hawaii Press, 2008, 175–206.

Glassman, Hank. *The Face of Jizō: Image and Cult in Medieval Japanese Buddhism*. Honolulu: University of Hawaii Press, 2012.

Glenn, Evelyn Nakano. "Social Constructions of Mothering: A Thematic Overview." In *Mothering: Ideology, Experience, Agency*, ed. by Grace Chang, Evelyn Nakano Glenn, and Linda Rennie Forcey. New York: Routledge, 1994, 1–29.

Glenn, Evelyn Nakano, Grace Chang, and Linda Rennie Forcey, eds. *Mothering: Ideology, Experience, Agency*. New York: Routledge, 1994.

Gluck, Carol. *Japan's Modern Myths: Ideology in the Late Meiji Period*. Princeton, NJ: Princeton University Press, 1985.

Gombrich, Richard. "'Merit Transference' in Sinhalese Buddhism: A Case Study of the Interaction between Doctrine and Practice." *History of Religions* 11(2) (1995): 183–230.

Gómez, Luis O. "Unspoken Paradigms: Meanderings through the Metaphors of a Field." *Journal of the International Association of Buddhist Studies* 18(2) (1995): 183–230.

Goodwin, Janet R. "Shooing the Dead to Paradise." *Japanese Journal of Religious Studies* 16(1) (1989): 63–80.

Goodwin, Janet R. *Alms and Vagabonds: Buddhist Temples and Popular Patronage in Medieval Japan*. Honolulu: University of Hawaii Press, 1994.

Gordon, Beate Sirota, *The Only Woman in the Room: A Memoir*. New York: Kodansha International, 1997).

Goss, Robert E. and Dennis Klass. *Dead but Not Lost: Grief Narratives in Religious Traditions*. Walnut Creek, CA: AltaMira Press, 2005.

Graham, Hilary. "The Social Image of Pregnancy: Pregnancy as Spirit Possession." *Sociological Review* (May 1976): 291–308.

Grapard, Allan G. "Japan's Ignored Cultural Revolution: The Separation of Shintō and Buddhist Divinities in Meiji (*Shinbutsu Bunri*) and a Case Study: Tōnomine." *History of Religions* 23(3) (February 1984): 240–265.

Grapard, Allan G. "Visions of Excess and Excesses of Vision: Women and Transgression in Japanese Myth." *Japanese Journal of Religious Studies* 18(1) (1991): 3–22.

Grapard, Allan G. *The Protocol of the Gods*. Berkeley: University of California Press, 1992.

Grimes, Ronald L. "Defining Nascent Ritual." *Journal of the American of Religion* 50(4) (1982): 539–555.

Grimes, Ronald L. *Ritual Criticism: Case Studies in Its Practice, Essays on Its Theory*. Columbia: University of South Carolina Press, 1990.

Grimes, Ronald L., ed. *Readings in Ritual Studies*. Upper Saddle River, NJ: Prentice Hall, 1996.

Grimes, Ronald L. *Ritual*. In Guide to the Study of Religion, ed. by Willi Braun and Russell T. McCutcheon. London: Cassell, 2000.

Griswold, Eliza. "How Rachel Carson Gave Voice to the Modern Environmental Movement—and Ignited its Opposition," *The New York Times Magazine*, September 23, 2012.

Griswold, Susan. "Sexuality, Textuality, and the Definition of the 'Feminine' in Late Eighteenth-Century Japan." *U.S.-Japan Women's Journal* (English Supplement) 9 (1995): 59–76.

Grossberg, John Barth. "Formulating Attitudes towards Death: A Study of Elderly Japanese Jōdo Shin Buddhists." Urbana-Champaign: University of Illinois, 1981.

Guthrie, Stewart. *A Japanese New Religion: Risshō Kōsei-kai in a Mountain Hamlet*. Ann Arbor: Center for Japanese Studies, University of Michigan, 1988.

Habino, Yuri. "Postabortion Spirituality in Women: Insights from Participants in the Japanese Ritual of *mizuko kuyo* over the Internet." *Journal of the Japanese Society of Psychosomatic Obstetrics and Gynecology* 13(1) (2008): 73–85.

Hall, John Whitney. "The Confucian Teacher in Tokugawa Japan." In *Confucianism in Action*, ed. by David S. Nivison and Arthur F. Wright. Stanford, CA: Stanford University Press, 1959, 268–301.

Hall, John Whitney. "Education and Modern Development." In *Twelve Doors to Japan*, ed. by John Whitney Hall and Richard K. Beardsley. New York: McGraw-Hill Book Company, 1965, 384–426.

Hamabata, Matthews Masayuki. *Crested Kimono: Power and Love in the Japanese Business Family*. Ithaca, NY: Cornell University Press, 1990.

Hane, Mikiso. *Peasants, Rebels, & Outcastes: The Underside of Modern Japan*. New York: Pantheon Books, 1982.

Hane, Mikiso, ed. *Reflections on the Way to the Gallows: Rebel Women in Prewar Japan*. Berkeley: University of California Press, 1988.

Hanley, Susan B. "Toward an Analysis of Demographic and Economic Change in Tokugawa Japan: A Village Study." *Journal of Asian Studies* 31 (1971–72): 515–537.

Hanley, Susan B. and Arthur P. Wolf, eds. *Family and Population in East Asian History*. Stanford, CA: Stanford University Press, 1965.

Hanley, Susan B. and Kozo Yamamura. *Economic and Demographic Change in Preindustrial Japan 1600–1868.* Princeton, NJ: Princeton University Press, 1977.

Hardacre, Helen. "The Transformation of Healing in the Japanese New Religions." *History of Religions* 21(4) (1982): 305–320.

Hardacre, Helen. *Lay Buddhism in Contemporary Japan: Reiyūkai Kyōdan.* Princeton, NJ: Princeton University Press, 1984.

Hardacre, Helen. *Shintō and the State, 1868–1988.* Princeton, NJ: Princeton University Press, 1989.

Hardacre, Helen. "Japanese New Religions: Profiles in Gender." In *Fundamentalism and Gender,* ed. by John Stratton Hawley. New York: Oxford University Press, 1994, 111–133.

Hardacre, Helen. *Marketing the Menacing Fetus in Japan.* Berkeley: University of California Press, 1997.

Harding, Esther. *The Way of All Women.* Boston: Shambhala Publications, Inc., 1970.

Harrison, Beverly Wildung. *Our Right to Choose: Toward a New Ethic of Abortion.* Boston: Beacon Press, 1983.

Harrison, Elizabeth G. "Women's Responses to Child Loss in Japan: The Case of Mizuko Kuyō." *Journal of Feminist Studies in Religion* 11(2) (1995): 67–93.

Harrison, Elizabeth G. "Mizuko Kuyō: The Re-Production of the Dead in Contemporary Japan." In *Religion in Japan: Arrows to Heaven and Earth,* ed. by P. F. Komicki and I. J. McMullen. New York: Cambridge University Press, 1996, 250–266.

Harrison, Elizabeth G. "'I Can Only Move My Feet towards Mizuko Kuyō': Memorial Services for Dead Children in Japan." In *Buddhism and Abortion,* ed. by Damien Keown. Honolulu: University of Hawaii Press, 1999, 93–120.

Hatano Yoshihiro and Tsuguo Shimazaki. "Japan (Nippon)." In *The International Encyclopedia of Sexuality,* ed. by Robert T. Francoeur. New York: Continuum, 2004, 1–86.

Hendry, Joy. *Becoming Japanese: The World of the Pre-School Child.* Honolulu: University of Hawaii Press, 1986.

Hibino Yuri. "Postabortion Spirituality in Women: Insights from Participants in the Japanese Ritual of *mizuko kuyo* over the Internet." *Journal of the Japanese Society of Psychosomatic Obstetrics and Gynecology* 13(1–2) (2008): 73–85.

Higuchi Keiko. *Bringing up Girls: Start Aiming at Love and Independence: Status of Women in Japan.* Kyoto: Shōkadoh Booksellers, 1985.

Higuchi Keiko. "Women at Home." *Japan Echo* 12 (1985): 51–57.

Hobsbawn, Eric and Terence Ranger, eds. *The Invention of Tradition.* Cambridge: Cambridge University Press, 1983.

Hockey, J., J. Katz, and N. Small. *Grief, Mourning and Death Ritual.* Buckingham, UK: Open University Press, 2001.

Hodge, Robert W. and Naohiro Ogawa. *Fertility Change in Contemporary Japan.* Chicago: University of Chicago Press, 1991.

Holden, Karen C. "Changing Employment Patterns of Women." In *Work and Lifecourse in Japan*, ed. by David W. Plath. Albany: State University of New York Press, 1983, 34–46.

Holt, John C. "Assisting the Dead by Venerating the Living: Merit Transfer in the Early Buddhist Tradition." *Numen* 28(1) (1981): 1–28.

Homans, Peter. *The Ability to Mourn: Disillusionment and the Social Origins of Psychoanalysis*. Chicago: University of Chicago Press, 1989.

Homans, Peter, ed. *Symbolic Loss: The Ambiguity of Mourning and Memory at Century's End*. Charlottesville: University Press of Virginia, 2000.

Hopkinson, Deborah, Michele Hill, and Eileen Kiera. *Not Mixing up Buddhism: Essays on Women and Buddhist Practice*. Fredonia, NY: White Pine Press, 1986.

Hori Ichiro. *Folk Religion in Japan; Continuity and Change*. Chicago: University of Chicago Press, 1968.

Horton, Sarah J. *Living Buddhist Statues in Early Medieval and Modern Japan*. New York: Palgrave Macmillan, 2007.

Hoshino Eiki and Takeda Dōshō. "Indebtedness and Comfort: The Undercurrents of *Mizuko Kuyō* in Contemportary Japan." *Japanese Journal of Religious Studies* 14(4) (1987): 305–320.

Hoshino Eiki and Takeda Dōshō. "Mizuko Kuyō and Abortion in Contemporary Japan." In *Religion and Society in Modern Japan*, ed. by Shimazono Susumu, Mark R. Mullins, and Paul L. Swanson. Berkeley, CA: Asian Humanities Press, 1993, 171–190.

Hrdy, Sarah Blaffer. *Mother Nature: A History of Mothers, Infants, and Natural Selection*. New York: Pantheon Books, 1999.

Hsüan Hua, Jing Heng, and Ch'ih Heng. *Sutra of the Past Vows of Earth-Store Bodhisattva: The Collected Lectures of Tripiṭaka Master Hsüan Hua*. Trans. Bhiksu Heng Ching. New York: Institute for Advanced Studies of World Religions, 1974.

Hubbard, Jamie. "The Yamaguchi Story: Buddhism and the Family in Contemporary Japan." *60 Minutes*. London and Washington, D.C.: BBC/Educational Communications International, 1988.

Hubbard, Jamie. *Yielding to the New: Buddhism and the Family in Contemporary Japan*. Florence, MA: J&M Information Systems, 1988.

Hubbard, Jamie. "Premodern, Modern, and Postmodern: Doctrine and the Study of Japanese Religion." *Japanese Journal of Religious Studies* 19(1) (1992): 3–37.

Hubbard, Jamie. "Review of Jan Nattier, Once Upon a Future Time." *Eastern Buddhist*, New Series, 26(1) (1993): 138–146.

Hubbard, Jamie. "Embarrassing Superstition, Doctrine, and the Study of New Religious Movements." *Journal of the American Academy of Religion* 66(1) (1998): 59–92.

Hur, Nam-lin. *Death and Social Order in Tokugawa Japan: Buddhism, Anti-Christianity, and the Danka System*. Cambridge, MA: Harvard University Press, 2007.

Hurvitz, Leon. *Scripture of the Lotus Blossom of the Fine Dharma (The Lotus Sūtra).* Trans. from the Chinese of Kumārajīva. New York: Columbia University Press, 1976.

Igeta Midori. "A Response." *Journal of Feminist Studies in Religion* 11(2) (1995): 95–100.

Iijima Yoshiharu. "Folk Culture and the Liminality of Children." *Current Anthropology* 28(4) (1987): S41–S48.

Imai Yasuko. "The Emergence of the Japanese Shufu: Why a Shufu Is More than a 'Housewife.'" *U.S.-Japan Women's Journal* (English Supplement) 6 (1994): 44–65.

Imamura, Anne E. "The Active Housewife: Continuity and Change in the Status of Shufu." *Transactions of the Asiatic Society of Japan* 23 (1978): 85–98.

Imamura, Anne E. *Urban Japanese Housewives: At Home and in the Community.* Honolulu: University of Hawaii Press, 1987.

Imamura, Anne E., ed. *Re-imaging Japanese Women.* Berkeley: University of California Press, 1996.

Inagaki Hisao, ed. *Sutra on the Heavy Indebtedness to One's Parents.* Trans. John Doami. Kyoto: Ryūkoku Translation Center, Ryūkoku University, 1965.

Irokawa Daikichi. *The Culture of Meiji Japan.* Princeton, NJ: Princeton University Press, 1985.

Itami Juzo, Tsutomu Yamazaki, and Nobuko Miyamoto. "The Funeral." [Videocassette, 124 minutes.] Los Angeles: Republic Pictures Home Video, 1988.

Ivy, Marilyn. *Discourses of the Vanishing: Modernity, Phantasm, Japan.* Chicago: University of Chicago Press, 1995.

Ivy, Marilyn Jeanette. "Discourses of the Vanishing in Contemporary Japan.". (Ph.D, diss., Cornell University, Ithaca: NY, 1988). Ann Arbor, MI, University Microfilms International, 1988.

Iwamura Miki, Kunishige Atsuko, Tanaka Hiroshi, Tomiie Emiko, and Yamamoto Itsuki. "A Comparative Analysis of Gender Roles and the Status of Women in Japan and the U.S." *U.S.-Japan Women's Journal* (English Supplement) 3 (1992): 36–53.

Iwao Sumiko. "The Quiet Revolution: Japanese Women Today." *Japan Foundation Newsletter* 19(3) (1991): 1–9.

Iwao Sumiko. *The Japanese Woman: Traditional Image and Changing Reality.* New York: Free Press, 1993.

Jaggar, Alison M. and Susan R. Bordo, eds. *Gender/Body/Knowledge: Feminist Reconstructions of Being and Knowing.* New Brunswick, NJ: Rutgers University Press, 1989.

Jaworski, Jan. "L'avalambana sutra de la terre pure." *Monumenta Serica: Journal of Oriental Studies* 1 (1935): 82–107.

Johnson, Elizabeth L. "Grieving for the Dead, Grieving for the Living: Funeral Laments of Hakka Women." In *Death Ritual in Late Imperial and Modern China,* ed. by James L. Watson and Evelyn S. Rawski. Berkeley: University of California Press, 1987, 135–163.

Jolivet, Muriel. "Derrière les représentations de l'infanticide ou mabiki ema (間引き絵馬)." *Bulletin of the Faculty of Foreign Studies, Sophia University* 37 (2002): 82–116.

Jolivet, Muriel. *Japan: The Childless Society?: The Crisis of Motherhood.* Trans. Anne-Marie Glasheen, English language ed. London: Routledge, 1997.

Jonte-Pace, Diane. "At Home in the Uncanny: Freudian Representations of Death, Mothers, and the Afterlife." *Journal of the American Academy of Religion* 64(1) (1996): 61–88.

Jordan, David K. *Gods, Ghosts & Ancestors: Folk Religion in a Taiwanese Village,* 2d ed. Taipei, Taiwan: Cave Books, Ltd., 1985.

Kaibara Ekken. "Onna daigaku (1672)." In *Women and Wisdom of Japan,* ed. by Takaishi Shingoro. London: John Murray, 1905, 33–46.

Kaji Chizuko. "The Post-War Wife—No Longer Incompetent: Civil Code Revisions and Equality for Women." *Japan Quarterly* 31(1) (1984): 11–18.

Kaji Nobuyuki. "Japan and the Confucian Cultural Sphere." *Japan Echo* 23 (Special Issue) (1996): 72–78.

Kamens, Edward. *The Buddhist Poetry of the Great Kamo Priestess: Daisaiin Senshi and 'Hosshin Wakashū'.* Ann Arbor: Center for Japanese Studies, University of Michigan, 1990.

Kamens, Edward. "Dragon-Girl, Maidenflower, Buddha: The Transformation of a Waka Topos, 'the Five Obstructions.'" *Harvard Journal of Asiatic Studies* 53(2) (1993): 389–442.

Kaminishi Ikumi. *Explaining Pictures: Buddhist Propganda and Etoki Storytelling in Japan.* Honolulu: University of Hawaii Press, 2006.

Kamstra, J. H. "Skilful Means as a 'Germinative Principle': Some Remarks on a Concept in Mahayana Buddhism." *Numen* 27(2) (1980): 270–277.

Kanazu Hidemi. "The Criminalization of Abortion in Meiji Japan." *U.S.-Japan Women's Journal* 24 (2003): 35–58.

Kaneko, Sachiko and Robert E. Morrell. "Sanctuary: Kamakura's Tōkeiji Convent." *Japanese Journal of Religious Studies* 10(2–3) (1983): 195–228.

Kaneko, Satoru. "Dimensions of Religiosity among Believers in Japanese Folk Religion." *Journal for the Scientific Study of Religion* 29(1) (1990): 1–18.

Kano Masanao. "Changing Perspectives on the Family in Post-War Japan." *Review of Japanese Culture and Society* 1(1) (1986): 78–84.

Kapferer, Bruce. *A Celebration of Demons: Exorcism and the Aesthetics of Healing in Sri Lanka.* Bloomington: Indiana University Press, 1983.

Katō Bunnō, Yoshirō Tamura, and Kojirō Miyasaka, eds. *The Three Fold Lotus Sutra.* New York: Weatherhill/Kōsei Publishing Company, 1975.

Kato, Masae. "Silence between Patients and Doctors: The Issue of Self-Determination and Amniocentesis in Japan." *Genomics, Society and Policy* 3(3) (2007): 1–15.

Kato, Masae. "Quality of Offspring? Socio-Cultural Factors, Pre-Natal Testing and Reproductive Decision-Making in Japan." *Culture, Health & Sexuality* (2009): 1–13.

Kato, Masae. *Women's Rights? The Politics of Eugenic Abortion in Modern Japan*, International Institute for Asian Studies (IIAS) Publication Series: Monographs 2. Leiden, The Netherlands: Amsterdam University Press, 2009.

Kato, Masae and Margaret Sleeboom-Faulkner. "Dichotomies of Collectivism and Individualism in Bioethics: Selective Abortion Debates and Issues of Self-Determination in Japan and 'the West.'" *Social Science and Medicine* 73 (2011): 507–514.

Kato, Masae and Margaret Sleeboom-Faulkner. "Meanings of the Embryo in Japan: Narratives of IVF Experience and Embryo Ownership." *Sociology of Health & Illness* 33(3) (2011): 434–447.

Katō Mieko. "Women's Associations and Religious Expression in the Medieval Japanese Village." In *Women and Class in Japanese History*, ed. by Hitomi Tonomura, Anne Walthall, and Wakita Haruko. Ann Arbor: Center for Japanese Studies, University of Michigan, 1999, 119–134.

Kawabata Yasunari. *Beauty and Sadness*. Trans. Howard Hibbett. Tokyo: Charles E. Tuttle Company, 1975.

Kawahashi Noriko. "Feminist Buddhism as Praxis: Women in Traditional Buddhism." *Japanese Journal of Religious Studies* 30(3–4) (2003): 291–313.

Kawahashi Noriko. "Japan's Traditional Buddhism and the Gender Issue." *Dharma World* 38 (2011): 20–22.

Kawai Hayao. *The Japanese Psyche: Major Motifs in the Fairy Tales of Japan*. Dallas, TX: Spring Publications, Inc., 1988.

Kawakami Gentarō. *I'd Like to See Their Parents' Faces*. Tokyo: Goma Shobō, 1975.

Kawakami Mitsuyo. "The View of Spirits as Seen in the Bon Observances of the Shima Region." *Japanese Journal of Religious Studies* 15(2–3) (1988): 121–130.

Kelly, William W. "Directions in the Anthropology of Contemporary Japan." *Annual Review of Anthropology* 20 (1991): 395–431.

Kelly, William W. "Finding a Place in Metropolitan Japan: Ideologies, Institutions, and Everyday Life." In *Postwar Japan as History*, ed. by Andrew Gordon. Berkeley: University of California Press, 1993, 189–216.

Kelsey, W. Michael. "The Raging Deity in Japanese Mythology." *Asian Folklore Studies* 40(2) (1981): 213–236.

Kelsey, W. Michael. *Konjaku Monogatari-Shū*. Boston: Twayne Publishers, 1982.

Kenyon, Edwin. *The Dilemma of Abortion*. London: Faber & Faber, 1986.

Keown, Damien. *The Nature of Buddhist Ethics*. New York: St. Martin's Press, 1992.

Keown, Damien. *Buddhism and Bioethics*. New York: St. Martin's Press, 1995.

Keown, Damien, ed. *Buddhism and Abortion*. Honolulu: University of Hawaii Press, 1999.

Kerner, Karen. "The Malevolent Ancestor: Ancestral Influence in a Japanese Religious Sect." In *Ancestors*, ed. by William H. Newell. The Hague: Mouton Publishers, 1974, 205–217.

Kim Seong Nae. "Chronicle of Violence, Ritual of Mourning: Cheju Shamanism in Korea." Ph.D. diss., University of Michigan, Ann Arbor, 1989.

Kim Seong Nae. "Lamentations of the Dead: The Historical Imagery of Violence on Cheju Island, South Korea." *Journal of Ritual Studies* 3(2) (1989): 251–285.

King, Sallie B. *Journey in Search of the Way: The Spiritual Autobiography of Satomi Myōdō*. Trans. Sallie B. King. Albany: State University of New York Press, 1987.

King, Sallie B. "Egalitarian Philosophies in Sexist Institutions: The Life of Satomi-San, Shinto Miko and Zen Buddhist Nun." *Journal of Feminist Studies in Religion* 4 (1988): 7–26.

Kinsley, David. *Hindu Goddesses: Visions of the Divine Feminine in the Hindu Religious Tradition*. Berkeley: University of California Press, 1986.

Kirby, R. J. "Ancestral Worship in Japan." *Transactions of the Asiatic Society of Japan* 38 (1910): 233–267.

Kitada Sachie. "Contemporary Japanese Feminist Literary Criticism." *U.S.-Japan Women's Journal* (English Supplement) 7 (1994): 72–97.

Kiyoka Eiichi. *The Autobiography of Yukichi Fukuzawa*. Trans. Eiichi Kiyooka. New York: Columbia University Press, 1966.

Kiyoka Eiichi, ed. *Fukuzawa Yukichi on Japanese Women*. Tokyo: University of Tokyo Press, 1988.

Kiyomi Morioka. "The Appearance of 'Ancestor Religion' in Modern Japan: The Years of Transition from the Meiji to the Taishō Periods." *Japanese Journal of Religious Studies* 4(2–3) (1977): 183–212.

Klass, Dennis. *Parental Grief: Solace and Resolution*, ed. by Robert Kastenbaum, The Springer Series on Death and Suicide, Vol. 9. New York: Springer Publishing Company, 1988.

Klass, Dennis. "Ancestor Worship in Japan: Dependence and the Resolution of Grief." *Omega: Journal of Death and Dying* 33(4) (1996): 279–302.

Klass, Dennis. "Continuing Bonds in the Resolution of Grief in Japan and North America." *American Behavioral Scientist* 44(55) (2001): 742–763.

Klass, Dennis and R. Goss. "Spiritual Bonds to the Dead in Cross-Cultural and Historical Perspective: Comparative Religion and Modern Grief." *Death Studies* 23 (1999): 547–567.

Knecht, Peter. "Funerary Rites and the Concept of Ancestors in Japan: A Challenge to the Christian Churches?" *Japan Missionary Bulletin* 39(3) (1985): 32–45.

Kojima Hideo. "Japanese Concepts of Child Development from the Mid-Seventeenth Century to the Mid-Nineteenth Century." *International Journal of Behavioral Development* 9(3) (1986): 315–329.

Kon, Igor. "Sexuality and Culture." In *Sex and Russian Society*, ed. by Igor Kon and James Riordan. Bloomington: Indiana University Press, 1993.

Kondo, Dorinne K. *Crafting Selves: Power, Gender, and Discourses of Identity in a Japanese Workplace*. Chicago: Chicago University Press, 1990.

Koschmann J. Victor, Ōiwa Keibō, and Yamashita Shinji, eds. *International Perspectives on Yanagita Kunio and Japanese Folklore Studies*. Ithaca, NY: Cornell University East Asia Program, 1985.

Koyama Shizuko. "The 'Good Wife and Wise Mother' Ideology in Post-World War I Japan." *U.S.-Japan Women's Journal* (English Supplement) 7 (1994): 31–52.

Krauss, Ellis S., Thomas P. Rohlen, and Patricia G. Steinhoff, eds. *Conflict in Japan*. Honolulu: University of Hawaii Press, 1984.

Kretschmer, Angelika. *Kuyō in Contemporary Japan: Religious Rites in the Lives of Laypeople*. Göttingen: Cuvillier Verlag, 2000.

Ku Cheng-mei. "The *Mahisasaka* View of Women." In *Buddhist Thought and Ritual*, ed. by David Kalupahana. New York: Paragon House, 1991, 104–124.

Kubo Tsugunari. "Contemporary Lay Buddhist Movement in Japan: A Comparison between Reiyūkai and Sokagakkai." In *Buddhica Britannica*, ed. by Tadeusz Skorupski. Hertfordshire, UK: Tring, 1989, 193–218.

Kubler-Ross, Elisabeth. *On Children and Death*. New York: Collier Books, 1983.

Kubler-Ross, Elisabeth. *On Death and Dying*. New York: Macmillan Publishing Co., Inc., 1969.

Kuroda Toshio. "Shintō in the History of Japanese Religion." *Journal of Japanese Studies* 7(1) (Winter 1981): 1–21.

Kuroda Toshio. "The World of Spirit Pacification: Issues of State and Religion." *Japanese Journal of Religious Studies* 23(3–4) (1996): 321–351.

Kurosawa Kozo. "Myths and Tale Literature." *Japanese Journal of Religious Studies* 9(2–3) (1982): 115–125.

Kuzume Yoshi. "Images of Japanese Women in U.S. Writings and Scholarly Works, 1860–1990." *U.S.-Japan Women's Journal* (English Supplement) 1 (1991): 6–50.

LaFleur, William R. *The Karma of Words: Buddhism and the Literary Arts in Medieval Japan*. Berkeley: University of California Press, 1983.

LaFleur, William R. "Paradigm Lost, Paradigm Regained: Groping for the Mind of Medieval Japan." *Eastern Buddhist*, New Series, 18(2) (1985): 99–113.

LaFleur, William R. "Hungry Ghosts and Hungry People: Somaticity and Rationality in Medieval Japan," in *Fragments for a History of the Human Body*, ed. by Ramona Naddaff, Nadia Tazi and Michel Feher. New York: Urzone, Inc., 1989, 271–303.

LaFleur, William R. *Liquid Life: Abortion and Buddhism in Japan*. Princeton, NJ: Princeton University Press, 1992.

LaFleur, William R. "Abortion in Japan: Towards a 'Middle Way' for the West?" In *Buddhism and Abortion*, ed. by Damien Keown. Honolulu: University of Hawaii Press, 1999, 67–92.

Lai, Whalen. "Buddhism and the Manners of Death in Japan: Extending Aries' Histoire de mentalite de la mort." *Pacific World*, New Series, 9 (1993): 69–89.

Lamotte, Étienne. *History of Indian Buddhism*. Trans. from French by Sara Webb-Boin (under the supervision of Jean Dantinne). Louvain-La-Neuve: Institut Orientaliste, 1988.

Layne, Linda L. "'Never Such Innocence Again': Irony, Nature, and Technoscience in Narratives of Pregnancy Loss." In *The Anthropology of Pregnancy Loss*, ed. by Rosanne Cecil. Oxford: Berg Publishers Limited, 1996, 131–152.

Layne, Linda L. "Breaking the Silence: An Agenda for a Feminist Discourse of Pregnancy Loss." *Feminist Studies* 23(2) (1997): 289–315.

Layne, Linda L. "True Gifts from God': Motherhood, Sacrifice, and Enrichment in the Case of Pregnancy Loss." In *Transformative Motherhood: On Giving and Getting in a Consumer Culture*, ed. by Linda L. Layne. New York: New York University Press, 1999, 167–214.

Layne, Linda L., ed. *Transformative Motherhood: On Giving and Getting in a Consumer Culture*. New York: New York University Press, 1999.

Layne, Linda L. *Motherhood Lost: A Feminist Account of Pregnancy Loss in America*. New York: Routledge, 2003.

Lebra, Takie Sugiyama. "Ancestral Influence on the Suffering of Descendents in a Japanese Cult." In *Ancestors*, ed. by William H. Newell. The Hague: Mouton Publishers, 1974, 219–230.

Lebra Joyce, Joy Paulson, and Elizabeth Powers, eds. *Women in Changing Japan*. Stanford, CA: Stanford University Press, 1976.

Lebra, Takie Sugiyama. *Japanese Women: Constraint and Fulfillment*. Honolulu: University of Hawaii Press, 1984.

Lebra, Takie Sugiyama. *Above the Clouds: Status Culture of the Modern Japanese Nobility*. Berkeley: University of California Press, 1993.

Lebra, Takie Sugiyama. "Fractionated Motherhood: Status and Gender among the Japanese Elite." *U.S.-Japan Women's Journal* (English Supplement) 4 (1993): 3–25.

Lee, Jung Young, ed. *Ancestor Worship and Christianity in Korea*. Lewiston, NY: Edwin Mellen Press, 1988.

Lee, Kwang Kyu. "The Concept of Ancestors and Ancestor Worship in Korea." *Asian Folklore Studies* 43 (1984): 199–214.

Lemert, Charles C. and Garth Gillan. *Michel Foucault: Social Theory as Transgression*. New York: Columbia University Press, 1982.

Leon, Irving G. *When a Baby Dies: Psychotherapy for Pregnancy and Newborn Loss*. New Haven, CT: Yale University Press, 1990.

Lifton, Robert Jay. *The Broken Connection: On Death and the Continuity of Life*. New York: Basic Books, Inc. Publishers, 1983.

Lippit, Noriko Mizuta and Kyoko Iriye Selden, eds. *Stories by Contemporary Japanese Women Writers*. Armonk, NY: M.E. Sharpe Inc., 1982.

Lock, Margaret. "Protests of a Good Wife and Wise Mother: The Medicalization of Distress in Japan." In *Health, Illness, and Medical Care in Japan: Cultural and Social Dimensions*, ed. by Edward Norbeck and Margaret Lock. Honolulu: University of Hawaii Press, 1987, 130–157.

Lock, Margaret. "The Selfish Housewife and Menopausal Syndrome in Japan." In *Working Papers in International Development*. East Lansing: Michigan State University, 1987, 1–5.

Lock, Margaret. "New Japanese Mythologies: Faltering Discipline and the Ailing Housewife." *American Ethnologist* 15(1) (1988): 43–61.

Lock, Margaret. *Encounters with Aging: Mythologes of Menopause in Japan and North America*. Berkeley: University of California Press, 1993.

Long, Susan Orpett. "Family Change and the Life Course in Japan." In *Cornell East Asia Papers*. Ithaca, NY: Cornell University, 1987.

Loughbridge, Mark Page. "Sculptured Friends: A Living Japanese Folk Religion." A.B. thesis in East Asian Studies, Harvard University, Cambridge, MA, 1988.

Luker, Kristin. *Abortion and the Politics of Motherhood*. Berkeley: University of California Press, 1984.

Mackie, Vera. "Division of Labour: Multinational Sex in Asia." In *The Japanese Trajectory: Modernization and Beyond*, ed. by Gavan McCormack and Yoshio Sugimoto. Cambridge: Cambridge University Press, 1988, 218–232.

Mackie, Vera. "Feminist Politics in Japan." *New Left Review* 167 (1988): 53–76.

Maeda Takashi. "Ancestor Worship in Japan: Facts and History," in *Ancestors*, ed. by William H. Newell. The Hague: Mouton Publishers, 1974.

Marcure, Kenneth A. "The Danka System." *Monumenta Nipponica* 40(1) (1985): 39–67.

Marra, Michel. "The Development of Mappō Thought in Japan." *Japanese Journal of Religious Studies* 15(1) (1988): 25–54; 15(4) (1988): 287–305.

Marsella, Anthony, George DeVos, and Francis L.K. Hsu, eds. *Culture and Self*. New York: Tavistock Publications, 1985.

Martin, Emily. "Gender and Ideological Differences in Representations of Life and Death." In *Death Ritual in Late Imperial and Modern China*, ed. by James L. Watson and Evelyn S. Rawski. Berkeley: University of California Press, 1988, 164–179.

Masami Ohinata. "The Mystique of Motherhood: A Key to Understanding Social Change and Family Problems in Japan." In *Japanese Women: New Feminist Perspectives on the Past, Present, and Future*, ed. by Kumiko Fujimura-Fanselow and Atsuko Kameda. New York: Feminist Press, 1995, 199–212.

Masuda Kokichi. "Bride's Progress: How a Yome Becomes a Shutome." In *Adult Episodes in Japan*, ed. by David W. Plath. Leiden: E.J. Brill, 1975, 10–19.

Mathews, Gordon. *What Makes Life Worth Living: How Japanese and Americans Make Sense of Their Worlds*. Berkeley: University of California Press, 1996.

Matsunaga, Daigan and Alicia Matsunaga. *The Buddhist Concept of Hell*. New York: Philosophical Library, Inc., 1972.

McCarthy, Paul. "Images of Woman as Mother in Tanizaki's Fiction." *Transactions of the Asiatic Society of Japan* Fourth Series, 1 (1986): 23–44.

McClain, Yoko. "Eroticism and the Writings of Enchi Fumiko." *Journal of the Association of Teachers of Japanese* 15(1) (1981): 32–46.

McCormack, Gavan and Yoshio Sugimoto, eds. *The Japanese Trajectory: Modernization and Beyond*. Cambridge: Cambridge University Press, 1988.

McDaniel, Justin T. "Transformative History: Nihon Ryōiki and Jinakalamalipakaranam." *Journal of the International Association of Buddhist Studies* 25(1–2) (2002): 151–207.

McDonnell, Jane Taylor. *News from the Border: A Mother's Memoir of Her Autistic Son.* New York: Ticknor and Fields, 1993.

McDonnell, Kathleen. *Not an Easy Choice: A Feminist Re-Examines Abortion.* Boston: South End Press, 1984.

McKinstry, John A. and Asako Nakajima McKinstry. *Jinsei Annai (Life's Guide): Glimpses of Japan through a Popular Advice Column.* New York: M.E. Sharpe, 1991.

McMullin, Neil. "Historical and Historiographical Issues in the Study of Pre-Modern Japanese Religion." *Japanese Journal of Religious Studies* 16(1) (1989): 3–40.

Meyerhof, Barbara. "Rites of Passage: Process and Paradox." In *Celebration: Studies in Festivity and Ritual*, ed. by Victor Turner. Washington, DC: Smithsonian Institute Press, 1982, 109–135.

Millen, Leverett and Samuel Roll. "Solomon's Mothers: A Special Case of Pathological Bereavement." *American Journal of Orthopsychiatry* 55(3) (1985): 411–418.

Miller-McLemore, Bonnie J. *Also a Mother: Work and Family as Theological Dilemma.* Nashville, TN: Abingdon Press, 1994.

Minamoto Junko. "Buddhism and the Historical Construction of Sexuality in Japan." *U.S.-Japan Women's Journal* (English Supplement) 5 (1993): 87–115.

Miura Domyo. *The Forgotten Child: An Ancient Eastern Answer to a Modern Problem.* Trans. Jim Cuthbert. Henley-on-Thames, Oxfordhsire, UK: Aidan Ellis Publishing Ltd., 1983.

Miyake Yoshiko. "Doubling Expectations: Motherhood and Women's Factory Work under State Management in Japan in the 1930s and 1940s." In *Recreating Japanese Women, 1600–1945*, ed. by Gail Lee Bernstein. Berkeley: University of California Press, 1991, 267–295.

Miyazaki Fumiko and Duncan Williams. "The Intersection of the Local and the Translocal at a Sacred Site: The Case of Osorezan in Tokugawa Japan." *Japanese Journal of Religious Studies* 28(3–4) (2001): 399–440.

Mizuta Noriko. "Symposium on Women and the Family: Post-Family Alternatives." *Review of Japanese Culture and Society* 3(1) (1989).

Modell, Judith. "Review Article of *Haruko's World and the Women of Suye Mura*." *Journal of Japanese Studies* 12(1) (1986): 141–150.

Moffat, Mary Jane and Charlotte Painter, eds. "Unknown Japanese Woman (1866–1900)." In *Revelations: Diaries of Women*. New York: Vintage Books, 1974, 163–177.

Molony, Barbara. "Activism among Women in the Taishō Cotton Textile Industry." In *Recreating Japanese Women, 1600–1945*, ed. by Gail Lee Bernstein. Berkeley: University of California Press, 1991, 217–238.

Momoko Yakemi. "Menstruation Sutra Belief in Japan." *Japanese Journal of Religious Studies* 10(2–3) (1983): 229–245.

Moore, Jean Frances. "A Study of the Thirteenth Century Buddhist Tale Collection 'Senjūshō'." *Asian Literature*. New York: Columbia University, 1982, 229–245.

Mori Masato. "Konjaku monogatari-shū: Supernatural Creatures and Order." *Japanese Journal of Religious Studies* 9(2–3) (1982): 147–170.

Morioka Kiyomi. "The Appearance of "Ancestor Religion" in Modern Japan: The Years of Transition from the Meiji to the Taishō Periods." *Japanese Journal of Religious Studies* 4(2–3) (1977): 183–212.

Morley, Patricia. *The Mountain Is Moving: Japanese Women's Lives*. New York: New York University Press, 1999.

Morrell, Robert E. *Sand and Pebbles (Shasekishū): The Tales of Mujū Ichien, a Voice for Pluralism in Kamakura Buddhism*. Albany: State University of New York Press, 1985.

Morrison, Toni. *Beloved*. New York: New American Penguin Library, Inc., 1988.

Moskowitz, Marc L. *The Haunting Fetus: Abortion, Sexuality, and the Spirit World in Taiwan*. Honolulu: University Press of Hawaii, 2001.

Mulhern, Chieko Irie. "Japanese Harlequin Romances as Transcultural Woman's Fiction." *Journal of Asian Studies* 48(1) (1989): 50–70.

Mullins, Mark R. "The Place of Ancestors in Buddhism and Christianity." *Dharma World* 34 (July–September 2007): 8–11.

Mullins, Mark R. "From 'Departures' to 'Yasukuni Shrine': Caring for the Dead and the Bereaved in Contemporary Japanese Society." *Japanese Religions* 35(1–2) (2010): 101–112.

Murakami Yasusuke. "Ie Society as a Pattern of Civilization." *Journal of Japanese Studies* 10(2) (1984): 281–363.

Murray, Julia K. "Representations of Hārītī, the Mother of Demons, and the Theme of 'Raising the Alms-Bowl' in Chinese Painting." *Artibus Asiae* 43 (1981–82): 253–284.

Muta Kazue. "Images of the Family in Meiji Periodicals: The Paradox Underlying the Emergence of the 'Home.'" *U.S.-Japan Women's Journal* (English Supplement) 7 (1994): 53–71.

Nagai Michio. "Westernization and Japanization: The Early Meiji Transformation of Education." In *Tradition and Modernization in Japanese Culture*, ed. by Donald H. Shively. Princeton, NJ: Princeton University Press, 1971, 35–76.

Nagy, Margit Maria. "'How Shall We Live?': Social Change, the Family Institution and Feminism in Prewar Japan." Ph.D. diss, Department of History, University of Washington, 1981.

Nagy, Margit. "Middle-Class Working Women During the Interwar Years." In *Recreating Japanese Women, 1600–1945*, ed. by Gail Lee Bernstein. Berkeley: University of California Press, 1991, 199–216.

Nakamaki Hirochika. "Continuity and Change: Funeral Customs in Modern Japan." *Japanese Journal of Religious Studies* 13(2–3) (1986): 177–192.

Nakamura, Kyoko Motomochi, trans. *Miraculous Stories from the Japanese Buddhist Tradition: The Nihon Ryōiki of the Monk Kyōkai.* Cambridge, MA: Harvard University Press, 1973.

Nakamura Kyoko. "Women and Religion in Japan: Introductory Remarks." *Japanese Journal of Religious Studies* 10(2–3) (1983): 115–121.

Nakane Chie. *Japanese Society.* Berkeley: University of California Press, 1970.

Namihira Emiko. "Pollution in the Folk Belief System." *Current Anthropology* 28(4) (1987): S65–S74.

Napier, Susan J. *Escape from the Wasteland: Romanticism and Realism in the Fiction of Mishima Yukio and Ōe Kenzaburō.* Cambridge, MA: Harvard University Press, 1991.

Naquin, Susan. "Funerals in North China: Uniformity and Variation." In *Death Ritual in Late Imperial and Modern China,* ed. by James L. Watson and Evelyn S. Rawski. Berkeley: University of California Press, 1987, 37–70.

Nara Yasuaki. "May the Deceased Get Enlightenment! An Aspect of the Enculturation of Buddhism in Japan." *Buddhist–Christian Studies* 15 (1995): 19–42.

Nathan, John. "Ōe Kenzaburō: Mapping the Land of Dreams." *Japan Quarterly* 42(1) (1995): 89–97.

Nathanson, Sue. *Soul Crisis: One Woman's Journey through Abortion to Renewal.* New York: New American Library, 1989.

Nattier, Jan. *Once Upon a Future Time: Studies in a Buddhist Prophecy of Decline.* Berkeley, CA: Asian Humanities Press, 1991.

Nelson, John. "Social Memory as Ritual Practice: Commemorating Spirits of the Dead at Yasukuni Shinto Shrine." *Journal of Asian Studies* 62(2) (2003): 443–467.

Nelson, John. "Household Altars in Contemporary Japan: Rectifying Buddhist 'Ancestor Worship' with Home Décor and Consumer Choice." *Japanese Journal of Religious Studies* 35(2) (2008): 305–330.

Newell, William H. "Good and Bad Ancestors." In *Ancestors,* ed. by William H. Newell. The Hague: Mouton Publishers, 1974, 17–28.

Nishikawa Yuko. "Japan's Entry into War and the Support of Women." *U.S.-Japan Women's Journal* (English Supplement) 12 (1997): 48–83.

Nishiyama Shigeru. "Indigenization and Transformation of Christianity in a Japanese Rural Community." *Japanese Journal of Religious Studies* 12 (1985): 17–61.

Niwa Akiko. "The Formation of the Myth of Motherhood in Japan." *U.S.-Japan Women's Journal* (English Supplement) 4 (1993): 70–82.

Nolte, Sharon and Sally Ann Hastings. "The Meiji State's Policy toward Women, 1890–1910." In *Recreating Japanese Women, 1600–1945,* ed. by Gail Lee Bernstein. Berkeley: University of California Press, 1991, 151–174.

Nolte, Sharon H. "Women, the State, and Repression in Imperial Japan." Office of Women in International Development, Michigan State University, 1983, 1–11.

Norgren, Tiana. "Abortion before Birth Control: The Interest Group Politics Behind Postwar Japanese Reproduction Policy." *Journal of Japanese Studies* 24(1) (1998): 59–94.

Norgren, Tiana. *Abortion before Birth Control: The Politics of Reproduction in Postwar Japan*. Princeton, NJ: Princeton University Press, 2001.

Norwood, Vera L. "The Nature of Knowing: Rachel Carson and the American Environment," *Signs: Journal of Women in Culture and Society* 12 (1987).

Nyanasobhano Bhikkhu. "A Buddhist View of Abortion." *Bodhi Leaves*, no. 117 (1989): 1–29.

O'Connor, Thomas P. "Consoling the Infants: For Whose Sake?" *Japan Christian Quarterly* (Fall 1984): 206–214.

O'Connor, Thomas P. "Death, Fear and Folk Religion in Japan: An Episode in Dialogue." *Bulletin Secretariatus pro Non-Christianis* 21 (1986): 62–79.

Oaks, Laury. "Fetal Spirithood and Fetal Personhood: The Cultural Construction of Abortion in Japan." *Women's Studies International Forum* 17(5) (1994): 511–523.

Ochiai Emiko. "The Modern Family and Japanese Culture: Exploring the Japanese Mother-Child Relationship." *Review of Japanese Culture and Society* 3(1). Special Issue on Women and the Family) (1989): 7–15.

Ochiai Emiko. "The Reproductive Revolution at the End of the Tokugawa Period." In *Women and Class in Japanese History*, ed. by Anne Walthall, Wakita Haruko, and Tonomura Hotomi. Ann Arbor: Center for Japanese Studies, University of Michigan, 1999, 187–215.

Ōe Kenzaburō. *A Personal Matter*. Trans. John Nathan. New York: Grove Press, Inc., 1968.

Ogino Miho, facilitator. "Symposium—Women and the Family: Post-Family Alternatives." *Review of Japanese Culture and Society* 3(1) (1989): 79–96.

Ohnuki-Tierney, Emiko. *Illness and Culture in Contemporary Japan: An Anthropological View*. Cambridge and New York: Cambridge University Press, 1984.

Ohnuki-Tierney, Emiko. "Health Care in Contemporary Japanese Religions." In *Healing and Restoring: Health and Medicine in the World's Religious Traditions*, ed. by Lawrence E. Sullivan. New York: MacMillan Publishing Co., 1989, 59–87.

Okamoto Kanoko. "A Mother's Love." In *Rabbits, Crabs, Etc.: Stories by Japanese Women*, ed. by Phyllis Birnbaum. Honolulu: University of Hawaii Press, 1982, 51–97.

Omine Akira. "The Geneology of Sorrow: Japanese View of Life and Death." *Eastern Buddhist*, New Series, 25(2) (1992): 14–29.

Omori Maki. "Gender and the Labor Market." *Journal of Japanese Studies* 19(1) (1993): 79–102.

Ooms, Emily Groszos. *Women and Millenarian Protest in Meiji Japan: Deguchi Nao and Omotokyō*. Ithaca, NY: East Asia Program, Cornell University, 1993.

Ooms, Herman. "The Religion of the Household: A Case Study of Ancestor Worship in Japan." *Contemporary Religion in Japan* 8 (3–4) (1967): 201–333.

Ooms, Herman. "A Structural Analysis of Japanese Ancestral Rites and Beliefs." In *Ancestors*, ed. by William H. Newell. The Hague: Mouton Publishers, 1974, 61–90.

Orenstein, Peggy. "Mourning My Miscarriage: In Japan, I Find a Culture Willing to Acknowledge My Loss." *New York Times Magazine*, April 21, 2002.

Orenstein, Peggy. *Waiting for Daisy.* New York: Bloomsbury, 2007.

Otake Emiko. "Two Categories of Chinese Ancestors as Determined by Their Malevolence." *Asian Folklore Studies* 39(1) (1980): 21–31.

Ōtō Osamu. "Life and Death, Funeral Rites and Burial Systems in Early Modern Japan." *Early Modern Japan: An Interdisciplinary Journal* 19 (2011): 3–20. Trans. and Introduction Timothy D. Amos and Scot Hislop.

Parker, Rozsika. *Mother Love/ Mother Hate: The Power of Maternal Ambivalence.* New York: BasicBooks, 1995.

Pas, Julian F. "Journey to Hell: A New Report of Shamanistic Travel to the Courts of Hell." *Journal of Chinese Religions* 17 (1989).

Passin, Herbert. *Society and Education in Japan.* New York: Columbia University Teachers College and East Asian Institute, 1965, 43–60.

Paul, Diana Y. *Women in Buddhism: Images of the Feminine in Mahayana Tradition.* Berkeley, CA: Asian Humanities Press, 1979. Reprint, *Images of the Feminine in Mahayana Buddhism.* Berkeley: University of California Press, 1985.

Paulson, Joy. "Evolution of the Feminine Ideal." In *Women in Changing Japan*, ed. by Joy Paulson, Joyce Lebra, and Elizabeth Powers. Westview, CO: Westview Press, Inc., 1976, 1–23.

Paz, Octavio. *Conjunctions and Disjunctions.* Trans. Helen R. Lane. New York: Viking Press, 1974, 10.

Peri, Noël. "Hārītī la mère-de-démons." *Bulletin de l'École Française d'Extrême-Orient* 17(3) (1917): 1–102.

Perry, Linda L. "Being Socially Anomalous: Wives and Mothers without Husbands." In *Adult Episodes in Japan*, ed. by David W. Plath. Leiden: E.J. Brill, 1975, 32–41.

Pharr, Susan J. *Political Women in Japan: The Search for a Place in Political Life.* Berkeley: University of California Press, 1981.

Pharr, Susan J. "The Japanese Woman: Evolving Views of Life and Role." In *Asian Women in Transition*, ed. by Sylvia A. Chipp and Justin J. Green. University Park: Pennsylvania State University Press, 1980, 36–61.

Picone, Mary J. "Buddhist Popular Manuals and the Contemporary Commercialization of Religion in Japan." In *Interpreting Japanese Society: Anthropological Approaches*, ed. by Joy Hendry and Jonathan Webber. Oxford: JASO Occasional Papers, 1986, 157–161.

Picone, Mary J. "The Ghost in the Machine: Religious Healing and Representations of the Body in Japan." In *Fragments for a History of the Human Body, Part Two*, ed. by Michel Feher. New York: Urzone Inc., 1989, 467–489.

Plaskow, Judith and Carol P. Christ, eds. *Weaving the Visions: New Patterns in Feminist Spirituality.* San Francisco: Harper & Row, 1989.

Plath, David W. "Where the Family of God Is the Family: The Role of the Dead in Japanese Households." *American Anthropologist* 66 (1964): 300–317.

Pounds, Wayne. "Enchi Fumiko and the Hidden Energy of the Supernatural." *Journal of the Association of Teachers of Japanese* 24(2) (1990): 167–183.

Premasiri, P.D. "Significance of the Ritual Concerning Offerings to Ancestors in Theravāda Buddhism." In *Buddhist Thought and Ritual*, ed. by David Kalupahana. New York: Paragon House, 1991, 151–158.

Pye, Michael. *Skilful Means: A Concept in Mahayana Buddhism*. London: Gerald Duckworth & Co, Ltd., 1978.

Rambelli, Fabio. "Home Buddhas: Historical Processes and Modes of Representation of the Sacred in the Japanese Buddhist Family Altar (Butsudan)." *Japanese Religions* 35(1–2) (2010): 63–86.

Rand, Yvonne. "Jizo: Protector of Travelers into and out of Life" (rev., 2012): 1–3.

Reader, Ian. "Letters to the Gods—The Form and Meaning of Ema." *Japanese Journal of Religious Studies* 18(1) (1991): 23–50.

Reader, Ian. "Recent Japanese Publications on New Religions: The Work of Shimazono Susumu." *Japanese Journal of Religious Studies* 20(2–3) (1993): 229–248.

Reader, Ian. "Review of Liquid Life: Abortion and Buddhism in Japan by William R. LaFleur." *Journal of Japanese Studies* 21(1) (1995): 195–200.

Reader, Ian. "Social Action and Personal Benefits in Contemporary Japanese Buddhism." *Buddhist–Christian Studies* 15 (1995): 3–17.

Reader, Ian and George J. Tanabe Jr. *Practically Religious: Worldly Benefits and the Common Religion of Japan*. Honolulu: University of Hawaii Press, 1998.

Reid, David. "Japanese Christians and the Ancestors." *Japanese Journal of Religious Studies* 16(4) (1989): 259–283.

Remennick, Larissa I. "Patterns of Birth Control." In *Sex and Russian Society*, ed. by Igor Kon. Bloomington: Indiana University Press, 1993, 45–63.

Reuther, Rosemary. *Women-Church: Theology and Practice of Feminist Liturgical Communities*. San Francisco: Harper and Row, 1988.

Reynolds, Frank E. and Mani B. Reynolds. *Three Worlds According to King Ruang: A Thai Buddhist Cosmology*. Berkeley, CA: Asian Humanities Press, 1982.

Rhodes, Lorna Amarasingham. "Time and the Process of Diagnosis in Sinhalese Ritual Treatment." *Contributions to Asian Studies* 18 (1984): 46–58.

Roberts, Glenda S. *Staying on the Line: Blue Collar Women in Contemporary Japan*. Honolulu: University of Hawaii Press, 1994.

Roberts, Jennifer. "The Shingaku Woman: Straight from the Heart." In *Recreating Japanese Women, 1600–1945*, ed. by Gail Lee Bernstein. Berkeley: University of California Press, 1991, 88–107.

Rodd, Laurel Rasplica. "Yosano Akiko and the Taishō Debate over the 'New Woman.'" In *Recreating Japanese Women, 1600–1945*, ed. by Gail Lee Bernstein. Berkeley: University of California Press, 1991, 175–198.

Rose, Barbara. *Tsuda Umeko and Women's Education in Japan*. New Haven, CT: Yale University Press, 1992.

Rosenberger, Nancy. "Fragile Resistance, Signs of Status: Women between State and Media in Japan." In *Re-imaging Japanese Women*, ed. by Anne E. Imamura. Berkeley: University of California Press, 1996, 12–45.

Rosenberger, Nancy. *Gambling with Virtue: Japanese Women and the Search for Self in a Changing Nation*. Honolulu: University of Hawaii Press, 2001, 277.

Rosenblatt, Paul C. *Bitter, Bitter Tears: Nineteenth-Century Diarists and Twentieth Century Grief Theories*. Minneapolis: University of Minnesota Press, 1983.

Rosenblatt, Paul C. *Parent Grief: Narratives of Loss and Relationship*. The Series in Death, Dying, and Bereavement. Philadelphia, PA: Brunner/Mazel, a member of the Taylor & Francis Group, 2000.

Rowe, Mark. "Grave Changes: Scattering Ashes in Contemporary Japan." In *The Buddhist Dead: Practices, Discourses, Representations*, ed. by Bryan J. Cuevas and Jacqueline Ilyse Stone. Honolulu: University of Hawaii Press, 2007, 405–437.

Rowe, Mark. "Where the Action Is: Sites in Contemporary Sōtō Buddhism." *Japanese Journal of Religious Studies* 31(2) (2004): 357–388.

Ruch, Barbara. "Coping with Death: Paradigms of Heaven and Hell and the Six Realms in Early Literature and Painting." In *Flowing Traces: Buddhism in the Literary and Visual Arts of Japan*, ed. by James H. Sanford, William R. LaFleur, and Masatoshi Nagatomi. Princeton, NJ: Princeton University Press, 1992, 93–130.

Ruch, Barbara. "Medieval Jongleurs and the Making of a National Literature." In *Japan in the Muromachi Age*, ed. by John Whitney Hall and Takeshi Toyoda. Berkeley: University of California Press, 1977.

Ruch, Barbara, ed. *Engendering Faith: Women and Buddhism in Premodern Japan*. Ann Arbor: Center for Japanese Studies, University of Michigan, 2002.

Russo, Ann. "Conflicts and Contradictions among Feminists over Issues of Pornography and Sexual Freedom." *Women's Studies International Forum* 10(2) (1987): 103–112.

Sadakata Akira. "The Buddhist View of the Universe Today." *Dharma World*, November–December 1994.

Saddhatissa, Hammalawa. "The Significance of *Paritta* and Its Application in the Theravada Tradition." In *Buddhist Thought and Ritual*, ed. by David Kalupahana. New York: Paragon House, 1991, 125–137.

Saikaku Ihara. *The Life of an Amorous Woman, and Other Writings*. Norfolk, CT: New Directions, 1963.

Saitō Osamu. "Infanticide, Fertility and 'Population Stagnation': The State of Tokugawa Historical Demography." *Japan Forum* 4(2) (1992): 369–381.

Salamon, Sonya. "'Male Chauvinism' as a Manifestation of Love in Marriage." In *Adult Episodes in Japan*, ed. by David W. Plath. Leiden: E.J.Brill, 1975, 20–31.

Sanford, James H., William R. LaFleur, and Masatoshi Nagatomi, eds. *Flowing Traces: Buddhism in the Literary and Visual Arts*. Princeton, NJ: Princeton University Press, 1992.

Sasaki Shōten. "Shinshū and Folk Religion: Toward a Post-Modern Shinshū 'Theology.'" *Nanzan Bulletin* 12 (1988): 23–35.

Savage, Judith A. *Mourning Unlived Lives: A Psychological Study of Childbearing Loss.* Wilmette, IL: Chiron Publications. 1989.

Sawayama Mikako. "The 'Birthing Body' and the Regulation of Conception and Childbirth in the Edo Period." *U.S.-Japan Women's Journal (English Supplement)* 24 (2003): 10–34.

Sawicki, Jana. *Disciplining Foucault: Feminism, Power, and the Body.* New York: Routledge, Chapman and Hall, Inc., 1991.

Schalow, Paul Gordon and Janet A. Walker, eds. *The Woman's Hand: Gender and Theory in Japanese Women's Writing.* Stanford, CA: Stanford University Press, 1996.

Schopen, Gregory. *Bones, Stones, and Buddhist Monks: Collected Papers on the Archeology, Epigraphy, and Texts of Monastic Buddhism in India.* Honolulu: University of Hawaii Press, 1997.

Scott, David. *Formations of Ritual: Colonial and Anthropological Discourses on the Sinhala 'Yaktovil'.* Minneapolis: University of Minnesota Press, 1994.

Scott, James C. *Weapons of the Weak: Everyday Forms of Peasant Resistance.* New Haven, CT: Yale University Press, 1985.

Scott, James C. *Domination and the Arts of Resistance: Hidden Transcripts.* New Haven, CT: Yale University Press, 1990.

Seckel, Dietrich. "Kariteimo: Die 'Buddhistische Madonna' in der Japanischen Kunst." *Deutsche Gesellschaft für Natur- und Volkerkunde Ostasiens* (1943): 1–53 and Plates 1–20.

Seftel, Laura. *Grief Unseen: Healing Pregnancy Loss through the Arts.* London: Jessica Kingsley Publishers, 2006.

Seraphim, Franziska. *War Memory and Social Politics in Japan, 1945–2005.* Cambridge, MA: Harvard University Press, 2006.

Sered, Susan. "The Domestication of Religion: The Spiritual Guardianship of Elderly Jewish Women." *Man*, New Series, 23(3) (1988): 506–521.

Sered, Susan. "Mother Love, Child Death and Religious Innovation: A Feminist Perspective." *Journal of Feminist Studies in Religion* 12(1) (1996): 5–23.

Sered, Susan Starr. "Childbirth as a Religious Experience?: Voices from an Israeli Hospital." *Journal of Feminist Studies in Religion* 7(2) (1991): 7–18.

Sered, Susan Starr. *Women as Ritual Experts: The Religious Lives of Elderly Jewish Women in Jerusalem.* Oxford: Oxford University Press, 1992.

Sered, Susan Starr. *Priestess, Mother, Sacred Sister: Religions Dominated by Women.* Oxford: Oxford University Press, 1994.

Shibata Chizuo. "Some Problematic Aspects of Japanese Ancestor Worship." *Japanese Religions* 13(1) (1983): 25–48.

Shigematsu Setsu. "'The Law of the Same' and Other (Non)-Perversions: Woman's Body as a 'Use-Me/Rape-Me' Signifier." *U.S.-Japan Women's Journal (English Supplement)* 12 (1997): 154–177.

Shimazu Yoshiko. "Unmarried Mothers and Their Children in Japan." *U.S.-Japan Women's Journal (English Supplement)* 6 (1994): 83–110.

Shinno Toshikazu. "From Minkan-shinkō to Minzoku-shūkyō: Reflections on the Study of Folk Buddhism." *Japanese Journal of Religious Studies* 20 (2–3) (1993): 187–206.

Shiokawa Kanako. *Children of the Bright Light: A Folkloric Inquiry into a "True-Light" Religious Sect in Japanese Cosmological Contexts* in Graduate School of Arts and Sciences. Philadelphia: University of Pennsylvania, 1994.

Shively, Donald H. "Motoda Eifu: Confucian Lecturer to the Meiji Emperor." In *Confucianism in Action*, ed. by David S. Wright, David S. Nivison, and Arthur F. Wright. Stanford, CA: Stanford University Press, 1959.

Shively, Donald H. "The Japanization of the Middle Meiji." In *Tradition and Modernization in Japanese Culture*, ed. by David S. Nivison and Arthur F. Wright. Princeton, NJ: Princeton University Press, 1971, 77–119.

Sievers, Sharon L. "Feminist Criticism in Japanese Politics in the 1880s: The Experience of Kishida Toshiko." *Signs: Journal of Women in Culture and Society* 6(4) (1981): 602–616.

Sievers, Sharon L. *Flowers in Salt: The Beginnings of Feminist Consciousness in Modern Japan*. Stanford, CA: Stanford University Press, 1983.

Silverberg, Miriam. "The Modern Girl as Militant." In *Recreating Japanese Women, 1600–1945*, ed. by Gail Lee Bernstein. Berkeley: University of California Press, 1991, 239–266.

Slater, Philip E. *The Glory of Hera: Greek Mythology and the Greek Family*. Boston: Beacon Press, 1968.

Smith, Bardwell. "Buddhism and Abortion in Contemporary Japan: Mizuko Kuyō and the Confrontation with Death." *Japanese Journal of Religious Studies* 15(1) (1988): 3–24.

Smith, Bardwell. "The Social Contexts of Healing: Research and Grieving in Japan." In *Innovations in Religious Traditions: Essays in the Interpretation of Religious Change*, ed. by Michael A. Williams, Collett Cox, and Martin S. Jaffee. Berlin: Mouton de Gruyter, 1992, 285–317.

Smith, Jonathan Z. *To Take Place: Toward Theory in Ritual*. Chicago: University of Chicago Press, 1987.

Smith, Robert J. *Ancestor Worship in Contemporary Japan*. Stanford, CA: Stanford University Press, 1974.

Smith, Robert J. "Who Are the 'Ancestors' in Japan?: A 1963 Census of Memorial Tablets." In *Ancestors*, ed. by W. H. Newell. The Hague: Mouton Publishers, 1974, 33–60.

Smith, Robert J. *Kurusu: The Price of Progress in a Japanese Village, 1951–1975*. Stanford, CA: Stanford University Press, 1978.

Smith, Robert J. and Ella Lury Wiswell. *The Women of Suye Mura*. Chicago: University of Chicago Press, 1982.

Smith, Robert J. "Making Village Women into 'Good Wives and Wise Mothers' in Prewar Japan." *Journal of Family History* 8(3) (1983): 70–84.

Smith, Robert J. "Ancestor Worship in Contemporary Japan." *Nanzan Bulletin* (1983): 30–40.

Smith, Robert J. *Japanese Society: Tradition, Self, and the Social Order.* Cambridge: Cambridge University Press, 1983.

Smith, Robert J. "Gender Inequality in Contemporary Japan." *Journal of Japanese Studies* 13(1) (1987): 1–25.

Smith, Robert J. "The Living and the Dead in Japanese Popular Religion." In *Lives in Motion: Composing Circles of Self and Community in Japan,* ed. by Susan O. Long. Ithaca, NY: Cornell University, 1999, 255–281.

Smith, Ruth L. "Feminism and the Moral Subject." In *Women's Consciousness, Women's Conscience: A Reader in Feminist Ethics,* ed. by Barbara Hilkert Andolsen, et al. San Francisco: Harper and Row, 1985.

Smith, Thomas C. *Nakahara: Family Farming and Population in a Japanese Village, 1717–1830.* Stanford, CA: Stanford University Press, 1977.

Sono Ayako. *Watcher from the Shore.* Trans. Edward Putzar. Tokyo: Kodansha International Ltd., 1990.

Souder, William. *On a Farther Shore: The Life and Legacy of Rachel Carson.*
New York: Crown Publishers, 2012.

Spelman, Elizabeth V. *Inessential Woman: Problems of Exclusion in Feminist Thought.* Boston: Beacon Press, 1988.

Stoesz, Willis. "Death and the Affirmation of Life: Robert Lifton's 'Sense of Immortality.'" *Soundings: An Interdisciplinary Journal* 62(2) (1979): 187–208.

Stone, Jackie. "Seeking Enlightenment in the Last Age: Mappō Thought in Kamakura Buddhism (Part I)." *Eastern Buddhist,* New Series, 18(1) (1985): 28–56.

Stone, Jacqueline I. and Mariko Namba Walter, eds. *Death and the Afterlife in Japanese Buddhism.* Honolulu: University of Hawaii Press, 2008.

Stone, Jacqueline I. and Mariko Namba Walter, eds. "Introduction." In *Death and the Afterlife in Japanese Buddhism.* Honolulu: University of Hawaii Press, 2008, 1–26.

Strong, John S. *The Legend and Cult of Upagupta: Sanskrit Buddhism in North India and Southeast Asia.* Princeton, NJ: Princeton University Press, 1992.

Sūtra of the Past Vows of the Earth-Store Bodhisattva: The Collected Lectures of Tripiṭaka Master Hsüan Hua. Trans. Heng Ching. New York: Buddhist Text Translation Society and the Institute for Advance Studies of World Religions, 1974.

Suzuki Hikaru. *The Price of Death: The Funeral Industry in Contemporary Japan.* Stanford, CA: Stanford University Press, 2000.

Suzuki, Kentarō. "Divination in Contemporary Japan: A General Overview and an Analysis of Survey Results." *Japanese Journal of Religious Studies* 22(3–4) (1995): 249–266.

Swanger, Eugene R. "A Preliminary Examination of the Omamori Phenomenon." *Asian Folklore Studies* 40(2) (1981): 237–252.

Swyngedouw, Jan. "In Search of a Church with a Japanese Face: The Problem of Ancestor Veneration." *Japan Missionary Bulletin* 37 (1983): 360–366.

Swyngedouw, Jan. "The Japanese Church and Ancestor Veneration Practices: The Mahayanization of Japanese Catholicism?" *Japan Missionary Bulletin* 39(2) (1985): 56–65.

Tabata Yasuko. "Women's Work and Status in the Changing Medieval Economy." In *Women and Class in Japanese History*, ed. by Anne Walthall, Tonomura Hotomi, and Wakita Haruko. Ann Arbor: Center for Japanese Studies, University of Michigan, 1999, 99–118.

Tadesco, Frank M. "Rites for the Unborn Dead: Abortion and Buddhism in Contemporary Korea." *Korea Journal* 36(2) (1996): 61–74.

Taeuber, Irene B. *The Population of Japan*. Princeton, NJ: Princeton University Press, 1958.

Takahashi Michiko. "Working Mothers and Families." *Review of Japanese Culture and Society* 3(1), (Special Issue on Women and the Family) (1989): 21–30.

Takahashi Tetsuya. "Legacies of Empire: The Yasukuni Shrine Controversy." In *Yasukuni, the War Dead, and the Struggle for Japan's Past*, ed. by John Breen. New York: Columbia University Press, 2008, 105–124.

Takakusu, Junjirō. *The Essentials of Buddhist Philosophy*, 3d ed., ed. by Wing-tsit Chan and Charles A. Moore. Honolulu: University of Hawaii, 1956.

Takeda Choshu. "'Family Religion' in Japan: Ie and Its Religious Faith." In *Ancestors*, ed. by William H. Newell. The Hague: Mouton Publishers, 1974, 119–128.

Takemi Momoko. "'Menstruation Sutra' Belief in Japan." *Japanese Journal of Religious Studies* 10(2–3) (1983): 229–246.

Takenaka Akiko. "Politics of Representation or Representation of Politics? Yasukuni the Film." *Review of Japanese Culture and Society* 21 (December 2009): 117–136.

Tama Yasuko. "The Logic of Abortion: Japanese Debates on the Legitimacy of Abortion as Seen in Post-World War II Newspapers." *U.S.-Japan Women's Journal (English Supplement)* 7 (1994): 3–30.

Tamamuro Fumio. "Local Society and the Temple-Parishioner Relationship within the Bakufu's Governance Structure." *Japanese Journal of Religious Studies* 28(3–4) (2001): 261–292.

Tamamuro Fumio. "The Development of the Temple-Parishioner System." *Japanese Journal of Religious Studies* 36(1) (2009): 11–26.

Tamanoi Mariko Asano. "Songs as Weapons: The Culture and History of Komori (Nursemaids) in Modern Japan." *Journal of Asian Studies* 50(4) (1990): 793–817.

Tamanoi Mariko Asano. "Women's Voices: Their Critique of the Anthropology of Japan." *Annual Review of Anthropology* 19 (1990): 17–37.

Tamanoi Mariko Asano. *Under the Shadow of Nationalism: Politics and Poetics of Rural Japanese Women*. Honolulu: University of Hawaii, 1998.

Tamanoi Mariko Asano. "Japanese Nationalism and the Female Body: A Critical Reassessment of the Discourse of Social Reformers on Factory Women." In

Women and Class in Japanese History, ed. by Anne Walthall, Tonomura Hotomi, and Wakita Haruko. Ann Arbor: Center for Japanese Studies, University of Michigan, 1999, 275–298.

Tambiah, Stanley. *Culture, Thought, and Social Action: An Anthropological Perspective.* Cambridge, MA: Harvard University Press, 1985, especially pp. 123–166.

Tanabe, George. "Review of *Liquid Life: Abortion and Buddhism in Japan* by William F. Lafleur." *Japanese Journal of Religious Studies* 21(4) (1994): 437–440.

Tanabe, George J. "The Orthodox Heresy of Buddhist Funerals." In *Death and the Afterlife in Japanese Buddhism*, ed. by Jacqueline I. Stone and Mariko Namba Walter. Honolulu: University of Hawaii Press, 2008, 325–364.

Tanaka Masako. "Categories of Okinawan 'Ancestors' and the Kinship System." *Asian Studies Folklore* 36(2) (1977): 31–64.

Tanaka, Mark Makoto. "Mizuko Kuyō, Memorial Rites for Aborted and Miscarried Fetuses in Japan: An Anthropological Study." Cambridge, MA: Harvard University, 1991.

Taniguchi Shoyo. "A Study of Biomedical Ethics from a Buddhist Perspective." Berkeley, CA: Graduate Theological Union and Institute of Buddhist Studies, 1987.

Taniguchi Shoyo. "Biomedical Ethics from a Buddhist Perspective." *Pacific World: Journal of the Institute of Buddhist Studies,* New Series, 3 (1987): 75–83.

Tanizaki Junichiro. "Bridge of Dreams." In *Seven Japanese Tales*, ed. by Tanizaki Junichiro. London: Secker and Warburg, 1963.

Taylor, Charles. *The Ethics of Authenticity.* Cambridge, MA: Harvard University Press, 1992.

Teiser, Stephen F. "Ghosts and Ancestors in Medieval Chinese Religion: The Yü-Lan-P'en Festival as Mortuary Ritual." *History of Religions* 26(1) (1986): 47–67.

Teiser, Stephen F. "'Having Once Died and Returned to Life': Representations of Hell in Medieval China." *Harvard Journal of Asiatic Studies* 48 (1988): 433–464.

Teiser, Stephen F. *The Ghost Festival in Medieval China.* Princeton, NJ: Princeton University Press, 1988.

Teiser, Stephen F. *The Scripture on the Ten Kings and the Making of Purgatory in Medieval Chinese Buddhism.* Honolulu: Kuroda Institute, University of Hawaii Press, 1994.

Teiser, Stephen F. *Reinventing the Wheel: Paintings of Rebirth in Medieval Buddhist Temples.* Seattle: University of Washington Press, 2006.

Ten Grotenhuis, Elizabeth. *Japanese Mandalas: Representations of Sacred Geography.* Honolulu: University of Hawaii Press, 1999.

Tonomura Hitomi, Anne Walthall, and Wakita Haruko, eds. *Women and Class in Japanese History.* Ann Arbor: Michigan Monograph Series in Japanese Studies, Center for Japanese Studies, University of Michigan, 1999.

Toshitani Nobuyoshi. "The Reform of Japanese Family Law and Changes in the Family System." *U.S.-Japan Women's Journal* (English Supplement) 6 (1994): 66–82.

Traphagan, John W. *The Practice of Concern: Ritual, Well-Being, and Aging in Rural Japan*. Durham, NC: Carolina Academic Press, 2004.

Traphagan, John W. "Heroes of the Antimodern: 'Respect for the Elderly Day' and Writing the Narrative of the Elder Generation in Japan." *Journal of Ritual Studies* 19(2) (2005): 99–113.

Tsurumi, E. Patricia. *Factory Girls: Women in the Thread Mills in Meiji Japan*. Princeton, NJ: Princeton University Press, 1990.

Tsurumi Kazuko. *Social Change and the Individual: Japan before and after Defeat in World War II*. Princeton, NJ: Princeton University Press, 1970.

Tucker, Mary Evelyn. "Religious Aspects of Japanese Neo-Confucianism: The Thought of Nakae Tōju and Kaibara Ekken." *Japanese Journal of Religious Studies* 15(1) (1988): 55–69.

Tucker, Mary Evelyn. *Moral and Spiritual Cultivation in Japanese Neo-Confucianism: The Life and Thought of Kaibara Ekken, 1630–1714*. Albany: State University of New York, 1989.

Turner, Victor. "Death and the Dead in the Pilgrimage Process." In *Religious Encounters with Death*, ed. by Frank E. Reynolds and Earle H. Waugh. University Park: Pennsylvania State University Press, 1977, 24–39.

Turner, Victor. *Process, Performance and Pilgrimage: A Study in Comparative Symbology*. New Delhi: Concept Publishing Company, 1979.

Turner, Victor. *From Ritual to Theatre: The Human Seriousness of Play*. New York: Performing Arts Journal Publications, 1982.

Turner, Victor, ed. *Celebration: Studies in Festivity and Ritual*. Washington, DC: Smithsonian Institution Press, 1982.

Turner, Victor. "Body, Brain, and Culture." *Zygon* 18 (1983): 221–245.

Turner, Victor. "Liminality and the Performative Genres." In *Rite, Drama, Festival, Spectacle*, ed. by John J. MacAloon. Philadelphia: Institute for the Study of Human Issues, 1984, 19–41.

Turner, Victor W. "Dewey, Dilthey, and Drama: An Essay in the Anthropology of Experience." In *The Anthropology of Experience*, ed. by Victor W. Turner and Edward M. Bruner. Urbana: University of Illinois Press, 1986, 33–44.

Ueda Makoto, ed. *The Mother of Dreams, and Other Short Stories: Portrayals of Women in Modern Japanese Fiction*. Tokyo: Kodansha International, Ltd., 1986.

Ueno Chizuko. "The Position of Japanese Women Reconsidered." *Current Anthropology* 28(4) (1987): S75–S84.

Ueno Chizuko. "The Japanese Women's Movement: The Counter-Values to Industrialization." In *The Japanese Trajectory: Modernization and Beyond*, ed. by Gavan McCormack and Yoshio Sugimoto. Cambridge: Cambridge University Press, 1988, 167–185.

Ueno Chizuko. "Collapse of 'Japanese Mothers.'" *U.S.-Japan Women's Journal* (English Supplement) 10 (1996): 3–19.

Ueno Chizuko. "In the Feminine Guise: A Trap of Reverse Orientalism." *U.S.-Japan Women's Journal* (English Supplement) 13 (1997): 3–25.

Ueno Chizuko. *The Modern Family in Japan: Its Rise and Fall*. Trans. Ayako Kono. Melbourne: Trans Pacific Press, 2009.

Underwood, Meredith. "Strategies of Survival: Women, Abortion, and Popular Religion in Contemporary Japan." *Journal of the American Academy of Religion* 67(4) (1999).

Uno, Kathleen S. *Day Care and Family Life in Industrializing Japan, 1868–1926*. Berkeley: University of California, 1987.

Uno, Kathleen S. "'Children Are Treasures': A History of Children in Modern Japan." In *Children in Historical and Comparative Perspective: An International Handbook*, ed. by Joseph Hawes and N. Ray Hiner. Westport, CT: Greenwood Press, 1990, 389–419.

Uno, Kathleen S. "Women and Changes in the Household Division of Labor." In *Recreating Japanese Women, 1600–1945*, ed. by Gail Lee Bernstein. Berkeley: University of California Press, 1991, 17–41.

Uno, Kathleen S. "The Death of 'Good Wife, Wise Mother?'" In *Postwar Japan as History*, ed. by Andrew Gordon. Berkeley: University of California Press, 1993, 293–322.

Uno, Kathleen. "Questioning Patrilineality: On Western Studies of the Japanese Ie." *Positions* 4(3) (1996): 569–594.

Uno, Kathleen S. *Passages to Modernity: Motherhood, Childhood, and Social Reform in Early Twentieth Century Japan*. Honolulu: University of Hawaii Press, 1999.

Ury, Marian. *Tales of Times Now Past: Sixty-Two Stories from a Medieval Japanese Collection*. Berkeley: University of California Press, 1979.

Vogel, Suzanne H. "Professional Housewife: The Career of Urban Middle Class Japanese Women." *Japan Interpreter* 12(1) (1978): 16–43.

Wakita Haruko. "Marriage and Property in Premodern Japan from the Perspective of Women's History." *Journal of Japanese Studies* 10(1) (1984): 7–99.

Wakita Haruko. "Women and the Creation of the Ie in Japan: An Overview from the Medieval Period to the Present." *U.S.-Japan Women's Journal (English Supplement)* 4 (1993): 83–105.

Wakita Haruko, Narita Ryūichi, Anne Walthall, and Hitomi Tonomura. "Appendix: Past Developments and Future Issues in the Study of Women's History in Japan: A Bibliographical Essay." In *Women and Class in Japanese History*, ed. by Hitomi Tonomura, Anne Walthall, and Wakita Haruko. Ann Arbor: Center for Japanese Studies, University of Michigan, 1999, 299–313.

Walter, Mariko Namba. "The Structure of Japanese Buddhist Funerals." In *Death and the Afterlife in Japanese Buddhism*, ed. by Jacqueline I. Stone and Mariko Namba Walter. Honolulu: University of Hawaii Press, 2008, 247–292.

Walter, Tony. "Emotional Reserve and the English Way of Grief." In *The Unknown Country: Death in Australia, Britain and the USA*, ed. by Kathy Charmaz, Glennys Howarth, and Allan Kellehear. New York: St. Martin's Press, Inc., 1997, 127–140.

Walter, Tony. *The Revival of Death*. London: Routledge, 1997.

Walthall, Anne. "The Life Cycle of Farm Women in Tokugawa Japan." In *Recreating Japanese Women, 1600–1945*, ed. by Gail Lee Bernstein. Berkeley: University of California Press, 1991, 42–70.

Walthall, Anne. "Matsuo Taseko and the Meiji Restoration: Texts of Self and Gender." In *Women and Class in Japanese History*, ed. by Anne Walthall, Tonomura Hitomi, and Wakita Haruko. Ann Arbor: Center for Japanese Studies, University of Michigan, 1999, 217–240.

Walthall, Anne. "The Life Cycle of Farm Women in Tokugawa Japan." In *Recreating Japanese Women, 1600–1945*, ed. by Gail Lee Bernstein. Berkeley: University of California Press, 1991, 42–70.

Welter, Barbara. "The Cult of True Womanhood: 1820–1860." *American Quarterly* (18) 1966: 151–174.

Werblowsky, R. J. Zwi. "Mizuko Kuyō: Notulae on the Most Important 'New Religion' of Japan." *Japanese Journal of Religious Studies* 18(4) (1991): 295–354.

White, Merry. "The Virtue of Japanese Mothers: Cultural Definitions of Women's Lives." *Daedalus* 116(3) (1987): 149–163.

White, Merry. *The Japanese Educational Challenge: A Commitment to Children*. Tokyo: Kodansha International, 1987.

Williams, Duncan Ryūken. "The Other Side of Zen: A Social History of Sōtō Zen Buddhism." In *Tokugawa Japan*, ed. by Stephen F. Teiser. Princeton, NJ: Princeton University Press, 2005.

Williams, Duncan Ryūken. "Funerary Zen: Sōtō Zen Death Management in Tokugawa Japan." In *Death and the Afterlife in Japanese Buddhism*, ed. by Jacqueline I. Stone and Mariko Namba Walter. Honolulu: University of Hawaii Press, 2008, 207–246.

Williams, Noel. *The Right to Life in Japan*. London: Routledge, 1997.

Wilson, Jeff. *Mourning the Unborn Dead: A Buddhist Ritual Comes to America*. New York: Oxford University Press, 2009.

Wilson, Michiko N. *The Marginal World of Ōe Kenzaburo: A Study in Themes and Techniques*. Armonk, NY: M.E. Sharpe, Inc., 1986.

Wilson, Michiko Niikuni. "Misreading and Un-Reading the Male Text, Finding the Female Text: Miyamoto Yuriko's Autobiographical Fiction." *U.S.-Japan Women's Journal* (English Supplement) 13 (1997): 26–55.

Wolf, Arthur. "Gods, Ghosts, and Ancestors." In *Studies in Chinese Society*. Stanford, CA: Stanford University Press, 1974, 131–182.

Yagi, Dickson K. "Protestant Perspectives on Ancestor Worship in Japanese Buddhism: The Funeral and the Buddhist Altar." *Buddhist–Christian Studies* 15 (1995): 43–59.

Yahata Takatsune. "Shinmo (Spirits of the Recently Deceased) and Community: Bon Observances in a Japanese Village." *Japanese Journal of Religious Studies* 15(2–3) (1988): 131–136.

Yamada, Patricia. "The Bodhisattva Jizō: Humanity's Refuge in the Six Realms of Existence." *Chanoyu Quarterly* 67 (1991): 35–56.

Yamakawa Kikue. *Women of the Mito Domain: Recollections of Samurai Family Life*. Trans. Kate Wildman Nakai. Tokyo: University of Tokyo Press, 1992.

Yanagita Kunio. *About Our Ancestors: The Japanese Family System*. Trans. Fanny Hagin Mayer. Tokyo: Japanese Society for the Promotion of Science, 1970.

Yasui Manami. "Research Notes: On Burial Customs, Maternal Spirits, and the Fetus in Japan." *U.S.-Japan Women's Journal* (*English Supplement*) 24 (2003): 102–114.

Yokota Fuyuhiko. "Imaging Working Women in Early Modern Japan." In *Women and Class in Japanese History*, ed. by Anne Walthall, Tonomura Hitomi, and Wakita Haruko. Ann Arbor: Center for Japanese Studies, University of Michigan, 1999, 153–167.

Yonemura Shoji. "Dozoku and Ancestor Worship in Japan." In *Ancestors*, ed. by William H. Newell. The Hague: Mouton Publishers, 1974, 177–203.

Yoshida Teigo. "Mystical Retribution, Spirit Possession, and Social Structure in a Japanese Village." *Ethnology* 6(3) (1967): 237–262.

Young, Richard Fox. "Abortion, Grief and Consolation: Prolegomena to a Christian Response to Mizuko Kuyo." *Japan Christian Quarterly* 55 (Winter 1989): 31–39.

Young, Richard Fox. "Magic and Morality in Modern Japanese Exorcistic Technologies—A Study of Mahikari." *Japanese Journal of Religious Studies* 17(1) (1990): 29–49.

Yu, Anthony C. "'Rest, Rest, Perturbed Spirit!': Ghosts in Traditional Chinese Prose Fiction." *Harvard Journal of Asiatic Studies* 47 (1987): 397–434.

Zelizer, Viviana A. *Pricing the Priceless Child: The Changing Social Value of Children*. Princeton, NJ: Princeton University Press, 1985.

Zhiru [Ng, Sok-keng Lilian] *The Making of a Savior Bodhisattva: Dizang in Medieval China*. Honolulu: University of Hawaii Press, 2007.

Index